Business Law

EIGHTH EDITION

First published by:
McGraw-Hill Book Company

Sixth edition published in 1995 by:
Stanley Thornes (Publishers) Ltd
Seventh edition 1998

Eighth edition published in 2002 by:
Nelson Thornes Ltd
Delta Place
27 Bath Road
CHELTENHAM
GL53 7TH
United Kingdom

02   03   04   05   06   /   10   9   8   7   6   5   4   3   2   1

A catalogue record for this book is available from The British Library.

ISBN 0 7487 6647 2

Page make-up by Acorn Bookwork
Printed and bound in Great Britain by Ashford Colour Press

Contents

Preface

This book was written initially to cover the law examinations of the Chartered Institute of Management Accountants, but in more recent years it has proved to be of value principally to all students who are required to study Business Law as part of a non- law course. It has therefore proved to be particularly useful for the examinations of other professional bodies, and for many BTEC courses.

The text is not divided into chapters according to subject, but into units, each containing a similar amount of material. It is hoped that this approach will help students to plan a programme of study.

The early units provide an outline of the English legal system, its procedures, and some fundamental concepts for those studying law for the first time, and there is a new unit on the law of the European Union. The law of agency, and the principles of tort and contract are then introduced, with reference to a lesser extent to the relevant criminal law, since these principles underlie most business activities. Further units deal with specific legal problems arising from the sale of goods, product liability and consumer credit. Finally, there are two more substantial groups of units: the law relating to business associations, partnerships and particularly companies is covered in Units 22–25, and employment law is covered in Units 26–29.

Questions are included at the end of each unit to provide the opportunity for written practice, which many candidates appear to lack.

J. Soulsby
January 2002

Table of Cases

Table of Statutes

Unit 1. The Nature and Development of English Law

A. The nature of law

The word 'law' suggests the idea of rules; rules affecting the lives and activities of people.

In any community or group, rules made by people will develop to control the relationships between members. These rules are essential if the community is to work and will be found in all forms of activity which depend upon some form of cooperation—in games, in schools, in clubs. The rules come into existence in varying ways, although in most cases there must have been agreement between at least some of the members of the community that the rule was desirable. When a person or persons having power in the community enforces the rule, then that rule will acquire the status of a 'law' in the generally accepted meaning of the word.

Even in primitive societies, traditions and customs will affect conduct. Such customary rules tend to be too vague and imprecise at this stage to merit the use of the term 'law' although they may provide the basis of later law. As the society develops and becomes more complex, rules of a more definite nature emerge and a body of law comes into existence. At the same time some machinery for its enforcement must be established.

B. Civil and criminal law

As legal systems develop, the different rules tend to fall into two main categories, criminal law and civil law, and the objectives of each, although closely connected, are different. Criminal law is concerned with conduct of which the state disapproves so strongly that it will punish the wrongdoer. It is felt that society cannot work if people are allowed to take the property of others at will; therefore theft is forbidden and thieves are punished to deter them, and others of a like mind, from repeating this conduct. It is not the objective of criminal law to compensate the victim, except perhaps incidentally.

Civil law has a complementary function. If a dispute arises between two individuals, each believing himself to be in the right, a quarrel may ensue and violence or other criminal conduct may result. To prevent this, rules of civil law were developed in order to determine which of the two parties was in the right. The party in the wrong was then obliged to make redress by compensating the other for any loss the wrongdoer might have caused. The object of the civil law therefore is to resolve disputes and give a remedy to the persons wronged, not to punish wrongdoers.

Most countries, including England, find it convenient to set up separate systems of criminal courts and civil courts. In England, a criminal prosecution is usually begun in the name of the Crown (i.e., the state) through the machinery of the police and the Crown Prosecution Service, and the decision as to whether or not to press the prosecution is not the concern of the victim. In a civil case, the law is set in motion by a private individual, or a firm, who has the right to determine how far the action shall continue.

Thus the parties and the terminology differ. In the criminal case of *R.* v. *Smith*, the Crown (*R.* signifying *Regina* or the Queen) prosecutes the accused, who may also be referred to as the prisoner or defendant. In the civil case of *Jones* v. *Smith*, the claimant sues the defendant (see also page 16).

Differences also exist in the rules of evidence and procedure, reflecting the fact that a criminal conviction is likely to be far more damaging to a person's character than failure in a civil action. The rules of evidence are much stricter in criminal cases; for example, a confession will be carefully examined to see if any pressure was brought to bear upon the accused, but an admission in a civil case will be freely accepted. The standard of proof required in criminal cases is greater, for the accused must be proved guilty beyond all reasonable doubt. A claimant in a civil action will succeed on the balance of probabilities, that is if he can convince the court that he has only a marginally stronger case than the defendant.

Finally, it is important to note that the same series of events may sometimes give rise to both criminal and civil proceedings. For instance, if an employer is alleged to have left dangerous factory machinery unguarded causing injury to a worker, two types of issue arise. Failure to guard such machinery is conduct which has been made a criminal offence and the employer may be prosecuted in a criminal court and, if found guilty of the offence, punished. The issue of whether the employer caused loss to the injured worker through negligence and failure to comply with his statutory duty will be determined in a separate civil action brought by the worker in a civil court, where the worker will claim compensation (damages) from his employer. There are many other situations, such as road accidents, assaults, frauds, and the sale of mis-described goods, where the same incident may give rise to both criminal and civil actions.

C. The development of English law

Origins of English law

Most legal systems in Europe, including that of Scotland, and indirectly those in many other parts of the world were strongly influenced by Roman law. In England and Wales, on the other hand, Roman law has had much less influence except in a few specialized fields. The body of law which at present applies in England and Wales developed very gradually over a long period. Like so many of our institutions, it was not systematically created. Drawing upon many different sources, the English common law system finally emerged and has become the basis of law not only in this country but also in the United States and in many Commonwealth countries.

The period of local justice

Until and for some time after the Norman Conquest, it could scarcely be said that there was such a thing as English law. The population was small, settlements were often widely separated and travel was difficult. Justice and other aspects of administration tended to be local. Each local community would have its own court in which, for the most part, *local customs* would be applied. These customs, the beginnings of legal rules, varied considerably from one area to another.

The emergence of the common law

The Norman Conquest made little immediate impact upon English law. William I promised that the English should keep their rights and their law, which meant the customary law. At the same time, the Normans developed a strong central government and over the following 200 years greatly increased central control over the administration of the law. This was a gradual process bringing with it the decline of the local courts.

Central courts, eventually sitting permanently at Westminster, developed when special committees of the King's Council were entrusted with jurisdiction over legal disputes. At the same time, the practice grew up of sending royal judges to visit most parts of the country so as to establish closer royal control over the administration of justice. The sittings of these judges were known as Assizes.

These new institutions, particularly the travelling judges, brought with them a most important change in the law itself, the unification of the varying local customs. As they went around the country on circuit the judges tended to select and apply certain customary rules in all cases rather than rely in every case upon enquiring into local customs. This process was assisted by the King who sometimes created new legal rules which were to apply nationally, and by the permanent courts which had nationwide jurisdiction. The different local customs were therefore replaced gradually by a body of rules applying throughout, or common to, the whole country and known eventually as the common law. This process was substantially completed by the end of the thirteenth century.

The formulation of the common law took place when there were few statutes or other forms of written law. The judges accordingly looked to previous decisions for guidance in order to maintain consistency. In other words the doctrine of precedent, to be discussed in Unit 2, began to emerge in the common law courts. If previous decisions were to be followed, it was essential that the judges' decisions be recorded and we see the beginning of law reporting, at first by anonymous lawyers in the Year Books. The main stream of English law, therefore, began with the unification of local customs to form the common law and has been developed down to the present day by the judges as precedent has been built upon precedent.

Equity

A legal rule aims at making provision for a large number of cases of a particular kind. It is impossible to provide for every eventuality, however, and some special situations will arise where the application of the rule will cause hardship. Since 'hard cases make bad law', most legal systems develop some machinery to deal with these special cases which would otherwise bring the law into disrepute.

As the common law courts became separated from the King's Council, they became increasingly reluctant or unable to grant remedies for new and unfamiliar types of wrong. As conditions changed and new forms of property and interests in property developed, there came to be many types of wrong for which the courts could grant no remedy.

Subjects unable to obtain a remedy, therefore, would sometimes petition the King asking for justice, and these petitions were usually passed to the Chancellor. The latter was empowered to order the parties to appear before him under penalty (*subpoena*) for refusal and, after hearing the petition, he could make such order as appeared to him to be fair, just or 'equitable'. These sittings of the Chancellor became more regular and by the end of the fourteenth century had developed into a new Court of Chancery, administering its own form of justice known as equity.

The early Chancellors were clergymen, and for a long time each petition was simply dealt with at the entire discretion of the individual Chancellor on the basis of what he himself felt to be just. It gradually came to be recognized, however, that there were some situations in which the Chancellor would almost always grant relief and a doctrine of precedent began to appear even in the Court of Chancery. This process quickened from the seventeenth century onwards when the office of Chancellor was held by lawyers trained in the common law. By the early nineteenth century, equity was as much tied by precedent as was common law and we had the unique system of two bodies of legal rules administered in two sets of courts, each with its own particular procedure and remedies. Many litigants were not only disappointed if they eventually found that they had chosen the wrong court but were utterly bewildered.

A number of reforms were introduced culminating in the Judicature Acts 1873–75. These statutes swept away the common law courts and the Court of Chancery and replaced them by one Supreme Court of Judicature in which each branch had the power to administer both common law and equity according to the same rules of procedure. The rule that equity should prevail in the event of a conflict was also restated.

The administration of the two systems was therefore combined, although it is still necessary to distinguish between them for some purposes. Thus the common law remedy of damages may be claimed as of right but the action will be barred after a fixed period, normally six years. On the other hand, the award of equitable remedies still remains partly at the discretion of the court and will be refused if it is felt that the claimant has delayed unnecessarily, even for a short time, in seeking them.

Equity was never a comprehensive system of law as was common law, but was for the most part a collection of individual rules or principles. If common law was the book, equity was a page of errata. Nevertheless, equity played an important part in developing certain aspects of law. It recognized and protected the trust by compelling the trustees, the legal owners, to deal with the property on behalf of the beneficiaries, the equitable owners. It treated the mortgage as the parties intended it to be treated, as a device for borrowing money, and would not allow the lender to exercise his full legal rights over the property if repayment was not made on the *exact* contractual date. It granted relief where a contract was entered into as a result of misrepresentation or undue influence by allowing the innocent party to abandon the contract and be returned to his original position—the remedy of rescission. It also provided the remedies of specific performance and injunction which are court orders compelling the performance or non-performance respectively of certain acts under pain of fine or imprisonment for contempt if not obeyed.

It should be noted that the phrase 'common law' is sometimes used today to describe the whole body of judge-made rules of law whether the rules originated in equity in the Court of Chancery or were common law rules in the strict sense, emanating from the old common law courts. In this wider sense, common law is contrasted with statute law which is discussed later.

Law merchant

The early common law courts were concerned largely with problems of land tenure and gave little attention to the growing number of mercantile transactions and the disputes arising therefrom. Procedure in the common law courts was slow and, in order to give the quick decisions which the merchants needed, many markets and boroughs were allowed to set up their own special tribunals. There were various types. Courts of Pie Powder were found widely, and possibly derived their name from the *pieds poudrés* or dusty feet of the traders who used them before moving on to the next fair. Courts of Staple were found in certain larger towns which had been allowed to act as trading centres for particular 'staple' products such as wool, and where foreign merchants were likely to be involved.

The rules administered in these courts were based upon mercantile customs and became known as the law merchant. Some of these customs became internationally recognized, while others were applied only in a particular locality or trade.

5

The common law courts realized the growing importance of this work and gradually took it over. Various types of commercial documents and procedures were recognized in legal decisions, thereby forming precedents and becoming part of the common law itself. At the same time the modern law of contract was developed. The law merchant had been incorporated into the common law by about the end of the eighteenth century and the mercantile courts had disappeared. Even today, however, the ordinary courts will often take account of business practice in reaching a decision and this still plays a part in the evolution of English law.

Statute law

Statute law, or legislation, consists of rules which are formally enacted by a body which has constitutional power to do so. Parliament is the body with inherent power to legislate under English law and statutes today take the form of Acts of Parliament. Sometimes legislative powers are delegated to subordinate bodies.

From earliest days, legislation, often in the form of royal decrees, played some part in the growth of English law. The early statutes would supplement or amend the rules of common law, and later equity, but the main framework of law grew through the decisions of the courts.

Over the last two centuries, the Government has concerned itself to an unprecedented degree with such matters as public health, education, transport, the use and conservation of natural resources, the management of the economy and the concept of the welfare state. Industrialization, the population explosion and the growth of large conurbations created social, economic and human problems to which the common law and equity could not adapt. New institutions and new legal rules and concepts had to be created quickly and this was done through Parliament. Vast numbers of statutes have been enacted creating new areas of law and, as will become apparent in later units, legislation has become a major source of new legal rules.

The courts have recognized the legislative sovereignty of Parliament and will always obey and apply an Act of Parliament even where it conflicts with or abolishes the rules of common law or equity (but subject now to European Community law). Legislation as a source of law today will be examined in the next unit.

D. Entry into Europe

One of the most potentially important legal developments in the history of this country took place in January 1972 when the United Kingdom signed the Treaty of Accession in Brussels. By this Treaty, the United Kingdom and two other states joined the original six member states in the enlarged European Communities as from 1 January 1973. Six more states have since joined giving a membership now of 15, and further expansion is very probable.

The Treaty was made by the Government under the Crown's prerogative power to enter into agreements with other states. The United Kingdom thereby accepted an international obligation but, since the internal law of this country was not affected, the approval of Parliament was not strictly required. Membership of the Communities, however, requires that Community law shall become part of the internal law of the member states and shall be accepted and applied by the national courts. It was therefore necessary to change our internal law by Act of Parliament and this was subsequently done by the European Communities Act 1972.

The Act provides that the Treaties, and some secondary legislation, shall become part of the law of the United Kingdom. This includes legislation already made and that which may be made in the future. As regards new Treaties and regulations, no further enactment by Parliament is necessary. Thus while Parliament may devise a procedure whereby draft regulations are considered and representations made to the Commission or Council, there is no direct Parliamentary control over whether or not such regulations become law.

As a condition of the United Kingdom becoming a member state, Parliament has therefore been obliged to give up its sovereignty so far as Community matters are concerned. In theory, there is no reason why the 1972 Act should not be repealed by a later Act but this would mean the renunciation of membership.

The subject of English law and the European Union is addressed in Unit 6.

Specimen questions

1. Rogue defrauds Victim and takes £5m of Victim's property. Explain what legal consequences may follow.
2. Distinguish between common law and statute law. Why is statute law a major source of new legal rules today?
3. What was the 'law merchant'? Do the specialized and complex business disputes of today justify special courts and procedures to deal with them? (See also Unit 4.)
4. (a) Explain the emergence of 'equity' as a source of English law.
   (b) What are the main differences between common law remedies and equitable remedies?
5. Explain each of the following:
   (a) claimant;
   (b) prosecution;
   (c) European Community law;
   (d) legislation;
   (e) R. (as in 'R. v. Smith').

Unit 2. Sources of Law

The expression 'sources of law' can mean several different things. It can refer to the historical origins from which the law has come, such as common law and equity which were discussed in the last unit. Secondly, it can also refer to the body of rules which a judge will draw upon in deciding a case, and where these rules are to be found. In this second sense there are two main sources of English law today: legislation and precedent.

A. Legislation

The nature and effect of legislation

Legislation is the body of rules which have been formally enacted or made. Many bodies in England have power to lay down rules for *limited* purposes, for example social clubs, but fundamentally the only way in which rules can be enacted so as to apply *generally* is by Act of Parliament. For various reasons, some of Parliament's legislative functions are delegated to subordinate bodies which, within a limited field, are allowed to enact rules. Local authorities, for instance, are allowed to enact by-laws. But local authorities can only do this because an Act of Parliament has given them the power to do so.

In constitutional theory, Parliament is said to have legislative sovereignty and, provided that the proper procedure is followed, the statute passed must be obeyed and applied by the courts. However, this conventional view has been affected more recently by the UK membership of the European Communities (see page 9).

In this respect England differs from many countries which have written constitutions. In the United States, for instance, the Supreme Court has power to declare legislation passed by Congress to be invalid if it is, in the opinion of the Court, inconsistent with the written constitution. The conventional attitude of the courts in this country, on the other hand, has best been expressed in words attributed to Holt, C.J., in a report of *City of London* v. *Wood* in 1702: 'An Act of Parliament can do no wrong, though it may do several things that look pretty odd.'

This conventional view is now subject to a major qualification. While the UK is a member of the European Union, law enacted or created by the European Union Treaties has priority over law made or enacted in this country. Therefore even an Act of Parliament, whenever made, is invalid unless it is compatible with European Union law.

> In *R.* v. *Secretary of State for Transport, ex parte Factortame Ltd* (1991), Spanish fishermen were claimed to be catching part of the UK 'quota' of European fishing stocks by forming British companies and having their boats registered in the United Kingdom. The Merchant Shipping Act 1988 and regulations made under it tried to prevent this. The European Court held that part of this UK legislation was incompatible with European Union law. The House of Lords made an order restraining the UK Government from applying part of the Act pending this decision, and eventually the Government was held liable to compensate the fishermen.

Although the courts cannot *generally* question the validity of an Act of Parliament, they do always have the task of applying it to specific problems. The Government, by Act of Parliament, states what the law is to be but, having done so, it must then abide by the words which it has used. What those words *mean* is a matter for the courts to decide. If the Government disapproves of the interpretation it must pass another Act in an attempt to state its intentions more clearly. The courts have, in fact, evolved rules of interpretation which they will use to discover the 'true' meaning of the words of a statute. Parliament helped the courts to some extent by passing the Interpretation Act 1889, which was repealed and replaced by the Interpretation Act 1978 (see page 16).

The legislative process

The process by which an Act is passed is a long one. The first and most important step in most cases is for the Government to decide that it wishes the legislation to be passed. Once this decision has been taken, and so long as public opinion does not cause the Government to change its mind, the legislation will pass through Parliament and become law, because of the Government's effective command of a majority in the House of Commons. On some issues the Government will first seek the response of interested parties by the publication of a consultative paper. After considering the response, advance notice of the more definite proposals is given in a White Paper.

A formal requirement is that the bill must be approved by both Houses of Parliament, with ample opportunity for debate both in the Commons and in the Lords. In spite of Government control of the Commons, Parliament is not a mere rubber stamp, because it gives opportunities for members to question, criticize, publicize, explain and amend the detailed provisions of the bill, and few bills emerge without at least some amendment.

Finally, a bill must receive the Royal Assent, which today is never refused. It thereupon becomes an Act of Parliament and, unless otherwise provided, takes effect from the day of Assent. Many Acts now contain a section delaying commencement and providing for the Act to be brought into effect, if necessary part by part, by delegated legislation. Those affected by the Act are thereby given time to adapt to the change in the law.

The legislative sources of European Community law are described in Unit 6.

Amendment and repeal

A statute, once enacted, remains in force permanently unless and until it is *repealed*, and it can only be repealed by another statute. The Distress Act of 1276 still appears in the current edition of Halsbury's *Statutes of England* for instance. Similarly, a statute can only be *amended* by another Act of Parliament unless, as rarely happens, an Act delegates to a Minister or some other body the power to make minor changes. Most Acts today, in fact, do have to repeal or amend some earlier statutory provisions, and they will usually contain a schedule specifying what earlier provisions have been affected.

Conversely, Parliament can never take away its own power to amend or repeal earlier legislation. Nor can it abandon its own freedom to legislate in future as it thinks fit. The European Communities Act 1972 does at present limit the power of Parliament to legislate in a manner inconsistent with the European Treaties. Nevertheless, the European Communities Act could always be repealed by a future Parliament, although this would mean withdrawal of the United Kingdom from the European Union.

Consolidating and codifying Acts

Governments have always tended to introduce legislation as and when some specific need arises, and several closely connected Acts on a particular topic may well exist side by side. In such circumstances the Government will often do some tidying up. A *consolidating* Act will be passed which will repeal all of the piece-meal provisions, and re-enact them in one logically arranged Act. This is periodically done, for instance, with tax legislation. Other examples include Acts dealing with road traffic, social security, safety at work, and companies.

Sometimes a Government may decide not only to consolidate all of the legislation, but also to replace some of the *case law* on the subject by a new Act. Such an Act is called a *codifying* one. It reduces most of the law on the subject into a single code. There are good examples in commercial law, particularly the Bills of Exchange Act 1882 and the Sale of Goods Act 1893. (The Sale of Goods Act 1893 was subsequently amended by several other Acts, and this legislation was consolidated in the Sale of

Goods Act 1979. Since then there have been further amendments, and perhaps another consolidating Act is due.)

B. Delegated legislation

Forms of delegated legislation

The vast extension of the functions of Government over the past 200 years was mentioned in Unit 1. The task of making the detailed rules needed to translate this new development into practice was beyond the capacity of any one legislative body. What the Government has often done, therefore, is to pass an 'enabling' Act setting up the main framework of the reform on which it has decided, and then empowering some subordinate body – often a Minister – to enact the detailed rules necessary to complete the scheme. Thus the Road Traffic Acts empower the Minister responsible to make regulations about the use of motor vehicles and trailers on the road, the construction of such vehicles, and the conditions under which they may be used. Rules enacted under such powers are called 'delegated legislation'. The following are the principal forms that this may take:

1. *Orders in Council* are enacted under powers delegated to the Privy Council. Most senior members of the Government are also Privy Councillors, and effectively determine what shall be enacted.
2. *Ministerial regulations* are made by individual Ministers within some limited sphere relating to their departmental responsibilities, for example, traffic regulations.
   Most orders and rules of both of these kinds are published through HM Stationery Office under the description of *statutory instruments*.
3. *Local authorities* are given powers by many Acts of Parliament to make *by-laws* which will have the force of law within the geographical area of the authority. Various non-elected governmental bodies are also given such powers within the scope of their functions.
4. *Certain professional bodies* are given power by Parliament to make rules governing the conduct of their members. The Law Society, for example, has this power under the Solicitors' Acts.

Advantages of delegation of powers

1. Parliamentary time is saved on relatively trivial matters.
2. Greater flexibility is assured by the ability to enact and change the rules quickly without lengthy Parliamentary proceedings.
3. In national emergencies it may sometimes be necessary for the Government to act at short notice.
4. Many regulations cover technical subjects which few Members of Parliament are competent to discuss adequately.

5. Local and specialist knowledge may be drawn upon when local authority by-laws are passed.

Criticisms of the growth of delegated legislation

In the past there were widespread criticisms of the growth of delegated legislative powers. It was felt to be an erosion of the constitutional role of Parliament to allow such wide powers to be given to other bodies, particularly to individual Ministries. Moreover, it was pointed out, delegated legislation need not ever be debated or even mentioned in Parliament, and might therefore become law without people really being aware of the fact. There are usually over 2000 different statutory instruments alone coming into force each year, and some of these can make substantial changes in the law.

It is generally felt today that these criticisms were exaggerated, and to some extent simply an expression of resentment at the sheer volume of legislation needed in a modern industrialized country. Certainly some safeguards do exist against abuse of delegated powers; how adequate these safeguards are is a matter which is still sometimes discussed.

Control of delegated legislation

1. *Parliamentary control*

   (a) Parliament, having given the power to legislate, can obviously take the power away at a future date.
   (b) Ministers are usually answerable to Parliament for the content of regulations made by their departments.
   (c) The enabling Act will sometimes require that an instrument be laid before Parliament thereby permitting limited Parliamentary debate.
   (d) Committees of Members of Parliament examine and report on statutory instruments, EC regulations and other delegated legislation.

2. *Judicial control*
   (a) *Ultra vires.* There is a vitally important distinction between the attitude of the courts to an Act of Parliament and their attitude to delegated legislation. The courts can never challenge the validity or reasonableness of a statute except if it contravenes European Community law. The courts can, and do, sometimes challenge the validity of delegated legislation. The delegate body has power to legislate only in so far as Parliament has given it this power, and the courts keep it firmly within this limit. If it exceeds its powers in any way, the rules are *ultra vires* (outside its powers) and therefore *void.*
   (b) *Unreasonableness.* The courts will sometimes take the view that Parliament has given the power only on the understanding that it be exercised *reasonably.* Some local authority by-laws have been held void, because the court felt that they were unreasonable.

(c) *European Community law*. In some limited circumstances, the courts in this country have power under EC law to restrain the application of UK legislation. This can apply to Acts of Parliament as well as to delegated legislation.

C. Judicial precedent

The nature of precedent

The idea of binding judicial precedent is a special feature of common law jurisdictions, that is to say, systems of law based on that of England. The doctrine is based on the general principle that once a court has stated the legal position in a given situation, then the same decision will be reached in any future case where the material facts are the same.

Whether a court is bound to follow a previous decision depends to a very large extent on which court gave the previous decision. Generally, if the decision was of a superior court then the lower court must follow it, but a superior court is not bound by the previous decisions of an inferior one. The following table outlines the main rules:

1. Decisions of the House of Lords bind all other courts for the future, and until 1966 were even binding on the House of Lords itself in subsequent cases. In that year, however, the Lord Chancellor issued a statement on behalf of the House that it would no longer regard itself as rigidly bound if this would cause injustice by reason of changing social circumstances.
2. The Court of Appeal is bound by previous decisions of the Lords and, in most circumstances, by its own previous decisions. Its decisions are binding on all lower courts but not upon the House of Lords.
3. A High Court judge is bound by decisions of the House of Lords and the Court of Appeal but not by other High Court decisions.
4. A County Court judge is bound by decisions of all higher courts. The decisions of the County Courts themselves are not binding in any future case, and they are not normally reported at all.

This does not mean that decisions of lower courts will be disregarded by higher courts. These decisions may not be *binding* precedents, but they will have *persuasive* value. They may be long standing, recognized by people as the law, and acted upon accordingly. Similarly, decisions of the House of Lords in appeals from Scotland or Northern Ireland, and decisions of the Judicial Committee of the Privy Council in appeals from some Commonwealth countries, while not binding in English courts, have strong persuasive influence. An English court may even turn for guidance to a decision in the United States or the Commonwealth, where the legal systems have the same basis as our own.

On matters of European Community law (of increasing importance), a court in this country can and sometimes must refer the issue to the European Court of Justice (see Unit 6). Although the European Court ruling is binding on the court here *in this particular case*, the European Court does not itself have a doctrine of binding precedent. Nevertheless, its decisions are reported, and a mass of highly persuasive European case law is developing.

When seen in operation, the doctrine of precedent works in quite a complex manner. When he gives his decision in a case the judge does, in effect, three things.

1. He gives his actual decision between the parties: 'I find for the claimant', or 'the appeal must fail'. This is obviously the part which is of most interest to the parties themselves.
2. He will also give his reasons for reaching that decision: what facts he regards as 'material', the legal principles which he is applying to those facts and why. This is called the *ratio decidendi* (the reasoning vital to the decision), and it is this part of the judgment which may bind future courts.
3. He may also, at the same time, discuss the law relating to this type of case generally, or perhaps discuss one or two hypothetical situations. These will be *obiter dicta* (other comments) and while they may have persuasive force in future cases, they are not binding.

Having become a precedent, a decision need not continue to be one indefinitely. It can cease to be binding in various ways. A decision can be *reversed* when the party who lost the case appeals to a higher court, which allows the appeal. Where similar facts come before the courts in a later case, then a higher court can *overrule* the previous decision of a lower one. This does not affect the parties of the earlier case; so far as they are concerned their decision still stands, but the earlier case is no longer binding in future. If a later court is not in a position to overrule a previous decision, for instance, because the legal principles involved are not the same, it may nevertheless *disapprove* it, usually by way of an *obiter dictum*. Disapproval by a higher court obviously casts doubt on the correctness of an earlier decision. Similarly, a later court which is not bound can simply *not follow* a previous decision, which will itself cast doubt on the earlier case. Finally, a previous decision can often be *distinguished* where the material facts of the earlier case differ from the present ones. There will always be some difference between the facts of two separate cases and if the later judge feels that the difference is sufficient to justify a different decision, he will distinguish the earlier case. In this way even a lower court can avoid holding itself bound by a previous higher decision.

Precedent or code?

Many other countries, particularly in Continental Europe, have no doctrine of binding precedent. Instead, the main source of law in these countries will be a code. Almost all of the rules of civil and of criminal law have been written out fairly simply, and then formally enacted by the legislature.

It is largely for historical reasons that the English legal system is based mainly on precedent rather than on a code, and each alternative has its advantages.

1. In favour of the English system of judge-made or case law, it is argued that it gives more flexibility. The law steadily grows as new cases come before the courts, and new rules develop to meet new situations. A code, once enacted, can be changed only by a complex legislative process, and can sometimes work injustice as the rules become outdated.

2. Systems based on precedent are claimed to be more realistic and practical in character, being based on actual problems that have come before the courts. On the other hand, it is sometimes necessary to wait until an actual dispute arises before the law can be known. This can lead to uncertainty, and bringing a case to find out the law can be a costly business. A code can, within limits, legislate in advance, so that the parties know what their legal position is without having to go to court to find out.

3. Finally, although case law provides us with many detailed rules, this can itself be a drawback. In English law there are over 1000 volumes of law reports in which precedents are to be found. The ease with which cases may now be discovered by computerized retrieval methods has already led to the courts expressing concern at the number of precedents being cited.

Law reporting

The development of a doctrine of precedent in this country has been very closely tied to the growth of good law reporting. Without a clear and reliable record of earlier decisions, a doctrine of precedent simply could not work.

Law reporting in England began in the thirteenth century with the Year Books, which were very brief notes written by anonymous lawyers, often in curious mixtures of English, Latin and Norman French. From about 1530 the Year Books were replaced by private reports published under the names of those compiling them. These continued until the nineteenth century, but they vary considerably in value according to the accuracy of the reporter. In 1865, the Council of Law Reporting was established by the legal profession to provide for systematic publication of professionally prepared and officially revised volumes of reports.

Today, the main reports are still produced by what is now the Incorporated Council of Law Reporting. It now publishes only one volume each year of reports of decisions in the Queen's Bench Division of the High Court, one of Chancery Division cases, and one of Family Division decisions. Court of Appeal cases are included in the volumes for the High Court Division from which the appeal came, but House of Lords decisions are found in a separate volume of Appeal Cases. Since 1953 the Council has also issued the Weekly Law Reports, to enable reports of certain cases to be available more quickly.

Some private reports did survive after the nineteenth century; the main general ones now issued are the All England Law Reports, published now in four volumes each year, and also periodically, about weekly. An increasing number of more specialized private reports also continues in fields such as commercial law, taxation and employment law.

A further development in recent years has been the collection of case reports and statutes in computer programs. Access can be bought on computer terminals through schemes such as Lexis.

The report of a civil case is referred to by the names of the parties as, for example, *Bolton* v. *Stone*, but in speech the 'v.' is said as 'and' (*not* 'versus'). The claimant's name is placed first and the defendant's second. If the case goes to appeal the parties are known as the appellant and the respondent, but the order is not changed unless it is a House of Lords case, when the appellant's name is placed first. After the name of the case will be found details for each reference: the year, the series of reports with the volume number if necessary, and the page. Thus in the Law Reports, the House of Lords decision in *Bolton* v. *Stone* [1951] AC 850 is to be found on page 850 of the Appeal Cases reports for 1951. The Court of Appeal decision in the same case was reported under the name *Stone* v. *Bolton* [1950] 1 KB 201 (Miss Stone being the original claimant), and is found on page 201 of the first volume of King's Bench Division Reports for 1950. In the All England Law Reports, the Court of Appeal decision in this case is reported under the reference *Stone* v. *Bolton* [1949] 2 All ER 851, and the House of Lords decision as *Bolton* v. *Stone* [1951] 1 All ER 1078.

D. The judges and statutes

Construction and interpretation of statutes

Another major way in which the judges contribute to the development of English law is in interpreting and construing the words used in statutes and other legislation. Once a higher court has decided that the words of an Act apply in a particular way to a set of facts, this decision will form a precedent to be followed should a similar problem arise in a future case. Sometimes a complex body of case law may arise out of the interpretation of a single statute, as has happened with parts of the Sale of Goods Acts, for example.

The Interpretation Act 1978 gives certain statutory rules of interpretation, for example that the masculine gender shall include the feminine, and the singular shall include the plural, and vice versa, unless a contrary intention is obvious. Moreover, almost all Acts contain a series of definitions of technical and other terms which the enactment contains.

Subject to this, it is for the judges to say what the words of an Act mean should any doubt arise. Words will be given their literal or everyday meaning unless this would lead to absurdity. If particular words are followed by general words, the general words are restricted to things similar to those specified particularly. Thus 'wheat, barley and other crops' would include oats but not potatoes. On the other hand, if there is particular mention only, nothing else is included. Thus 'wheat and barley' would not include oats.

It is the words of the Act alone which constitute the law but, if the words used are ambiguous, or if their application is uncertain, more difficult questions of construction can arise. The courts will look at the Act as a whole; often the way in which a word is used in other parts of the Act will make it plain what it is intended to mean here. If the meaning is still not clear, the courts will try to discover from the wording of the Act what 'mischief' the Act was designed to deal with, and will try to interpret the words so as to give effect to what the Act was intended to achieve. Exceptionally, following the House of Lords decision in *Pepper* v. *Hart* (1993), the courts may look at Ministerial statements in Parliament *before* the bill was enacted, as printed in Hansard, in order to discover its purpose. They will not, however, ask the Government *after* the bill becomes an Act what it was intended to achieve, largely because a Government might be tempted to give an answer best suited to its own immediate purpose.

Finally, there are certain presumptions which a court will make. Thus it is presumed that a statute is not intended to bind the Crown unless the statute expressly so provides. Since 'the Crown' includes all crown servants (e.g., civil service departments) this presumption can be very important. Similarly, it is presumed that an Act is not intended to create a strict criminal offence; the courts will assume that the defendant is guilty only if he *intended* to commit the offence, or acted carelessly. This presumption will, of course, be rebutted if the words of the Act make it plain that the legislature wishes to impose strict liability (see page 72).

E. Other sources of law

Law of the European Communities

By section 2 of the European Communities Act 1972, Community law is incorporated in English law. The sources from which Community law is derived are discussed in Unit 6.

Codes of practice

Section 45 of the Road Traffic Act 1930 provided that 'The Minister shall ... prepare a code (in this section referred to as the "Highway Code") comprising such directions as appear to him to be proper for the guidance of persons using roads ...'. This code is *not* a piece of legislation; it does not have binding force, it is not a criminal offence to break it, nor will breach of it give rise to civil liability. It can always, however, be cited in evidence, and a person who breaks it is much more likely to be held negligent, or guilty of careless driving, than a person who observes the provisions. The code must be treated as a source of law to the extent that a court must accept its provisions in evidence.

In addition, there are many non-statutory codes of practice, produced by professional bodies, making recommendations as to safety in such matters as handling chemicals or other materials. Unlike statutory codes of practice, these are not sources of law, in that the courts have no *duty* to accept them in evidence. Nevertheless, they may, in practice, influence a court in deciding whether or not particular conduct is reasonable.

17

Human Rights

In 1950, various west European countries made a European Convention of Human Rights, which set out and adopted a series of agreed 'rights and freedoms'. It also created a European Court of Human Rights (ECHR), at Strasbourg, to hear complaints of breach. Although the UK ratified it in 1951, the Convention was not made part of English law until the Human Rights Act 1998, which largely came into force in 2000. The Act provides that UK legislation must be interpreted by the UK courts, as far as possible, in a way which is compatible with the Convention. The UK courts can, where appropriate, make a 'declaration of incompatibility', but this does not have much direct effect on statutes. In particular, it does not make UK Parliamentary legislation invalid. It largely gives the government a power (not a *duty*) to overrule an Act of Parliament by ministerial order.

The courts do sometimes have power to declare the conduct of executive public authorities to be unlawful and, exceptionally, to award damages. The ECHR in Strasbourg also has power to award compensation, but these awards can only be enforced by the states themselves, at their discretion. The main effect of the Human Rights Act may well continue partly to be persuasive, in that it will set standards and exert moral pressures.

Custom

Historically, custom formed the basis of common law. General customs, almost without exception, have now fallen into disuse or been recognized by the courts and incorporated into precedent. Occasionally, a local custom may be put forward as still being law but the court will accept this only on very stringent conditions. More frequently, the courts will take into consideration what amount to special customs, such as commercial and business practice, in cases where they have to decide how existing legal rules should be applied in business situations.

Books by legal authors

These are not cited very frequently in the English courts, contrary to the practice in many other countries. At one time this practice was seldom allowed here, and was restricted to a few notable authorities. More recently the rule has been relaxed and the number of acceptable authors increased.

Specimen questions

1. Outline the sources from which a judge may draw the legal rules when deciding a case.
2. Many of the statutory rules governing business operations were not laid down by Parliament but by other bodies to whom Parliament had delegated the power to legislate.

Explain: (a) the reasons for this delegation;
    (b) the forms that delegated legislation may take;
    (c) the ways in which this delegated power is controlled.

3. A local authority by-law is preventing the expansion of your company. On what grounds, if at all, may the validity of the by-law be challenged?

4. Your company is considering whether or not to sue a supplier of faulty goods. There is a precedent when, on similar but not identical facts, the supplier was held to be liable. Explain the extent to which reliance may be placed upon this precedent.

5. Paula is suing Derek for breach of contract. In support of her case, Paula cites a decision of the Court of Appeal and an Act of Parliament. In his defence, Derek puts forward a decision of the House of Lords, a statutory instrument and a regulation from the European Community.

   You are required to explain the meaning and the importance as a source of law of:

   (a) a decision of the Court of Appeal;
   (b) an Act of Parliament;
   (c) a decision of the House of Lords;
   (d) a statutory instrument;
   (e) a European Community regulation.

Unit 3. The English Court System

A. County Courts

After the medieval local courts had largely disappeared, there was little provision for the hearing of minor civil claims until the County Courts were created in 1846. They were originally designed for the settlement of small claims and the collection of debts where the amount at stake did not exceed £20, but their jurisdiction has subsequently been extended by many statutes. Consolidating Acts have been passed from time to time, and they are now governed by the County Courts Act 1984.

There are some 400 of these courts in England and Wales. They have no connection either with the earlier courts which carried the same name or with the geographical counties. County Courts are grouped in circuits varying from as many as 15 courts in country areas to one court in almost continuous session in parts of London. They are presided over by Circuit judges, of whom there are some 550, and, while it is usual for there to be one judge to each circuit, the busier courts may have more than one judge.

The majority of civil cases in this country are disposed of in the County Courts by the judge sitting without a jury. Procedure tends to be quicker and less formal than in the High Court and, particularly since the cases are heard locally, less costly. Solicitors, wearing gowns but not wigs, have a right of audience as well as barristers.

Limits to the jurisdiction of County Courts were formerly based almost entirely on the amount of the claim. Actions in contract and tort, such as the collection of debts and accident claims, could be brought where the amount claimed did not exceed £5000. This was not altogether satisfactory, since even a small claim can raise difficult issues of law and the amount at stake does not necessarily measure the complexity of the case. There is now much greater flexibility between the County Courts and the High Court.

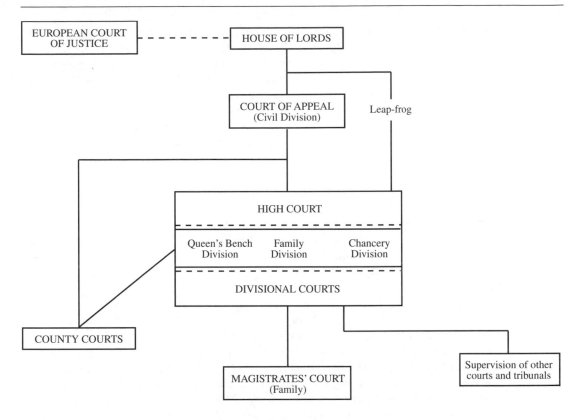

Figure 3.1 The Civil Courts

The Courts and Legal Services Act 1990, as amended, now governs the position. As a *general* rule, there is now no financial limit on the *jurisdiction* of a County Court to hear actions in contract and tort. In this respect, the County Courts and the High Court are now the same.

There are then a number of qualifications to this rule. In particular, there are detailed provisions as to where the hearing should actually take place. This is a matter for the 'District Judges' (formerly the County Court Registrars and the District Registrars of the High Court). Wherever the action starts, the claim is subject to an allocation procedure. 'Small claims' for under £5000 will usually be heard by the District Judge himself. Claims for between £5000 and £15 000 are assumed to be 'fast track' claims. They will normally be heard by a Circuit Judge in a County Court and be subject to special rules to speed up the process. Claims for over £15 000 are normally treated as 'multi-track', and can vary vastly in amount and complexity. Claims begun in the High Court for less than £50 000 are likely to be transferred to the County Court. If the amount claimed is £50 000 or more, it is presumed that it should be heard by a High Court Judge, normally in the Queen's Bench Division (see page 23). This Division may sit at 26 'first tier' regional centres as well as in London. It

21

should be emphasized that the figures in this paragraph are only presumptions; for any amount, the District judge will ultimately decide according to: (a) the financial substance of the action; (b) whether the action is otherwise important and, in particular, whether it raises important questions for other people or in the public interest; (c) the complexity of the facts and legal issues involved; and (d) whether transfer is more likely to result in a speedy trial.

Similar considerations now apply to the so-called Family Court, attached to and following the hierarchy of the Civil Courts but with an independent structure running from the Magistrates' Court through the County Court to the High Court. The complexity of the case largely determines whether the dispute shall be heard in the High Court or the County Court and, if the latter, whether it will be dealt with by a Circuit judge or a District judge.

There have been other changes of detail but the rest of the County Courts' jurisdiction remains basically as before. There are still financial limits as regards most actions concerning land. The new limits are no longer based on rateable value (which has been abolished for domestic property) but on the 'capital value of the land or interest in land'. The County Courts have jurisdiction if the value does not exceed £30 000. Above this figure, only the High Court has jurisdiction, although further changes may be introduced gradually. Similar £30 000 limits apply to most actions based on trusts, mortgages, the administration of estates and the dissolution of partnerships. Many of these are actions where the High Court's jurisdiction is exercised by the Chancery Division which, for the most part, sits only in London.

Certain County Courts can deal with insolvencies and the winding up of companies whose paid-up share capital does not exceed £120 000. Some courts near the coast can hear Admiralty cases, particularly small salvage claims. Many statutes confer other jurisdiction, including hire-purchase, extortionate credit bargains (without financial limit), rent restriction, and claims of racial discrimination. On the other hand there are still some cases where the County Courts have no jurisdiction; for example, actions for judicial review of administrative action must be in the High Court; so must most actions for defamation, which normally require trial by jury.

Further flexibility has been achieved by some new venue rules which, in general, give a claimant a choice of court and should allow cases to be moved to courts which are less busy. There were previously territorial limits which restricted cases to districts where the defendant lived or carried on business, or where the reason for the action arose or, if land was claimed, where the land was situated.

The administration of County Courts is supervised by District judges (formerly the Registrars), normally solicitors of at least seven years' standing. As we have seen, the District judges now have additional functions in deciding where a case shall be heard. They can also try certain cases themselves, if the action is not defended, if the amount at stake does not exceed £5000, and in other cases if the judge and parties agree.

In relation to small claims, it is sometimes felt that the County Courts are no longer fulfilling the purpose for which they were originally created. Although procedure is much quicker and cheaper than that in the High Court, it is still expensive. A defended County Court action could now cost hundreds of pounds in fees and disbursements and many solicitors would advise against suing if only a small sum were at stake. The 'small claims track' (which replaces an older County Court arbitration scheme) is much cheaper, but costs of legal representation in court are not awarded to a successful party where the amount involved does not exceed the normal limit of £5000.

B. The High Court

The Judicature Acts 1873–75 reorganized the system of civil courts by sweeping away the many separate courts which then existed and replacing them by the Supreme Court of Judicature (divided into the Court of Appeal and the High Court of Justice). The system then established has remained in operation with only minor alterations to the present day. It is now governed by the Supreme Court Act 1981, as amended.

As we have seen, there is greater overlap than hitherto in the jurisdiction of the High Court and the County Courts. Certain types of action must be *commenced* in a County Court, particularly claims for £50 000 or less for personal injuries. Most other claims of any amount can be commenced in the High Court. It is then for a District judge to decide where the case should be sent for *trial*. For cases begun in the High Court, the District judges are the former District Registrars. They apply the same criteria as above in deciding where to send a case for hearing.

The High Court is divided into three divisions, the Queen's Bench Division, the Chancery Division and the Family Division with some 100 judges in total. Any division is legally competent to deal with any matter arising, but in practice cases must be assigned to the division specializing in that particular type of action.

Before 1972, High Court cases outside London were tried at Civil Assizes. The cases were heard by High Court judges, mainly from the Queen's Bench Division, drawing their power from a special commission. The Courts Act 1971 abolished Civil Assizes and provided that the High Court may sit throughout the country wherever convenient. In practice this will be at 26 'first-tier' centres where almost any type of High Court case may be heard. An exception concerns Chancery matters which will be confined to London and certain centres in the North of England.

Queen's Bench Division

This division, presided over by the Lord Chief Justice, has succeeded to the jurisdiction formerly exercised by the old common law courts of Queen's (or King's) Bench, Common Pleas, and Exchequer. It deals with the greatest number of cases, notably those arising out of breaches of contract, the commission of torts and claims for the recovery of land. Typical cases would include an action for non-performance of a contract, an allegation that the defendant has published a defamatory statement, and a large claim for damages arising out of a road accident or any injury suffered at work. An action not specifically assigned to one of the other two divisions will be heard in the Queen's Bench Division.

23

In this division are to be found the few remaining civil juries. While most actions are now tried by a judge sitting alone, a jury will normally be empanelled whenever a person's character is likely to be in issue, as in actions based upon fraud or defamation. Majority verdicts can now be accepted.

Two specialized courts sit within the Queen's Bench Division, the Admiralty Court and the Commercial Court. Judges may be assigned to these courts and thereby specialize in these types of case.

Chancery Division

This division inherited the jurisdiction formerly exercised by the old Court of Chancery and other matters have since been allocated to it by statute. It is concerned with probate and the administration of the estates of deceased persons, trusts, mortgages, partnerships, companies, bankruptcies and revenue and planning matters. The nominal president is the Lord Chancellor but his many other duties prevent him from taking any direct part in the work of the division: the organization of the day-to-day business is carried out by a senior judge, the Vice-Chancellor. The Patents Court, the Companies Court, and the Court of Protection (for the estates of mentally disordered persons) are specialized courts within this division.

Family Division

This division was created in 1970 to deal with matters arising out of marriage, divorce, matrimonial property and children. The senior judge in the division is known as the President.

In 1970, probate cases were transferred to the Chancery Division, except for non-contentious matters which remained within the Family Division for administrative reasons. Jurisdiction over minors, for example wardship, was transferred from the Chancery Division to the Family Division.

C. Appeals in civil cases

The High Court and Divisional Courts

Under the Access to Justice Act 1999, many appeals from County Courts are now made to a single judge of the High Court, and not directly to the Court of Appeal as hitherto.

In addition, two or three judges may sit together to form a Divisional Court. In the Queen's Bench Division, this may exercise criminal and civil jurisdiction. Criminal appeals are heard by way of 'case stated' from Magistrates' Courts and the Crown Court (see page 28). Civil appeals are heard from the decision of certain tribunals. Single judges in the Chancery Division hear appeals from the County Courts on bankruptcy questions.

The Divisional Court in the Queen's Bench also hears applications for various prerogative orders, through which various special courts and tribunals are kept under review (Unit 4). Thus if an administrative tribunal exceeds its jurisdiction or otherwise acts wrongfully, its decision can be quashed by the Divisional Court. This is not strictly an appellate jurisdiction, but in many cases it is so similar as to be almost indistinguishable.

Court of Appeal (Civil Division)

Appeals from the High Court and certain tribunals, for example the Lands Tribunal, are normally heard by three judges of this court. The court, for all practical purposes, is constituted by the Master of the Rolls and 35 Lords Justices of Appeal, though judges from the High Court may also be asked to sit if necessary. An appeal may generally be made as of right but leave is required in some cases. In County Court cases the permission of the trial judge or of the Court of Appeal may sometimes be given.

The appeal takes the form of a rehearing of the case through the media of the judge's notes and the transcript of the official shorthand writer's notes, and by listening to argument from counsel. Witnesses are not heard again nor is fresh evidence usually admitted. The court has all the powers of the court below and it may uphold or reverse the decision in whole or in part, may alter the sum of damages awarded, and may make a different order as to costs. In certain prescribed circumstances, for example the discovery of fresh evidence, a new trial may be ordered.

House of Lords

A further right of appeal exists from the Court of Appeal to the House of Lords; leave is required from the Court of Appeal or from the Appeals Committee of the House itself.

The House of Lords, when it sits as a judicial tribunal, differs in constitution from the legislative body which forms one of the Houses of Parliament. All the lay peers are now excluded, by convention if not by law, and the judges are drawn from the Lord Chancellor, peers who have held or are holding high judicial office such as ex-Lord Chancellors, and the 12 life peers who are known as Lords of Appeal in Ordinary or Law Lords. Some of the Law Lords are appointed from Scotland and Northern Ireland since the House is also the highest civil court of appeal for these countries and the highest criminal court of appeal for Northern Ireland.

Appeals heard by the House of Lords require a minimum of three judges but in practice five will normally sit. Exceptionally, as in *Pepper* v. *Hart* (1993) (see page 17) there may be seven. Since the court is technically part of the House, the judgments are given in the form of 'speeches', not usually read aloud today. If their lordships disagree, the view of the majority will prevail, and an appellant or respondent may succeed by only three votes to two. This was so in the case of *Donoghue* v. *Stevenson* (Unit 9).

It had long been felt that two appeals from the High Court to the Court of Appeal and then to the House of Lords were unnecessary. Accordingly, there is now a 'leap-frog' procedure whereby the Court of Appeal can be avoided and the appeal can go direct from a trial judge in the High Court to the House of Lords.

The trial judge must grant a certificate that the case is suitable for a direct appeal to the House of Lords, on the grounds that it involves a point of law of general importance, which either relates to a matter of statutory interpretation or is a case in which the judge was bound by a previous decision of the Court of Appeal or the House of Lords. The parties must also consent to the 'leap-frog'. Finally, the House of Lords must grant leave for the direct appeal. It is worth noting that since this change was introduced there have been relatively few instances where it has been used.

Finally, any court or tribunal faced with a point of Community law which it feels is both uncertain and yet necessary for judgment to be given *may* refer the matter to the European Court for a preliminary ruling. Where there is no further right of appeal internally, such reference is obligatory if requested by one of the parties to the action.

D. Criminal courts (see Figure 3.2)

Magistrates' Courts

These courts are held in most centres of population; the number of courts and the frequency of their sitting depend upon the amount of work to be done. They deal with over 98 per cent of all criminal offences.

The court must be composed of at least two justices of the peace or magistrates, but three will usually sit so that a majority decision can be given in the event of a disagreement. Justices are appointed by the Lord Chancellor on the recommendation of local advisory committees, and no legal qualifications or knowledge of law are required. The justices decide upon guilt or innocence, without the assistance of a jury, and upon the appropriate sentence to be imposed. Advice on questions of law is given by the Clerk to the Justices, or by the court clerk who will also be legally qualified. In a few towns the place of the unpaid lay justices is taken by one full-time District Judge who must be a barrister or solicitor.

The jurisdiction of Magistrates' Courts is regulated closely by statute. In general, there is the power to try all minor offences which will include, for example, most breaches of the Road Traffic Acts, many employment safety offences, false trade descriptions and sales of adulterated food. The power of punishment depends upon the offence but a fine of more than £5000 may not normally be imposed nor imprisonment exceeding 6 months. An offender may be committed to the Crown Court for sentence if the justices feel that their powers of punishment are inadequate.

Justices have another function to perform in the case of more serious crimes, which they cannot try, of deciding whether there is a prima facie or reasonable case to go forward for trial. Their so-called committal proceedings avoid wasting the time of higher courts on frivolous charges. These proceedings are now usually a formality with the prosecution merely handing in written statements of witnesses. Justices must

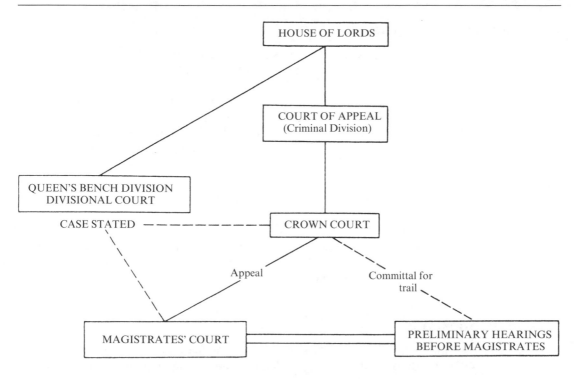

Figure 3.2 The Criminal Courts

also decide whether the accused should be remanded in custody pending trial or allowed freedom on bail.

The Crown Court

The Courts Act 1971 reorganized a criminal structure dating back to the Middle Ages. Courts of Assize and Quarter Sessions were abolished and replaced by a system of Crown Courts, with unrestricted criminal jurisdiction, sitting at convenient centres and trying cases committed for trial by Magistrates' Courts.

Criminal offences have been classified into four groups for the purpose of trial. The first class which comprises the most serious offences must be tried by a High Court judge. Less serious offences will be tried by (lesser) Circuit judges or by Recorders (barristers sitting as part-time judges). In some cases lay justices may form part of the bench.

The judge conducts the trial and decides any points of law that may arise. The guilt or innocence of the accused is determined by a jury of 12 laymen and women and, if the verdict is guilty, the judge will pass sentence.

27

E. Appeals in criminal cases

An appeal may be made from a Magistrates' Court against either the conviction or the severity of the sentence. The appeal takes the form of a complete re-hearing of the case in the Crown Court.

An appeal may be made on a point of law by either the prosecution or the defence to the Divisional Court of the Queen's Bench Division. This is known as 'case stated' since the magistrates are required to state their findings on the facts before them. The Divisional Court will decide the law applicable to those facts and, if necessary, remit the case to the justices, instructing them to decide the case again on the basis of this ruling on the law.

An appeal against a conviction or sentence in the Crown Court may be made by the defendant to the Criminal Division of the Court of Appeal where it will be heard by a bench of three judges. A further appeal by either the prosecution or the defence is possible to the House of Lords but this occurs infrequently. A point of law of general public importance must be involved and permission to appeal must be given by either the Court of Appeal or the House itself.

Specimen questions

1. Explain the jurisdiction of the County Courts in matters likely to affect a business. What are the advantages and disadvantages of bringing an action in the County Court instead of the High Court?
2. 'The Divisional Court yesterday upheld the conviction of John Bull for selling oats at a price higher than the price which had been fixed by statutory instrument issued by the Minister of Agriculture. This follows a European Community directive under which maximum prices are to be fixed for the sale of wheat, barley and other such products.'
   You are required to explain briefly:
   (a) whether this was a civil or criminal case;
   (b) the place of the Divisional Court in the court structure;
   (c) how the case would have reached the Divisional Court;
   (d) the relevance of the decision for future cases of a similar nature;
   (e) the meaning and effect of a directive (see Unit 6); and
   (f) why the court was able to deal with oats, which were not specifically mentioned.
3. (a) Explain the difference between criminal law and civil law.
   (b) Because of a fault in the manufacturing process, some tins of food are marketed which contain impurities. In consequence, a number of consumers become seriously ill.
      (i)   What legal proceedings may arise?
      (ii) What courts would hear the cases?
      (iii) What is the likely outcome of the proceedings?
4. Explain, with reasons, which court would hear the following cases:
   (a) a claim for damages for negligence which has caused an alleged loss of £50 000;

(b) a petition to wind up a company with a capital of £100 000;

(c) a prosecution for applying a false trade description;

(d) a claim for £20 000 for breach of trust.

State in each instance the court to which an appeal might lie.

5. There is widespread concern about the number of unqualified persons giving incorrect advice on taxation problems. To remedy this, an Act could be passed empowering the Department of Trade and Industry, after consultation with the appropriate professional bodies, to issue regulations specifying the qualifications which must be held by 'tax consultants'.

Suppose that this happens and such regulations are later made.

Alice, whose professional body has not been consulted and whose qualification has not been recognized, feels that this change in the law is unfair.

You are required to explain to Alice:

(a) the meaning of 'Act' and 'regulations' and the relationship between them;

(b) whether the validity of (i) the Act, or (ii) the regulations, may be challenged in the courts and, if so, on what grounds;

(c) in which court she may seek a remedy and the channels of appeal open to her if the decision is unfavourable.

6. Assume that an Industrial Safety Act empowers the Secretary of State for Employment to issue regulations for guarding factory machinery in order to protect the operators from personal injury. In the exercise of this power, the Woodworking (Type X Machines) Regulations are issued. These provide that all Type X machines must be fitted with a secure guard. There is a maximum fine of £2000 for default.

Edward, an employer, installs a Type XY machine, a later model, which the manufacturers claim has a built-in guard. He does not therefore fit a guard. Unfortunately, William, an employee, is injured when operating the machine, and Edward is subsequently prosecuted, convicted and fined £2000 in a Magistrates' Court.

You are required to explain:

(a) the court to which Edward may appeal and the possible grounds for his appeal;

(b) the court in which William may claim compensation and the grounds upon which his claim may be based;

(c) the relevance in both of these cases of earlier court decisions on similar facts.

Unit 4. Other Courts and Tribunals

A. Modern special courts and tribunals

The existence of special courts outside the ordinary system has always been a feature of the English legal system throughout its history. The mercantile courts and the Court of Chancery itself in its early days are examples which were mentioned in Unit 1. Most of these older special courts have been incorporated into the ordinary system, although there are still a few which, for various reasons, did not perish in the nineteenth-century reforms or in the Courts Act 1971.

More recently, in the last 100 years, governments have created a large number of new special courts and tribunals. This was another result of the great expansion of government into social and economic fields. The special nature of some of the disputes arising from these new activities makes the composition and procedure of the ordinary courts inappropriate for this purpose.

Reasons for their creation

1. The ordinary courts are courts of *law*, and are not equipped to deal with the economic, social, business, industrial relations and other considerations that lie behind certain types of dispute.
2. The procedure of the ordinary courts tends to be slow. Administrative decisions often have to be acted upon fairly quickly, otherwise the job will never be done. Special tribunals may therefore be set up to hear and decide on appeals very quickly. In other circumstances, delay can cause great financial hardship to the claimant. A person claiming to have been wrongly refused social security benefits can hardly be expected to starve while an appeal awaits hearing in the ordinary

courts. Such appeals, therefore, now go to special social security appeal tribunals which operate relatively quickly.

3. Procedure in the ordinary courts is also very expensive, again for reasons which will be discussed later. The quick and less formal procedure of special tribunals can be much cheaper, and this can outweigh the fact that evidence may sometimes be presented and examined less thoroughly.

4. The formal atmosphere of the ordinary civil courts can be very forbidding, and can often deter claimants from pursuing certain types of claim. Most special tribunals operate in a much more relaxed and informal manner.

5. Finally, the rules of common law and equity concentrate on protecting and enforcing *individual* rights, and on giving the individual the right to help himself. The social legislation, which has played such an important part in the development of English law in the last century, has a rather different basic objective, and concentrates more on those who are not very good at helping themselves. This difference in approach has sometimes influenced governments in deciding that disputes over social legislation should normally go to special tribunals.

A description of some of the special courts and tribunals which have been created may help to illustrate some of these points.

B. Administrative tribunals

Types of tribunal

In most cases where special courts were established, it was not felt necessary to set up a powerful body like the courts just described. The nature of the disputes likely to arise made smaller 'administrative' tribunals more appropriate, and very many of these have been created. The Franks Committee on Tribunals and Inquiries in 1957 estimated that there were even then over 2000 different tribunals in existence. These differ from each other in many respects, but they do have some common features: the members are usually not lawyers, although most chairmen are legally qualified; they operate informally, cheaply, and fairly quickly; most of them sit locally; there is usually no appeal to the courts on a point of fact, and only sometimes on a point of law. It is not possible here to describe all of these tribunals, but a few of the main categories will serve as examples.

1. *Social security*

The Social Security Acts 1992, as amended, provide that benefits shall be payable to people out of state funds, subject to certain conditions, in the event of sickness, death, unemployment, maternity or similar situations giving rise to financial problems; there may also be entitlement to income support or family credit. Under the industrial injuries provisions of these Acts, benefits may be paid to persons suffering injury or disease arising out of and in the course of employment. Disputes can often arise as to whether a claimant is entitled to benefit, and as to the amount due.

If the local insurance officer rejects a claim, the claimant can appeal to a local social security appeal tribunal, of which there are some 200 in England and Wales. The tribunal will have three members: a chairman who will be a barrister or solicitor, and two lay members.

A further right of appeal on a point of law lies from the local tribunals to one of the full-time Social Security Commissioners, who are barristers or solicitors of at least 10 years' standing. Some decisions of the Commissioners are published in a series of reports and a system of precedent has now been developed. A further appeal lies to the Court of Appeal on a question of law.

Other types of tribunal in this broad category include medical appeal tribunals, disability appeal tribunals and child support tribunals. In 1991, responsibility for administration passed to a new Independent Tribunal Service. This marked an important step in the rationalization of the tribunal system.

2. *Tribunals dealing with employment*

These are some of the busiest and most important of all tribunals, and their constitution is governed by the Employment Tribunals Act 1996 (as amended). Their main work arises from disputed claims for redundancy payments, complaints of unfair dismissal, and with allegations of discrimination in employment on grounds of race or sex. They sit locally, with a legally qualified chairman and normally two other members, one from a panel representing employers, the other from a panel representing employees. They work informally and fairly quickly.

An appeal on a point of law lies to the Employment Appeal Tribunal, where again three members usually sit. The chairman will be a Judge with special experience in this field, from the High Court in England and Wales or from the equivalent courts in Scotland and Northern Ireland. There will also be two lay members chosen from a special panel. This is therefore a very important body, and some of its decisions are reported and published in the Industrial Relations Law Reports (IRLR). A further direct right of appeal on a point of law lies to the Court of Appeal (Civil Division).

3. *Competition law*

The Competition Act 1998, which replaces earlier legislation, is based very closely on European Community law. By s.2, agreements between undertakings which (a) may affect trade within the UK, and (b) have as their object or effect the prevention, restriction or distortion of competition within the UK, are prohibited. This applies, for example, to agreements which directly or indirectly fix purchase or selling prices or other trading conditions; or limit or control production, markets, technical development or investment; or distort share markets or sources of supply. Some agreements may also be affected by s.18, which prohibits any conduct on the part of one or more undertakings which amounts to the abuse of a dominant position (such as a monopoly) in a market, if it may affect trade within the UK.

A party affected can apply for questions of infringement to be referred to the Director General of Fair Trading. An applicant who is dissatisfied may then appeal to the Competition Commission, which has its appeal tribunal for this purpose. Sittings of the tribunal will have a legally qualified chairman and two lay members. Chairmen will be professionally qualified with at least 7 years' experience. There must also be a President of the Competition Commission Appeal Tribunals, with at least a 10-year legal qualification. He must arrange for training of the chairmen, and choosing lay members.

An appeal on a point of law, or as to the amount of any penalty, can then be made direct to the Court of Appeal (Civil Division).

4. *Revenue*

Examples here include the Special Commissioners (civil servants) and the General Commissioners (lay people) who hear appeals against income tax assessments, and VAT Tribunals which hear appeals against valued added tax decisions. Valuation Tribunals have jurisdiction over non-domestic rates and the local council tax.

Control over tribunals

Administrative tribunals have sometimes come in for criticism; it is suggested that the legal and lay members appointed by a Minister might be more likely to give a decision favourable to the Government and civil service than would the independent judges in the ordinary courts; and that the looser procedure might sometimes make a wrong decision seem more likely. There is little evidence that these criticisms are justified, but in any event tribunals are subject to two main controls.

1. *Judicial control by the courts.* In the first place there is usually a provision for an appeal on a point of law to the ordinary courts. This can cause delay, however, and occasionally no right of appeal is allowed.

    Secondly, the courts exercise some other controls, often by an extended use of very old 'prerogative' orders. *Mandamus*, which means 'we command', is used to compel the performance of some duty, such as the duty of a tribunal to allow an appeal when it ought to do so. *Prohibition*, as the name suggests, is used to prevent a tribunal exceeding its jurisdiction or otherwise acting wrongfully. *Certiorari*, the most important of these orders, is used to compel a tribunal to inform the High Court of the facts of the case under discussion so that the High Court may certify whether the tribunal has acted wrongfully, in which event the decision will be quashed. It is no longer necessary to ask the High Court for a specific order; instead a request is made for a 'judicial review' of the decision in question and the High Court is able to make such order as it deems appropriate.

    These controls can be exercised if a tribunal has acted *ultra vires*, i.e., exceeded its powers. The tribunals only have the powers conferred on them by statute, and can only exercise them in the ways and for the purposes intended by Parliament. The courts can, therefore, intervene if these powers are, in the opinion of the court, exceeded or seriously abused. Thus the courts can insist that tribunals observe the principles of 'natural justice', for instance that no man shall be judge in his own cause, that is, that no member of the tribunal shall have any personal interest in the subject-matter under discussion, and that all legally interested parties shall have a right to be heard.

This supervisory jurisdiction of the courts is exercised largely by the Queen's Bench Division, usually by a Divisional Court.

If a tribunal is alleged to have acted in a way that is incompatible with the European Convention on Human Rights then this too can be raised by an appeal or application for judicial review.

2. *The Council on Tribunals.* A Council on Tribunals keeps under review the constitution and working of administrative tribunals. The members of the Council are appointed by the Lord Chancellor, and report to him on matters referred to it. The Council also has an important power to examine any rules of procedure that a tribunal may introduce. Thus, in most cases, tribunals must now give reasons for their decision upon request from one of the parties and give a right of appeal on a point of law to the ordinary courts. This is now governed by the Tribunals and Inquiries Act 1992.

C. Domestic tribunals

When people form an association, they usually prescribe rules which members must obey, and provide a committee or other machinery for enforcement where necessary. All persons joining the association agree to be bound and to submit to the judgment of the committee in the event of a dispute.

Thus, allegations of unprofessional conduct against solicitors, medical practitioners, dentists and architects are heard by disciplinary committees set up for this purpose within the profession. Trade associations often set up tribunals to enforce uniform trading practices on their members and trade unions ensure discipline in powers given to their committees.

Many such disciplinary bodies exercise wide powers, particularly where membership of the association may be a condition for carrying on the particular trade, profession or business, so that expulsion can take away a person's ability to earn a living in that field. The ordinary courts do exercise some controls where domestic tribunals exceed or abuse the power given them by the rules of the association, in much the same way as the courts can review the actions of administrative tribunals.

D. Arbitration

Arbitration is a means of settling disputes otherwise than by court action and it arises when one or more persons are appointed to hear the arguments submitted by the parties and to give a decision on them. The type of arbitrator depends upon the nature of the case. In some instances a legal practitioner may be chosen, while in others of a highly technical nature it may be more appropriate to appoint a person with knowledge or experience of the subject-matter.

The most common way in which arbitration arises is by the voluntary agreement of the parties either before or after a dispute has arisen. Many commercial contracts, for example insurance policies, contain a clause providing for this method of settling disputes. It is often preferred to court action for it is usually cheaper, quicker, more informal, and does not involve publicity.

Provided that the submission is in writing, which is usually the case, arbitration procedure is now governed by the Arbitration Act 1996 which consolidates three earlier Acts; current statute law is re-enacted, together with codification of the more important arbitration principles developed through the courts. Once arbitration has been agreed upon and is being carried out in a proper manner, the court will not interfere nor hear the dispute itself. An arbitration award properly arrived at will be enforced by the court. Points of law which arise may be submitted separately to the court for decision, by means of *case stated*. In these ways the court allows the parties to settle their own disputes, but at the same time maintains a supervisory role.

Various statutes provide for reference of certain types of issue to arbitration, and the courts themselves can refer a matter to arbitration where, for instance, the case requires prolonged examination of documents, scientific investigation or involved accounting.

In 1973 an arbitration service was set up within the County Court structure. From 1999 this was replaced by a new 'fast claims track' for claims not exceeding £5000 (£1000 for most personal injuries). A District Judge will usually refer the claim to this 'track' even against the wishes of the parties, and claims for more than this amount can be referred with the agreement of the parties. The District judge himself usually hears the case. Legal representation is permitted but discouraged since the fees of a lawyer cannot be recovered as costs and must be paid by the litigants themselves even if they win the case. Awards are enforceable in the same ways as a County Court judgment. This procedure allows small claims to be settled informally, without rigid adherence to the rules of evidence and procedure, and now covers a large proportion of all County Court cases. There can be no appeal on most issues.

A specialized use of arbitration, which has sometimes been important in recent years, is for the purpose of settling industrial disputes. This is arbitration in a slightly different sense, in that the award here is not usually legally enforceable, although it can be none the less effective.

E. The Judicial Committee of the Privy Council

This body does not form part of the court structure of this country but, since it corresponds in structure with the House of Lords and its decisions have a strong persuasive influence, it is more conveniently dealt with here. The Judicial Committee is the final court of appeal from the Commonwealth in both civil and criminal matters, except where self-governing countries have exercised their right to abolish such appeals; most countries have now done this. The Committee also hears appeals from the Channel Islands, the Isle of Man, the Ecclesiastical Courts, the Prize Courts in wartime, and from certain other tribunals such as the Disciplinary Committee of the General Medical Council.

In practice, membership is restricted to those persons holding high legal qualifications and it is very similar in composition to the House of Lords when that body sits as a court of appeal, with the addition of certain judges from Commonwealth countries. Although its judgments are not binding upon English courts, they are treated with great respect in view of the Committee's composition. The judgment takes the form of advice to the Crown which is then formally implemented by Order in Council. Dissenting opinions can be delivered.

F. Other Courts

The European Court of Justice

This is an important institution of the European Union, and its decisions on European Community law must be accepted by national courts. There is also a Court of First Instance, which has limited jurisdiction, and from which appeals can be made to the full Court (see Unit 6).

The European Court of Human Rights (ECHR)

This must not be confused with the European Court of Justice above. The Human Rights Court has no connection with the European Union. It sits in Strasbourg, and hears claims that the European Convention on Human Rights has been broken. An individual may petition it, but sometimes its judgments have only persuasive effect in the UK, despite the Human Rights Act 1998.

Both of the above courts must be distinguished from the International Court of Justice, which sits in the Hague as an organ of the United Nations and offers a means of settling disputes between states.

Specimen questions

1. Many industrial and commercial disputes are today settled by administrative tribunals.
   (a) What is an administrative tribunal?
   (b) Why are tribunals established?
   (c) How are tribunals controlled?
2. (a) A change in the law may necessitate some new provision for the settlement of disputes. What are the advantages of making such provision a reference to some tribunal instead of leaving it to the courts?
   (b) Indicate which court or tribunal would settle the following matters and any provisions existing for an appeal:
      (i) a claim for a social security benefit which has been rejected by the local insurance officer;
      (ii) a dispute concerning an alleged restrictive trade agreement.

3. Write short notes on:
   (a) Competition Commission Appeal Tribunals;
   (b) Employment Tribunals;
   (c) Social Security Appeal Tribunals;
   (d) Council on Tribunals;
   (e) Judicial Committee of the Privy Council.

4. (a) Your company is revising its standard form of contract, which is used for its car-hire business, and is considering the insertion of an arbitration clause.
   Draft a report explaining the effect of such a clause and the benefits that might arise from it in the event of a dispute.

   (b) Many contracts do not include an arbitration clause. Explain when a dispute concerning such a contract may be submitted to arbitration.

5. (a) Which court or tribunal would hear the following cases:
   (i) a prosecution for breach of the Health and Safety at Work Act;
   (ii) a claim for breach of a contract to supply goods to the value of £60 000;
   (iii) an action for unfair dismissal;
   (iv) an action to re-possess goods following the breach of a hire-purchase agreement?
   State in each instance the court to which an appeal might lie.

   (b) In what circumstances might a commercial dispute be more appropriately settled by arbitration rather than a court action?

Unit 5. Court Proceedings

This unit will be concerned primarily with the course taken by typical civil proceedings, including matters likely to arise before trial, the trial itself, and the ways in which any judgment given by the court may be enforced. It will conclude with a brief outline of criminal proceedings.

Civil proceedings vary according to the type of action. It is not possible here to deal with petitions for divorce, for the bankruptcy of a private individual or for the winding up of a company. Cases in the Chancery Division and the Family Division are also governed by special rules. The emphasis here will be on common law actions in the Queen's Bench Division or the County Court, such as are likely to arise following a breach of contract or an accident at work or on the road. It should be remembered that many such actions take place in the County Courts, but the more important are heard in the High Court. In any event the problems facing a litigant in either Court are very similar.

The Courts and Legal Services Act 1990 did simplify procedure and many more changes followed the 1996 report and recommendations of Lord Woolf. These were aimed at flexibility, reduction of delay and expense, and greater simplicity. Under the Civil Procedure Act 1997, the Civil Procedure Rules 1998 now govern all civil proceedings in England and Wales (from 1999).

A. Preliminary considerations

To sue or not to sue

Any person may begin and conduct proceedings himself without legal assistance, but because of the difficulties involved it is highly desirable to obtain legal advice by consulting a solicitor. The solicitor may advise that further legal action is not worth while at all. It has been said that only lawyers benefit from the law, and the litigant might be best advised simply to drop the matter. The following factors may be relevant.

1. Is the other party worth suing? There is always the possibility that, because of lack of means, he will not be able to pay any damages that may be awarded against him. Even if he has the means it might be difficult to enforce the judgment against him; the methods of enforcing judgments will be discussed later in this unit. If there are two possible defendants, for example, a bus driver whose negligence caused the accident and his employers who are responsible for his actions, it is desirable to bring the action against the one more likely to be able to pay the damages, in this example the bus company.

   If the other party is insured against liability then justice is more likely. This is why the Road Traffic Acts make it an offence to use a motor vehicle on a road unless the driver is insured against liability for personal injury to third parties. Note also the Employers' Liability (Compulsory Insurance) Act 1969.

2. A major consideration is the likely cost of the proceedings. The claimant's costs in a defended High Court action may run to many hundreds of thousands of pounds, more on appeal. Even the costs of a defended County Court action may be high. Moreover, unless there are good reasons for deciding otherwise, the unsuccessful party will be required to pay not only his own costs, but also those of his opponent, at the discretion of the court. The cost of losing an action can, therefore, be very substantial indeed.

   The winner does not, in fact, get all of his costs from the unsuccessful party. The actual legal costs incurred by the winner will be scrutinized by a court official, and anything not strictly essential to winning the case, such as a very high fee paid to counsel, will be struck out. Even winning the action, therefore, can still be expensive, and the action might not be worth while if the damages recovered are small. There may, of course, be good reasons for bringing an action at a loss, for example a business firm does not wish to acquire a reputation among its debtors that it does not bother to collect small debts.

3. The length of time which proceedings will take must also be borne in mind, particularly in cases where an appeal is likely. The claimant might have to wait several years for his remedy which, depending upon the type of loss suffered, might make it hardly worth the effort. Negotiations for a settlement can also prolong matters greatly.

4. The possibilities of mediation and arbitration should be explored. If successful, these will be quicker and cheaper.

5. A final consideration may be the publicity which a court action will bring. Even a successful action by a business may have a bad effect upon its public reputation or on its relations with customers, employees, creditors or shareholders.

Assistance with legal costs

If, taking account of the above considerations, it is decided to proceed with the action, the next step is to consider how to finance the proceedings. A private person of limited means will find this difficult.

The Access to Justice Act 1999 replaces the old legal aid scheme with a new Community Legal Service. This provides substantially for legal advice and help in preventing or settling disputes. It does not, however, deal with most court proceedings. It does not cover proceedings for under £5000. Moreover, unlike the former legal aid scheme, it does not give financial help with most accident proceedings arising from negligence. Tribunal cases are not covered, although free initial advice might be available.

Many accident proceedings and private contract claims are now funded by 'conditional' fees, where the client pays no fee if the action is lost (no-win–no-fee). If the action is won, however, he pays the solicitor's normal fee and probably also a 'success' fee calculated as a percentage of the normal fee. He will usually be entitled to recover most of these fees from the losing party. Conversely, if he should lose he may have to pay the other side's costs, but he can insure against this. The solicitor may help with the premium, which is then recoverable from the other side if he wins.

Other sources of assistance may be available. A worker may be helped to bring an action by his trade union, or a body such as the Equal Opportunities Commission may act to remedy a grievance (page 310).

B. Civil procedure before trial

Negotiating a settlement

As a first step it is customary for the solicitor to try to settle the dispute without litigation by writing to the opposing party or his solicitor. If no opportunity at all is given to the other party to settle, a successful claimant might be penalized by not getting some of his costs from the other side. In most cases this initial letter will be followed by other correspondence, and possibly meetings between representatives of the two sides with a view to reaching a settlement. In an accident claim the negotiations will usually be between the injured person's solicitor and the other party's insurance company.

Simultaneously with this, each side will be concerned with collecting evidence. In accident claims this will normally include medical reports, statements from witnesses, and possibly technical reports about, for example, the condition of the motor vehicle or the defective premises. Medical reports, in particular, can be extremely important, because the amount of any settlement will depend upon how bad, and how permanent, the injuries prove to be. Where the injuries take some time to heal, doctors cannot always answer these questions immediately, and this is often a major reason for delay in reaching a legal settlement. During this period, the solicitor will usually also obtain 'counsel's opinion' on any difficult points of law or of evidence which might arise.

The vast majority of claims in tort or for breach of contract are in fact settled without actual resort to the courts. As a rule, it is only where a settlement proves impossible that proceedings have to be started.

Commencing proceedings

In civil proceedings the first formal steps, referred to as *statements of case*, are designed to do two things: to bring the parties together before the court, and to ensure that everyone concerned clearly understands what issues are in dispute. The claimant, normally through his solicitor, will file a claim in the County Court or High Court. A claim form is then served on the defendant, notifying him of the claim. Particulars of claim must state briefly the facts and wrongs that are alleged, and the remedies (including amounts if possible) that are sought.

If the defendant does not admit the claim, he may enter a defence. He may also make a counterclaim ('Part 20 claim') alleging that it is the claimant who is at fault and claiming redress for himself. The court has power to require further information of allegations made and obtain disclosure of documents. All claims, defences, etc. must be 'verified' by the person putting them forward. This is a statement that the maker genuinely believes facts that he alleges. A dishonest answer is a contempt of court and may be punished. Time limits are fixed for all of these matters, and delay by one party may lead to judgment against him. At any stage a party can withdraw from the action, though may then have to pay the other's costs.

Meanwhile, even at this stage, a claimant might have to ask for some temporary order to protect his position pending the main hearing. He might ask for a 'freezing injunction' restraining the defendant (usually a company) from removing assets from the country, or a 'search order' to seize documents and thereby safeguard evidence.

Before the trial can take place there must be a decision about where and how the case will be heard. This is made by a District Judge (or by a 'Master' in the High Court in London). An allocation questionnaire is sent to each party asking him, for example, to identify witnesses and expert evidence, estimate trial time, state desired locations, and estimate overall costs. There may sometimes be a hearing if required. On the basis of this and the original statement of claim the Judge allocates the case to one of the following 'tracks':

- There is a 'small claims' track for cases up to £5000, which will then be heard by the District Judge himself; this is very like the former County Court arbitration service (see page 23).
- There is a 'fast track' for most claims between £5000 and £15 000. Most of these will be heard by a Circuit Judge in a County Court, with special rules to increase speed

of the trial itself and of pre-trial proceedings. Cases of greater complexity or general legal significance can be sent to the High Court.

- 'Multi-track' cases are normally ones exceeding £15 000. They will vary widely in amount and complexity, and the courts are given wide discretion as to how they handle cases. Claims begun in the High Court for less than £50 000 may well be transferred to a County Court, depending upon complexity, etc.

The District Judge will also fix a date for the trial. He will examine the evidence that the parties intend to call: some allegations may be ones which the other side is willing to admit, and therefore formal proof is unnecessary; other matters can be proved by sworn written statements (*affidavits*) so that attendance of witnesses in person is unnecessary. He can restrict the number of expert witnesses, so as to save time. He will decide whether the case is one of the rare instances where there should be a civil jury (e.g. fraud, defamation).

All of these preliminary or *interim* stages can be justified in that they save the time of judges and witnesses at the trial itself. On the other hand, their complexity may deter a litigant from conducting a case himself, and oblige him to seek expensive legal assistance.

C. The civil trial

At the trial both parties are usually represented by barristers and/or solicitors and, since the burden of proving the case generally rests upon the claimant, counsel for the claimant begins. He outlines the facts of the case and the evidence he proposes to call in support of these facts. This evidence is then produced, and any witnesses who are examined may be cross-examined by the defence. The defence will then put its case to the court in the same manner. After the defence case has been completed, each counsel will address the court in turn, first the counsel for the defendant and then the counsel for the claimant. It is usually during these closing speeches that any points of law will be argued before the judge.

In the rare cases where a jury is present in civil proceedings, the judge will sum up the case, outlining the evidence, giving any directions on questions of law, and telling them what questions of fact are for their decision and the various conclusions open to them. If there is no jury, the judge will deliver his judgment, either immediately or, if the case is particularly complicated, at a later date. The latter is known as a *reserved judgment*.

A defended action in the County Court follows a similar pattern, except that in most areas the parties will usually be represented in court by solicitors rather than barristers. Reserved judgments, and indeed detailed arguments on points of law, are not very common.

If the claimant is successful in proving his case, there are several remedies which the judge may grant. The most common will be an order for the defendant to pay damages to the claimant, a fixed sum of money by way of compensation. If he has been asked to do so by the claimant, the judge has power to grant an injunction or to make various other orders, such as an order for the possession of land or goods.

Immediately after judgment has been given it is usual for counsel for the successful party to ask for costs and, as mentioned earlier, this is a matter for the judge's discretion. If damages awarded are less than a sum offered or paid into court during the pre-trial negotiations, the claimant will not normally be awarded costs. If an appeal is to be made against the judgment it must be made within a limited period of time.

D. Enforcement of civil judgments

It is one thing to obtain judgment; it can be another thing to force the defendant to comply with it. If the judgment orders the defendant to pay damages to the claimant, for instance, what happens if the defendant still refuses to pay? Or if he simply has not the means to pay? Equally important, what happens if the defendant fails to comply with an injunction, or an order to return land or goods to the claimant?

Money judgments

Various legal steps can be taken if a judgment debtor fails to pay.

1. A first step is often to find out what income or assets the debtor has. An individual debtor can be called before the court for an *oral examination*, at which he can be questioned about his assets (property, bank accounts, savings, etc.) and sources of income (such as job, employer, wages/salary).
2. Under the Attachment of Earnings Act 1971, a judgment creditor may be able to obtain an *attachment of earnings* order from the court. Where the defendant is in employment, his employer can be ordered to deduct a specified sum each week or month from the defendant's wages or salary, and to pay this into court for the claimant. The defendant will of course always be left with at least a basic living allowance.
3. The claimant can obtain a *warrant of execution*, by which a court officer is ordered to seize the defendant's goods (car, etc.) and, if necessary, to sell them to pay the claimant out of the proceeds. This might be useful if the defendant has his own privately owned business or practice.
4. The court may grant a *garnishee order*, under which money owed to the defendant by someone else must be paid directly to the claimant. In this way, the claimant can obtain direct payment from the debtor's bank account if it is in credit, or from his savings if any.
5. The claimant can apply to the court for a *charging order* on the defendant's land or shares held by him in a company. If the money is still not paid, the claimant can ultimately have the house or shares sold, and recover his damages from the proceeds.

In addition to these methods of enforcement, the judgment creditor can also threaten to make the defendant bankrupt in certain circumstances and, if need be, carry out the threat.

Non-money judgments

If the defendant fails to obey an injunction, which is an order of the court to refrain from doing something, then he is in contempt of court, and the court can, on application by the claimant, punish him. If he still refuses to comply, the defendant can ultimately be imprisoned. An order to deliver land to the claimant, or to deliver goods, can be carried out by a court officer if necessary.

E. Criminal proceedings

Procedure before trial

In the case of less serious offences, a summons is served upon the accused directing him to appear before the court at a specified time, date and place. Proceedings against companies for such offences as false trade descriptions, unguarded factory machinery and incorrect weights and measures are invariably begun in this way. If the offence is more serious and the accused is unlikely to appear voluntarily, a warrant for his arrest will be signed by a magistrate and executed by the police. For some offences, usually the most serious ones, the offender may be arrested without a warrant.

As already mentioned, Magistrates' Courts deal with 98 per cent of all criminal prosecutions and therefore, once the attendance of the offender has been secured, the court may proceed to trial. If the offender has only recently been arrested, an adjournment may first be necessary to allow time for both parties to prepare their cases. The prosecution is normally conducted by a legal practitioner of the Crown Prosecution Service, but various statutes give the power to prosecute to such officials as factory inspectors, inspectors of trading standards and public health inspectors in respect of offences against statutes which it is their duty to enforce. If the offence is one that must be tried in the Crown Court, committal proceedings will be held to determine whether or not there is a sufficiently strong case against the accused to justify a trial. If he is committed for trial, the magistrates can determine whether he is to be held in custody pending the trial or released on bail.

The trial

In both the Magistrates' Court and the Crown Court the accused will be asked to plead guilty or not guilty. If the plea is guilty, the prosecution will summarize the evidence and give details of the background of the accused, the defence may plead for mitigation, and sentence is passed.

If the plea is not guilty, the prosecution will outline the case against the accused and call witnesses to give evidence on oath to support this; these witnesses may be cross-examined by the defence. The defence case will then be put in a like manner. After closing speeches by both sides, the verdict of the court will be given, either by the magistrates or by the jury following a summing-up by the judge. A verdict of guilty will place a duty upon the court of imposing the most appropriate form of sentence, for example a custodial sentence of imprisonment or the payment of a monetary sum by way of a fine.

Compensation

The punishment of the offender will not of itself compensate the victim of a crime. It is always possible for the latter to bring a civil action, normally in tort, but this may not be worth while. To avoid hearing the same evidence twice in different courts it would seem desirable to settle small amounts of compensation in the same (criminal) proceedings.

A criminal court may, therefore, at its discretion, award compensation for personal injury, loss or damage, excluding loss arising from fatal and road traffic accidents. In Magistrates' Courts there is a restriction of £5000 for each offence for which there is a conviction. Any compensation ordered is deducted from any damages subsequently awarded in a civil action arising from the same facts.

This power is now contained in the Powers of Criminal Courts Act 1973. It has been used to compensate some victims of offences under the Trade Descriptions Act (Unit 18) who might not have brought a separate civil action because of the time and cost involved. Wide powers are also given to order the restitution of stolen goods or money which represents the proceeds of their sale.

A further means of securing compensation since 1964 is through the Criminal Injuries Compensation Board. Awards from £1000 upwards may be paid to the victims of criminal violence.

Specimen questions

1. Many possible rights of action are not enforced through the courts and, even when court proceedings are begun, very few cases reach the appeal stage.

   Why do you think this is so? Take as an illustration a debt owing to your company and explain at what stage and for what reasons the case may be settled or further action for enforcement abandoned.

2. (a) Why, in civil proceedings, is there normally a long period of time between the first consultation with a solicitor and the trial of the case?

   (b) Outline the course of proceedings in the trial of a civil case.

3. Your company has been successful in a claim for damages for breach of contract. What action may be taken if the judgment debtor refuses to pay?

4. You have suffered loss by reason of a false trade description. Compare the right to recover damages by a civil action with an award of compensation following a criminal prosecution.

5. Explain each of the following terms:
    (a) freezing injunction;
    (b) multi-track claims;
    (c) reserved judgments;
    (d) warrant of execution;
    (e) garnishee order.

Unit 6. Law of the European Union

A. The European Union

The Treaties creating the European Union date historically from the Treaty of Paris 1951, when the European Coal and Steel Community was established (ECSC). Another special community, to do with nuclear energy, was created in 1957 (Euratom). The main European Economic Community (EEC) was established by the first Treaty of Rome 1957. It had six member states at the outset. The United Kingdom joined with two others in 1972/3, and others joined later. There are currently 15 member states. The Treaties became part of English law by the European Communities Act 1972.

The provisions of the EEC Treaty of Rome still form the basis of European Community law: the main institutions; the forms that the legal rules take (EC legislation, etc.); and some of the rules themselves. Nevertheless, the EEC Treaty has been added to and amended in many respects over the years, notably by the Single European Act 1986 (SE), by the Treaty on European Union 1993 enacted at Maastricht (TEU), and by the Treaty of Amsterdam 1997 (ToA).

After the 1993 Maastricht Treaty, the 1957 EEC Treaty was renamed simply the European Community Treaty (EC). More importantly, the title 'European Union' was officially adopted. The Treaty of Amsterdam, among many other things, renumbered the EC Treaty Articles, but did not substantially alter them.

The aims of the Treaties have gradually become more extensive. In 1957, the aims included 'approximating the economic policies of member states' and promoting 'closer relations between the states'. The Single European Act 1986 went much further, and aimed to establish a single internal market, without frontiers, in which goods, persons, services and capital could circulate freely. The Maastricht Treaty (TEU) 1992 provided three main pillars for this: (i) the European Communities, based on the original treaties as extended; (ii) a common foreign policy and cooperation on security; and (iii) cooperation on judicial matters and policing. (This unit will concentrate mainly on the first 'pillar', the provisions of which can still be referred to as EC law.) In the European Union, citizens of the member states also become 'citizens of the EU'. One of the main economic aims of the Maastricht Treaty and the Union has been the creation of a European Monetary Union (EMU) and a common currency. Certain countries, including the UK, opted out of the new currency, although the UK might join later. Both the Maastricht and the Amsterdam Treaties extended the provisions for employment. All the Treaties have had and are having a growing influence on UK business and constitutional law.

B. The Institutions of the European Union

The Institutions responsible for carrying out the functions of the Union date, for the most part, from 1957.

1. *The Council*

This is composed of one minister of government from each member state. He must be authorized to commit the government of that state. A government can choose to send any minister, and if a specific topic is to be dealt with, such as agriculture or employment, the appropriate minister from the national government will be sent. Otherwise the Council will be composed of the foreign ministers. Council meetings are monthly, and member states take it in six-monthly turns to hold the Presidency and take the chair. In general it can act by a majority.

The Council is the formal legislative body for the Communities, although usually it can only act on proposals put forward by the Commission. It also makes the final decision on a large number of EU issues, including foreign and security policy, and judicial and policing matters.

Between the monthly meetings of ministers, a *Comité des Représentants Permanents (Coreper)* carries on the work of the Council. This is composed of ambassadors and senior diplomats of the member states, and can deal with many vitally important matters, such as examining and proposing agreement of regulations, many economic and budgetary issues, and even some foreign affairs. It is not formally an institution or part of the Council, but in practice it carries out very important functions.

In addition to the monthly ministerial Council meetings described above, there is a full European Council 'summit' twice a year. This is composed of the Heads of Government, the Foreign Ministers, the President of the Commission (see below) and another Commissioner. It provides the political impetus for the EU, and it reports to the European Parliament.

2. *The Commission*

This is the executive body, and has 20 members, two each from the larger states and one each from the smaller. Members are appointed by their own national governments, and serve five-year terms. A Commission President must be chosen by the member states unanimously, so that each state has a veto. Commissioners are required to act solely on behalf of the Union, and independently of their own member governments. The Commission acts as a whole, but in practice each Commissioner is given responsibility for one aspect of Community work, such as transport or employment, and each will have his own administrative department.

The Commission has vital functions in relation to new legislation. In particular, it prepares and agrees new drafts to be sent to the Council for enactment. ('The Commission proposes and the Council disposes.') Its executive functions then include ensuring that the obligations of all concerned under the Treaties and under secondary legislation are carried out, and it can institute proceedings in the Court of Justice against any institution, body, member or member state that it considers to be in default. It can also rule on and enforce some matters itself in areas such as competition policy. Another extremely important task is to administer and apply the EU budget.

3. *The European Parliament*

This was formerly called the 'Assembly'. It represents the peoples of the member states, and the number of seats allocated to each country is fixed according to population. Each state can choose its own electoral system. The Parliament usually meets for one week each month. It is not a Parliament as understood in the UK, since it is not the formal legislature. It is largely an advisory and consultative body in which Union issues may be discussed. Council legislation must be submitted to it for consideration, and it can make recommendations, but the Council need not accept these. Nevertheless, the suggestions will have some persuasive influence.

The Parliament does have some limited powers over the Commission. It can reject a *whole* new Commission (not an individual Commissioner), or it can pass a motion of censure on a whole Commission; it has not yet done either. It also has powers to block some fairly limited items of expenditure, and it did use these powers 1999 to make the whole Commission resign.

Members of the Parliament organize themselves into political groups (Christian Democrat, Socialist, etc.) rather than national ones.

4. *The European Court of Justice*

The Court sits in Luxembourg and its decisions on EU matters, from which there is no appeal, must be accepted by national courts. There are at present 15 judges, one from each member state. An odd number is maintained so that a majority decision can be reached on a full sitting of the Court, and business is often heard before all the judges. They may be professional judges in their own countries, or academic lawyers or public servants. The judges are assisted in each case by an advocate-general (there are nine in total), who delivers a lengthy opinion at the close of proceedings and in advance of judgment.

Compared with English procedure, much greater emphasis is placed upon written submissions or pleadings than upon oral argument, and the judges play a much more active and inquisitorial part in the hearing. It gives a single judgment without dissenting opinions. Various remedies, including monetary, may be awarded, but there is no machinery for enforcing judgments and, where this is necessary, it must be done by the member states through their national courts.

In an attempt to relieve the burden upon the Court and reduce delays, a Court of First Instance was established in 1989 under the provisions of the Single European Act. This Court has 15 judges appointed by member states, and three or five of these will sit together to hear some cases. Jurisdiction is limited to disputes between the Community and its servants and to applications for judicial review of certain actions of the Council or Commission. It also hears some complex questions of competition law. There is a right of appeal to the full Court on a point of law.

The jurisdiction of the European Court of Justice is set out by the Treaties, principally by the EEC Treaty 1957.

(i)   Actions may be brought against member states either by other member states or by the Commission on the grounds that Treaty obligations are not being fulfilled. The Court will give a declaratory judgment and it is a matter of good faith for the member state to comply with it; see *Commission of the European Communities* v. *United Kingdom* (1982) (Unit 27).

(ii) Actions may be brought against Community institutions by other institutions, by member states or by private individuals or corporate bodies who are directly concerned. In this way the legality of an act of even, for example, the Commission may be challenged. The Court may declare the act to be void and, if appropriate, award compensation.

(iii) The Court may settle disputes between the Communities and their employees arising from the employees' contracts of employment. It may also deal with non-contractual liability of Community institutions for damage caused by their servants in the performance of their duties.

(iv) One of the most important functions of the European Court is to give preliminary rulings on questions of EC law for the benefit of national courts. The European Court does not wholly decide the case. It simply gives a ruling on the disputed question of EC law and then refers back the case to the national court to be decided according to this and other issues before that court. By the EC Treaty Article 234, any court may refer a question if necessary, and this procedure has been used by many national courts at different levels. The *Factortame* case (page 9), for example, was initially referred by an English Divisional Court, to which an application for judicial review had been made. Where such a question arises in a national court from which there is no further right of appeal (such as the House of Lords), it *must* be referred to the European Court of Justice. Where a point of EC law is clear and reasonably free from doubt, the English court can simply apply it without referral; the same applies if the point has recently been ruled upon by the European Court of Justice.

5. *The Court of Auditors*
This court is another formal institution. It must examine the accounts of all EU bodies, and report at least annually.

In addition to the formal institutions, many other consultative groups have been set up by the Treaties, and some of these are very influential.

One example is the Economic and Social Committee (ECOSOC), set up by the 1957 EEC Treaty. It provides a body to represent various social and economic interests and groups, such as producers, carriers, farmers, professions, and the general public. It has over 200 members, appointed by the Council on the nomination of member states. It can be consulted by the Commission, for example when new legislation is proposed and prepared, and also by the Council and the Parliament.

Another example, set up by the Maastricht Treaty, is the Committee of the Regions (CoR), which can be consulted on many matters, including cross-border cooperation.

C. Sources of law in the European Union

The Treaties

These are the 'primary' source. They include the three foundation Treaties (of Paris and Rome) with their supplementary schedules and appendices. To these must be added all further Treaties made between member states, such as the Single European Act 1986, the Maastricht Treaty on European Union 1992, and the Treaty of Amsterdam 1997, as well as treaties such as trade agreements between the Union and states in the outside world. The Treaties are 'self-executing' in that the provisions automatically become part of the law of the member states, without the states having the right to decide whether or not to implement them by their own legislation. Thus the courts in the UK accept and apply Article 81 (formerly Art. 85) of the EC Treaty, which prohibits specified restrictive practice agreements between commercial under-takings. Rights given by the Treaties can be relied upon by individuals.

> *Macarthy's* v. *Smith* (1981), for example, arose from a provision in the EC Treaty 1957 that requires member states to maintain 'the principle that men and women should receive equal pay for equal work'. In this case, a male stockroom manager, who was paid £60 per week, left the firm. After an interval, he was replaced by Mrs Smith, doing the same job for only £50 per week. The UK Equal Pay Act at that time only applied to work done at the same time, and Mrs Smith's equality claim failed in the UK. However, the European Court of Justice held that the treaty had been broken, and Mrs Smith's claim finally succeeded (see also page 310).

Secondary legislation

In addition to the Treaties themselves as sources of law, various forms of 'secondary' legislation can be enacted by the Council (and Commission) to enable the broad objectives of the Treaties to be achieved.

Regulations are one of the main forms. They are of general application, binding in their entirety, and directly applicable in all member states without the need for further legislation.

> In *Commission* v. *UK* (1979) (Case 128/78), a regulation required that tachographs be installed in vehicles carrying goods or passengers by road, to record the duration of driving

51

and rest periods. The UK proposed to introduce a partial and voluntary scheme, whereby drivers could choose whether or not to have tachographs. The European Court held that this was insufficient, and it emphasized that the whole of the EC regulation was already part of English law.

Directives also have general scope, but they are addressed simply to member states requiring them to make changes in their own law to bring it into line with EU requirements. Each state will decide how this is to be done. In the UK it is sometimes done by Act of Parliament, or sometimes by delegated legislation such as Orders-in-Council or ministerial regulations.

The main difficulty can lie when a government does *not* implement a directive. If an individual who should have benefited from the directive wishes to claim a remedy against the government, should the government be able as a defence to rely on its own misconduct in not carrying out its EU obligations?

To avoid this, the European Court of Justice has given some limited *direct* effect to directives. An unimplemented directive can be relied upon by an individual in so far as it defines rights that the individual *should* have been able to assert against the state.

> In *Van Duyn* v. *Home Office* (1974), the applicant wished to come to the UK from Holland. She was excluded on public policy grounds because she was a member of a religious sect that was considered undesirable. This was contrary to a directive the UK had not implemented. She could claim the benefit of the directive against the UK.

> In *Marshall* v. *Southampton & S.W. Hampshire Area Health Authority* (1986), male employees had to retire at 65, female at 60. This was contrary to an EC Equal Treatment Directive, which the UK should have implemented but had not. Miss Marshall, an employee, objected to this, but English law *appeared* to give her no remedy. The House of Lords referred the question of the unimplemented directive to the European Court, which held that the claimant *was* entitled to the rights that the directive gave her.

These cases do, however, have some limits. First, they can only have 'vertical' effect, i.e. as regards rights that the individual should have *against the government*. The concept of 'government', however, has been construed very widely. A Local Authority, or an Area Health Authority, for instance, is regarded as being sufficiently part of government. It has even been held that the ruling body of a nationalized industry can be included. On the other hand, the direct effect rules do not have 'horizontal' effect, in that they do not give any rights for one private individual against another *private* body.

> In *Duke* v. *GEC Reliance Ltd* (1988), the claimant was not entitled to the benefit of the unimplemented Equal Opportunities Directive against her private employer.

Second, if member states have been given a time limit in which to implement the directive, the direct effect rules do not apply until the time limit has expired.

In addition to the radical 'direct effect' rules, a directive can also have an on-going indirect effect, in that national legislation must be construed by the national courts in a manner consistent with the directive, if at all possible.

Decisions, like regulations, take effect immediately without further implementation, but they are only binding upon those to whom they are addressed and they do not have general legislative effect. Decisions adopted by the Commission in application of the competition rules in the EC Treaty Art. 81 (formerly Art. 85) are an example of decisions addressed to individuals or undertakings.

The European Court of Justice has in *theory* relatively few law-*making* powers. It interprets and gives rulings on the *effect* of all aspects of EC law, and its rulings can be binding both on the Community and in the member states. It is therefore an exceptionally important institution. However, in theory at least, there is no doctrine of binding precedent. Nevertheless, the court is generally consistent in its judgments, and in practice is very reluctant to depart from its own previous decisions. Indeed it sometimes expressly uses phrases such as 'as the Court has repeatedly held . . .'. Judgments of the Court are published here in the Common Market Law Reports, in much the same way as important judgments of the UK courts are published.

Specimen questions

1. Describe the main effects of each of the following:
   (a) the Treaty of Paris 1951;
   (b) the first Treaty of Rome 1957;
   (c) the European Communities Act 1972;
   (d) the Treaty of European Union (Maastricht Treaty) 1993.
2. (a) Describe the composition and work of the Council of the European Union.
   (b) In this context, describe:
       (i) the *Comité des Représentants Permanents (Coreper)*; and
       (ii) a Council 'Summit'.
3. (a) Describe the effect of directives as sources of EC law.
   (b) In English law, if a directive has been made, but has not been implemented yet, what effect could it have:
       (i) in an action by a citizen against the government; or
       (ii) in an action between one private company and another?
4. Indicate whether each of the following statements is accurate. Explain your answers.
   (a) The European Parliament makes regulations that are binding in the UK;
   (b) Members of the EU Commission are elected to office by elections in each member state;
   (c) The Council is the formal legislative body of the EU;
   (d) Members of the Council are chosen by the majority political party in the European Parliament.
5. How far is each of the following binding in English law:
   (a) an EU regulation;
   (b) Article 81 of the EC Treaty;
   (c) a ruling by the European Court of Justice about how Article 81 should be interpreted;
   (d) a decision by the Commission as to whether a specific arrangement contravenes Article 81?

Unit 7. Legal Personality, Capacity and Agency

A. Natural and legal persons

Legal personality

A legal person is anything recognized by law as having legal rights and duties. With one main exception, a legal person in this country is simply a person in the ordinary sense: a human being. In general, his or her rights begin at birth and end at death and, subject to rules such as those of capacity (below), the same rules apply to everyone.

In one important instance, English law also grants legal personality to an artificial person. This arises where a group of persons together form a *corporate* body of some sort. The corporate body can acquire a personality separate from that of its members, with some of the legal powers of a natural person. It can, for example, own property and make contracts, even with its own members, in its own name. The ways in which such *incorporation* can occur are described later.

Capacity

English law limits the legal capacity of certain categories of natural person. For example, special rules protect minors, i.e. those under 18 years of age. A minor is not generally liable on his contracts (Unit 13) and may escape liability in tort (Unit 8). He may own personal property, such as books or even a car, but he cannot own land except indirectly as beneficiary under a trust. He cannot make a will to dispose of his property on death unless he is on active military service. Other special rules apply at different ages: a person under 16 cannot marry, and there are special provisions for young criminal offenders. A young person is not allowed a full driving licence until the age of 17.

The legal capacity of some *mentally disordered* persons is restricted, mainly under statutory provisions, depending on the nature and seriousness of the disorder.

Many of the restrictions formerly placed on *aliens* have been removed, but generally they still do not have a right of free entry to the country. They remain liable to deportation in some circumstances, and they cannot vote or become MPs. There are now also restrictions on entry and powers to deport some Commonwealth citizens, but new rights of entry for citizens within the European Union. *Foreign sovereigns* and some diplomatic staff are normally granted the privilege of immunity from legal actions.

The main limits on the capacity of *corporate bodies* arise from their very nature. First, there are things which they cannot physically do, such as marry. Second, they are the creation of law and, therefore, only have such powers as the law gives them; anything outside those powers (*ultra vires*) is void, although there is now special provision for companies (Unit 22).

B. Corporations

Corporations may come into being in one of these ways.
1. The earliest form of incorporation was by Royal Charter, issued under the Royal prerogative upon the advice of the Privy Council. This form of incorporation was used to create early trading companies (long gone) such as the East India Company and the Hudson's Bay Company, and also the Bank of England. The issue of a Charter today is largely confined to non-commercial bodies such as universities or the BBC.
2. A corporation may be created by Act of Parliament. This method was used for the early railway and gas companies and for later nationalized corporations such as the coal, steel and electricity boards. Many of these have more recently been 'privatized' into registered companies (see below). Some of the most important statutory corporations today are the local authorities, which owe their existence to the Local Government Acts. Some towns had earlier acquired corporate status by Royal Charter and, although they are now statutory bodies, they have regained their 'Borough' status by new Charters. Other statutory corporations include the Independent Broadcasting Authority.
3. It was found in the nineteenth century that the cumbersome and expensive method of forming chartered and statutory corporations was not ideal for private business concerns. Hence the Companies Act 1844 provided a third and easier method of incorporation, by registration following a few relatively simple formalities. In 1855, limited liability was introduced, whereby shareholders who invested in companies could only be called upon for the amount they had agreed to contribute and were not liable to creditors to the extent of all their wealth. Formation by registration and limited liability together helped provide the capital which the increasing scale of business then needed. The law governing companies is now largely contained in the Companies Act 1985. This consolidated many earlier Acts, but has itself since been amended. Several other Acts allow incorporation by

55

registration today. Building societies are created under the Building Societies Acts 1986 and 1997, and organizations such as working men's clubs and cooperative societies are incorporated under the Industrial and Provident Societies Acts.

As we have seen, a corporation, once formed, acquires *separate legal personality*. It can sue its own members and be sued by them. It can employ its own members. Its property belongs to the corporation, not to the members. This gives the advantage of *perpetual succession*, in that ownership of the corporation's property does not have to be changed when the human participants come and go. *Limited liability* developed naturally with this: the corporation's debts and liabilities are its own and, in general, members are not responsible for them; see *Salomon* v. *Salomon & Co Ltd* (1897) in Unit 22. However, a corporation's powers are limited. If it exceeds its powers, the act in question is *ultra vires* and void. While a natural person can do whatever the law does not prohibit, a corporation is an artificial person and can only do what the law and the documents creating it will permit. The *ultra vires* rule has been relaxed for registered companies, but it still applies for other statutory and registered corporations. For example, most powers of a local government authority are limited by its geographical boundaries, and even within its own borders it can only spend its money for authorized purposes and in authorized ways.

> In *London Borough of Bromley* v. *Greater London Council* (1982), for example, it was held *ultra vires* and unlawful for the (then) GLC to subsidize public transport out of rates in the way it had done.

Most of the above corporations comprise many human beings who *combine* to form a further artificial person, the corporation. Because this is in reality the activity of a group, the corporation is sometimes called a *corporate aggregate*. By contrast, some corporations comprise only one individual. The post of Public Trustee, for example, is held by one person at a time. However the *post* of Public Trustee is a statutory corporation. It has perpetual succession, so that when one holder of the office retires, there is no need to transfer its property, rights and powers to his successor. The *post* is known as a *corporation sole*.

C. Unincorporated associations

People may combine to further a common interest without creating an independent legal personality. Such interests may be sporting, social, political or business. In the absence of incorporation, the law does not normally recognize the association as a separate entity but regards it instead as a number of individual persons. Any property belongs to the members jointly, not to the association.

In some instances, however, limited recognition is given to the association.

1. If its property is held by trustees on behalf of the members, the trustees are then the legal owners, and they may bring and defend actions and do other things necessary to safeguard it.

2. If the management of affairs is entrusted to a committee, all the members of that committee may be liable for an act done with their authority.
3. Under the rules of court it is possible for some members to sue or be sued on behalf of all the others in a representative action. In *Bolton and Others* v. *Stone* (Unit 9), Miss Stone sued Bolton, the secretary, and three other committee members of the cricket club, which was an unincorporated association.

Special rules exist for particular types of unincorporated association. For example, most *trade unions* are unincorporated. In the early nineteenth century, they were unlawful, and members could be prosecuted for the crime of conspiracy. Gradually their status was recognized by law and, since 1871, their status (if not always their activities) has been regarded as lawful. Today they can acquire some features similar to those of corporations, particularly if they register with the Certification Officer under the Trade Union and Labour Relations (Consolidation) Act 1992.

Most unincorporated associations for *business* purposes are governed by the Partnership Act 1890 (see Unit 22).

D. The Crown

At common law, the Crown was above the law, and no action could be brought against the King in the King's courts. This was summarized in the maxim, 'The King (or Queen) can do no wrong'. This legal immunity applied also to public acts carried out in the King's name by Ministers and Government departments.

As the activities of state vastly increased, the extent of this immunity brought many cases of injustice. Thus, the Crown was not liable for the negligent driving of an army lorry or for a dangerous post office floor, as an ordinary employer would have been; nor were Government departments liable if they broke their contracts. At common law there was, in practice, some mitigation of this severe position, but the important changes were made by the Crown Proceedings Act 1947, which now largely governs the matter.

In tort (see Unit 8), the Crown can now be liable for the wrongful acts of its servants, for injuries arising out of the ownership and control of premises and, where the statute expressly states that the Crown is to be bound, for breach of statutory duty. An immunity preserved by the 1947 Act that no action would lie for death or personal injury suffered during service in the armed forces if the Minister responsible certified this injury ranked for entitlement to pension was removed by the Crown Proceedings (Armed Forces) Act 1987.

In contract, similarly, the Crown can be liable, particularly for commercial agreements. It is doubtful if it is bound by the service contracts of its employees (civil servants) but, in any event, they are now protected by the unfair dismissal provisions of the Employment Rights Act 1996.

Civil actions may now be brought against the appropriate departments or against the Attorney-General, who is empowered to defend such actions on the Crown's behalf. There is still no legal way of enforcing judgments against the Crown, although this is normally not necessary. The Crown (i.e., the Government) can still stop disclosure of certain evidence for which Crown privilege is claimed. The Queen in her private capacity still enjoys complete immunity.

E. Agency

An agent is a person authorized or empowered by another (the 'principal') to bring the principal into legal relations with a third party. Most commonly, the agent's task is to bring about a contract between his principal and a third party. Thus, an estate agent is engaged by the householder to find a buyer for the house, and a travel agent brings about contractual relations between the would-be holidaymaker and the airline and hotel companies. Agents may do other things on behalf of the principal, without creating a contract for him. A solicitor may take steps to bring or defend his client's legal proceedings, and some accountants communicate with the Inland Revenue on behalf of their clients.

An agent is not necessarily an independent person. The greatest volume of agency work is almost certainly done, on behalf of employers, by employees such as shop assistants, bank managers, executives of large businesses, college admissions tutors, hospital administrators and ticket clerks. There are other possible relationships between principal and agent: a company director may have authority to make contracts on behalf of the company, and a partner has general authority to act on behalf of his fellow partners (see Unit 22). A corporate body, having no physical existence, can *only* act through its organs or agents.

Normally there will be a contract between principal and agent, and the agent will be paid by salary, fees, commission or share of profits. This is not always the case however; the person who acts for a friend as a favour, the member of a family who is given authority to act for another, and the unpaid helper at a jumble sale can all be agents. Generally, an agent can be appointed in any way, orally or in writing, and anyone, even a minor, can validly be an agent. Quite often, the agent will be a corporate body.

The concept of 'authority'

An agent's acts can bind his principal if, and only if, the agent has authority to do so. The word authority, however, can be used in at least two different senses, and the subject can best be tackled with this as a first step.

As between principal and agent, 'authority' means what the principal has expressly or impliedly instructed the agent to do. 'Authority', therefore, means what the agent has been given a *right* to do.

As between principal and third party, the issue is slightly different. The third party wants to know what the agent has *power* to do. The important question is: 'Will the principal be bound by what the agent does?' The third party cannot be expected to know everything that has gone on between principal and agent, and he is, therefore, normally entitled to rely on appearances. So long as the agent is doing what he *appears* to have the right to do, then the third party need usually enquire no further. An agent may have 'ostensible' or 'apparent' authority even if (unknown to the third party) he is exceeding or disobeying his actual instructions. In this sense, therefore, 'authority' means what the agent has *power* to do, whether or not he has a *right* to do it.

Actual authority

This is what the principal expressly or impliedly gives the agent the *right* to do on his behalf. It is important chiefly between principal and agent, because if an agent exceeds his actual authority then he will be liable to his principal.

Express authority comes from the principal's specific instructions. If these are ambiguous, the agent must seek clarification but, if he cannot contact the principal, he is justified in acting in good faith on a reasonable interpretation of his instructions, even if this turns out not to be what the principal intended.

Implied authority. An agent also has implied authority to do things which are normally incidental to carrying out his express instructions, such as incurring necessary postal, telephone and travelling expenses. More importantly, where by ordinary business practice it is *usual* for a particular type of agent to carry out certain functions, the principal, will be taken impliedly to have authorized this. There are cases below on the 'usual authority' and powers of people from pub managers to solicitors.

Apparent or ostensible authority

This is important between principal and third party because, as explained above, sometimes an agent can have power to do things which he has no right to do.

1. This can occur particularly where there have been undisclosed restrictions on a professional or business agent's 'usual' authority. The principal can restrict the usual authority (rights) of a particular type of agent simply by telling the agent not to do what he would normally expect to do. If the agent then disobeys his instruction, *he* is liable to the principal (see page 65). However, this restriction will not affect a third party who deals with the principal through the agent in good faith and without notice of the unusual restriction. The principal has placed the agent in a position where he appears to the world to have the powers usual to such an agent. If there are no suspicious circumstances, the principal is bound to the third party.

   In *Waugh* v. *Clifford & Sons Ltd* (1982), solicitors were acting for a building firm in a dispute concerning property. The other side suggested a compromise involving an independent valuer. The solicitors sought their client's instructions. In fact their client did not want to settle on these terms, but his instructions to this effect were not passed on within the firm of solicitors to the partner dealing with the case. Therefore, he did agree a compromise. It was held that the builder was bound by it. It was within the

59

usual authority of a solicitor to agree such a compromise, and the other side could rely on the solicitor's ostensible powers.

Other examples discussed later include *Folkes* v. *King* (Unit 19), and *Mercantile Credit* v. *Garrod* (Unit 22).

2. A third party can also rely on an agent's 'usual' and apparent authority when the agent has misused his position.

    In *Panorama Developments Ltd* v. *Fidelis Fabrics Ltd* (1971) a company secretary hired cars in the company's name but then used them for his own purposes. The company still had to pay the bill.

3. Sometimes ostensible authority can arise from estoppel. The principal has 'held out' another as having authority and, as a result, a third party has been deceived.

    In *Eastern Distributors Ltd* v. *Goldring* (1957), a private car owner prepared documents which falsely stated that a named dealer was the owner. This was part of a scheme to enable the private owner to borrow money unlawfully. The scheme fell through, but the dealer, who had obtained the documents and was in possession of the car, was able fraudulently to sell the car to a third party who bought in good faith.

    See also *Freeman and Lockyer* v. *Buckhurst Park Properties Ltd* (page 286).

4. Something similar can occur even if the principal is undisclosed. If the principal allows the agent (*A*) to appear to be acting for himself (*A*), whereas in reality *A* is only acting for the principal, then *A* may have all of the usual powers of a person acting for himself. Restrictions on *A*'s actual rights will not affect a third party who has been allowed to believe that he is dealing solely with *A*, and who, therefore, cannot know of the restraints.

    In *Watteau* v. *Fenwick* (1893), Mr Humble ran a public house. His name appeared as licensee, and he appeared to be dealing for himself. He ordered cigars from a supplier, *W*, for re-sale in the bar. In fact he had been forbidden to order cigars by Fenwick, the owner, but there was nothing to make *W* suspect this. Fenwick was, therefore, liable to *W* for the price.

In all of the above situations it must be remembered that if there are suspicious circumstances then ostensible or apparent authority will not apply. The third party can only rely on a *genuine* appearance of authority.

In *Reckitt* v. *Barnett, Pembroke and Slater Ltd* (1929), an agent with authority to draw cheques on his principal's bank account used such a cheque to pay his private debts. It was obvious from the cheque that this was not the agent's own money. The principal could, therefore, recover the money from the creditor, who should have been suspicious.

Moreover, ostensible authority only arises if the *principal* has given the agent the appearance of authority. An agent cannot give it to himself.

In *Armagas Ltd* v. *Mundogas SA* (1986), an agent negotiated an unusual three-year charter of a ship, purportedly for his principal. This was clearly outside of the agent's usual powers (contrast *Waugh* v. *Clifford* and *Panorama* v. *Fidelis* above), and the principal had not held out the agent as having power to make it. The principal therefore was not bound.

Agency of necessity

Exceptionally, a person (the 'agent') may acquire authority from the pressure of necessity. Four conditions must be satisfied: First, the 'agent' must have been placed in control of something belonging to the principal. Second, a genuine emergency must have arisen, which threatens the property. This may occur, for example, where the thing is perishable, and storage or transport facilities break down. Third, it must be impossible for the 'agent' to obtain the principal's instructions in time. Fourth, the 'agent' must have acted in good faith in a genuine attempt to protect the property.

> In *Great Northern Railway Co.* v. *Swaffield* (1874) the railway company, through no fault of its own, was unable to deliver a horse consigned by rail. Unable to contact the owner, the company put the horse in livery stables, and was held entitled to recover the cost from the owner.

Agency of necessity will rarely arise today because, with improved communications, it should normally be possible to obtain the owner's instructions quickly.

Ratification

In some situations, a principal can choose to adopt and ratify transactions which were made entirely without his authority. Where someone has pretended to be his agent and used his name, the principal can subsequently ratify the transaction so as to obtain the benefit and undertake the obligations agreed. Four conditions must be satisfied:

1. The 'agent' must have used the principal's name and claimed to act for him.

   > In *Re Tiedemann and Ledermann Frères* (1899), an agent who periodically bought and sold wheat on behalf of a principal, used the principal's name, for financial reasons, in a contract which he made for himself. The principal could ratify and adopt this transaction.

   > Conversely, in *Keighley, Maxted & Co.* v. *Durant & Co.* (1901), an agent agreed to buy wheat in his *own* name. He intended this to be on behalf of a principal, but the seller did not know this. The principal purported to ratify, but later refused to take delivery. He was not bound to do so. The seller had been content to deal with the agent, and the principal's 'ratification' was inoperative.

2. The principal must have existed and had contractual capacity at the time when the agent acted. A principal cannot ratify something which he could not himself have done or authorized at the time when it happened.

   > In *Kelner* v. *Baxter* (1866), three promoters of a company bought goods on the company's behalf *before it was incorporated*. When it *was* formed, the company purported to ratify the transaction, but was held not entitled to do so.

In this situation, by the Companies Act 1985, section 36C, the company promoter will be *personally* bound by the contract (see Unit 23).

3. The principal must have known all material facts when he ratified.

> In *Marsh* v. *Joseph* (1897), a rogue purported to be acting on behalf of a solicitor in transactions which turned out to be fraudulent. He then gave a partial account of what he had done to the solicitor who, believing the transactions to be legitimate, ratified the rogue's action. The ratification was held inoperative.

4. An illegal or void act cannot be ratified. A firm cannot normally ratify a contract based on a forged (not merely unauthorized) signature. A corporation cannot extend its powers by ratifying something which is *ultra vires* (although as regards *companies*, see Unit 22).

Ratification *relates back* to the time of the agent's act, so that the position is the same as if the agent had had authority in the first place. The effect of ratification is *retrospective*.

> In *Bolton Partners* v. *Lambert* (1889), Lambert made an offer to an agent of Bolton Partners which the agent, acting without authority, purported to accept on behalf of Boltons. Lambert then sought to revoke his offer. *After* this, Boltons ratified the agent's act. Lambert was bound by the contract, because ratification related back to the agent's acceptance, so that Lambert's revocation was too late.

The main limit on 'relation back' is that vested rights cannot be divested, so that ratification cannot affect a third party who has acquired rights to the property before ratification.

> In *Bird* v. *Brown* (1850), goods were in transit from seller to buyer when the seller's agent heard that the buyer was insolvent. The agent, without authority, sent a notice of 'stoppage in transit' giving the seller a right to re-take the goods (see Unit 18). By the time that the seller ratified this, however, the goods had been delivered to the buyer's trustee in bankruptcy. Ratification was held ineffective, because it would defeat the rights over the goods which the trustee had now acquired.

Effect of the agent's acts

As a general rule, the agent simply drops out as soon as the contract (or other legal relationship) comes into existence between principal and third party. The agent incurs no personal liability; nor can he sue the third party.

> In *Gran Gelato Ltd* v. *Richcliff (Group) Ltd* (1992), *R*'s solicitors, acting within their apparent authority, negligently gave a false answer to *G*'s question about *R*'s property. The solicitors gave the answer on behalf of their client (*R*), but without consulting him. Nevertheless *R* was liable to *G*, and the solicitors were not.

Exceptions are fairly rare. First, some do arise in trades where, by special custom, particular types of agent do take personal responsibility (often for a higher fee). Secondly, if an agent *signs a document* in his own name, without indicating that he is doing so merely as agent, the courts have sometimes been reluctant to admit or believe oral evidence that the document, which appears to bind the agent, in fact only binds someone else, the principal. Normally, it is best if, as a precaution, the agent for an unnamed principal adds words like '*as* agent' after his signature.

The undisclosed principal is the main exception. Here the third party believes throughout that the agent is acting solely on his own behalf (see *Watteau* v. *Fenwick* earlier). The principal is not just *unnamed* (where the third party knows that he is dealing with an agent, but does not know the identity of the principal); here the very *existence* of the principal is undisclosed. In this situation, the agent does not automatically drop out. The third party has an option to sue *either* the agent (with whom he thought he was contracting) *or* the principal. However he cannot sue both. He can ask both for a remedy, but if he receives none he must choose which to sue, and if the one whom he sues cannot pay, he cannot sue the other.

Conversely, the undisclosed principal *can* normally sue the third party on the contract (so long as the agent had at all stages intended to contract on the undisclosed principal's behalf). There are some exceptions however. First, the contract itself may expressly provide that the person making it is the true and only principal, thereby expressly excluding any possible undisclosed party. Secondly, the terms of the contract may be inconsistent with agency, for example where the identity of the parties is important. A person of whom the third party is known to disapprove might be refused the right to come in as undisclosed principal. If an employee accepted a job and then stepped aside and revealed that he was only doing so on behalf of his younger brother, the employer would not be bound to employ the younger brother.

> In *Said* v. *Butt* (1920), a critic who had quarrelled with the theatre management was unable to get a ticket for the first night of a play. A friend, therefore, bought a ticket in his own name, and gave it to the critic, who appeared on the night. The management rightly refused admission, because the critic was claiming to step in as undisclosed principal in circumstances where identity was material.

Finally, if an undisclosed principal is allowed to sue, he can be met with any defence or set-off which the third party had against the agent before the principal appeared.

Payment via the agent follows the general rules. Payment by the third party to the agent is deemed to be payment to the principal if, but only if, it is within the actual or apparent/ostensible authority of the agent to take such a payment in such a way. Therefore payment to the employee at the cash-desk of a supermarket for goods chosen in the usual way from the shelves is treated as payment to the supermarket company (the principal). If it is *not* within the authority of the agent to take such a payment on behalf of the principal, then the principal is not treated as having received the money; see *Waugh* v. *Clifford* earlier. Where the principal owes money to a third party, it is not enough for him merely to hand the money to his own agent. If his agent fails to pass on the money, the principal is still normally liable to the third party.

Torts committed by a agent *in the course of his authority* can render the principal liable to the third party, even if the principal himself is innocent. (Torts are civil wrongs such as negligence and deceit, and are discussed in Units 8–10.) The agent too may be liable to the third party if the agent himself commits a tort against the latter, for example by knowingly being deceitful. Otherwise, however, the agent simply drops out and incurs no personal liability to the third party; see *Gran Gelato* v. *Richcliff* earlier, where the agent himself owed no legally actionable duty of care to the third party, and therefore did not himself commit a tort against them. (The solicitors would, however, be liable to their own client, the principal.)

The agent's warranty of authority

A person who acts as agent is taken to promise to the third party that he does have authority, and that his principal will be bound. If the agent lacks authority, or exceeds his powers so that the principal is not bound, *the third party* can sue the agent for damages for breach of warranty of authority. The third party must show that he has acted in some way in reliance on the agent's implied warranty, so as to give consideration for it.

> In *Penn* v. *Bristol and West Building Society* (1997), a house was owned by a husband and wife. The husband wished to sell it and instructed a solicitor. The wife's consent was necessary, but she did not give it and in fact knew nothing of this. The solicitor, therefore, did not have authority. A prospective purchaser and his building society with whom the solicitor dealt both incurred expense in the belief that he did have authority. In fact, the wife prevented the sale. The solicitor was held liable to both the 'purchaser' and his building society for breach of warranty of authority.

The warranty of authority is strict, and the agent may be liable even if he acted in all innocence, and believed that he did have authority.

> In *Yonge* v. *Toynbee* (1910), solicitors, acting for their client, defended proceedings started by Yonge and thereby put him to considerable expense. Unknown to the solicitors, their client had become insane, thereby ending their authority. Yonge recovered his legal expenses from the solicitors personally.

Finally, the third party must have been deceived by the agent's warranty of authority. If the third party knows that the agent is exceeding his authority, he has no remedy against either principal or agent.

Termination of agency

Agency can come to an end in the following ways:

1. *Performance*. If the agent is engaged for a specific task, his authority ends as soon as his task is completed. Thus, an estate agent engaged to find a buyer for the house has no further authority once the sale is completed.
2. *Withdrawal of authority*. In general, the principal can withdraw his agent's authority at any time, although he may have to pay damages to his agent if this involves breach of a contract between principal and agent (for example, if the agent is employed by the principal and is wrongly dismissed from his employment without notice).

   In two exceptional situations the principal cannot revoke his agent's authority. First, powers of attorney may be rendered irrevocable under the Powers of

Attorney Act 1971. Secondly, authority 'coupled with an interest' may be irrevocable. This could arise where a principal who owes money to his agent gives the agent authority to collect the principal's debts and keep the money. The agent has an interest in the subject-matter, and his authority is irrevocable.

3. *Death of either party* ends the agency.
4. *Bankruptcy* of the principal ends the agency, as will bankruptcy of the agent if (as is usual) this renders him unfit for his duties.
5. *Insanity* can end the agency: the agent's insanity if it renders him unfit for his duties, the principal's if it renders him incapable of making the transactions contemplated.
6. *Frustration* of the agency can occur in other ways: supervening illegality can end it, for example, where the agent becomes an enemy alien; illness of either party might frustrate it if the illness makes commercial nonsense of the agency.

The effect of termination *as between principal and agent* is that the agency is terminated for the future, but existing rights, such as the agent's rights to commission already earned, are not affected.

The effect *as between principal and third party* depends largely upon how the termination occurred. Where the principal consciously withdraws his agent's authority, this does *not* affect a third party unless and until the third party knows of the termination or of circumstances which should make him suspect this. He can still rely on the agent's ostensible authority.

Duties of agent to principal

An agent owes certain implied duties to his principal. These are matters between principal and agent themselves and, for the most part, do not affect third parties. In the event of breach, the agent must normally compensate his principal for loss which results. If breach is serious, the principal may also end the agency without notice or compensation. There are further remedies if there has been fraud; see below.

1. *Obedience*. An agent must obey his principal's instructions and not exceed them. He must do so reasonably promptly. There are only a few situations where an agent is entitled to disobey, although he can always refuse to act fraudulently or otherwise illegally.
2. *Personal performance*. An agent cannot validly delegate or sub-contract his duties without the principal's consent, although he may have implied authority to entrust mere secretarial and routine tasks to employees. Authority to delegate may also arise from trade custom, or necessity. In some cases, however, it might even be wrongful for an agent to pass the work to another office or member of his own firm, for example if personalities are important.

> *In Pilbrow* v. *Pearless de Rougement & Co.* (1999), a client asked the firm to provide the services of a solicitor. The adviser provided was a legal executive, not a solicitor, and the firm did not tell the client this. The executive handled the matter competently, but the firm was not entitled to its fees.

65

If the agent does validly delegate or sub-contract, the sub-agent normally acts for the agent, not for the principal, so that if the agent becomes bankrupt, the sub-agent cannot normally recover his fees from the principal.

3. *Care and skill*. An agent must show such care and diligence as is reasonable in all the circumstances. If he has professed some special skill, he must show the degree of care and skill ordinarily expected in his profession; see also the section on professional liability in Unit 9.

4. *Good faith*. An agent must never permit an undisclosed *conflict of interest*, that is, he must never allow his own interests to conflict with those of his principal. For example:

(a) An agent must not personally buy from or sell to his own principal without full disclosure. He must also disclose other connections which might prejudice his good faith such as close family relations with the third party, or a large shareholding in it.

> In *Armstrong* v. *Jackson* (1917), a stockbroker was engaged to buy certain shares for his principal. The stockbroker held some such shares himself and, without disclosing this to his principal, transferred his own shares. The principal could rescind the contract, and recover what he had paid for the shares (even though they had since fallen in value).

(b) An agent must not act for both sides without full disclosure.

> In *Fullwood* v. *Hurley* (1928), an agent was engaged by the owner to sell a hotel. The agent found someone who wanted a hotel and, without disclosing his connection with the owner, arranged the sale and claimed commission from both. He was held not entitled to commission from the buyer.

Some of these rules can cause great difficulty for large firms with many offices, or even large departments within offices. Large firms of accountants have branches throughout the world. Even moderately large solicitors have branches throughout the UK, with different departments within each. The interests of one client might conflict with those of another client in another office far away, unknown to both branches at first.

> In *Bolkiah (Prince Jeffri)* v. *KPMG* (1999), the conflict was foreseen, but KPMG, an accountancy firm, claimed to be able to raise a 'Chinese Wall' between the accountants of one client and those of another. The House of Lords did not believe that they could do this on an *ad hoc* basis. The first client obtained an injunction against KPMG acting for the others where the clients' interests conflicted. Any 'wall' would have to have been convincing, and clearly arranged before any conflict could arise.

(c) The agent must not compete with his principal by setting up a rival business of his own, without the principal's full knowledge and consent; compare the Partnership Act 1890, section 30 (Unit 22).

(d) An agent must not make any secret profit from an unauthorized use of his position.

> In *Hippisley* v. *Knee Bros.* (1905), an advertising agent obtained discounts from printers with whom he regularly dealt. It was held that these had to be passed on to his principal. On the other hand, the agent had not been fraudulent, and was still entitled to his commission.

5. *Honesty.* An agent must not act fraudulently; for example he must not take a bribe or other inducement to favour the donor third party. For breach, the principal has remedies against the third party as well as the agent. The principal can rescind any contract with the third party. He can also recover damages both from the donor and from the agent, but not double damages; sums recovered from one would be set off against sums recovered from the other. He can also refuse commission to the agent.

> In *Mahesan* v. *Malaysia Government Officers' Housing Society* (1978), *M* was engaged by the Society to find building land. He found a cheap and suitable site, but accepted a bribe by a property speculator to keep silent about it. This enabled the speculator to buy the land cheaply, and then re-sell it to the Society at a huge profit. The Society was entitled to recover the bribe and the speculator's profit from *M*.

6. *Confidentiality.* An agent must not use for his own or another's benefit confidential information obtained on his principal's behalf, and this duty can probably extend after the agency has ended.
7. *Disclosure.* During the course of his agency, any information which the agent obtains which is relevant to his duties must be disclosed to his principal (except information which he has only obtained in confidence from another principal – but here he must disclose any potential conflict of interest).

> In *Keppel* v. *Wheeler* (1927), an estate agent who told his principal of a £6150 bid for his house, but did not tell him in time of a better bid of £6750, was liable to the principal for the £600 difference when the principal accepted the lower bid.

When an agent acts for both sides in a transaction (with the full knowledge and consent of both, so that there is no *secret* conflict of interest), his duties of disclosure to each side can be limited to what he has expressly been instructed and authorised to do.

> In *National Home Loans Corp.* v. *Giffen Couch & Archer* (1997), an owner wanted a *second* mortgage on his house. The solicitor acted for both the home owner and the lender. His instructions from the lender were to investigate the owner's title to the property and its adequacy as security for *this* loan, and to draft the relevant documents. He incidentally discovered that the owner was still in arrears on his *first* mortgage loan, but he was not obliged to disclose this to the second lender.

8. *Duty to account.* An agent must account to his principal for all moneys received on the principal's behalf. He must keep proper records, and take care not to mix his own money and property with that of the principal (compare Partnership Act, section 28).

Duties of principal to agent

1. *Payment of commission.* Agency can be gratuitous, without payment, but *if* commission or other payment is agreed (expressly or impliedly) the principal must pay the agreed amount. If the agent is in business, and would not ordinarily act gratuitously, there may be an implied obligation to pay a reasonable sum, normally by reference to usual commercial or professional rates.

   The agent must, however, have *earned* his commission, that is, the event for which he was engaged must have occurred, and occurred through his actions. Thus, as a general rule, an estate agent does not earn his commission until the sale is completed, and no commission is payable if the vendor finds a buyer privately, not through the agent.

   When the agency is terminated, the agent is entitled to payment for transactions which he brought about before termination, but not (unless otherwise agreed) for transactions thereafter, even with continuing customers whom he initially introduced. Similar problems arise when the principal ends his business, thereby depriving the agent of further opportunities. The general rule again is that the agent has no redress unless there was an express or implied term in the agency agreement that the principal would so conduct the business as not to deprive the agent of commission for a given period.

   > In *Turner* v. *Goldsmith* (1891), Turner was engaged *for five years* to sell shirts manufactured or sold by Goldsmith on a commission basis. Within the five years, Goldsmith's factory was burnt down. Turner was held entitled to damages for commission lost for the rest of the five-year term. (He might also today have had a remedy under the Commercial Agents Regulations, below.)

2. *Indemnity.* The principal must indemnify his agent for expenses properly and legally incurred in exercising his duties.

Commercial agents

The Commercial Agents (Council Directive) Regulations 1993 were introduced as a result of an EC Directive. They apply to *independent* agents (i.e. not employees, directors or partners) who have *continuing* authority in connection with the *sale or purchase* (not hire or charter) of *goods*. Their title, therefore, is misleading, in that they do *not* apply to most business agents. They would not have affected any of the cases in this unit, with one possible exception. They apply mainly to firms *dealing in goods* who, rather than employing salesmen or selling to separate distribution companies, choose to engage long-term selling agents who are paid by commission or fees. They do not apply when an agent is engaged on an isolated occasion. Credit-brokers under the Consumer Credit Act are specifically excluded (see Unit 21). Mail-order catalogue agents are normally excluded, as are others 'whose activities as commercial agents are considered secondary'.

Where the regulations do apply, they have no effect on the authority of the agent, or on the relations between principal and third party. They do have some effect on relations between principal and agent, and give limited protection to these specialized selling (or buying) agents. The principal must give all necessary documentation and information to such an agent, inform the agent within a reasonable time whether the principal has accepted the third party's proposals, warn the agent within a reasonable time of any anticipated fall in business, and generally act dutifully and in good faith.

As at present, the agent must receive reasonable remuneration for work done. *During* the agency, the agent must receive the agreed commission if the transaction is concluded as a result of his action; or if it is a repeat order from a customer previously found by the agent; or, in cases where the principal has given the agent exclusive rights, where the customer is from the region or type over which the agent has such rights. Commission must be paid at the agreed time, even if the principal has not yet received his money from the third party. The principal must give a detailed statement enabling the agent to check the amounts due. *After* the agency, the agent must receive commission for a contract made reasonably soon afterwards which was substantially the result of his efforts; or which was a repeat order soon afterwards from a customer found by the agent. These terms cannot be excluded, and can protect agents from being deprived of commission by being sacked immediately after introducing a potentially valuable customer.

On ending the agency, the principal must give the agent at least one month's notice for each year served, to a maximum of three. The parties can contract for longer, but not less. The agent is entitled to compensation if the principal ends the contract early otherwise than for serious breach by the agent, or if the agent ends it because of serious misconduct by the principal (compare 'constructive dismissal' in employment). There must also be compensation if the agency ends because of the agent's age, illness or death. The principal must be notified of a claim within 12 months.

In return for these protections, such agents owe statutory duties of obedience and good faith similar to those owed already at common law (see earlier). In addition, the principal of such an agent now has statutory power to impose a restraint of trade clause, which can protect the principal against an agent who, having built up much goodwill and many contacts while working for him, is now tempted to take these assets elsewhere. In his contract with the agent, the principal can include a clause restraining him from acting as agent for anyone else, so long as the clause is in writing and is reasonable. The restraint must only apply within the scope of the present agency (area, customers, type of goods), and can only last up to two years after the end of the agency (compare the common law rules for restraints of trade in employment in Units 17 and 27).

Specimen questions

1. Explain briefly the meaning of the following:
   (a) separate legal personality;
   (b) *ultra vires*;

    (c) a minor;

    (d) an unincorporated association;

    (e) a corporation sole.

2. 'The Queen can do no wrong.' Explain the legal meaning of this phrase, and discuss whether it is true today.

3. What is meant by an agent's ostensible authority? Give examples, and say why it is important.

4. (a) Discuss the nature of an agent's obligations to his principal and the remedies available to the principal if these are not fulfilled.

    (b) Paul engages Arthur as his agent to sell three cars for the best price possible but for not less than £2000 each. The agent's commission is to be 10%. Arthur informs Paul that he has found a buyer for the first car for £2000 and, after deducting his commission, remits £1800. In fact, Arthur has bought this car himself. There are two potential buyers for the second car, offering £2200 and £2400, respectively. Arthur carelessly loses the address of the second buyer and, to avoid extra work, sells the car for £2200 and again remits the money to Paul, after deducting his commission. Arthur cannot find a buyer for the third car and, therefore, sends it to his friend, Terry, who lives in another town, asking Terry if he will attempt to sell the car. Terry is unable to sell and returns the car to Paul who then discovers that Terry's carelessness has caused damage to the car to the extent of £400. Advise Paul.

5. (a) Under what circumstances may an agent incur personal liability to third parties with whom he contracts on behalf of his principal?

    (b) A, the purchasing officer of an electrical goods manufacturer, is authorized to buy materials for the company at prices which must not exceed those laid down by the directors. A agrees to buy copper wire from X at a price that is higher than the prescribed maximum. A also enters into an agreement to buy switches from Y in return for which Y promises to pay a commission to A, which A is not authorized to accept. Details of these two transactions are now known to the company. Discuss:

    (i) whether the manufacturer is bound by these contracts; and

    (ii) whether the manufacturer has any remedies against A and, if so, what remedies.

Unit 8. Liability for Wrongful Acts

A. Crimes and torts

As it has been noted in Unit 1, conflicts can arise in many ways in a complex society, and the law aims to regulate conduct in various different ways. First, certain conduct is deemed so undesirable that the law prohibits it, makes it a criminal offence, and provides that offenders may be punished. Secondly, some conduct harms other members of society, and the rules of civil law provide for the victim to receive compensation or some other civil remedy. Civil liability for breach of contract will be discussed in Units 11–17. The law of tort is concerned with some of the other matters which can give rise to civil liability.

There is a large overlap between crime and tort. If a criminal act harms the victim, it will usually be a tort as well, thus making the offender liable both to be prosecuted and to be sued for damages by the victim. The factory occupier who fails to fence dangerous machinery commits both a criminal offence and, if an employee is injured, a tort against that employee. He may also be liable to the employee for breach of contract, because he owes a duty, under the contract of employment, to provide a reasonably safe system of work (Unit 27).

A second preliminary point must be made. Not all undesirable conduct, however much we disapprove of it, is necessarily either a crime or a tort. If a builder erects a block of flats on the field behind your house, he may not only ruin your view, but also cause your house to fall in value. Nevertheless, so long as he has planning permission, the builder has probably committed neither a crime nor a tort. A similar situation arises where a new supermarket deliberately cuts prices with the sole intention of driving the old corner shop out of business, thereby depriving the shop owner of his livelihood. No one is a criminal unless he has committed one or more of the crimes recognized by law; similarly, no one can be liable in tort unless he has committed one or more of the recognized torts.

Criminal offences and torts have either evolved through precedent, been created by statute, or arisen from a combination of both. Development has been influenced by external pressures, often of a political, social or economic nature. To a large extent, each crime has its own special features, as has each separate tort. On the other hand there are some common elements, and because many business situations give rise to both criminal and tortious liability, this unit is devoted to a comparison of the general features of each of these branches of law. The following two units deal with some aspects of tort in more detail.

B. Criminal liability

For convenience, criminal offences may be classified according to whether the crime is committed against the state and public order (treason, unlawful assembly), or against the person (murder, assault), or against property (theft, obtaining property by deception). There are, in addition, other offences, usually but not always of a minor nature, which do not fall neatly into any of these major categories and which may be of more direct concern to business people. Examples include unlawfully discharging polluting matters into a stream, applying a false trade description to goods in the course of business, or breach of statutory provisions for electrical appliances. Minor traffic offences are another example. These offences are frequently created by statute as part of a wider administrative scheme designed, for example, to control traffic or pollution, protect consumers or promote occupational safety.

The element of fault

Most criminal offences require some measure of moral culpability or fault so that, in addition to committing the wrongful act, the accused must be shown to have a wrongful intention or guilty mind (*mens rea*). It follows that an accused may have a defence if, because of insanity or reasonable mistake of fact, he did not appreciate that his action was wrongful.

On the other hand, contrary to the general rule, in a growing number of statutory criminal offences there is no need for the prosecution to prove *mens rea*. The act alone constitutes the offence, and the very fact that the accused has done it, even without wrongful intent, is enough. These offences are sometimes called crimes of strict liability, and some of the statutory offences mentioned elsewhere fall into this category.

> In *Alphacell Ltd* v. *Woodward* (1972), a company accidentally polluted a river when poisonous liquid overflowed from some settling tanks because a valve was blocked by dead leaves. The company was found guilty even though it had acted neither intentionally nor carelessly.

Nevertheless, the difference between strict offences and other offences is not always so great as would appear at first sight. The statute creating the offence sometimes goes on to provide various defences if, for example, the accused can prove that he acted by mistake and was not careless in any way. In these instances, although the prosecution need not prove that the accused *did* have a guilty mind, it may be open for the defence to prove that he *did not*. Only the burden of proof is different.

> In *Tesco Supermarkets Ltd* v. *Nattrass* (1972), faulty supervision by a shop manager led to goods being sold with a false indication as to price, contrary to what is now the Consumer Protection Act 1987, section 20. Liability for this offence is strict, but the Act provides a defence if the *accused* can prove that the offence was due to the default of another person and that the accused had exercised all due care and diligence. The company succeeded in proving that it had exercised all due diligence, and that the shop manager, although employed by the company, was 'another person'. The conviction, therefore, was quashed.

In addition, there is always a presumption that *mens rea* must be proved unless the statute clearly dispenses with the need for such proof. When a man is convicted of a criminal offence the consequences can be very severe, involving possible loss of liberty and probably social disgrace, and the courts are reluctant to contemplate such sanctions in the absence of moral guilt.

C. Liability in tort

Infringement of rights

The law recognizes certain rights, both personal and in respect of property, which it will protect by compelling anyone who infringes the right to pay damages to the victim. In appropriate cases the court will issue an injunction restraining the wrongdoer from repeating his act.

Infringement of one of these rights is known as a tort. Interference with the person of another, causing physical harm, could give rise to an action for the torts of battery or negligence. Damaging the reputation of another could lead to an action for defamation. Interests in land are protected by the torts of trespass and nuisance, and interests in goods by trespass to goods and conversion.

The element of fault

As with crime, liability in tort normally requires an element of fault or blame on the part of the wrongdoer or 'tortfeasor'. On the other hand, the degree of moral fault required is normally smaller. Thus *careless* conduct which harms others will often constitute the tort of negligence without giving rise to criminal liability.

There are some torts of strict liability which, like strict criminal offences, can be committed without fault. Examples occur in the case of dangerous things escaping from land (*Rylands* v. *Fletcher*) and breach of some statutory duties (Unit 10).

73

Loss suffered by the claimant

An essential element of most torts is that the claimant must have suffered some physical or financial harm as a result of the defendant's conduct. Thus if someone drives negligently and commits a criminal offence, he does not necessarily commit the tort of negligence against anyone. It is only if the negligent driver harms or injures someone that the tort has been committed.

On the other hand, harm and tort do not always go together. First, there are still some torts where the defendant's wrongful act itself is sufficient to constitute the tort, without the claimant having to show loss. Notable examples are the torts of trespass and libel. These are said to be actionable *per se*, for themselves, without proof of loss. The man who stands on your lawn without permission commits the tort of trespass even if he does not damage the lawn (although in practice it might not be worth while to sue him for damages because, with no loss, damages might only be nominal; you might want an injunction, however).

Conversely, it must again be emphasized that merely causing harm to someone does not necessarily constitute a tort. There may be no infringement of a legal right. In many situations it is impossible to act without harming someone; for example, every sale by a shopkeeper means one less for his competitors.

> In *Bradford Corporation* v. *Pickles* (1895), the defendant, in order to induce the corporation to buy his land at a high price, dug wells and extracted water that would otherwise have found its way into the town's water supply. Although the corporation had suffered loss, there had been no infringement of a legal right, for Pickles had only done what he was at that time fully entitled to do on his own land.

D. Parties

Subject to only a few exceptions, everyone may sue or be sued in tort or be liable to criminal prosecution. Reference has already been made in Unit 7 to some exceptional cases such as the Crown. In addition, foreign sovereigns may avoid liability for criminal prosecution or civil action, as may ambassadors and their staffs who claim 'diplomatic immunity'. To protect the administration of justice, actions for defamation cannot be brought in respect of statements made in the course of court proceedings, nor can actions be brought for false imprisonment against those executing court orders.

Minors are normally fully liable for their torts, but they may escape liability in some instances. First, the court will not allow an action in tort to be used as an indirect way of obtaining a remedy for a contract which would otherwise not be actionable (see Unit 13).

> In *Leslie Ltd* v. *Shiell* (1914), a minor fraudulently pretended to be of age in order to obtain a loan of money. The lender could not sue on the contract of loan, so he sued the minor for the tort of deceit. It was held that this was merely an indirect attempt to recover for breach of contract, and the action therefore failed.

On the other hand, if the minor does something quite outside the contract, then the general rule applies and he can be liable in tort.

In *Ballet* v. *Mingay* (1943), a minor had an amplifier under a contract of loan. He could not have been sued for the tort of conversion for simply refusing to return the goods. He was held liable in tort, however, for parting with the goods to someone else, because this was quite outside the original contract of loan.

Secondly, a minor may escape liability if the tort requires a mental element, as with fraud and negligence, and the minor is too young for this to be present. A minor who is alleged to have been negligent will be judged by what might reasonably have been expected of a person of that age and not by what might have been expected of an adult. Thus a minor may escape liability where an adult would not.

In criminal law, a minor is given rather more protection as to the age at which he is deemed capable of *mens rea*, the courts in which cases will be heard and the sanctions which may be imposed.

Trade unions and their members have, since 1906, enjoyed varying degrees of immunity from actions in tort as regards things done in contemplation or furtherance of a trade dispute. This is now governed by the Trade Union and Labour Relations (Consolidation) Act 1992.

In general, trade unions and their members are subject to the criminal law in the same way as everyone else, except that there is limited protection for peaceful picketing that might otherwise constitute an offence.

Joint wrongdoers

When a tort is committed by two or more persons acting together, for example if *A* and *B* assault or defraud *C*, the position is governed by the Civil Liability (Contribution) Act 1978. Liability is 'joint and several', in that the claimant may sue both tortfeasors, or each separately, or only one of them. If *A* is sued and cannot pay, another action can be brought against *B*, provided that the total damages recovered do not exceed the amount awarded in the first action.

If *A* has to pay the whole of the damages, he can claim a *contribution* from *B*. The court will, if called upon to do so, apportion liability as between *A* and *B*, either in the course of *C*'s action, or in a separate action by *A* against *B*. In some circumstances, *B* might be ordered to *indemnify A* completely. None of this, however, affects *C*'s right to claim the whole amount from either of the defendants.

If several persons act together and commit a criminal offence, all or any of them may be prosecuted.

E. Liability for the acts of others in tort

Vicarious liability

In some situations, a person may be held liable for torts committed by others, even though the wrongful act was no fault of his. This is known as *vicarious liability*. Thus a principal may be liable for the torts of his agent, and a partner may be liable for the torts of another partner in connection with the partnership business (see Unit 22).

A director can, exceptionally, be personally liable for torts committed by the company (see Unit 25) and, in certain circumstances, a trade union can be vicariously liable for torts by its members. In *League Against Cruel Sports* v. *Scott* (1985), even a master of hounds was held vicariously liable for the acts and omissions of hunt servants and mounted followers, over whose conduct he could exercise control.

The most important example is the liability of an employer for the torts of his employee committed by the latter in the course of employment. It depends upon two conditions.

1. *The employee must have been acting under a contract of service.* An employer will only be vicariously liable for the torts of employees, and not normally for those of independent contractors. The distinction between employees and independent contractors is sometimes straightforward: a chauffeur is an employee, a taxi-driver is an independent contractor. It is not always so simple, however, and it is discussed in more detail in Unit 26.

2. *The tort must have been committed in the course of employment.* There has been considerable litigation upon what constitutes the course of employment, and the following rules are suggested.

   (a) Where the employee (servant) *deliberately* defrauds a third party, the employer's liability depends upon whether the servant appeared to be acting with the employer's authority. The employer must have 'held out' this employee as being authorized to make such arrangements or transactions on the employer's behalf. Having given the employee such *ostensible* authority, the employer must now take responsibility if the employee uses the position fraudulently and for his own benefit.

   > In *Lloyd* v. *Grace, Smith & Co.* (1912), solicitors were held liable when their managing clerk, while dealing with some property in the course of his duties, fraudulently induced a client to make over the property to him. The solicitors had put the clerk in a position where he appeared to the client to be acting on behalf of the firm. Therefore the firm must take responsibility for the clerk's misdeeds.

   This only applies where it is the *employer* (or principal in an agency context) who has given the impression to the third party victim that the employee was acting with the employer's authority.

   > In *Armagas Ltd* v. *Mundogas SA* (1986), an *agent* claimed to be acting on behalf of the defendant, but nothing which the *defendant* did gave that impression. Therefore the defendant was not vicariously liable (see Unit 7).

   If, therefore, an employee commits a fraud which the victim should have realized was outside of the employee's normal powers, the employer/principal will not generally be liable (see *Reckitt* v. *Barnett, Pembroke & Slater Ltd* in Unit 7).

   (b) An employer will less often be vicariously liable for deliberate physical violence by his employee. It may not be often that an employer will be held to have authorised this. The rules therefore depend less upon authority than upon how close a connection there was between the job and the tort. There will have to be a *very* close connection. The tort must effectively be an integral part of the job.

In *Warren* v. *Henlys Ltd* (1948), a petrol pump attendant mistakenly thought that a driver was trying to avoid paying for petrol. An argument developed and the attendant lost his temper and struck the claimant. The employer was not vicariously liable. The fight arose from the employment, but was not really part of it.

In *Lister* v. *Hesley Hall Ltd* (2001), a private residential school had undertaken to care for disturbed boys. *G* was employed as a teacher/carer, but he sexually abused some of the boys. These torts were committed in the time and at the premises of the school while *G* was busy caring for the children in performance of his duties. The House of Lords held that the school was vicariously liable.

(c) As regards *carelessness* by the employee, the rules are wider. The mere fact that the employee was acting carelessly or foolishly does not take him outside the course of his employment. It is sufficient if he was acting *in connection with* what he was employed to do (not necessarily as *part* of it).

In *Century Insurance Co. Ltd* v. *Northern Ireland Road Transport Board* (1942), the respondents *were* held liable for the act of a driver who, while delivering petrol to a garage, lit a cigarette, threw away the lighted match and caused an explosion. (No one would assume that the employer had expressly authorized that!)

In *Harrison* v. *Michelin Tyre Co. Ltd* (1985), *H* fell and was injured when *S*, a fellow employee, indulged in some horseplay by pushing his truck against the duck-board on which *H* was standing. The employer was vicariously liable for *S*'s negligence.

In *Ricketts* v. *Thos. Tilling Ltd* (1915), a bus driver negligently allowed the conductor to drive and the claimant, a passenger, was injured. The employer was vicariously liable for the *driver's* negligent irresponsibility.

(d) The employer cannot escape liability merely by prohibiting the wrongful method of working. He can be liable to third parties injured even if the employee was acting in breach of express instructions.

In *Limpus* v. *London General Omnibus Co.* (1862), an accident occurred when the defendant's bus driver raced with and obstructed a driver from another company. Although the defendant had expressly forbidden such conduct, the driver's unauthorized and wrongful act was clearly in the course of his employment. The defendant was therefore vicariously liable.

In *Rose* v. *Plenty* (1976), a milkman, in breach of express instructions, allowed a thirteen-year-old to help him and to ride on the float. The boy was injured by the milkman's negligent driving. The employer was vicariously liable.

(e) On the other hand, the employer will not be vicariously liable for something which is wholly outside the scope of the worker's employment, particularly if the third party should have realized this.

In *Twine* v. *Bean's Express Ltd* (1946), a van driver gave a lift and the passenger was killed through negligent driving. The driver had been forbidden to give lifts,

77

and there was a notice to this effect on the dashboard. Moreover, the passenger was not helping the driver to do his job, unlike the boy in *Rose* v. *Plenty*. The employer was not vicariously liable.

Sometimes the employee is said to be on a frolic of his own, as where a lorry driver deviates widely from his authorized route for entirely his own purposes.

> In *Hilton* v. *Thomas Burton Ltd* (1961), demolition workers were allowed to use the employer's van for reasonable purposes. At 3.30 p.m. one day they drove seven miles to a cafe to pass the time until they finished work at 5.30 p.m. On the way back, the driver drove negligently and injured the claimant. The employer was not vicariously liable.

Loaned employees may give rise to problems, as when an employer hires out a worker, with or without equipment, to another employer. Which employer will be vicariously liable for torts committed by the worker during the hiring? There is a strong presumption that liability will remain with the permanent or general employer unless there is clear evidence that control over the *method* of working (as opposed to the tasks to be done) has passed to the temporary or special employer. This will depend upon the facts of each particular case, and will be determined by such matters as the specialized skill of the worker and the intricacy of machinery hired out at the same time. Thus, responsibility is more likely to remain with the general employer if a complex piece of earthmoving equipment and a skilled operator are involved than if a lorry and driver are hired.

> In *Mersey Docks and Harbour Board* v. *Coggins and Griffith Ltd* (1947), the harbour authority hired a crane and driver to a firm of stevedores. The contract of hire provided that the authority should pay and have power to dismiss the driver, but that he should be regarded as the servant of the stevedores. The stevedores had power to direct the work, but had no power over the way the driver operated the crane. The House of Lords held that the harbour authority was vicariously liable for the driver's negligence.

The contract between the employers may provide which of them will ultimately bear the loss, but this will not affect the above rules regarding which of them is vicariously liable *to the injured third party*.

Two further matters merit comment. First, it is worth repeating that the vicarious liability of the employer is in addition, and not an alternative, to the personal liability of the worker who committed the wrongful act. The worker may be sued by the injured party if the latter so chooses, but, since employers are more likely to be able to pay the damages because of their obligation to insure against such liability, the action is usually brought against the employer. If the employer is successfully sued he may, under the Civil Liability (Contribution) Act 1978, be entitled to indemnity from the worker.

> In *Lister* v. *Romford Ice and Cold Storage Ltd* (1957), Lister was employed as a lorry driver. He reversed the lorry carelessly, and injured his father, a fellow employee, who recovered damages from the employer. The employer (at the insistence of the insurance company) sued for and obtained indemnity from Lister. (In practice, however, employers do not usually seek indemnity from employees.)

Second, a distinction must be drawn between an employer and a superior servant. Vicarious liability for the misconduct of a bank clerk will rest upon the bank itself and not upon the bank manager. The latter will be liable only if he himself has contributed to the wrongful act.

The torts of independent contractors

The person who engages an independent contractor is not, as a general rule, vicariously liable for the contractor's torts. In general, only the contractor himself is liable for torts which he commits while carrying out the contract.

There are, however, some exceptional situations where the principal and the contractor may both be liable. The principal is not vicariously liable for the *contractor's* torts, but he will be liable if *he himself* has also committed a tort, or if the law imposes on him a duty to ensure that he chooses a contractor carefully.

Liability may arise in the following instances:

1. *Where the principal is negligent* in that he has engaged an incompetent contractor, or failed to give proper instructions.

   > In *Robinson* v. *Beaconsfield Rural Council* (1911), the Council had a statutory duty to clear cesspools. The Council engaged a contractor to do the work, but gave him no instructions as to disposal of the filth, and he deposited it on the appellant's land. The Council was held liable.

2. *Where strict liability is imposed by law*, the person who bears the responsibility cannot escape liability by engaging an independent contractor to do the job. Strict liability may arise at common law, as under the rule in *Rylands* v. *Fletcher* (Unit 10), or it may be imposed by legislation, for example some of the duties arising from occupational safety legislation.

3. *Where a contractor is engaged to do ultra-hazardous acts* which by their very nature involve special danger to others.

   > In *Sumner* v. *William Henderson & Sons Ltd* (1964), a fire was caused in a department store by the defective installation of an electric cable, and 11 people were killed. The respondents were held liable for the negligence of the contractors who installed the cable.

   > In *Holliday* v. *National Telephone Co.* (1899), the defendants, who were laying telephone cables along a highway, engaged a plumber to solder joints. They were held liable when a passer-by was injured by the negligent use of a blow lamp by the contractor.

4. *Where the person who engaged the contractor interferes with the work or actively participates in the wrong.*

   > It is possible for the principal to impose liability on the contractor by contract. While this will not affect the claim of a third party against the principal, it will give him a right to claim indemnity from the contractor later.

79

F. Liability for the acts of others in criminal law

The concept of vicarious liability does not generally apply in criminal law. Thus, if your employee, in the course of his employment, drives carelessly and injures someone, you will be vicariously liable for the driver's tort, but you will normally incur no criminal liability. Only the driver can be prosecuted. There are some statutory exceptions to this general rule, but these depend on the wording of the statutes concerned.

Problems arise where the offender is a corporation. As it has been noted, a corporation has no physical existence, and can only act through its organs (such as the board of directors), agents or employees. For most offences, the corporation cannot be held vicariously liable for the crimes of its employees.

For the purposes of criminal law, however, certain human persons are treated as the 'mind' of the corporation. These normally include executive directors and very senior management. The acts and decisions of these individuals are treated as the acts of the corporation, and can render the corporation criminally liable. Other less senior employees and agents are treated as separate persons, for whose acts the company is not criminally liable. We have seen how, in *Tesco Supermarkets Ltd* v. *Nattrass*, mentioned earlier, the branch manager in a supermarket chain was treated as 'another person', for whose misdeeds in the course of his employment the company was not criminally liable. To some extent this case turned on the particular wording of the Trade Descriptions Act, but it does reflect the general position. On the other hand, had the manager committed a *tort* in the course of his employment, there is no doubt that the company would have been vicariously liable for this.

If the company *does* commit a criminal offence, many statutes expressly provide that, in some circumstances, directors and/or senior managers may also be convicted (for example, see page 288).

G. Limitation of actions

The Limitation Act 1980 provides that in general no action in tort may be brought after six years have elapsed. There are exceptions to this period, in particular, 12 years are allowed for the recovery of land, whereas an action which includes a claim for damages for personal injuries or which arises from a fatal accident must be brought within three years. Actions for defamation must be brought within one year.

The time is calculated from the time when the cause of action accrued, that is from the date when the action could first have been brought. This could sometimes work injustice to a claimant who did not, for good reason, realize that he had a cause of action. He might not have realized that he was so ill, or that the foundations of his house were negligently built. Therefore there are exceptions.

1. In cases of personal injury or death, the Act sometimes permits an action on an otherwise statute-barred claim for up to three years after the discovery of material facts of which the claimant was previously unaware.

2. Under the Latent Damage Act 1986, there are similar rules as regards actions for negligence resulting from the loss of or damage to property. The limitation period of 6 years remains, but a further 3-year period can run if there is any latent damage that is not initially discernible. This added period runs, effectively, from the time when the claimant knew or should reasonably have known that he had a cause of action. There is a 15-year 'long-stop' time after which no action will lie.

3. There are similar rules to those in contract (Unit 16) for postponing the start of limitation periods until the end of a disability such as minority or insanity, or because of fraud.

There are no equivalent limitation periods in criminal law, and a prosecution may be brought at any time, even for an offence committed very much earlier. There are some exceptions to this general rule, the most important of which is that prosecutions for summary offences must normally be brought within six months of their commission.

Specimen questions

1. (a) In general any person may sue or be sued in tort. Discuss.
   (b) Smith, aged 17, hired a car for one day. On the following day, he failed to return the car as he had agreed. Instead he drove the car on another journey and damaged it through careless driving. Advise Smith as to his liability, if any, to the car owners.

2. Sparks is employed by Power & Co. as an electrician. While carrying out certain repairs at the department store of Harridges, Sparks lights a cigarette and throws away the lighted match. This badly damages the fur coat of Mrs Lamb, a customer. Can Mrs Lamb sue Sparks or Power & Co. or Harridges? Would your answer be different if Sparks had been forbidden to smoke during the course of his work?

3. (a) In what circumstances is an employer liable for the wrongful acts of his employees?
   (b) Eric, an accountant, is sent by his employer to audit the accounts of a client. Eric's instructions prohibit him from giving any advice on the investment of surplus funds. However, he does give such advice carelessly and, in acting upon it, the client suffers loss.
   To what extent is the employer liable for this loss?

4. A firm of contractors is engaged in road repairs. During the course of the work, the following incidents take place:
   (a) A labourer employed by the contractors omits to fence a hole in the road. A cyclist falls into the hole and is injured.
   (b) A lorry with a driver is hired to carry away waste material. While doing this, the driver knocks down and injures a pedestrian.
   (c) A subcontractor is engaged for work with electric cables. His carelessness leads to a small boy being electrocuted.
   Discuss the possible liability of the contractors for these injuries.

5. Road Contractors Ltd engages a number of drivers to move earth and rubble during the construction of a motorway. Each driver provides his own lorry and payment is made on a piecework basis subject to guaranteed minimum earnings. During prescribed hours of work the drivers are subject to control by the company's supervisors. One driver overloads his lorry, contrary to instructions given by a supervisor, and this is the cause of an accident in which a third party is injured. Advise Road Contractors Ltd as to its possible liability.

Unit 9. Negligence

Negligence is perhaps the most important of all torts, affecting many aspects of life. It arises when damage is caused to the person or property of another by failure to take such care as the law requires in the circumstances of the case. To succeed in an action for negligence, the claimant must prove three things:

1. The defendant owed him a legal duty of care.
2. The duty was broken.
3. Damage was suffered in consequence.

Each of these requirements is discussed further below.

A. The duty of care

1. Foreseeability

There are specific situations where a duty of care has long been recognized. A road user must show care towards other users, and an employer owes duties to employees for their safety at work. These duties were created and extended by judicial decisions. In *Donoghue* v. *Stevenson* (1932) (see page 89) Lord Atkin tried to replace this piecemeal approach by suggesting a general duty of care which could be applied in all situations. His view was that reasonable care should always be taken to avoid injury to your 'neighbour', that is, any person so closely affected by your conduct that you should *reasonably foresee* might be injured by it.

This 'neighbour' principle was increasingly applied by the courts in the next 50 years. It became the general test for examining whether a duty of care existed. An outstanding example came in 1963, when the House of Lords said *obiter* that, contrary to what had previously been believed, liability for negligence could extend to careless words as well as to deeds, and that damages could sometimes be awarded for purely financial loss as well as for physical injury to persons and property.

> In *Hedley Byrne* v. *Heller and Partners* (1963), a firm of advertising agents gave credit to a client in reliance upon a reference from the client's bank, which had known the purpose for which the reference was required. The reference was given carelessly but, since the bank had expressly disclaimed liability when giving it, the action failed. Nevertheless the above *obiter dicta* were made, and have since been followed.

> In *Smith* v. *Eric S. Bush* (1989), a surveyor employed by a building society to value a house knew that his report would be relied upon by a specific buyer who had a right to see it. The House of Lords held the surveyor liable to the buyer (who was not his client) for careless omissions.

> Even in *Spring* v. *Guardian Assurance plc* (1994), the House of Lords held that an employer giving a personal reference for an employee owed a duty *to the employee* to take reasonable care over the accuracy of facts upon which the employer's opinions were based.

Although the law did move towards a general duty of care, this position was never reached. The assumption that there *was* a duty could always be limited by issues of public policy, as Lord Wilberforce emphasized in *Anns* v. *Merton LBC* (1977). More recently, particularly after *Murphy* v. *Brentwood DC* (1990) (see page 88) and *Caparo* v. *Dickman* (1990) (this page, below), the emphasis has changed, and there will *not* be a duty unless the claimant can show at least three inter-related things: the damage must be foreseeable; there must be a close and direct connection, a 'proximity', between claimant and defendant which enables the claimant to show that the duty was owed towards him (see below); and it must be fair, just and reasonable that the law should impose a duty on the defendant in these circumstances. This brings the law much closer to the piecemeal approach of former years.

2. Proximity

The need to show that there is sufficient proximity arises particularly when the number of potential claimants is large and/or uncertain; see cases such as *D & F Estates* v. *Church Commissioners* (1988) and *Murphy* v. *Brentwood D C* (1990) (page 88). A duty for financial loss usually arises only from an assumption of responsibility by a person rendering professional services, and acting in his professional capacity, towards a person (other than the client) for whose benefit the services were rendered or who was known to be relying on them for a specific purpose.

> In *White* v. *Jones* (1995), the House of Lords held that a solicitor was liable to the intended beneficiary from his client's will when, because of the solicitor's undue delay, the client died before the intended will was ready to be signed.

> In *Caparo Industries plc* v. *Dickman* (1990), the accountants engaged by a company to audit its annual accounts were alleged to have done so negligently, so that the accounts looked misleading. As a result, the claimants made a successful but unwise takeover bid and suffered financial loss. The House of Lords held that the ordinary annual audit was not for the benefit of potential buyers of a company's shares. Nor was it carried out in

order to influence existing individual shareholders in deciding whether or not to buy more shares in the company. Therefore, even if the auditors had been negligent, they did not owe an actionable duty of care to the claimants. (To have held otherwise might have made them liable to a very large number of people; contrast *Hedley Byrne* and the other cases)

In *ADT Ltd* v. *Binder Hamlyn* (1995), it was held that there *was* a breach of duty when the auditors said *specifically to ADT*, knowing that their statement would be relied upon, that the accounts of a company which ADT wished to take over were reliable. In fact, the accounts were not reliable. ADT suffered huge loss and was awarded damages in tort.

In The *Law Society* v. *KPMG* (2000), the accountants, KPMG, had a contract with a firm of solicitors to prepare the firm's annual accounts to the Law Society. The accounts were negligently prepared, and defective. The solicitors became insolvent, and the Law Society had to pay clients' claims from its compensation fund. KPMG were held liable to the Law Society, who they knew would rely on the accounts.

Many of the other important decisions on this point have involved 'nervous shock'.

In *Bourhill* v. *Young* (1942), a pregnant woman who suffered a miscarriage from shock after hearing a nearby accident to a stranger and seeing blood on the road was not awarded damages.

In *McLoughlin* v. *O'Brian* (1982), the claimant saw and was in physical contact with her badly injured husband and children very shortly after a road accident caused by two lorries. Another of her children was killed. She was awarded damages against the lorry drivers and their employers, even though she was at home when the accident occurred.

In *Alcock* v. *Chief Constable of S. Yorks Police* (1991), Liverpool supporters were killed by overcrowding in part of Hillsborough football ground, Sheffield. It was claimed that senior police officers at the scene had been negligent. The claimants were relatives and a fiancée who suffered illness from shock after seeing the accident at a distance or on live TV. Their actions failed. Some were less closely related to the main victims, and none saw the bodily injuries closely or immediately. A distinction was drawn between the 'primary' and 'secondary' victims of such a disaster. Primary victims were those who had themselves been injured or in danger of bodily injury, and suffered 'shock' illness because of this. Secondary victims were never themselves in bodily danger, but suffered shock from seeing bodily injury to others. Secondary victims are much less likely to be sufficiently proximate.

In *White* v. *Chief Constable of S. Yorks Police* (1998), it was held that police officers who suffered psychiatric injury while attempting rescue at Hillsborough were secondary victims and, on the facts, not entitled to damages.

3. 'Fair, just and reasonable'

This requirement is often closely associated with issues of public policy. It might not be reasonable to impose a duty that could make the defendant liable to a vast number of people (see *Caparo* v. *Dickman* again); nor a duty that would inhibit the exercise by a public person of his public duties; or there might be other considerations.

In *Hill* v. *Chief Constable of W. Yorkshire* (1989) the relatives of one of the later victims of a serial murderer claimed damages from the police for their allegedly negligent investigation of earlier deaths. The House of Lords held that the police owed no duty to the claimants on public policy grounds (and also because of the lack of proximity with persons who were unidentifiable at the time of the alleged negligence).

In *Mulcahy* v. *Ministry of Defence* (1996), the claimant alleged that he had been injured by the negligence of a fellow soldier while engaging the enemy (in the Gulf War). The claim failed.

However in *Hall* v. *Simons* (2000), the House of Lords held, contrary to the existing rule, that advocates – barristers or solicitors – could be liable for negligently conducting a case in court. By a majority, this was applied to criminal as well as to civil proceedings. There was no overriding public policy reason for preventing such actions. The seven Law Lords in this case effectively reversed the former House of Lords decision of *Rondel* v. *Worsley* (1969).

B. Breach of duty

1. The standard of care

In deciding whether or not the duty of care has been broken, the standard against which the defendant's conduct will be measured is that of the so-called 'reasonable man'. Negligence will be deemed to be present if the defendant did not act in a reasonable manner in the circumstances of the situation. What is reasonable will depend upon factors such as the magnitude of the risk involved, for the greater the risk the greater the care required.

In *Bolton* v. *Stone* (1951), a batsman hit a ball out of the ground during a cricket match. It struck and injured Miss Stone, who was in the street. The top of the fence surrounding the ground was 17 feet higher than the pitch at the point where the ball crossed, and Miss Stone was about 100 yards from the batsman. It was only proved that a cricket ball had been hit out of the ground on six occasions in 30 years, and there was evidence that the shot was exceptional. It was held that, in the circumstances, the cricket club had taken reasonable care, and was not liable. It would have been otherwise if balls had landed in the road frequently.

Greater care will be expected *from* persons having or professing special skills, such as accountants and lawyers; also from persons who are in a position of responsibility, such as employers. The standards expected are those of the reasonable accountant, lawyer, or employer.

Greater care will be expected *towards* persons who are seen to be especially vulnerable, such as children and blind persons; similarly if the person exposed to the risk possesses known characteristics which, if an injury occurs, make the consequences more serious.

In *Paris* v. *Stepney Borough Council* (1951), a fitter with only one good eye was employed on work which involved some danger to the eyes from fragments of metal. No goggles were provided. It was held that the employer acted unreasonably, and hence negligently, in not taking extra precautions.

It may sometimes be reasonable to take less care in an emergency, such as driving an urgent case to hospital.

In *Watt* v. *Hertfordshire County Council* (1954), a fireman failed to recover damages when he had been injured by the movement of a heavy lifting jack which was not properly secured on a lorry. The vehicle was not properly equipped to carry the jack, but it was the only lorry available to carry the jack to free a trapped woman in danger of losing her life. The defendants had taken a reasonable risk in the circumstances.

2. Proof of breach

A major problem connected with breach of duty is the *onus of proof*. Normally it is for the claimant to show that the defendant did not act in a reasonable manner, and in the absence of reliable evidence his action will fail. This can sometimes occur when the claimant is unable to say what happened, and there is no other evidence.

In *Wakelin* v. *London and South Western Railway Co.* (1886), the body of a man was found on the railway, near a level crossing, at night. He had been hit by a train, and it seemed quite possible that the railway company had been careless. On the other hand, it was equally possible that the accident was entirely the man's own fault. In the absence of evidence either way, the action failed.

There are, however, some situations where an accident happens of which the only or most likely cause must be negligence. Unattended cars do not normally run away, train doors do not normally fly open, nor do cakes contain stones. The court may then apply the maxim *res ipsa loquitur* (the thing speaks for itself) and, upon proof of the accident by the claimant, infer negligence from this fact, unless the *defendant* offers a reasonable explanation. The onus of proof, at this point, is reversed, and the defendant is effectively left to prove that he was *not* negligent.

This rule of procedure can be of considerable assistance to the claimant in situations of obvious negligence, which are normally those where the claimant knows little of why the accident occurred, but the defendant is (or should be) able to explain what has happened.

In *Richley* v. *Faull* (1965), the defendant's car skidded violently, turned round, and collided with the claimant's car on the wrong side of the road. It was held that this, of itself, was sufficient evidence of negligent driving. Since the defendant was unable to give a satisfactory explanation of his skid, he was held liable.

C. Resulting damage

1. Types of loss

The claimant must prove that he has suffered loss as a result of the defendant's breach of duty of care. Loss can include damage to property, personal injury and, in some circumstances, financial loss. Policy considerations may also apply here in determining whether the loss may be recovered.

At one time it was not clear whether personal injuries could include nervous shock because of the difficulties of linking cause and effect. Medical and psychological advances have overcome this difficulty, and it is now established that nervous shock may be compensated if it gives rise to physical or mental illness, and it is just as much a form of injury as a broken leg.

Financial or economic loss is recoverable in only some cases. It may be recovered as a result of a careless act if it is closely connected with physical harm which has occurred. Thus damages for personal injuries may include compensation for medical expenses and loss of earnings. Similarly in damage to property cases, financial loss very *directly* caused by the damage may be recoverable.

In *Spartan Steel & Alloys Ltd* v. *Martin & Co. Ltd* (1972), careless excavation during road work damaged an electricity cable and cut off the power supply to the claimant's foundry for 14 hours. Metal currently melted in a furnace had to be removed to prevent it from solidifying. Damages were awarded for physical harm to the metal, and for financial losses on *that* operation. The court refused to award damages for loss of profits from future operations while the power was off, however, because this was not directly connected with the 'melt' in progress.

In *Muirhead Ltd* v. *Industrial Tank Specialities Ltd* (1985), a wholesale fish merchant, *M*, wished to keep live lobsters in a seawater tank. Pumps had to circulate the water regularly. The pumps broke down and *M* lost his lobsters. He sued the firm which had installed the pumps, but it became insolvent. He therefore brought an action for negligence against the manufacturer from whom the pumps had been acquired indirectly. The manufacturer was held liable for the value of the lobsters and the financial loss directly connected with this. But it was not liable for the fact that the tank was worth less than it should have been, nor for the future profits that *M* had hoped to make from it. These were purely economic losses.

Purely financial loss is rarely recoverable for the tort of negligence. Since the *Hedley Byrne* case, liability for it can arise from an assumption of responsibility by a person rendering professional or quasi-professional services, coupled with a concomitant reliance by the person for whom the services were rendered. There are always strict limits on the duty of care; see *Caparo Industries* v. *Dickman* earlier. A negligent act or omission, such as bad workmanship, which only causes economic loss in the sense that a product is worth less than it should have been, or needs repair, will generally not give rise to liability for the tort of negligence. (If, however, there is a *contract* between the parties, then financial loss can readily be recovered for breach of contract, and there is no need to rely on the tort of negligence; see Unit 15.)

In *D & F Estates Ltd* v. *Church Commissioners* (1988), the plastering work was done negligently when a block of flats was built. The House of Lords held that the present tenants, who had no direct connection with the builders or plasterers, could not recover damages from them for the cost of repairing the defects. This was purely economic loss in that the product (the plasterwork) was worth less than it should have been.

In *Murphy* v. *Brentwood DC* (1990), a local authority approved plans for building a house on an 'infill' site which might later subside. The plans contained inadequate precautions and when subsidence occurred much later, the house was damaged and lost much of its value. The house owner sued the council for its negligence in approving plans which turned out to be inadequate. The action failed. The House of Lords held that the owner's loss was purely economic, and the fact that the house was *potentially* dangerous to live in did not alter this. It was undesirable that, when approving plans, a council should owe a transferable duty to compensate future owners for purely financial risks.

2. Remoteness

Finally, the resulting damage must not be too remote. Since the *Wagon Mound* case in 1961 (Unit 10), this means that the type of damage should reasonably have been foreseen by the defendant at the time when he acted carelessly.

> In *Doughty* v. *Turner Manufacturing Co. Ltd* (1964), the claimant was injured by an explosion caused by an asbestos cement lid being carelessly knocked into a cauldron of molten metal. His action failed because, according to the state of knowledge at the time, an explosion was not to be expected, and his injuries were not therefore reasonably foreseeable. The decision could well have been different if his injuries had been caused by a foreseeable splash of metal.

D. Liability for defective goods

A person who hands over dangerous or defective goods can owe several duties at common law. He may be liable for breach of contract to the recipient himself if the latter bought or gave value for the goods (see Units 15, 18 and 20). He may also be liable for the tort of negligence to other persons into whose hands the goods may come.

> In *Donoghue* v. *Stevenson* (1932), a woman drank some ginger beer which had been bought for her by a friend. The beer was in an opaque bottle and, when the last of it was poured out, it was found to contain what were thought to be the decomposed remains of a snail. The woman suffered shock and became ill. The House of Lords decided that a manufacturer owes a duty of care to the consumer of his products when they are marketed in the form in which the consumer will receive them. The snail was in an opaque bottle, and there was no reasonable possibility of its being discovered between leaving the manufacturer and reaching the consumer. The manufacturer could therefore be liable for negligence.

This rule has become more important in recent times, particularly with goods which are technically complex and/or pre-packaged by a producer, so that they reach the eventual user unopened and unchecked. The common law rules have been supplemented by the Consumer Protection Act 1987, particularly when the victim is a private consumer, and they are discussed more fully in Unit 20.

One problem facing a customer is the difficulty of proof. He is often in no position to know whether a manufacturer has been careless. The courts have sometimes, therefore, applied the maximum *res ipsa loquitur* and reversed the onus of proof.

> In *Steer* v. *Durable Rubber Co. Ltd* (1958), a girl aged six was scalded when a hot-water-bottle split soon after being bought. The Court of Appeal held that it was for the manufacturers to prove that they had *not* been negligent, which they were unable to do.

The above cases have involved the sale or supply of goods. There can be similar situations if a person repairs a customer's goods or does other work on them. If the repairs are done under a contract, the repairer can be liable for breach of contract to his customer. The repairer can also owe a duty of care to any other person likely to be injured by his negligence.

In *Stennett* v. *Hancock* (1939), Mrs Stennett, a pedestrian injured by part of a lorry wheel which had broken away, recovered damages from the defendant garage, which had not carried out repairs to the lorry in a proper manner.

It should be noted that all of the above cases have involved bodily injury to the claimant. In actions for negligence the courts will also give damages for physical harm to the claimant's other property caused by the defective goods, but not normally for mere economic loss; see *Muirhead* v. *Industrial Tank Specialities* again.

E. Employer's liability

This is another aspect of the general principles of negligence, which deserves special mention in view of the large number of actions which arise out of injuries suffered at work. An employer owes a duty to his employees to take reasonable care to provide a safe system of work. This includes an obligation to provide reasonably competent staff, to provide reasonably safe equipment, and to provide a reasonably safe method of working. It covers both the physical and the mental health of employees, and can extend to illnesses arising from stress. This duty of care has been reinforced by a number of statutory duties imposed in the interests of safety.

F. Liability for defective premises

Occupiers' liability

As regards *lawful visitors* to his premises, the duty of care owed by an occupier was formerly based upon complex rules which had evolved from the general principles of the tort of negligence. This duty was simplified and restated by the Occupiers' Liability Act 1957 which now largely governs the position.

The Act imposes a duty of care upon those in physical occupation and control of premises, who may not necessarily be the owners. Even temporary control can be enough, as where a builder occupies part of a site during construction work. It is possible for the duty to be owed by two (or more) people in respect of the same premises, for example the occupier of a house and a builder working there, if both have some degree of control over the work being done.

The duty is owed to all lawful visitors who enter with the express or implied permission of the occupier. It covers also those who enter in exercise of a right at law, for example a police officer executing a search warrant. This Act does not apply to trespassers whose position is discussed below.

The duty concerns the state of the premises and things done or omitted to be done on them. The occupier's obligation, described as the 'common duty of care', is 'to take such care as in all the circumstances of the case is reasonable to see that the visitor will be reasonably safe in using the premises for the purposes for which he is invited or permitted by the occupier to be there'. The occupier can protect himself by warning the visitor of specific dangers but this warning must, in the circumstances, be enough to enable the visitor to be reasonably safe.

90

As under the previous law, the occupier must be prepared for children to be less careful than adults. What constitutes adequate warning or protection for an adult may not be deemed so for a child. In addition, some dangerous things may attract a child and these traps or allurements must be guarded against.

> In *Glasgow Corporation* v. *Taylor* (1922), a boy of seven died after eating attractive looking poisonous berries in a park. The berries were within easy reach and it was held that the warning notice was insufficient so far as young children were concerned.

Conversely, the occupier may expect that experts, for example electricians entering to repair an electrical fault, will appreciate the special risks likely to arise from their work.

> In *Roles* v. *Nathan* (1963), two sweeps were killed by carbon monoxide fumes while cleaning the flues of a coke boiler. It was held that this was a risk of which they should have been aware, and that the occupier had discharged his duty under the Act by passing on a warning he had been given by an expert.

The duty imposed by the 1957 Act may not now be excluded or modified by contract in so far as death or personal injury is concerned (Unfair Contract Terms Act 1977). The occupier may contract out of liability for other loss or damage, for example to property, but only if he can show that it is reasonable to do so.

Trespassers, at common law, were deemed to take the premises as they found them and could not, in general, complain if they were injured. At the same time the occupier had to act in a reasonable and civilized manner and could not inflict intentional harm upon trespassers. Thus, while he could erect a fence of barbed wire as a reasonable means of deterring entry and would not be liable for any injury thereby caused, he could not set deliberate traps designed to cause injury after trespassers had obtained entry. In addition, if an occupier knew that trespassers were on his land or were likely to be there, he could not disregard their presence and endanger them by acting recklessly, for example by shooting where they were likely to be.

More recently, the courts have given greater protection to trespassers, particularly children, on humanitarian grounds.

> In *British Railways Board* v. *Herrington* (1972), children regularly played in a field next to an electrified railway. The fence guarding the line was broken down in one place, and people were known to use the gap for a short cut across the line. The Board was held liable to a boy aged six, who wandered from the field on to the line, and was badly injured by a live rail.

The Occupiers' Liability Act 1984 replaced these common law rules and attempted to clarify the liability of occupiers towards unlawful visitors. An occupier now owes a statutory duty to a trespasser if he knows or should know that a danger exists, that the trespasser is or may be in the vicinity of the danger and that it is reasonable for him to offer some protection. The duty is to take such care as is reasonable in all the circumstances to see that the trespasser does not suffer *personal* injury. Greater care may, therefore, be required towards a hiker who has lost his way than towards a burglar. It may be reasonable in appropriate cases to discharge the duty by a warning or by some other way of discouraging would-be trespassers.

Finally, acquiescence in a trespass may result in the trespasser being regarded as a lawful visitor. Again, this frequently applies to children.

In *Lowery* v. *Walker* (1911), passengers had crossed a farmer's field regularly for the last 30 years on their way to the station. It was held that, although the farmer had never expressly given permission, he had acquiesced for so long that the people were no longer regarded as trespassers. The farmer could have built a large fence, or otherwise made it clear that he no longer acquiesced, but he did not do so. Instead he put a savage horse in the field, and was held liable to someone it attacked.

Liability of builders

A builder's main duty is to the person who engages and pays him, to whom he can be liable for breach of contract. However, a builder can also be liable in tort to other people injured by his negligence.

In *Billings* (*A.C.*) *& Sons Ltd* v. *Riden* (1958), a builder was engaged to make alterations at the front of a house. He left access to the house unsafe overnight, and was held liable for negligence to an elderly visitor who fell and was injured.

A major difficulty in this area of the tort of negligence is the type of loss or harm for which damages can be recovered; see *D & F Estates* v. *Church Commissioners* (page 88). Damages are recoverable if someone is injured, or if property other than the builder's work is harmed; but financial loss arising from defective work is normally recoverable only by the person who contracted with the builder.

Another difficulty is that defects in buildings are usually latent, and may not become apparent until after the victim's rights of action have been barred by the Limitation Act 1980. The Latent Damage Act 1986 may help in these circumstances (page 80).

As regards *dwelling* houses, these rules are supplemented by the Defective Premises Act 1972. A person taking on work for or in connection with the provision of a dwelling owes a strict duty 'to see that the work which he takes on is done in a workmanlike or, as the case may be, professional manner, with proper materials and so that as regards that work the dwelling will be fit for habitation when complete'. This part of the 1972 Act does not apply, however, to houses built under the National House Building Council (NHBC) scheme, and therefore is of limited importance. Most professional builders belong to the NHBC scheme which provides, in effect, a limited guarantee and insurance cover to the buyers of new houses.

Liability of vendors

In general, the private seller of an existing building owes no duties of care to his buyer as regards the state of the premises. The general rule is *caveat emptor* (let the buyer beware). Under the Defective Premises Act, however, the seller of a house might owe duties if he has himself done work on it before selling. If his work has left the house unsafe, he could be liable for injuries to any 'persons who might reasonably be expected to be affected', which could include a buyer and/or the buyer's visitors.

Specimen questions

1. Express Carriers has an office at which goods are received for onward shipment. Alan enters this office and places on the counter a large package, wrapped in brown paper with no indication of its contents. Brian, the receiving clerk, completes the necessary paperwork and picks up the package. This slips from his grasp and falls to the floor when, since it contains highly dangerous fireworks, it explodes. Injuries are caused to Alan, Brian, Charles (another customer) and David (a passer-by, who has come into the office to avoid a heavy rainstorm).

   Discuss the legal position.

2. Albert is the proprietor of a large garage. What is his liability, if any, in each of the following situations?

   (a) One of his employees is taking a car for a test drive when it skids out of control on to the wrong side of the road and damages another car coming in the opposite direction.

   (b) A car that has just been repaired is being driven away by a customer when the car door falls off and injures a pedestrian.

   (c) Albert suggests that a customer changes his vehicle insurance company in order to get better terms. The customer does so and suffers loss when the recommended company later fails and is unable to meet his claim.

3. The heating plant at your employer's factory is operated by smokeless fuel. One consignment of fuel contained explosive that seriously damaged the plant and caused the factory to be closed for three weeks. In addition to loss of normal production, a particularly profitable contract was lost. Both the supplier and the manufacturer of the fuel disclaim responsibility, each blaming the other. Advise your employer.

4. (a) To what extent may an action for negligence be based upon:

   (i) a careless statement; and

   (ii) financial or economic loss?

   (b) Bernard was given a lump sum payment by his employer when he retired and he invested this by buying shares in three companies. The shares in Company X were bought on the advice of his bank manager, given during an interview at the bank to discuss his financial position. Company Y shares were recommended by his accountant in a brief conversation at a party and Company Z shares were recommended by his neighbour who sells insurance.

   Unfortunately, all the companies have failed and Bernard's money has been lost.

   You are required to advise Bernard as to whether he may have a remedy against those who advised him.

5. The proprietor of an hotel asks for your advice on the possible liability of the hotel for each of the following accidents:

   (a) Albert, a guest, has broken a tooth on a bone in a fishcake supplied to him in the restaurant.

(b) A lift engineer has carelessly repaired the lift and Bernard, another guest, has received a severe electric shock when he pressed the lift button.

(c) Charles came into the hotel to visit his friend, Albert, and tripped and broke his leg on a worn carpet in the hotel lobby.

Advise the proprietor.

Unit 10. Further Principles of Liability in Tort

A. Specific torts

The tort of negligence was discussed in detail in the previous unit because of its special importance. It is not possible to treat other torts in the same depth here, but the first part of this unit will be devoted to an outline of some other specific torts.

Torts against the person

Any direct interference with the person or liberty of another without lawful justification is actionable as a *trespass to the person*. This may take three forms: *assault*, where a person is threatened with violence; *battery*, where force is actually applied; and *false imprisonment*, where a total restraint is unlawfully placed upon the liberty of another. All forms may be present, for example, if a suspected shoplifter is forcibly and wrongfully taken into custody by a store detective.

Torts against land

The tort of *trespass to land* is committed by *direct* interference with the land of another. Trespass to land is only a tort, and trespassers cannot generally be criminally prosecuted, except in a few instances such as trespass upon railway or military property. In its simplest form it is unauthorized entry upon land. It can also be trespass to use land for an unauthorized purpose, to remain on land when permission to be there has ended, or to place, dump or throw things on to another's land. Thus unauthorized car parking on private land is trespass, as is unauthorized dumping of rubbish or litter there. 'Land' includes not only the surface and any buildings upon it,

95

but also the air space above within the area of ordinary use (tree branches, overhanging structures, etc. but not aeroplanes flying over; also the ground (including minerals) beneath.

Someone expressly invited on to the land will not be a trespasser, nor will someone with implied authority to be there, for example a sales representative entering business premises in the hope of selling something. In both cases, however, they must leave if asked to do so. Even against the wishes of the occupier, police officers have various powers of entry, and many officials such as public health inspectors and inspectors for health and safety at work have statutory powers to enter certain premises. In addition to a remedy through the courts by way of damages or an injunction, an occupier has a right to ask the trespasser to leave (or to remove his car or rubbish) and, if he refuses, to use such force as is reasonably necessary to effect a removal.

If the interference with a person's use or enjoyment of land is *indirect*, an action may lie for *private nuisance*. Indirect interference with the enjoyment of land can take many forms, such as noise, smoke, smells, vibrations, fumes, etc. Interference with specific rights over land, such as blocking a right of way or taking away a right of light, can also be a nuisance. On the other hand, not all interference will be actionable; the law expects some 'give and take' and an action for nuisance will lie only if the interference is unreasonable. In an urban area, for example, a certain amount of noise is accepted as inevitable. All circumstances, such as the locality and the duration, frequency and nature of the alleged nuisance must be considered. In *Hunter* v. *Canary Wharf Ltd* (1996), interference with TV reception caused by a new tower block gave no right of action to nearby London residents, for example.

If the annoyance or harm affects the public generally, a *public nuisance* may have been committed. This is not a tort against land, but is mentioned here for convenience. It is primarily a crime but an action in tort is also possible if the claimant has suffered loss over and above that suffered by the public as a whole. Thus, a road-user cannot recover damages simply because of the smell from a factory which he passes, but he may do so if acid smuts from the factory damage his car.

Torts against goods

A third form of trespass, *trespass to goods*, arises when there is direct and unauthorized physical interference with goods in the possession of another. It usually arises when the goods are removed or damaged; strictly, the slightest interference will suffice, but an action is unlikely unless there is substantial damage or serious inconvenience (unjustified wheel-clamping or vehicle seizure perhaps). There can be liability without fault, and it can be sufficient if goods are taken or moved by mistake. There need be no dishonest intent (unlike for the crime of theft).

If a person deals in the goods of another in such a way that the other's *right* or title to the goods is called in question, an action will lie for *conversion*. The most common forms arise when someone wrongfully purports to sell goods which do not belong to him, or wrongfully refuses to return goods to their rightful owner. Thus, it would be conversion for the hirer of goods to try to sell them to someone else, or to refuse to return them when the hiring expires. Again, there can be liability without fault, and the tort can be committed by mistake or in ignorance of the true ownership; in *Cundy* v. *Lindsay* (Unit 13), the innocent buyer of goods from a rogue was liable to the true owner for conversion when the true owner traced the goods.

By the Torts (Interference with Goods) Act 1977, the court may order the return of the goods in a successful action for conversion; or it can award damages, particularly if return is impracticable because the goods have been altered or re-sold; or the court can give the defendant the choice of either returning the goods or paying damages.

Torts against reputation

The publication of a (false) statement which tends to injure the reputation of another may constitute the tort of *defamation*. The test is whether, in consequence of the statement, right-thinking members of society might regard the claimant with hatred, ridicule or contempt, or tend to shun or avoid him, or hold him in lower esteem. A company can sue for defamatory statements about its business or property. The statement must clearly refer to the claimant, either expressly or by necessary implication. Moreover, it must be published to a third party other than the claimant's spouse; a person's reputation depends upon the opinion of others.

Defamation in a permanent form, such as writing, is *libel*; in a temporary form, such as speech, it is *slander*. The distinction is important because slander is only actionable if the claimant proves that the statement caused him financial loss, whereas libel is actionable even without such loss. There are exceptional cases of slander where loss need not be proved, for example allegations that the claimant has committed a serious criminal offence, or that a person in any office, trade or profession is unfit to hold his position or practise his trade.

Several defences are available. If the defendant can show *unintentional defamation*, he may avoid liability by apologizing, publishing a suitable correction and paying any legal costs or other expenses that the claimant has reasonably incurred. It is always a defence to show that the allegations are *true*, for no one can fairly claim a reputation which he does not deserve. In the interests of free speech and criticism, opinions passed on matters of public concern may be defended if they constitute *fair comment on a matter of public interest*, and are made in good faith. Finally, statements made in some situations are *privileged*, and therefore not actionable. Statements in court or in Parliament have absolute privilege, and are completely protected. Some other situations attract only qualified privilege, where there is protection only in the absence of malice, for example where the publisher has a duty to make the statement and the recipient has an interest in receiving it. Thus a reference or testimonial is protected from liability for defamation if it is honestly, though mistakenly, made. However an employer who was careless with facts alleged in a reference might be liable to his employee for the tort of *negligence*; see *Spring* v. *Guardian Assurance* in Unit 9.

The rule in *Rylands* v. *Fletcher*

This rule takes its name from the case in which it was first formulated. It provides that, if a person brings on to his land and keeps there something likely to do damage if it escapes, he keeps it there at his peril and will be strictly liable for any damage which follows from an escape, even if there has been no negligence. In *Rylands* v. *Fletcher* (1868), the defendant was liable when water leaked from his reservoir and flooded a neighbour's mines. The rule applies only where keeping the dangerous thing constitutes a 'non-natural' use of the land, and more recently it has been suggested that some industrial processes are natural uses of land, and so not within the rule. On the other hand, some industrial discharges, or the escape of toxic waste from private tips, may still come within the rule.

Breach of statutory duty

Many statutes impose duties on individuals, firms or public authorities, breaches of which are primarily *criminal* offences. In certain cases, particularly where the purpose of duty is to protect people from physical danger, there may also be a further sanction: a person injured as a result of breach may be allowed to recover damages for the *tort* of breach of statutory duty. An important example is where someone is injured as a result of breach of a statutory duty as regards safety at work.

The nature of the duty depends upon the wording of the legislation. Some statutory duties are *strict*, and there can be liability without fault (for example, under some sections of the occupational safety legislation). Other provisions simply impose a statutory duty of reasonable care.

Furthermore, as far as possible, Acts and delegated legislation must now be read and given effect in a way that is compatible with the European Convention on Human Rights; see Human Rights Act 1998.

Deceit

In Unit 9 we examined how, in limited situations, liability can arise for negligent misstatements; the tort of deceit (fraud) is concerned with *intentional* or *reckless* falsehood. The tort has five main elements:

1. There must be a false statement of *fact*, not merely an expression of opinion.
2. It must be made fraudulently, that is knowingly, or without belief in its truth, or recklessly, not caring whether it be true or false.
3. The claimant must be intended to act on the statement.
4. He must actually act in reliance on it.
5. He must thereby suffer loss.

Where the maker of a deceitful statement thereby induces the claimant to make a *contract* with him, the claimant will also be entitled to recover damages under section 2(1) of the Misrepresentation Act 1967 (Unit 13). To this extent, there can be an overlap between misrepresentation and deceit, but the tort can also apply more widely.

Interference with business interests

There are a number of actions in tort which may be used to protect business interests and prevent unfair competition. Thus, the remedy of *passing off* may be available where the public are misled by using a name for a business or for a product which is the same or nearly like an existing name. Maliciously publishing a false statement about a person or his property, for example that a competitor has gone out of business, may bring liability for *injurious falsehood.*

It is wrongful to *induce a breach of contract* intentionally and without lawful justification; an inducement to terminate a contract is not actionable provided unlawful means are not used. *Conspiracy* may arise when two or more persons combine wilfully to injure another and *intimidation* when loss is intentionally inflicted upon another by means of violence or unlawful threats. Some of these common law actions have been modified by statute, particularly where trade disputes are concerned.

B. Defences in tort

Many defences may be raised in an action in tort. In the first place, the defendant can argue simply that the alleged tort has not been committed; for example, in the tort of negligence, the defendant may claim (a) that he owed no duty of care, (b) that in any case he was not careless, and (c) that even if he was careless, his negligence did not cause the defendant's loss. Secondly, certain torts such as defamation have their own special defences. Finally, there are some 'general' defences which apply to almost all torts, and it is these which are discussed here.

Statutory authority

Generally, nothing authorized by statute is unlawful. Much, therefore, depends upon the interpretation of the statute, which may sanction an act even though it involves what would otherwise be a tort. Thus the train companies, that have statutory authority to run the trains, could not be sued for making such noise as is an inevitable result of doing so, even though, but for the statutory authority, this might constitute the tort of nuisance.

On the other hand, the courts are reluctant to hold that Parliament authorized a harmful act unless the statute is quite unambiguous. So, if the statute gives someone power to do something, the courts will assume that the power was given only on the understanding that it be exercised carefully.

In *Fisher* v. *Ruislip–Northwood UDC* (1945), the local authority had, by statute, been given power to erect air-raid shelters on the highway. In the black-out, Fisher drove his motor cycle into such a shelter, and was injured. When sued for the tort of public nuisance, the

Council pleaded that it had statutory authority to put up the shelter. The defence failed, because the Council could, even in the black-out, have put up small, shaded warning lights for motorists. The Council only had statutory authority on condition that it was exercised with care for the safety of others.

Similarly, in *Metropolitan Asylum District* v. *Hill* (1881), the authority had statutory power to erect a smallpox hospital. It chose to put it in a residential part of Hampstead, and it was held that statutory authority was no defence. The authority could have exercised its powers so as to cause much less danger.

It is presumed that an act authorized by statute will be carried out with reasonable care, and statutory authority is rarely a defence if there is negligence. It should also be noted that when a statute takes away a right of action, it may at the same time make provision for some compensation to be paid.

Again a statute is now subject to the Human Rights Act; see page 98.

Consent (*Volenti*)

If a person consents to suffer damage or run the risk of it, he cannot later bring an action. This defence is sometimes called voluntary assumption of risk, and expressed in the maxim *volenti non fit injuria*. The risk may be assumed by express agreement, for example by giving consent to an operation, or may be implied from the circumstances, as by participating in a vigorous game.

In *Hall* v. *Brooklands Racing Club* (1933), a spectator who was injured while watching a motor race was held to have agreed to take the risk of such injury.

In *Arthur* v. *Anker* (1996), a motorist who parked his car on private land after having been given notice that the landowner objected and might clamp the wheels, was deemed to have consented when this occurred.

However in *Vine* v. *Waltham B.C.* (2000), a car driver felt sick, turned hurriedly into a private car park, got out and was sick a short distance away. She returned to find the car wheels clamped. There was a warning notice, but it was partly obscured by another vehicle. She recovered damages because she had not consented to the risk of clamping.

1. It is not sufficient to prove merely that the claimant knew of the risk; there must be evidence of a willing consent to undergo it. For this reason the defence has normally failed when pleaded by employers in actions brought by employees for injuries suffered at work. The courts have demanded evidence of positive consent as opposed to mere acquiescence, and the nature of the employer–worker relationship has made this difficult.

In *Bowater* v. *Rowley Regis Corporation* (1944), a carter was injured by a dangerous horse which he took out under orders after protesting. It was held that he had not genuinely consented to run the risk.

In *Smith* v. *Charles Baker & Sons* (1891), a workman was injured by a falling stone when he worked under an overhead crane. He had not objected, even though he must have known that it was dangerous. He recovered damages nevertheless. His silence was evidence of acquiescence, not necessarily of consent.

2. This defence will also fail in 'rescue' cases where the claimant acted under a strong moral compulsion, if not a legal one.

> In *Haynes* v. *Harwood* (1935), a policeman succeeded in his claim for damages when he was injured while stopping a runaway horse and cart which was endangering the safety of people, including children, in a crowded street. He would not have been injured if he had stayed out of the way, but he could hardly be said to have freely consented. The legal position would have been different if he had acted in a similar voluntary manner in a country lane with no people about.

3. *Volenti* will not be a defence to an action for breach of a strict statutory duty. Therefore, even if an employee seems genuinely to consent to work an unguarded machine, he may still recover damages for any injury, if his employer is in breach of the occupational safety legislation. The employer cannot, in other words, persuade his workmen to consent to abandon their statutory protection.
4. Finally, the defence of consent may be excluded by statute on grounds of public policy. The Road Traffic Act 1988 prevents a car driver from relying upon this defence against a passenger who has suffered injury by reason of his negligent driving.

Contributory negligence

Although this defence is normally raised to actions for negligence, it is also applicable to most other torts, including breach of statutory duty, but not conversion. It arises when damage is suffered partly by the fault of the defendant and partly by the fault of the claimant. The defendant, therefore, attempts to reduce the damages by proving that the claimant was himself partly responsible. The Law Reform (Contributory Negligence) Act 1945 provides that in such cases the court shall reduce the damages by an amount proportionate to the claimant's share of responsibility. Thus if damages are assessed at £100 and the claimant is 30 per cent to blame, he will receive only £70.

> In *Sayers* v. *Harlow UDC* (1958), Mrs Sayers found herself locked in a public lavatory. Unable to summon help, she tried to climb out over the top of the door. She found this impossible and, when climbing back down, allowed her weight to rest on the toilet roll which 'true to its mechanical requirement, rotated'. Mrs Sayers fell and was injured. It was held that 75 per cent of her injury was the fault of the Council for providing a defective lock which jammed, and 25 per cent was her own fault.

> In *Stapley* v. *Gypsum Mines Ltd* (1953), two miners who worked, in breach of instructions, under a dangerous roof were held 80 per cent contributorily negligent.

> In *Froom* v. *Butcher* (1976), a front seat passenger injured in a car accident had his damages reduced by 25 per cent because he had not worn a seat belt.

C. Causation and remoteness

Where liability in tort depends upon loss, the claimant must show that his loss was legally *caused* by the defendant's conduct. Various problems can arise.

101

No causal connection

The defendant cannot be held liable for something to which his conduct has not contributed. The claimant may be the sole author of his own misfortune.

In *McWilliams* v. *Sir William Arrol & Co. Ltd* (1962), a steel erector fell to his death. His employer had not provided a safety belt, but evidence was given that he would not have worn one even had it been provided. The employers were held not liable because, on this evidence, their failure was not the cause of death.

In some such situations, on the other hand, an employer may be held liable for breach of his duty to supervise and enforce the use of safety equipment.

Remoteness of damage

It is possible for a wrongful act to give rise to a succession of events ultimately terminating in injury to another. Although logically the damage would not have occurred but for the defendant's wrong, a break may have to be made somewhere in the long chain of consequences. Some damage is too remote, and the general rule is that only damage which was *reasonably foreseeable* at the time of the wrong is taken into account.

In the *Wagon Mound Case* (1961), a ship negligently discharged oil while bunkering and the oil was carried under a wharf. A piece of cotton waste floating on the oil was set alight by sparks from welding operations. The oil caught fire and the wharf was severely damaged. The action failed because the fire was not reasonably foreseeable, particularly since there was expert evidence that oil would not normally ignite under these conditions.

If, however, the type of damage is foreseeable, there will be a liability for its full extent, even though the consequences are much more serious than could have been anticipated.

In *Smith* v. *Leech Brain & Co. Ltd* (1962), a labourer was splashed and burned by a piece of molten metal and, because of an existing pre-malignant condition, died later of cancer. It was held that the damage was not too remote since the burn was foreseeable, even though the ultimate consequences were not.

It is sometimes said that the defendant must take his victims as he finds them, in the sense that if a (slight) injury was foreseeable and the victim has, for example, a thin skull, there will be liability for all the (serious) consequences.

The damage will be too remote if the chain of events is broken by some unforeseeable independent or new act intervening between the wrongful act and the resulting injury (*novus actus interveniens*) over which the defendant has no control. A defendant whose negligence caused a road accident will not normally be liable for further injury suffered by the victim which is caused by negligent hospital treatment. The intervening act must be a conscious and independent act. It must not be an instinctive, or even a reasoned, attempt to deal with the danger which the defendant has created.

In *Sayers* v. *Harlow UDC*, mentioned earlier, the defendants pleaded that Mrs Sayers' attempt to climb over the door was a *novus actus interveniens*, so that it was this, and not the defective lock, which caused her injury. This defence failed.

D. Remedies

Damages

The principal remedy in tort is an award of *damages* to compensate the injured party for the loss he has suffered. The aim is to put the claimant back in his original position so far as money is able to do this. This can frequently be done satisfactorily where property has been damaged by assessing the value of the things destroyed or the cost of repairs.

Injuries to the person present more difficulties for much depends upon the individual in question. Fixed tariffs for compensation cannot be laid down and many things must be considered in attempting to arrive at an assessment of loss. These include pain and suffering, loss of ability to pursue previous activities or interests, loss of actual and prospective earnings, and medical expenses. By the Administration of Justice Act 1982, damages are no longer awarded for loss of expectation of life, although a claimant's knowledge that his life has been shortened may be relevant in assessing his pain and suffering. Payments received from other sources, such as social security benefits, may be set off against damages, and compensation for loss of earnings can take account of tax which would otherwise have been payable. The court can award interest on damages from the date when the cause of action arose, partly to deter defendants from trying to delay matters.

Although damages can still be assessed by a jury, this is usually done today by a judge sitting alone. Appeals may be made against the amount of damages awarded but the Court of Appeal is reluctant to interfere unless there has been an obvious error in the assessment.

Other remedies

In some situations, as with threatened or repeated trespass or nuisance, damages will not provide an adequate remedy. The court may then, at its discretion, grant an *injunction* ordering the defendant to refrain from committing or repeating the wrongful act. If the length of time before the case can come to trial might lead to irreparable damage being caused, it is possible to apply for an interlocutory or temporary injunction which will either be confirmed or discharged at the later trial.

E. The effect of death

At one time death effectively put an end to actions in tort by reason of two common law rules. One provided that the causing of death should not give rise to an action on the grounds that no one should profit out of another's death, and the second provided that a personal action died with the person. The effect of the first rule was the

103

anomalous situation that a tort causing injury was actionable but not one causing death, so that it could be cheaper to kill than to maim. The resulting hardship to dependants and the increase in the number of deaths from railway accidents led to the Fatal Accidents Act 1846. This was amended several times, and replaced by a consolidating Act in 1976.

The Fatal Accidents Act 1976 now provides that, if the deceased could have sued had he lived, his dependants will have a right of action arising from his death. The right to sue is limited to certain classes of dependants, who can claim for monetary loss that they have suffered as a result of the death. Thus claims may be made for expected maintenance and support and for additional expenses incurred in looking after children. The surviving spouse, or parents of an unmarried child, can claim a small amount for 'bereavement'.

There still remained the second rule, which prevented a claim for things such as pain and suffering which could have been claimed by the deceased had he lived. Furthermore, the death of the tortfeasor put an end to a claimant's claim. The increase in the number of road deaths led to the Law Reform (Miscellaneous Provisions) Act 1934 which provides that, on the death of any person, any causes of action existing in favour of or against him shall survive and exist in favour of or against his estate. Thus if *A* injures *B* and *B* dies, the estate of *B* may, in general, sue *A* for all that *B* could have claimed had he lived. On the other hand, if *A* were the one to die, his estate would be liable to *B* to the same extent as if he had lived. A few personal actions, in particular defamation, are excluded and are still brought to an end by the death of either party.

If the victim of a tort dies, there are, therefore, two possible claims, one by the dependants under the 1976 Act, as amended, and one by the estate under the 1934 Act. The two claims are quite distinct even though in practice they may be settled in the same action. If the same people are to benefit under both claims, an adjustment will be made to prevent duplication of damages. It can be to the advantage of the dependants to claim as much as possible under the Fatal Accidents Act, since these damages go directly to the dependants and not into the estate of the deceased, and are therefore not liable to inheritance tax payable on death.

Specimen questions

1. Explain, with reasons, what torts (if any) have been committed in each of the following circumstances:
   (a) Smoke from a factory chimney kills flowering plants in a nearby park.
   (b) An auctioneer sells *B*'s goods without *B*'s permission, believing that the goods belong to *A*.
   (c) An office manager dismisses a clerk saying, in the presence of others, that he is a thief.
   (d) An explosion in a nuclear power station releases radioactive material which kills animals on a neighbouring farm.
   (e) A worker is injured by an unguarded machine.

2. *X*, who has only one arm, is injured when unroping a load of timber that has been delivered to his employer's factory. When sued for damages by *X*, the employer pleads:
   (a) that *X* was negligent in not waiting for an inspection by a competent person to see that the load was safe;
   (b) that *X* willingly accepted what he knew to be a dangerous job; and
   (c) that, but for *X*'s disability, he could have prevented the timber from falling upon him.
   Discuss the validity of each of these defences.

3. Explain the considerations which a court will take into account in fixing the amount of damages to be awarded if the following claims have been successful:
   (a) by an employee who has suffered personal injuries in an accident at work;
   (b) by the widow of an employee who has been killed in an accident at work;
   (c) by another firm whose delivery van has been damaged by the careless driving of an employee.

4. Garish Garages Ltd overhauled a lorry belonging to Express Carriers Ltd. The work was carried out by Turner, an employee of Garish Garages Ltd. Shortly afterwards, while the lorry was being driven at an excessive speed by Driver, an employee of Express Carriers Ltd, the brakes failed because of Turner's negligent work. In the resulting accident injuries were suffered by Driver and by two pedestrians, Walker and Mort. Mort, before the accident, was in a very poor state of health and his injuries proved to be fatal. Nervy, an onlooker, fainted when he saw the accident and became seriously ill.
   Discuss the legal position.

5. (a) What defences may be put forward by a defendant who is being sued for negligence?
   (b) Driver parked his car on a slope and left it without securing the handbrake. Shortly afterwards, the car began to move down the slope. Walker, who was passing by, managed to stop the car but was injured in so doing. Advise Walker.

6. Clutch, who is employed as a lorry driver by Speedy Transport Ltd complains to his employer about the poor condition of the brakes on his lorry. He is told that the brakes will be repaired the following day, and is persuaded to make an urgent delivery. He is told to drive slowly and carefully and is also forbidden to give anyone a lift in the lorry. During the course of his journey Clutch gives a lift to Hiker. While driving far too fast, having regard to the state of the brakes, Clutch is involved in an accident in which Walker, a pedestrian, is seriously injured. Clutch and Hiker also receive injuries. Advise Speedy Transport Ltd as to their possible liability towards Walker, Clutch and Hiker.

Unit 11. The Nature of a Contract in English Law

A. Essential requirements

There are still misconceptions about this branch of law. For many people the word 'contract' suggests a visit to a solicitor's office and the signing of a formal document containing incomprehensible language. This is far from the truth. Most people make contracts every day of their lives, usually without realizing it. Every time they buy an article or pay for a service such as a haircut they are entering into a contract, while matters concerned with their work, such as holidays, wages and hours, are governed in part by the contract which they have made with their employer.

Another popular belief is that a contract must be in writing. Apart from a few exceptional instances (see page 113), this is not so. Most contracts are made by word of mouth. It may be desirable to have a written agreement where a lot is at stake, or where the contract has to last for a long time, but this is only for practical purposes of proof, and is usually not legally necessary.

A contract is simply *an agreement which the law will recognize*. It is of vital importance in business life, and forms the basis of most commercial transactions, such as the sale of goods and land, the giving of credit, insurance, carriage of goods, formation and sale of business organizations, and, to some extent, employment.

What agreements will the law recognize?

The law will not recognize all agreements. The law of contract is concerned mainly with providing a framework within which business can operate; if agreements could be broken with impunity, the unscrupulous could create havoc. English law will intervene, therefore, and make the person who breaks an agreement pay compensation (damages) to the other party, but only if the agreement has the following essential features:

1. *Intention to create legal relations.* Unless the courts are satisfied that the parties intended the agreement to be legally binding, the courts will take no notice of it (see page 108).
2. *Agreement.* The courts must be satisfied that the parties had reached a firm agreement, and that they were not still negotiating. Agreement will usually be shown by the unconditional acceptance of an offer (Unit 12).
3. *Consideration.* English law will only recognize a *bargain*, not a mere promise. A contract, therefore, must be a two-sided affair, each side providing or promising to provide some consideration in exchange for what the other is to provide (see page 109). Consideration is a special feature of the common law and is not required by most European legal systems, including Scotland.
4. *Form.* Certain *exceptional* types of agreement are only valid if made in a particular form, for example in writing (see page 113).
5. *Definite terms.* It must be possible for the courts to ascertain what the parties have agreed upon. If the terms are so vague as to be meaningless, the law will not recognize the agreement (Unit 12).
6. *Legality.* Certain types of agreements are so plainly 'contrary to public policy' that the law will have nothing to do with them. For example, the courts would not allow a hired murderer to recover damages if his principal refused to pay the agreed price (Unit 17).

Defective contracts

Discussion of these essential requirements must also include situations where, although English law will recognize the agreement, the contract will only be given limited effect or no effect at all.

Some defects will render a contract *unenforceable*, so that although the contract does exist, neither party can *sue* the other successfully. Examples include unregulated consumer credit agreements and guarantees which do not comply with certain formalities (see page 113). Goods or money which pass under an unenforceable contract are validly transferred and cannot be reclaimed, but the contract cannot be sued upon if one of the parties refuses to abide by its terms.

Other defects can render a contract *voidable*, where although English law will recognize the agreement, it will allow one of the parties to withdraw from it if he so wishes. Voidable contracts include most agreements made by minors or by persons incapacitated by drunkenness or insanity, and contracts induced by misrepresentation, duress or undue influence.

Finally, there are defects which can render a contract *void*, that is, destitute of all legal effect. The expression 'void contract' is really a contradiction in terms; if the contract is void it cannot be a contract. The expression is useful, however, to describe a situation where the parties have attempted to contract but the law will give no effect to their agreement at all. Thus a contract may be void if there is a common mistake on some fundamental issue, as where the parties agree to sell a cargo which, unknown to both, has already been completely destroyed. Agreements to sell land will not be recognized at all until the relevant documents have been signed (page 113).

The distinction between void and voidable contracts is important where the rights of third parties are concerned. If a contract of sale is void, ownership of the property sold will not pass to the buyer, and he cannot normally sell it to anyone else. The original seller will be able to recover the property from whoever has it. If the contract is merely voidable, it remains valid unless and until the innocent party chooses to terminate it; therefore, if the buyer re-sells *before* the contract is avoided, the sub-buyer becomes the owner, and can retain the property provided that he took it in good faith.

B. Intention to create legal relations

Many agreements are plainly never intended by the parties to be *legally* binding; there is no intention to take any dispute to a court of law.

In the case of agreements of a friendly, social or domestic nature there is a strong presumption that the parties did not intend to create a legal relationship. If friends agree to come to tea and they fail to turn up, or if a husband agrees to meet his wife and forgets, there can be no action for breach of contract, even though the complaining party may have incurred certain expenses.

> In *Balfour* v. *Balfour* (1919), a husband promised his wife an allowance before he left to take up a post abroad. When he stopped the payments, an action by the wife failed on the ground that this was not a binding contract but merely a domestic agreement with no legal obligations attached to it.

> Conversely, in *Simpkins* v. *Pays* (1955), three people sharing a house, the owner, her grand-daughter and paying lodger, regularly entered a competition in a Sunday newspaper. The entries were sent in the name of the grandmother, but all three contributed. When an entry won, the grandmother refused to share the prize of £750. It was held that the others *were* entitled to share, because their agreement to this effect was, in the view of the court, intended to be legally binding.

On the other hand, there is a strong presumption that business agreements are intended to create legal relations. This presumption can be rebutted, but only by very strong evidence such as a clear statement in a written contract.

> In *Rose and Frank* v. *Crompton Bros Ltd* (1925), an English company agreed to sell carbon paper in America through a New York firm. This marketing arrangement was for a renewable period of three years and provided that 'This arrangement is not entered into ... as a formal or legal agreement, and shall not be subject to legal jurisdiction in the Law Courts ...'. Therefore, when the English company withdrew, it was not liable for breach of contract, although it was held liable to honour orders placed before withdrawal.

> Similarly, in *Appleson* v. *Littlewood Ltd* (1939), the claimant sued to recover money which he claimed to have won on a football pool. His action failed, because the printed entry form contained a statement that the transaction was 'binding in honour only'.

Most collective agreements between employers and trade unions as to wages and other terms of employment will not be legally binding. The parties are assumed to have intended the agreement to be no more than a broad working arrangement, unless they expressly provide in writing that it is to be legally enforceable.

C. Consideration

As stated above, the English law of contract is concerned with *bargains*, not mere promises. Thus if *A* promises to *give* something to *B*, the law will not allow any remedy if *A* breaks his promise. On the other hand, if *B* promises to do (or does) something in return, so that *A*'s promise is dependent upon *B*'s, this reciprocal element, the *exchange* of promises, turns the arrangement into a contract. To use legal terminology, *A*'s promise (or action) is the 'consideration' for *B*'s, and vice versa. Thus, the promise of the seller to deliver the car is consideration for the buyer's promise to pay the agreed price.

Consideration may, therefore, be described broadly as something given, promised or done in exchange. The act, forbearance or promise of each party is the price for which the promise of the other is bought.

Consideration can be *executory* or *executed*. Executory consideration is a promise yet to be fulfilled, and most contracts start in this way, with the consideration executory on both sides. Executed consideration is the completed performance of one side of the bargain.

The existence of consideration

Consideration must exist and have some value; otherwise there is no contract. The following may have no value and may not, therefore, constitute consideration so as to render a promise actionable:

1. *Past consideration.* Something already done and completed by *B* at the time when *A* makes a promise to him cannot operate as consideration. *A* already has the benefit of what *B* has done, and *B* therefore receives nothing in exchange. Thus if, unasked, I paint my neighbour's house while he is away and, upon his return, he promises me £100 for doing so, I have no remedy if he later refuses to pay.

    In *Eastwood* v. *Kenyon* (1840), the claimant had been the guardian of a Miss Sutcliffe, and had spent money on her upkeep and education. When she came of age, the girl promised to repay her guardian, and her husband, Kenyon, repeated this promise when she married. It was held, however, that the guardian could not recover damages when these promises were broken, because the consideration for them was past. Any moral obligation to repay was irrelevant.

    Similarly, in *Roscorla* v. *Thomas* (1842), *after* Roscorla had bought a horse, the seller promised that it was sound and free from vice. It was held that Roscorla could not sue for breach of this undertaking, for which no new consideration had been given. (This would apply equally to promises made by a car salesman *after* the sale.)

A contrast must be drawn with those situations where, although the actual promise to pay a specific sum is made after the work has been carried out, there was an implied promise to pay (a reasonable sum) before the work was begun. If my

109

neighbour *asks* me to paint his house, he may be impliedly promising to pay me for my work.

> In *Stewart* v. *Casey* (1892), Stewart, who was joint owner of some patents, asked Casey to promote them. *After* Casey had done so successfully, Stewart promised him a share in them. It was held that this promise was binding, and that the consideration was not past. The original request carried with it an implied promise to pay a reasonable amount for Casey's services; the contract was made *then*. The subsequent promise to share in the profits merely put a figure to the original promise, which was given before Casey carried out his side of the bargain.

2. *A promise to perform an existing obligation*. This may not be consideration, because the promisor is only giving what he was already bound to give.

(a) This applies particularly if the promisor merely promises afresh to perform an existing contract *with the promisee*. Therefore, if a debtor promises to pay part of his debt in consideration of the creditor releasing him from the rest, the release is not binding. If *A* is owed £10 by *B* and agrees to take £9 in full satisfaction, *A* can still go back and demand the remaining £1. *B* gave no consideration for the promise to release him from the £1.

> In *D & C Builders Ltd* v. *Rees* (1966), the defendant owed £482 to the builders for work carried out, and refused to pay. Eventually the builders agreed to take a cheque for £300 in full satisfaction of the debt. It was held that they were still entitled to the remaining £182, because there was no consideration for the earlier promise to settle for less.

Similarly, if a debt is due *now*, an agreement to allow payment *later* (for example by instalments) is not binding; see *Foakes* v. *Beer* (1884).

> In *Re Selectmove Ltd* (1995), The Inland Revenue gave a debtor leave to pay arrears of taxes by instalments. This was not binding. The whole arrears were due now, and the debtor gave no consideration for the Revenue's promise of extra time.

The promise to forgo part of the debt will be binding, however, if the debtor gives some *new* consideration, by doing or promising something which he was not previously bound to do; for example paying the debt earlier than he was bound to do, or at a place other than where he was bound to do. These rules apply equally to obligations other than debts. Where new promises are made in return for *work* due, there may also be new consideration if: (i) circumstances have changed since the original contract, so as to make it especially difficult for one party to carry out his side of the bargain; (ii) the other party particularly needs to have the contract performed, and therefore promises extra money for this benefit; and (iii) there is no suggestion of fraud or duress.

> In *Williams* v. *Roffey Bros* (1989), builders had a contract to refurbish a block of flats. They subcontracted the carpentry work to the claimants for a fixed sum of £20 000. Before the carpentry work was done, the carpenters were in financial difficulties, and would be unable to complete their subcontract. The builders feared that they themselves would therefore be unable to complete the refurbish-

ment on time, and would therefore incur a large time penalty to the owners. To escape this, *on their own initiative*, they promised the carpenters extra money *to help them complete the carpentry* promptly. This promise was held binding even though the carpenters were only carrying out their original obligations. The promise had been given *for the builders' own benefit* and *on their own initiative*, and this was the consideration for the extra sum.

This case does not apply if the promisee's only obligation is to pay a debt (as in *D&C Builders* v. *Rees*, see page 110). Nor would it apply if a workman *demanded* extra payment from a builder who was desperate for prompt performance.

(b) The position is more simple as regards a promise to perform a contract which the promisor already has *with a third party*. This *can* be binding. The promisor is undertaking a new duty to the promisee in addition to the one which he already has to the third party. He now has two obligations, not just one, and this is the consideration.

> In *Pao On* v. *Lau Yiu Long* (1979), for example, the defendants gave Pao On a guarantee in consideration of Pao On promising to carry out a contract which Pao On had with *Fu Chip Ltd*. Pao On's promise was good consideration for the guarantee.

(c) A promise to perform *an existing public duty* will not usually be consideration. For example, it would be contrary to public policy to allow a public official to take (and, therefore, possibly demand) private payment for carrying out his public duty. However, a promise to do *more* than his duty *can* be enough.

> In *Glasbrook Bros. Ltd* v. *Glamorgan County Council* (1925), the police were offered £2000 to provide a special guard for a coal mine during a strike. It was held that they could recover this amount when the owners later refused to pay, because the special guard went beyond the ordinary police duty to protect property.

> In *Harris* v. *Sheffield United F.C. Ltd* (1987), the police authority was held entitled to payment for providing officers *inside* the football ground during matches.

If it can be shown that a promise to carry out a public or general duty is not contrary to public policy (e.g. a promise by a man or woman to maintain his or her family), then it might be consideration.

3. *A promise made to a third party.* Normally, only a person who has given consideration may sue on a contract. For example, *A* may promise to pay £1 to *B*, if *B* will give a book to *C*. If *B* refuses to deliver the book, *A* may sue, but not *C*, who has given no consideration and is not a party to the contract. However, by the Contracts (Rights of Third Parties) Act 1999, a third party ('*C*' in the above example) *can* enforce a term of the contract if (a) the contract expressly provides that he may; or (b) (normally) if the term purports to confer a benefit on him. Therefore, in the above example, *C might* have a right of action against *B*. This is discussed more fully in Unit 16.

4. *Vague promises*, which are incapable of monetary value, will not be consideration. A promise to show natural love and affection or to behave as a good son should behave will be of no effect in the law of contract.

111

The adequacy of consideration

Provided that the consideration has some value in the monetary sense, the court will not concern itself with whether or not the value is adequate, for the value of a particular article or service is largely a matter of opinion and for the parties to decide. The court will not make a man's bargain for him. The price paid may be relevant in determining whether goods are of a satisfactory quality at that price (Unit 18), but this does not directly affect the existence of the contract. The fact that goods are sold for a very high or low price may also be evidence, but no more than evidence, of fraud.

Promises made by deed

There is one major exception to the rules relating to consideration. Where a person embodies his promise in a formal document called a *deed*, it can be enforced against him whether or not the promisee has given any consideration. A deed is a document signed by the person making the promise; the signature must be 'attested' by a witness who also signs; and the document must be 'delivered' by the promisor. Delivery in this sense does not necessarily require the deed to be handed over but is merely conduct showing an intention to be bound by it. The Law of Property (Miscellaneous Provisions) Act 1989 removed the need for a deed to be 'sealed', provided that there is a clear intention to execute a deed and that the signature is witnessed; there is also, in the case of transfer of land, a conclusive presumption that a solicitor or licensed conveyancer has authority to 'deliver' the deed on behalf of the signatory. Promises made by deed are sometimes called *specialty* contracts, as opposed to *simple* contracts when a deed is not used.

Equitable estoppel

Although a promise made without consideration cannot be sued upon, and will not amount to a contract, it may have limited effect as a *defence*. If *A* promises not to enforce his rights against *B*, and the promise is intended to be binding, intended to be acted upon, and is in fact acted upon by *B*, then *A* may be estopped from later bringing any action inconsistent with his promise. This defence has been called promissory estoppel.

> In *Central London Property Trust* v. *High Trees House* (1947), the lease of a block of flats proved unprofitable to the tenant because of the war, and the landlord made a written promise to reduce the rent while the war lasted. After the war, the landlord withdrew this promise and started to charge the full rent again. It was held that he was free to do this for the future, because no consideration had been given for the wartime promise. On the other hand, the court said, *obiter*, that the landlord could not have recovered the full rent for the period between making his promise and the end of the war since the tenant had relied on the landlord's promise.

This defence is limited, and only applies where it would be unfair and inequitable to allow the claimant to succeed in spite of his promise.

In *D & C Builders Ltd* v. *Rees* (see page 110), it was also suggested that the builders should be estopped from going back on their promise to take £300 in full satisfaction. This defence failed because it was not grossly unfair to demand the balance. If anyone it was Rees who was unfair, in failing to pay the full amount and putting pressure on the builders, who had financial difficulties, to settle for less. Certainly Rees had not been made to act to *his* detriment as a result of the promise.

Moreover, in the light of *Williams* v. *Roffey Bros* (see page 110), there may now be fewer situations in which a party has to rely on promissory estoppel. In the *High Trees* case itself, for example, it might now be held that the tenant *had* given consideration for the landlord's promise to reduce the rent during the war. Circumstances had changed since the original lease; the landlord did, for his own benefit, still need to have a tenant to look after the property during the war; and there was no suggestion of fraud or duress by the tenant. Therefore, although the decision would probably be the same today, the *ratio decidendi* and *obiter dicta* might be different.

D. Form

In general, the form in which a contract is made does not matter and will have no effect upon the validity of the contract. However, there are certain exceptions.

Some contracts must be by deed. Promises for no consideration, and some bills of sale (mortgages of goods), are void unless in this form. Most conveyances of land must be completed by deed (see below).

Certain other contracts which must be in writing include bills of exchange, cheques and promissory notes, contracts of marine insurance, the transfer of shares in a company, and legal assignment of debts. Absence of duly signed writing renders such contracts *void*. Hire-purchase and other regulated agreements which come within the Consumer Credit Act 1974 may be unenforceable against the borrower unless they are made in writing and include the information required under the Act.

Contracts of guarantee, although not required to be in writing, are unenforceable in the courts unless there is written evidence of the essential terms, signed by the guarantor or his agent. This is a historical survival from the Statute of Frauds 1677.

Special rules apply to land. A conveyance, such as a sale or lease, is normally in two stages. First the parties *contract* to sell (or lease) the land. Under the Law of Property (Miscellaneous Provisions) Act 1989, this contract must be made in writing in a signed document which 'incorporates' all terms which the parties have expressly agreed; the terms can either be set out in the document itself or included by reference to some other document. Usually in practice two identical documents are prepared, one signed by the vendor (seller) and handed to the purchasers, the other signed by the purchasers and handed (with a deposit) to the vendor. The Act allows this, even though neither document is signed by both parties, so long as each copy incorporates all the express terms. None of these formalities applies to sales by public auction.

After the contract, the purchasers (through their solicitors) usually check the vendor's title to ensure that he does have the right to sell. If all is well, the transaction will then be 'completed' by conveyance of the title to the purchasers and payment by them of the (rest of the) price. This *conveyance* must be made by deed if the transaction is a sale or a lease for over three years.

Specimen questions

1. Explain, with examples:
   (a) the distinction between void, voidable and unenforceable contracts; and
   (b) the effect of this distinction when goods are subsequently transferred to third parties.
2. Explain whether or not Henry has a remedy in respect of each of the following agreements:
   (a) His daughter has a knitting machine and makes jerseys in her spare time. Henry promises to sell these in his shop and advertises them accordingly. His daughter then gives up knitting and fails to deliver any.
   (b) He agrees to buy a consignment of socks from a wholesaler. The contract contains a clause excluding the jurisdiction of the courts. The wholesaler fails to deliver the goods.
   (c) He agrees with a trade union regarding a productivity bonus scheme for his shop assistants. The union fails to honour the agreement.
3. Explain whether Paul is required by the law of contract to fulfil his promises in the following situations:
   (a) He promises to sell an expensive car to Arthur for £10.
   (b) He returns home to find that his house windows have been cleaned by Bernard and he promises to pay Bernard £10 for his work.
   (c) He agrees to pay Charles £100 for painting his house within three weeks and he later promises a further £20 if Charles finishes the job on time.
   (d) He promises to release Frank from a debt of £500 if Frank pays him £400.
4. Worsted, a clothing manufacturer, is in financial difficulties and is looking for short-term remedies which might help him. He has an order from Bernard for delivery on a fixed future date and he writes to Bernard saying that he cannot guarantee that delivery unless Bernard promises to pay an additional sum to cover overtime working; Bernard makes that promise.

   Worsted next approaches David, a debtor, and says that if David immediately pays 50% of the outstanding debt he will forget the balance; David makes that payment. Worsted also agrees to sell some of his stock to Eric for a ridiculously low price.

   You are required to explain whether Worsted may:
   (a) recover the additional sum promised by Bernard;
   (b) recover the balance of the debt from David;
   (c) refuse to deliver the goods to Eric.

Unit 12. Agreement

Unit 11 is concerned with some of the essential features which must be present in an agreement before English law will recognize it as a contract. This unit is concerned with how and when agreement is reached.

There is a difference between the situation where negotiations are in progress and the situation where a binding agreement has been reached. During negotiations, each side is free to withdraw without any sanction; after agreement has been concluded, withdrawal can amount to breach of contract. Agreement is usually shown in English law by the unconditional acceptance of an offer, and these elements will be examined in turn.

A. Offer

This is a statement of the terms on which the offeror is willing to be bound. If the offer is accepted as it stands, agreement is made.

An offer may be made to a specific person and only open to him to accept, as where *A* offers to sell his car to *B* for a stated price. An offer may be made to a class of persons, any one of whom may accept, as when the offer is only open to employees of a company or members of a particular club. An offer may, sometimes, be made to the whole world, as where the owner offers a reward to anyone who returns his lost canary; see also *First Sport Ltd* v. *Barclay's Bank*, later.

The following are *not* offers in this legal sense:

1. *A mere invitation to treat.* This is an indication that a person is willing to enter into negotiations, but *not* that he is yet willing to be bound by the terms mentioned.

115

In *Gibson* v. *Manchester City Council* (1979), Mr Gibson, a council tenant, received a letter from the Council saying that the Council '*may* be prepared to sell the house to you at the purchase price of ... £2180'. Mr Gibson formally applied to buy at this price, but meanwhile Council policy was changed and it refused to sell. It was held that the Council's letter was only an invitation to treat, not an offer. Therefore, there was no contract.

Catalogues or circulars advertising goods for sale constitute mere invitations. The same applies when a large undertaking invites tenders for the supply of goods or services. A company prospectus which invites investors to buy its shares is also an invitation to treat and not an offer, because the company can still refuse to allot the shares to those who apply for them.

In many cases where a person indicates that he is willing to deal with anyone in the world, as in the examples just given, this will be treated as a mere invitation to treat; otherwise there would be an impossible situation if, for example, an advertisement to sell a car were held to be a firm offer, and 20 acceptances were received. Only in cases where the advertiser very clearly intended to be bound will an advertisement be treated as a firm offer.

Perhaps the best examples of invitation to treat are goods in a shop window, even with price tickets attached. The shopkeeper does not undertake to sell the goods. They are on display merely to invite customers to come in and offer to buy at the price shown. The shopkeeper can always refuse, although obviously he rarely does so. The same rule applies to the display of goods in a self-service store.

In *Pharmaceutical Society of Great Britain* v. *Boots Cash Chemists* (1953), a criminal case, customers selected pharmaceutical goods from self-service counters, and paid later at the cash desk, where a pharmacist was in attendance with the cashier. It was held that the display on the shelves was a mere invitation to treat. The customer made the offer when he took the goods to the cashier, who could always refuse to sell. Therefore, the pharmacist was present where the sale took place.

2. A '*mere puff*' *or boast*, which no one would take too seriously, such as a claim on the packet that 'Brand X washes whitest', will not be treated as a firm offer. There can, however, be a narrow borderline between mere boasts, and promises which a reasonable man would take seriously.

In *Carlill* v. *Carbolic Smoke Ball Co.* (1893), the defendants advertised that they would pay £100 to anyone who caught influenza after using their smoke balls, and that, as evidence of their sincerity, they had deposited £1000 with a named bank. Mrs Carlill followed their instructions, but still caught influenza, and consequently claimed £100. One of the many defences put forward was that the advertisement was not an offer. It was held that, in the circumstances, it was an offer. A reasonable person would take the promise seriously, and assume that the advertiser intended to be bound on the terms stated.

3. A *declaration of intention* is, similarly, not intended to form the basis of a contract, and is not an offer.

In *Harris* v. *Nickerson* (1873), an auction sale was advertised and later cancelled, and the claimant, who had travelled to the place of sale, claimed his travelling expenses as damages. His action failed, for the advertisement was not an offer which he could accept by making the journey.

4. *Merely giving information* is not an offer.

> In *Harvey* v. *Facey* (1893), the claimant telegraphed 'will you sell us Bumper Hall Pen? Telegraph lowest price', and the reply was 'lowest price for Bumper Hall Pen £900'. This was held to be merely an answer to a request for information, and not an offer which could be accepted.

An offer must be communicated to the other party

Unless the offeree is aware of the offer he is unable to accept it. If *X* finds a wallet and returns it to the owner, he cannot claim any reward that may have been offered if he had no previous knowledge of this.

> In *Taylor* v. *Laird* (1856), the captain of a ship resigned his command in a foreign port, but later helped to work the ship home. The owners were entitled to refuse payment for this. They had not known that the captain was still willing to work, and they had neither accepted nor rejected his services.

Duration of the offer

An offer does not continue indefinitely. While the offeror may be content *at the moment* to deal on terms of the offer, circumstances may change. Once an offer has come to an end, it can no longer be accepted. It can end in the following ways:

1. It is possible for the offeror to *revoke* or withdraw his offer at any time up to acceptance. He is entitled to do this even if he has promised to keep the offer open for a specified time, unless the offeree had paid a sum of money or given some other consideration in return for such a promise (sometimes known as 'buying an option'). Even then, the offer can be withdrawn before the agreed time, but withdrawal will be a breach of this subsidiary contract to keep open the negotiations.

> In *Routledge* v. *Grant* (1828), Grant offered to buy Routledge's house, and gave him six weeks to decide whether to accept his offer. Before six weeks had elapsed, Grant withdrew his offer. He was held entitled to do so at any time before acceptance.

Revocation is only effective if it is communicated to the offeree, either by express words or by conduct which shows a clear intention to revoke. Selling the goods elsewhere would be an example of such conduct, but this will only revoke the offer when the first prospective buyer learns of the sale. Communication can be by the seller himself, or by another reliable source.

> In *Dickinson* v. *Dodds* (1876), the defendant had offered to sell a house to the claimant. Before the claimant accepted, the defendant sold the house to someone else. The claimant learned of this from a friend, Berry. It was held that, since the claimant had heard of the revocation from a reliable source, the original offer to him was revoked, and he could not now accept it. (On the other hand, a mere rumour would be much less likely to amount to reliable communication of revocation.)

117

2. An offer will *lapse* if the offeror imposes a time limit for acceptance, and the other party does not accept within that time. If no express time limit is imposed, the offer will lapse after a *reasonable* time. What is reasonable will depend on all the circumstances.

> In *Ramsgate Victoria Hotel Co.* v. *Montefiore* (1866), an investor offered in June to buy shares in the claimant company. He heard nothing until November, by which time he no longer wanted the shares. It was held that it was now too late for the company to accept his offer.

3. The *death* of either party before acceptance will normally terminate the offer, certainly from the moment when the other party learns of the death and, when the identity of the other party is vital, from the time of death.

4. Once the offeree has *rejected* an offer he cannot later go back and purport to accept it. A counter-offer will operate as a rejection.

> In *Hyde* v. *Wrench* (1840), an offer was made to sell a farm for £1000. A counter-offer of £950 was made and refused, whereupon the buyer tried to accept the original offer of £1000. It was held that the seller could refuse this, because the original offer had been rejected.

Acceptance subject to conditions will also be a rejection, because the offeree is trying to introduce new terms into the bargain.

> In *Neale* v. *Merrett* (1930), the defendant offered to sell land to the claimant for £280. The claimant 'accepted' this offer, sent a cheque for £80, and promised to pay the rest by instalments of £50. It was held that there was no contract; the purported acceptance introduced credit terms which the seller did not want.

However, a mere request for further information is not a rejection.

> In *Stevenson* v. *McLean* (1880), a prospective buyer *asked whether* the seller would be prepared to give more time for performance. This was an enquiry, not a rejection.

Rejection, like offer and revocation, must be communicated, and is only effective from the moment when the offeree learns of it. If, therefore, the offeree sends a letter of rejection, but then changes his mind and telephones acceptance before the rejection arrives, there will be a valid contract.

5. An offer may be *conditional* upon other circumstances. If the conditions are not fulfilled, the offer will lapse. The conditions may be express or implied.

> In *Financings Ltd* v. *Stimson* (1962), a customer offered to take a car on hire-purchase from Financings Ltd. Before the offer was accepted, the car was stolen from the dealer's garage where it was being kept, and badly damaged. Unaware of this, Financings Ltd purported to accept the offer. It was held that the company could no longer do so. The customer's offer was subject to the implied condition that the car remain in substantially the same state between offer and acceptance.

6. *Acceptance*, by completing the contract, will bring the offer to an end. If an offer, capable of acceptance by only one person, is made to a group of people and one accepts, the offer ceases to exist so far as the rest of the group is concerned.

B. Acceptance

This must take place while the offer is still open. It must be an absolute and unqualified acceptance of the offer, as it stands, with any terms that may be attached. As we have seen, anything else will amount to rejection.

On occasions, an acceptance may be made subject to a written or formal agreement. It is then a question of construction whether the parties intend to be bound by the initial agreement, and the writing is only for the purpose of recording this, or whether there is no intention to be bound until the more formal agreement is made. In contracts for land, correspondence expressed as being 'subject to contract' is not binding even if it incorporates all of the terms and is signed by or on behalf of the parties.

Acceptance completes the contract, and the place where acceptance is made is, therefore, the place of the contract. If negotiations take place between parties in different countries, the rule may help to determine which system of law applies.

The manner of acceptance

Acceptance may take the form of words, spoken or written, or it may be implied by conduct, as where the offeree performs some specific act required by the offeror. Mere mental assent is insufficient, nor is it possible in English law to dispense with acceptance altogether. There must be some positive act of acceptance, and mere silence will never be enough.

> In *Felthouse* v. *Bindley* (1863), negotiations were taking place regarding the price of a horse. The claimant eventually wrote, 'If I hear no more about him, I consider the horse mine at £30 15s.' The defendant did not reply. It was held that, although he had intended to accept and sell at this price, his silence could not constitute acceptance, and there was therefore no sale.

Thus where unsolicited goods arrive through the post with a note saying that unless they are returned within a specified time the recipient will be bound to pay the price, this note can be safely ignored. So long as the recipient does not treat the goods as his, by using or deliberately destroying them, his silence will not amount to acceptance. Indeed, under the Unsolicited Goods and Services Act 1971 as amended, the recipient will automatically become owner of the goods as against the sender, unless the sender collects them within 30 days. (Where the seller is a dealer, it can also be a criminal offence for him to demand payment.)

Where two businesses contract, an interesting 'battle of forms' can sometimes arise.

> In *Butler Machine Tool Co. Ltd* v. *Ex-Cell-O Corporation (England) Ltd* (1979), the claimant offered to sell tools to the defendant and sent a printed copy of the claimant's standard terms. The defendant 'accepted' this offer, enclosing a copy of the *defendant's* standard terms, which differed slightly from the claimant's. The claimant acknowledged this acceptance by sending back a tear-off slip from the defendant's copy probably without reading it. It was held that the defendant's 'acceptance' was really a counter-offer. The

119

claimant had accepted this counter-offer by sending back the tear-off slip and going on to perform the contract. When a dispute later arose, the defendant's terms were, therefore, applied.

Communication of acceptance

As a general rule, acceptance must be communicated to the offeror. There is no contract until the offeror knows that his offer has been accepted. The acceptance must, moreover, be communicated by the offeree himself or his authorized agent. Unlike revocation, acceptance cannot be communicated by an unauthorized third party, however reliable.

In *Powell* v. *Lee* (1908), the claimant had applied for a post as headmaster. The school managers decided to appoint him, and one of the managers, without authority, told him this unofficially. Later, the managers changed their minds. It was held that they were free to do so; there was no contract with Powell, because acceptance had not been communicated by the managers.

There are two main exceptions to the rule that acceptance is only effective on communication:

1. *The offeror may dispense with communication*, and indicate that the offeree should, if he wishes to accept, simply carry out his side of the bargain without bothering to inform the offeror. Thus if a customer wrote ordering fuel and, without further communication, the fuel was delivered in accordance with the order, the delivery would be acceptance of the offer to buy.

   In *Carlill* v. *Carbolic Smoke Ball Co.* (1893), another defence raised was that Mrs Carlill had not communicated to the company that she intended to use the smoke ball and catch influenza. This defence also failed; the nature of the offer made communication of acceptance inappropriate.

   In *First Sport Ltd* v. *Barclay's Bank plc* (1993), it was held that a 'cheque guarantee card', by which the bank promised that its client's cheque up to £50 would be paid, was an offer to the whole world. The retailer who allowed a customer to pay by cheque in reliance on the card had accepted the bank's offer, and did not need to tell the bank when doing so.

2. *Where the posting rule applies*, a letter of acceptance, properly addressed and stamped, is effective from the moment of posting, even if it never arrives. Three points must be emphasized about the posting rule. In the first place, the rule applies only where it must have been in the contemplation of the parties that the post would be used as a means of communicating the acceptance. This will not always be the case; if all the negotiations have taken place by telephone, and the offeror clearly expects a reply by telephone or fax, a letter of acceptance would not be effective until it arrived. Similarly, the posting rule would not apply if the offeror made it plain at the outset that he was only prepared to be bound when he *knew* of the acceptance.

   In *Holwell Securities Ltd* v. *Hughes* (1974), an offer to sell required that acceptance be made 'by notice in writing to the intending vendor' within six months. Notice was posted but never arrived. It was held that there was no contract. The words of the offer showed that the offeror was not prepared to be bound until he *received* the written notice.

Secondly, there must obviously be some evidence of posting. It is not enough to give the letter to some other person to post, or even to hand it to a postman; it must be put into the hands of the postal authorities in the normal way. Finally, the posting rule applies only to acceptance; an offer, or a letter of revocation or rejection, will be effective only on arrival.

In *Byrne* v. *Van Tienhoven* (1880), a firm in Cardiff offered by letter to sell tin plate to a firm in New York. Later, the firm sent another letter revoking this offer, but while this was in transit and before its delivery, the New York firm posted a letter of acceptance. It was held that the parties clearly intended the use of the post to communicate acceptance, and posting the letter of acceptance, therefore, brought the contract into existence, since this was done before the revocation arrived.

The posting rule applies to other non-instantaneous means of communication, but not to the use of the phone, fax, or telex. In these latter cases, the communication is virtually instantaneous and is inoperative unless and until it reaches the other party.

In *Entores* v. *Miles Far East Corporation* (1955), an acceptance sent by telex from Amsterdam to London was held to be effective only when it arrived in London, so that the contract, being made in England, could be brought before the English courts.

C. Certainty of terms

Even where offer and acceptance are apparently complete, there may still be no agreement. There can be no contract at all if it is not possible to say *what* the parties have agreed upon because the terms are too uncertain. In particular, this will be the case where the parties have still left essential terms to be settled between them. They are still at the stage of negotiation, and an agreement to agree in future is not a contract.

In *Scammell* v. *Ouston* (1941), Ouston agreed to take a van 'on the understanding that the balance of the purchase price can be had on hire-purchase terms over a period of two years'. It was held that this contract was void for uncertainty, because no one could say *what* hire-purchase terms were envisaged.

In *King's Motors (Oxford) Ltd* v. *Lax* (1969), an option to renew a lease 'at such rental as may be agreed upon between the parties' was similarly held void.

On the other hand, this rule is subject to some qualifications. Indeed the courts have often made every effort to resolve the uncertainty.

1. The parties may be bound if the unsettled terms are only part of a larger agreement, the rest of which is already being or has been performed, and which is agreed to be binding. This is particularly so if there has been some provision for arbitration to settle potential disputes.

In *Foley* v. *Classique Coaches Ltd* (1934), a garage sold land to the bus company on condition (*inter alia*) that the company buy all of its petrol from the garage 'at a price to be agreed between the parties ... from time to time'. A later clause provided that any dispute as to the subject-matter or content of the agreement should be referred to arbitration. The land was conveyed, and the bus company duly bought its petrol for three years, but then claimed that it need no longer do so. It was held bound. A reasonable price could be settled under the arbitration clause.

In *Sudbrook Trading Estate Ltd* v. *Eggleton* (1982), the claimant was tenant of some land, but had the right to buy it before his lease expired. The price was to be fixed by two arbitrators, one appointed by the landlord, the other by the tenant. The landlord refused to appoint an arbitrator. The House of Lords held that since the parties had clearly intended to be bound at the outset, and were already performing the lease, the *court* would make alternative arrangements to settle the sale price, and would order the transfer.

2. If the parties have agreed criteria according to which the price can be calculated, or have had previous dealings similar to the present transaction, the courts can use these matters to ascertain the terms of the contract.

In *Hillas & Co. Ltd* v. *Arcos Ltd* (1932), an option to buy 100 000 standards of softwood goods in 1931, without mention of detailed terms, was held binding because it was assumed to be on terms similar to those agreed in previous dealings between the parties.

In *Brown* v. *Gould* (1972), an option was given to renew a lease 'at a rent to be fixed having regard to the market value of the premises at the time of exercising this option taking into account ... structural improvement made by the Tenant ...'. This was held binding, because the court could, if necessary, discover the market price and the value of the improvements from independent valuers.

3. If only a fairly minor term is meaningless, it may simply be ignored, and the rest of the contract treated as binding.

In *Nicolene Ltd* v. *Simmonds* (1953), the defendant agreed to sell 3000 tons of steel bars at £45 per ton, and added that he assumed that 'the usual conditions of acceptance apply'. There were no usual conditions. The court held that he was bound; the rest of the agreement made good sense, and the meaningless phrase could, therefore, be ignored.

Note that in most of the above cases a *well drafted* arbitration and/or valuation clause could have prevented the expensive court proceedings.

If there is doubt about the meaning of any written term in a *consumer* contract (see page 147), the Unfair Terms in Consumer Contracts Regulations 1999 simply provide that the interpretation most favourable to the consumer shall apply.

Specimen questions

1. (a) Explain and illustrate the distinction between an offer and an invitation to make an offer in the formation of a contract.

(b) Brenda visits a self-service store and selects several articles which she places in the wire basket provided. She then changes her mind about some of these articles and replaces them on the shelves. The manager of the store claims that she has purchased the goods by placing them in the basket and that she must pay for them. Advise Brenda.

2. Outline the legal position of the parties and the principles of law involved in the following circumstances:

(a) *A* offers to sell a lorry to *B* who states that he will accept the offer if *A* will undertake to pay for any repairs that may be necessary during the next three months. *A* refuses this condition. *B* then states that he will buy the lorry without insisting upon this requirement, but *A* replies to the effect that he no longer wishes to sell.

(b) *C* offers to sell a van to *D* and states that he will give *D* a week to decide whether or not he wishes to buy. After three days, *D* is informed by *X* that *C* has sold the van to *E*. *D* writes to *C* accepting his offer.

3. (a) When may a contract be formed without the acceptance of the offer being specifically communicated to the offeror?

(b) Williams, a wholesaler, offered to sell a consignment of cheap tinned fruit to Roger, a retailer. Roger intended to accept this offer, but forgot to inform Williams. Roger did, however, arrange for the printing of leaflets advertising the sale of this fruit in his shop. Williams saw one of the leaflets when he happened to visit the printer. Williams now believes that he can obtain a better price for the fruit and has written to Roger withdrawing his offer. Advise Roger.

4. (a) Outline the rules applicable to the formation of contracts made by letters through the post. Do these rules apply equally to contracts made by telephone and e-mail?

(b) Martin telephones Nigel and offers to sell him a lorry. Nigel accepts the offer but Martin does not hear because of a bad line. Nigel changes his mind and writes to Martin saying that he does not wish to buy the lorry. Advise Martin.

5. (a) While a contract will not normally be valid if the terms are uncertain, it may still be possible to leave some of the terms to be decided at a later date. When may this be done?

(b) A supermarket contracted to buy the meat it required during 2002 from Henry at the then prevailing price. A clause in the contract gave the supermarket the option to extend the contract to cover its requirements for meat in 2003 but no mention was made of the price or any other terms.

The supermarket now seeks to exercise this option but Henry wishes to sell his meat elsewhere.

Advise Henry as to whether or not he is bound by this option.

6. Explain, with reasons, whether a valid contract has been formed between Sidney and Brian in each of the following situations:

(a) Sidney agrees to sell goods to Brian 'on the usual terms'.

(b) Sidney offers to sell goods to Brian for £500. Brian says he will pay £400 but Sidney refuses to reduce the price. Brian then says he will pay £500.

(c) Sidney offers to sell goods to Brian and gives him 10 days to decide whether he wishes to buy them. After five days Sidney sells the goods elsewhere. Two days later, Brian says that he accepts the offer.

Unit 13. Matters that Affect the Validity of Contracts

Some contracts that appear perfectly valid may nevertheless be wholly or partly ineffective because of some defect when they were formed. The vitiating factors discussed in this unit are mistake, misrepresentation, duress, undue influence, and lack of capacity in the formation of the contract.

A. Mistake

The general rule is that mistake does *not* affect the validity of a contract. For example, if a man is mistaken as to the nature or value of what he buys, this is simply his misfortune. The law will not help him unless he has been misled by the other party (see Misrepresentation, page 128).

> In *Leaf* v. *International Galleries* (1950), a picture was sold which both seller and buyer believed to be by Constable. In fact it was not. The contract was not affected by this mistake, because each side intended to deal with the physical thing sold; they were simply mistaken as to its quality and value.

A further preliminary point is that mistake of *law* will never affect the validity of a contract. Ignorance of the law is no defence. In certain circumstances, mistake of *fact* may affect the contract and, if sufficiently serious, render the contract void.

Mistakes of fact which render a contract void

1. *Mistakes concerning the subject-matter of the contract*, for example the property sold, can render the contract void if sufficiently serious. A mere mistake as to the nature or value of the subject-matter will not be enough (see above).

125

A mutual mistake as to the identity of the subject-matter will render the contract void. A mutual mistake will occur where the parties are, unknown to each other, thinking about different things. Neither is right, neither wrong; they are simply at cross purposes, and have never really agreed.

In *Raffles* v. *Wichelhaus* (1864), a cargo of cotton was described as being on the *SS Peerless* from Bombay. There were in fact two ships of that name sailing from Bombay with an interval of three months between them. The seller intended to put the cargo on the second ship, while the buyer expected it on the first. The contract was held void.

A fundamental common mistake about the subject-matter may, exceptionally, also render the contract void. A common mistake occurs where both parties are under the same misapprehension: both are wrong. The clearest instance of this is where, unknown to both parties, the subject-matter does not exist.

In *Associated Japanese Bank Ltd* v. *Credit du Nord S.A.* (1988), Mr *B* fraudulently 'sold' some machinery to Associated Japanese Bank ('*AJB*') and leased it back. Credit du Nord ('*CDN*') contracted with *AJB* to guarantee that Mr *B* would pay the rent. In fact, unknown to both *AJB* and *CDN*, there was no machinery. The contract of guarantee was held void for common mistake.

In *Couturier* v. *Hastie* (1856), the action was based on a contract to sell a cargo of wheat which, unknown to both seller and buyer, no longer existed. The action failed.

Similarly, in *Galloway* v. *Galloway* (1914), a separation agreement between 'husband' and 'wife', disposing of property between them, was held void when it was discovered that they had never legally been married.

In *Bell* v. *Lever Brothers Ltd* (1932), however, the common mistake was not sufficiently fundamental. Agreements to make large severance payments to senior employees who were losing their jobs were made on the assumption by all parties that the men were entitled to some payment. In fact, they could have been sacked for misconduct and without compensation. Nevertheless the compensation agreements were held valid. The mistake only affected the *value* of the old contracts of employment.

2. *Mistaken signing of written documents* may, exceptionally, be a nullity. Three elements must be present if the contract is to be void: the signing must have been fraudulently induced, the mistake must be fundamental, and the signer must prove that he or she has not been negligent. A person attempting to avoid liability under a contract on these grounds is said to plead *non est factum* (it is not my act).

In *Foster* v. *Mackinnon* (1869), a rogue induced Mackinnon, an old gentleman with weak sight, to sign a document which Mackinnon thought to be a guarantee. In fact he was indorsing a bill of exchange for £3000 thereby incurring personal liability for this amount. It was held that, so long as he had not been negligent, he was not liable on the bill.

Conversely, in *Saunders* v. *Anglia Building Society* (1971), a Mrs Gallie intended to assign the lease of her house so as to enable her nephew to borrow money. The assignment was prepared fraudulently by a rogue, Lee, who had promised to arrange the loan. The document which she signed transferred the lease to Lee himself, who mortgaged it to the building society and departed with the proceeds. Mrs Gallie and her nephew received nothing. Mrs Gallie claimed that the original assignment was void for mistake; she had not read it because her glasses were broken, and she had not realized its effect. Her plea failed. She had intended to assign her lease, and her mistake as to the way in which she was assigning it was not so fundamental as to avoid the contract.

3. *A mistake by one party as to the identity of the other* may sometimes invalidate the contract. If *A* contracts with *B* under the impression that he is really dealing with *C*, the contract will be void if *A* can prove that his mistake was material; he intended to deal with *C* and would not have dealt with anyone else. It may be exceptionally difficult for *A* to prove this, particularly where the parties dealt with each other face to face.

> In *Phillips* v. *Brooks* (1919), a rogue bought a ring in a jeweller's shop. He then persuaded the jeweller that he was Sir George Bullough, and was, therefore, allowed to take away the ring in return for a cheque. The cheque was dishonoured, and the ring was eventually traced to a pawnbroker. The jeweller claimed that his contract with the rogue was void for mistake, but his claim failed. The jeweller had dealt with the man facing him; the question of identity was only raised when it came to payment.

> Again, in *Lewis* v. *Averay* (1972), Lewis sold and parted with his car to a rogue who pretended to be Richard Greene, the film actor. The rogue paid by cheque which was dishonoured, and then re-sold the car to Averay. The contract between Lewis and the rogue was not void; Lewis could not prove that he was willing to sell only to Richard Greene and to no one else.

Where the parties did not deal with each other face to face, it may be easier for *A* to prove that the mistake was material.

> In *Cundy* v. *Lindsay* (1878), a rogue called Blenkarn ordered linen by post from Lindsay & Co. by pretending to be Blenkiron, a reputable dealer. Blenkarn re-sold the linen to Cundy. Lindsay & Co. were able to recover it (or its value) because the contract with Blenkarn was void. They satisfied the court that they intended to deal only with Blenkiron.

> In *King's Norton Metal Co. Ltd* v. *Edridge, Merret & Co. Ltd* (1897), on the other hand, the claimants sold goods to a firm called 'Hallam & Co.' which placed an order by post. Hallam & Co. turned out to be a complete fiction; the real buyer was a rogue called Wallis. The contract was not void. If the claimants were willing to deal with an unknown company, without checking, then the identity of the buyer was clearly not sufficiently material.

It will be apparent that most of the cases on mistake of identity are actions between two innocent parties. *A* will have parted with the goods to a rogue, who will have re-sold to *X* and departed with the proceeds. If the contract between *A* and the rogue was void for mistake, *A* can recover the goods or their value from *X* by an action for the tort of conversion (Unit 10); otherwise *X* will normally be entitled to keep the property.

Other consequences of mistake

Where there is a mistake as to the subject-matter, but the mistake is not so fundamental as to render the contract void, the court *may* nevertheless allow one

127

party the equitable remedy of *rescission*, that is, the right to have the contract set aside *if he so wishes*. The party claiming this remedy must show that he has not been at fault in any way, and the court may impose certain conditions on granting the remedy.

> In *Cooper* v. *Phibbs* (1867), Cooper agreed to lease a fishery from Phibbs. It later turned out that, unknown to both, the fishery already belonged to Cooper. The court allowed Cooper to rescind the lease, on condition that he compensate Phibbs for improvements which the latter had made.

> In *Grist* v. *Bailey* (1967), Grist contracted to buy Bailey's house for £850. Both parties believed that the house was occupied by a tenant protected under the Rent Acts. In fact, unknown to both, the tenant had died. This increased the value of the house to about £2250, and Bailey refused to carry out the contract, claiming that it was void for mistake. The contract was held *not* to be void at common law, but the court exercised its equitable power to set the original contract aside on condition that Bailey would now sell for the true value.

When an equitable remedy is claimed, mistake may exceptionally persuade the court to refuse the remedy. For example, specific performance of a contract may be refused if the defendant has made a mistake which renders it unfair and inequitable to enforce the agreement against him, as in *Malins* v. *Freeman* (see page 158).

Where, by mistake, the terms of a written document do not represent accurately what the parties agreed orally, the court may, at its discretion, order the rectification of the document so that it does express what was agreed.

B. Misrepresentation

The formation of a contract is often preceded by negotiations, in the course of which one party makes statements of fact intended to induce the other to enter into the contract. If any such statement is false, it is called a misrepresentation.

A misrepresentation, then, may be defined as a false statement of fact, made by one party to the contract to the other before the contract, with a view to inducing the other to enter into it. The statement must have been intended to be acted upon, and it must actually have induced the other party to make the agreement.

It must be a representation of fact, not law. A mere boast is not regarded as a statement of fact (otherwise advertisers might incur substantial liabilities). A distinction is also made between a statement of fact and a mere expression of opinion, although this can prove difficult. Statements about a car such as 'beautiful condition' and 'superb condition' have been held in criminal cases to be statements of fact, not mere expressions of opinion.

The statements must be by one party to the contract to the other. A statement by the manufacturer which induces a customer to buy from a retail shop will not give the customer any remedy for misrepresentation against either retailer or manufacturer.

The false statement must actually have deceived the other party and induced him to make the contract. Obviously it must be false, but even a misleading half-truth can be false.

> In *London Assurance* v. *Mansel* (1879), a person seeking life assurance was asked on the proposal form what other proposals for cover he had made. He answered, truthfully, that

he had made two proposals the previous year, both accepted. He did not mention, however, that he had also had several proposals rejected. This half-truth was held to be a misrepresentation. (See also non-disclosure, page 131.)

Many misrepresentations also amount to promises which are actually incorporated into the contract. In this event, the party deceived will normally sue for breach of contract rather than for misrepresentation because, once breach of contract is proved, damages will automatically be awarded. Where mere misrepresentation is proved, the person liable may still have a defence to an action for damages if he can prove that he reasonably believed himself to be telling the truth. The distinction between mere representations and contractual promises can be difficult, but in contracts of sale the court will often hold that statements by a seller who is a *dealer* are contractual promises, whereas statements by a seller who is not a dealer are mere representations.

> In *Oscar Chess Ltd* v. *Williams* (1957), the defendant was a private car owner, trading in his vehicle in part-exchange for another. He falsely stated that it was a 1948 model, whereas in fact it was a 1939 car. This statement was quite innocent, because the registration book had been falsified by a previous owner. It was held that his statement was a mere representation, so that his innocence was a defence.

> On the other hand, in *Dick Bentley Productions Ltd* v. *Harold Smith (Motors) Ltd* (1965), a dealer sold a car which appeared from the instruments to have travelled only 20 000 miles. In fact it had done about 100 000. This was held to be breach of contract, not a mere misrepresentation, so that the buyer was automatically entitled to damages. A dealer, who knows more about the goods than his customers do, is readily assumed to *promise* that his statements are true.

Remedies for misrepresentation

1. *Damages*. Under the Misrepresentation Act 1967, section 2(1), a party to the contract can recover negligence damages for loss arising from a misrepresentation; but the other party has a defence if he can prove that, up to the time of the contract, he believed that his statements were true, and had reasonable cause so to believe. This can be difficult to prove, and the onus of proving it is on the defendant.

> In *Howard Marine Ltd* v. *Ogden Ltd* (1978), the owners made false statements about the capacity of two barges to a company negotiating to hire them. The owners themselves were mistaken, basing their claims on incorrect entries in the official Lloyd's Register. Nevertheless the owners were liable to the company which hired the barges. Damages were awarded under section 2(1) because the owners *should* have known the correct capacity, and therefore could not prove that they had reasonable cause to believe their misrepresentations.

> In *Corner* v. *Mundy* (1988), the vendor of a house told a would-be purchaser that the central heating was in good order. At the time, this was true. However, before the contract was eventually made, the pipes froze and burst, and the purchaser was not told this. The vendor was liable for damages under section 2(1), because he could not prove that he had reasonable cause to believe *up to the time the contract was made* that his statement was true.

Damages under s.2(1) can be reduced for the claimant's contributory negligence.

Under section 2(2), damages may also be awarded as an alternative to rescission at the court's discretion and, in this event, even the defendant's innocence may be no defence.

If the misrepresentation was made fraudulently, the partly deceived can, alternatively, sue for damages for the tort of deceit (Unit 10), but since the onus of proving fraud is on the claimant, this will rarely be done.

2. *Rescission*. Any misrepresentation, even innocent, will give the other party a right to *rescind* the contract, that is, to end it if he so wishes. Each party must be restored to his original position; for example, the property must be returned to the seller and the price to the buyer. The contract is said to be *voidable* (Unit 11).

The right to rescind will be lost as soon as it becomes impossible to return the parties to their position before the contract. For example, if the property has been re-sold by the buyer, or has been destroyed by him, it will be impossible to return it to the seller.

Since rescission is an equitable right, it must be exercised reasonably promptly. It is undesirable for a contract to remain voidable for too long, because this leads to uncertainty as to the ownership of the property. If he delays unduly, therefore, the innocent party will lose his right to rescind, and be left to sue for damages. What is a reasonable time is a question of fact, and may in some cases be only a matter of days or hours.

> In *Leaf v. International Galleries* (1950), which was mentioned earlier, the picture was sold in 1944. The claimant only discovered in 1949 that it was not by Constable. Although the contract was not void for mistake, the claimant claimed the right to rescind for innocent misrepresentation. It was held that, after a lapse of five years, any right to rescind had been lost. (The claimant could have claimed damages for breach of contract, but did not in fact do so.)

Time may not run against the claimant, however, until he could with reasonable diligence have discovered the error.

Normally, rescission will only be effective from the moment when it is communicated to the party at fault. This would cause injustice, however, where the misrepresentation was fraudulent and the rogue had disappeared. In this event, therefore, the rule is relaxed.

> In *Car and Universal Finance Co. Ltd* v. *Caldwell* (1965), Caldwell was persuaded by a rogue to part with his car in return for a cheque which was dishonoured. On discovering this, Caldwell immediately told the police, but could do no more to rescind the contract because the rogue could not be found. It was held that, in the circumstances, Caldwell had done everything possible to make public his intention to rescind, and the rescission was, therefore, effective.

Finally, the right to rescind will be lost if the innocent party 'affirms' the contract, that is, elects to go on with it knowing of the misrepresentation. He cannot blow hot and cold, and once he has decided to go on, he cannot change his mind.

In addition to the civil remedies for misrepresentation, a false statement of fact may also give rise to criminal liability, for example under the Trade Descriptions Act 1968 or the Property Misdescriptions Act 1991.

Section 3 of the Misrepresentation Act makes it very difficult for a party to exclude his liability for misrepresentation (Unit 14). A term in the contract which would exclude or restrict any liability or remedy for misrepresentation will be of no effect unless the defendant can show that the clause is 'reasonable' within the meaning of the Unfair Contract Terms Act 1977.

C. Duty to disclose

There is, in general, no duty to *disclose* facts. Silence cannot normally constitute misrepresentation even when the silent party knows that the other is deceiving himself and does nothing about it. Each party must find out the truth as best he can, and in contracts of sale this rule is known as *caveat emptor*—let the buyer beware.

There is, however, a duty to correct statements which, although originally true, have subsequently become false before the contract was made. The facts have changed, and it would be unfair to let the original statement stand.

> In *With* v. *O'Flanagan* (1936), at the start of negotiations for the sale of a doctor's practice, the seller stated, truthfully, that the annual income was £2000. The seller then fell ill and, by the time that the sale took place some months later, the profits had fallen drastically. It was held that the early statement should have been corrected, and the fall disclosed.

Silence is also not enough in contracts of the utmost good faith (*uberrimae fidei*). These are, for the most part, contracts where one party alone has full knowledge of the material facts and, therefore, the law does impose on him a duty to disclose. The main examples are:

1. *Contracts of insurance.* There is a duty on the insured person to disclose to the insurance firm any circumstances which might influence it in fixing the premium or deciding whether to insure the risk. Failure to do this will render the contract voidable at the option of the insurance firm.
2. *In contracts for the sale of land*, the vendor must disclose all defects in *title*, but not in the property itself.
3. *Contracts to subscribe for shares in a company*. A prospectus issued by a company, inviting the public to make an offer to buy shares in the company, must disclose various matters set out in detail under the Companies Act. If it does not, the contract may be rescinded.
4. *In contracts of family arrangement*, each member of the family must disclose all material facts within his knowledge.

D. Duress and undue influence

At common law, duress arose when a party was induced to enter a contract by force or the threat of force. His consent was not freely given. Today, economic coercion can also be duress.

131

In *Universe Tankships Inc.* v. *ITF* (1982), a trade dispute arose involving a ship, the *Universe Sentinel*. The union stopped it from leaving port, and eventually only allowed it to do so on condition that the owners paid money into a welfare fund. This agreement was held voidable for duress, and the owners recovered the money.

However, the economic pressure must be such that the courts regard it as improper. There can be a narrow line between economic duress and legitimate commercial pressure.

In *D & C Builders Ltd* v. *Rees* (1966) (Unit 11), it was suggested, *obiter*, that even if there had been a valid contract, it would have been voidable for duress. Mr and Mrs Rees almost held the builders to ransom; the builders needed the money quickly, and the Rees family (who owed £482) said in effect, 'either agree to accept only £300 or we delay still further'.

In *Atlas Express Ltd* v. *Kafco Ltd* (1989), *K*, a small manufacturer, received a good order from a retail chain, Woolworth's. *K* contracted with Atlas, a road carrier, to deliver the goods at an agreed fee. After the first load, Atlas realized that it had miscalculated the delivery costs, and therefore told *K* that it would not make any further deliveries unless K almost doubled the agreed fee. *K*, desperate to fulfil its Woolworth's order and unable to find another carrier in time, had to agree—but later refused to pay the extra. It was held that *K* was not liable for the extra charge, which had been extorted from it by duress. (Moreover, there was no consideration for its promise to increase the fee; contrast *Williams* v. *Roffey*, Unit 11.)

On the other hand, in *Pao On v. Lau Yiu Long* (1979) (Unit 11), the defendant was the major shareholder in Fu Chip Ltd. He was persuaded to give a guarantee to Pao On by the latter's threat to break his contract with Fu Chip Ltd. This could have harmed the defendant. Nevertheless the guarantee was held valid. The full facts were complex, and Pao On's threat was ultimately regarded as legitimate commercial pressure.

Equity has long recognized less direct pressures, particularly where confidential or professional relationships are abused. Generally, improper pressure has to be proved.

In *Williams* v. *Bayley* (1866), a father was induced to give security for his son's debts to the bank by the bank's threats to prosecute the son. On proof of this, the father was held not to be bound.

In some instances equity goes further and *presumes* undue influence unless the contrary is proved. This can arise from the relationship between the parties: it is presumed there is such influence by a doctor over his patient, solicitor over his client, religious adviser over follower, parent over young child (but not necessarily by husband over wife or vice versa). The presumption can only be rebutted by proof that the weaker party used his own free will, fully understood the proposed transaction, and preferably had had independent advice.

There are also situations where, although the *relationship* does not necessarily suggest undue influence, the *circumstances* do. For example, there have been very many debt cases where wives (or husbands) have agreed to mortgage the family home as security for the spouse's business debts, or elderly parents have similarly been persuaded by adult children to give unwise security for the children's business debts. The undue influence will not always be exerted directly by the other party to the contract here, who is usually the bank (the creditor). Nevertheless, in these situations, the bank should foresee the possibility of its client (the debtor) putting undue pressure on the spouse or elderly parent to give some sort of security to the bank, and even telling lies in the process. Therefore, such a creditor has a duty to see that the person being asked to provide security is fully aware of what he or she is doing, and is free from undue influence either by the bank itself or by the main debtor. The bank should generally ensure that the guarantor takes independent advice, particularly where there might be manifest disadvantage. Documents should not normally be entrusted to the debtor himself to obtain the spouse or parent's signature. Unless the creditor can prove that it has taken all reasonable steps to safeguard the potential victim, then the guarantee or mortgage will be voidable.

> In *Lloyd's Bank Ltd* v. *Bundy* (1975), a son was in financial difficulty. The bank manager visited the father and persuaded him to give the bank a guarantee of the son's debts and a mortgage of the father's house as security. The father was old and was given no warning or opportunity to seek independent advice (which might have been against the contracts). Undue influence was presumed, and the contracts were set aside when the bank could not rebut the presumption.

> In *Barclay's Bank plc* v. *O'Brien* (1993), a husband persuaded his wife to mortgage the family home as security for his present and future business debts. He misled her into believing that her liability could be no more than £60 000, and she signed on that basis. In fact, the documents eventually enabled the bank to claim roughly double that amount. She was held liable for only £60 000. On equitable principles, the creditor who takes from a married person security for the spouse's business debts must take all reasonable steps to see that the potential liability is fully understood. The bank could not prove that it had done this.

> In *Credit Lyonnais Bank* v. *Burch* (1997), an employer required its employee to mortgage his flat to the Bank as security for all of the employer's debts, present and future. It was held that (1) the employment relationship did not raise the presumption of undue influence, but (2) the circumstances did. The mortgage was set aside.

There are other situations where the circumstances can raise a presumption of undue influence.

> In *O'Sullivan* v. *MAM Ltd* (1985), a young singer and composer (Gilbert O'Sullivan) made several contracts with a management company at a time when he had no business experience. Many of the contracts were unduly harsh, and they were later set aside as having been obtained by undue influence.

However, the court will only presume undue influence if the circumstances *do* make it seem likely. For example, a bank or building society which lends money to a married couple jointly, and takes a mortgage of the jointly owned family home as security, need not normally advise each of them to take independent advice. If the money is apparently sought by both, for the benefit of both, there is nothing to suggest that either of them is unduly pressurizing the other. The heavy burden of having to *dis*prove undue influence only falls on the lender who should have suspected it, as where the lender knows that the home is being used to secure the *business* debts of only one of them.

> In *National Westminster Bank plc* v. *Morgan* (1985), a couple in financial difficulty remortgaged their home to the bank. The house was jointly owned, and the bank

manager had to visit the wife to persuade her to sign. She did not realize that the new mortgage could also cover her husband's business debts, but this was not the main purpose of the loan. She received no independent legal advice at this stage. Nevertheless the mortgage was binding on her. The loan was in fact used to pay off earlier mortgagors of the house, so as to save the family home, albeit temporarily. The husband died leaving no business debts to the bank. The wife herself had wanted the loan and had benefited from it. Therefore equity would not intervene.

In *CIBC Mortgages plc* v. *Pitt* (1993), a married couple borrowed money jointly, and jointly told the lender that it was to be used to pay off their existing mortgage, and to buy a holiday home. In fact, unknown to the lender, the wife reluctantly allowed her husband to use the money to speculate in shares in a very risky manner. The court refused to set aside the mortgage. There was nothing in the circumstances known to the lender to make it presume undue influence.

Where undue influence is deemed to exist, either by proof or presumption, the contract is voidable either wholly or partly (see *Barclays Bank* v. *O'Brien* above). However, the right to rescind/avoid a contract is an equitable one, and it must therefore be exercised within a reasonable time.

In *Allcard* v. *Skinner* (1887), Miss Allcard joined a religious order and gave about £7000 to its leader during the years when she was a member. After leaving the order, she waited several years and then sued to recover the money. It was held that she had delayed for too long after the end of the undue influence, and her action failed.

E. Lack of capacity to contract

The general rule is that everyone is fully capable of entering into contracts, and that these contracts are enforceable by and against him. However, there are certain classes of people whose contractual capacity is limited.

Minors (infants)

A minor or infant is a person under the age of 18. As a general rule, he will be entitled to avoid his contracts and damages will not be awarded against him. For example, he will not be bound by trading contracts which he makes.

In *Cowern* v. *Nield* (1912), it was held that a minor who was a hay and straw merchant was not liable to repay the price of the goods which he failed to deliver.

In *Mercantile Union Guarantee Corporation Ltd* v. *Ball* (1937), an infant haulage contractor who took a lorry on hire-purchase was held not liable for arrears of instalments.

On the other hand, a minor *can* recover damages against an adult if the latter breaks the contract. The minor can *sue*, but cannot be *sued*.

There are, however, a few limits on this rule. First, as regards actions against the minor:

1. A minor must pay a reasonable price for necessary goods sold and delivered to him. He need not pay the contract price if this is exorbitant, and in any event he

can withdraw from the contract at any time before delivery. Furthermore, this rule only applies to 'necessaries', that is, goods suitable to the minor's condition in life and to his actual requirements at the time of sale and delivery.

> In *Nash* v. *Inman* (1908), an undergraduate ordered expensive clothes from a tailor, including 11 fancy waistcoats. The minor's father was a prosperous architect, and it was argued that the clothes were suitable to the minor's station in life. Since he was already well supplied with clothes, however, these goods were held not to be necessaries.

2. By the Minors' Contracts Act 1987, a court has a discretion, if it seems just and equitable, to require an infant to transfer to the other party any property acquired by the infant under the contract. (A court *might* now, therefore, order the return of the waistcoats, or of the lorry in *Mercantile Union Guarantee Corporation* v. *Ball* if such a case occurred today.) Before 1987, the court could only do this if the minor was proved to have been fraudulent when he made the contract.

3. Money lent to a minor cannot be recovered. However, if the money is lent to a minor specifically to enable him to buy necessaries, the lender can recover such part of the loan as is actually spent on necessaries at a reasonable price. The lender is said to be 'subrogated' to the rights of the supplier of the goods against the minor.

4. Contracts of employment, apprenticeship and education which, *taken as a whole*, are for the minor's benefit form the main full exception to the general rule. If as a whole the contract is beneficial, the court will enforce all of the clauses, even ones which, taken in isolation, are not beneficial.

> In *Doyle* v. *White City Stadium* (1935), an infant boxer was held bound by a clause in his contract which provided for forfeiture of his prize money if (as happened) he was disqualified. The contract as a whole was similar to apprenticeship.

5. Special rules apply to contracts of a continuing nature which can last after the minor reaches 18. A contract such as a lease, a partnership or the holding of shares in a company can be binding before 18 unless the minor repudiates it. It will continue to be binding after 18 unless the young person ends it within a reasonable time of reaching full age.

6. Other contracts made while one party was a minor can, under the 1987 Act, be ratified by him when he reaches full age. The contract was unenforceable against him when he made it, but his ratification – if he does choose to ratify – may now make it binding on him.

7. The Minors' Contracts Act makes it possible for an adult validly to guarantee a minor's obligations under a contract. The guarantor can be liable if the minor breaks his contract, even if the minor himself could not have been held liable.

Finally, as regards actions against the minor, the court will not hold him liable for damages in tort if this would merely be an indirect way of awarding damages for breach of contract.

There are also some exceptions to the rule that a minor can sue on his contracts. For example, since the remedy of specific performance will never be awarded *against* a minor, the court will not award it *to* a minor either (Unit 15). As another example, when a minor avoids the contract, as a general rule he can recover money or goods which he has handed over, but if he has received a benefit under the contract this will not be the case.

> In *Valentini* v. *Canali* (1889), a minor leased a house and agreed to buy some furniture, paying part of the price. After several months the minor left, and avoided the contract as he was entitled to do. He could not recover the payments which he made for the furniture, however, because he had received some benefit from the contract.

Other types of incapacity

Certain mental patients cannot validly enter into contracts. Contracts can be made on their behalf by the Court of Protection or receivers appointed for this purpose.

Ultra vires contracts are important examples of contracts that are void for incapacity; see Unit 7.

Specimen questions

1. (a) Explain the effect of mistake upon the validity of a contract.
   (b) David agrees to insure his premises with ERC Insurance after ERC Insurance has told him that he would be comprehensively covered against all risks. The contract includes a clause that David's cover will only continue if he obtains an annual fire certificate to the effect that all reasonable precautions against fire are being taken. David signs the contract without reading it and consequently does not obtain the requisite fire certificates each year.

      Some years later the premises are destroyed by fire and ERC Insurance refuses to reimburse David for his loss.

      Advise David.

2. *B* bought a business from *S*. Two years later, *B* realized that *S* had (probably unintentionally) made false statements to him about the business, which had persuaded *B* to buy. Discuss the remedies that *B* might have against *S*.

3. While negotiating to sell his business to Ivan, Henry made a true statement that gave total figures for turnover and profits for the previous five years. This created an impression that the business was in a healthy state. Henry did not disclose, nor did Ivan request, a breakdown of figures, which would have revealed a steady decline in profitability over the previous year. Ivan, having purchased the business, discovered the true state of affairs.

      What remedies, if any, does Ivan have? Discuss the possibilities.

4. Brian agrees to buy a computer from Stella. Explain how each of the following would affect the contract.
   (a) Brian believes that he is obtaining credit over six months, whereas Stella believes that it is a cash sale.

   (b) Both Brian and Stella believe that the contract price of £4000 represents the true value of the computer but, because of a latent defect in its manufacture, the computer is only worth £2000.

5. Husband and wife (*H* and *W*) own their house jointly. *W* wishes to borrow a specific sum to help her to expand her office machinery business. She approaches the bank, which is willing to lend as long as the house is mortgaged to the bank as security. *H* agrees to this without realising that the loan agreement allows *W* to borrow further sums if needed. The business is now insolvent, and *H* and *W* cannot repay the amount due. The bank seeks possession of the house. Discuss the legal issues.

Unit 14. The Terms of the Bargain

This unit deals with the rights and obligations which arise under a contract. It will also discuss one aspect of the idea of 'freedom of contract', that is, how far the parties can agree between themselves what their relations are to be, and how far the law determines their relations for them.

A. Express terms

Express terms are those specifically mentioned and agreed by the parties at the time of contracting, whether this be done in writing or by word of mouth. In simple agreements, such as small cash sales, the express terms may be very sketchy; the buyer will simply ask for what he sees before him at the price indicated, and the seller will agree to sell. There will be no need for detailed arrangements as to delivery or payment, because goods and cash will be handed over immediately.

Where the subject-matter is very valuable, where the agreement is complicated, or where the contract will last for some time, for example because credit is allowed, the parties are likely to be much more specific as to detailed terms. In these contracts, detailed terms will often be set out expressly, frequently in a written agreement. Thus, contracts of insurance, hire-purchase, or for the sale of land will be in writing and contain detailed express terms, whether or not this is required by statute or for the purpose of evidence (Unit 11).

If a written contract is signed, the signer is generally taken to have agreed to everything in the document, whether he has read it or not; see *Saunders* v. *Anglia Building Society* (Unit 13), and *L'Estrange* v. *Graucob Ltd* (page 143). Where there are *unsigned* documents, the position can be more complicated. First, it may be doubtful whether a document such as a ticket or notice is or is not part of the contract (see page 143). Secondly, if more than one document is used, containing slightly different terms, there may be 'a battle of the forms' as in *Butler* v. *Ex-Cell-O* (page 119). Thirdly, *unusually harsh* terms in an unsigned document may not automatically be part of the contract. Someone seeking to rely on such a term may have to show that he has done everything reasonable to bring it to the attention of the other party. In one case, Denning LJ expressed (*obiter*) the spectacular view that 'Some clauses which I have seen would need to be printed in red ink on the face of the document with a red hand pointing to it before the notice could be held to be sufficient'.

> In *Interfoto Ltd* v. *Stiletto Ltd* (1988), the defendant hired 47 photographic transparencies for 14 days. He did not notice that the delivery note provided for an unusually harsh penalty of £5 + VAT per transparency per day if the goods were returned late. He returned them about a fortnight late, and was therefore sued for £3783.50 plus interest. It was held that the claimant had not done everything reasonable to point out this clause to the hirer. The courts therefore ignored it, and assessed damages on a more sensible basis.

Contractual terms, oral or written, differ in importance, and may be classified into conditions and warranties. A *condition* is an important term which is vital to the contract, so that non-compliance will affect the main purpose of the agreement. Breach of condition will give the injured party a right to rescind or terminate the contract. Alternatively, the injured party may, if he so wishes, go on with the contract, but recover damages for his loss. A *warranty* is a less important term, non-compliance with which will cause loss but not affect the basic purpose of the contract. Breach of warranty will only give the injured party the right to sue for damages, not to rescind the contract.

> In *Bettini* v. *Gye* (1876), an opera singer agreed to attend for rehearsals six days before the first performance. He did not arrive until two days beforehand. The duty to attend for *rehearsals* was held to be only a warranty, and breach entitled the management to recover damages but not to terminate the contract.

> Conversely, in *Poussard* v. *Spiers & Pond* (1876), Madame Poussard, a singer, failed to turn up for the first few performances. The obligation for *performances* was held to be a condition, and breach entitled the management to end the contract.

Some express terms are difficult to classify so neatly in advance, and can only be classified by reference to the nature of the breach. A minor breach of the term might only be a breach of warranty, whereas a serious breach of the same term or a breach which has serious consequences might be breach of condition.

> In *Hong Kong Fir Shipping Co. Ltd* v. *Kawasaki Kisen Kaisha* (1962), the claimants chartered their ship to the defendants. The contract provided that the ship would be 'in every way fitted for ordinary cargo service'. This term could not be classified in advance as a condition or a warranty, because breach could be either a minor matter if the ship was slightly defective, or very serious if the ship was about to sink. In fact, the engines were old, the engine-room staff were inefficient, and the ship was delayed. This was held to be only a breach of warranty, which did not entitle the defendants to repudiate the contract.

139

The difficulty of such 'innominate' terms is that the parties may not know their rights and liabilities even after the contract is broken. One party may say that it was only a minor breach and that he is only liable for damages; the other may say that it was serious and that he can end the contract. The courts, and the parties themselves, often prefer that the remedies for breaking the term should be clear from the outset.

B. Implied terms

Terms implied by the courts

Where the parties have not made express provision on some point, the court will sometimes imply a term to cover the position. The court will impose such obligations as, in the court's view, the parties would reasonably have agreed had they thought of the matter.

> In *The Moorcock* (1889), the owner of a wharf contracted to provide a berth for a ship. The berth was unsuitable for the vessel, which was damaged when it hit a ridge of hard ground at low tide. There was no express undertaking that the berth was suitable, but the court implied a term to this effect, and the shipowner recovered damages.

The implication of additional terms is usually justified on the grounds that it is necessary in order to give business effect to the intentions of the parties; the agreement makes commercial nonsense without it. If, at the time of the contract, someone had said to the parties, 'What will happen in such a case?' they would both have said, 'Of course so and so will happen; we did not trouble to say that'.

> In *Liverpool City Council* v. *Irwin* (1977), the written tenancy agreements in a tower block of flats imposed no express duty on the landlord to keep the lifts and stairs in good repair! The court nevertheless implied such a term (but held that the landlord had not broken this on the facts).

In some instances the courts have gone beyond this, and implied terms largely because this was necessary to achieve substantial justice between the parties. In a tenancy of a furnished house, the courts will imply a term that the premises will be reasonably fit for human habitation when the tenancy begins. Under a contract of employment, the employer owes an implied duty to take reasonable care for the safety of his employees, and the latter owe a duty to show good faith and to exercise reasonable care and skill in the exercise of their duties. (A careless employer may also be liable for the tort of negligence; Unit 9.) In contracts for the carriage of goods by sea, there are implied undertakings that the ship is seaworthy, that it will proceed on its voyage with reasonable dispatch, and that there shall be no unnecessary deviation.

It should be remembered that, as a general rule, the courts will only imply terms where the parties have made no express provision. Most implied terms can be excluded or varied by the parties.

Terms implied by statute

In some types of contract, detailed terms are implied by Act of Parliament. In many instances this has resulted from codification of the common law rules relating to such contracts. Some provisions aim simply to standardize the obligations of the parties; others go further and aim to do justice between the parties.

Perhaps the best example is the Sale of Goods Act 1979. The terms implied by this Act were first developed by the courts and then codified by statute in 1893. There were subsequent changes, and the 1979 Act was a consolidating one (Unit 2). There have been further changes since then, notably in 1994.

Some of the implied terms are general rules which can be freely altered by the parties if they so wish. Thus delivery of the goods and payment of the price are concurrent conditions, that is to say, the general rule is 'cash on delivery'; but there is nothing to stop the parties from varying this implied term and expressly contracting that the buyer can take away the goods on credit.

Some other sections operate differently. They impose duties which the seller owes to the buyer and, in *consumer* sales, govern the parties *whether they wish it or not*. The seller cannot exclude them. There are four main examples. By section 12, there is an implied condition that the seller has a right to sell the goods. By section 13, where goods are sold by description, there is an implied condition that they shall correspond with the description. By section 15, where goods are sold by sample, the bulk must correspond with the sample. By section 14, where the seller sells in the course of a business, the goods must be of satisfactory quality, and reasonably fit for the buyer's purpose if he has made this known. These are discussed more fully in Unit 18.

Under the Supply of Goods (Implied Terms) Act 1973, obligations almost identical to these are imposed on the owner of goods who lets them on hire-purchase. By the Supply of Goods and Services Act 1982, similar terms are implied as regards the goods supplied under contracts of hire, and other contracts where possession or ownership of goods passes. Where the goods are supplied to a *consumer*, again, most of these implied terms cannot now be excluded; see the Unfair Contract Terms Act (page 145). Even where the goods are supplied to a business, not a consumer, the terms can only be excluded if the court considers it reasonable to allow this.

Other statutes which imply terms into certain types of contract include the Defective Premises Act 1972, and the Marine Insurance Act 1906.

C. Problems of unequal bargaining power

The law of contract, as we have seen it so far, has been based on the assumption that the parties freely negotiated the terms of their bargain. This is not always the case, particularly where one party is in a stronger economic position than the other.

The most obvious inequality arises where one of the parties enjoys a monopoly position. If someone wishes to acquire the goods or service which the monopolist supplies, he cannot genuinely negotiate terms to suit himself. He must either take the terms which the monopolist offers, or simply do without.

The position is very similar where there are only a few suppliers. The customer does not normally negotiate over the terms of an insurance contract, a hire-purchase agreement, or a mortgage. He contracts on a standard form prepared in advance by the company, which he can either take or leave. There will be little point in going to another company if all companies insist on more or less the same terms.

Other matters may affect the reality of bargaining power. A borrower who has no money is in a weaker position than a lender who has a lot. Unequal expertise may be relevant: in contracts for goods, it may be difficult to negotiate where the goods are so technically complex that the buyer is not competent to judge the quality or fitness of what he buys. The form which the agreement takes can be important: a standard form contract may be in intricate language and in small print, and it is probably unusual for a consumer to read through in detail the consumer credit or insurance forms which he signs.

Stronger parties have abused their position in various ways. They have imposed harsh terms such as extortionate rates of interest, or harsh 'penalty' clauses if the weaker party should be in breach. They have also included 'exemption' clauses, which attempt to limit or exclude altogether the potential liability of the stronger party should he be in breach. The next section of this unit deals with exemption clauses, and the approach of the courts and the legislature to them. The Unfair Contract Terms Act 1977, in spite of its wide name, only deals with exemption clauses. Other potentially harsh terms may be caught by special legislation such as the Consumer Credit Act (Unit 21). The Unfair Terms in Consumer Contracts Regulations 1999 (which implement an EU directive) apply more generally and are discussed in the last section of this unit.

D. Exemption clauses

While it may be acceptable for parties negotiating on an equal footing to exclude or limit their liability, both the courts and Parliament have been reluctant to allow exemption clauses which a stronger party has imposed on a weaker one.

Such clauses can take various forms. They may exclude one party's liability altogether. They may accept possible liability, but limit the damages to, say, £1000. They may exclude or restrict some remedy (e.g. 'no refunds'); or impose onerous conditions ('complaints must be made within 24 hours'); or exclude or restrict rules of evidence or procedure ('receipt must be produced'). There are many possibilities.

The approach of the courts

1. *Is the clause part of the contract?* The courts will require the person relying on an exemption clause to show that the other party agreed to it at or before the time when agreement was reached. Otherwise it will not form part of the contract.
    (a) Where a contract is made by signing a written document, the general rule is that the signer is bound by everything which the document contains, whether he has read it or not.

In *L'Estrange* v. *Graucob Ltd* (1934), Miss L'Estrange signed a contract to buy an automatic machine. The document provided that 'any express or implied condition, statement or warranty ... is hereby excluded', and the court commented that this clause was in 'regrettably small print'. Although Miss L'Estrange had not read the document, it was held that the clause bound her, and she had no remedy when the machine proved defective.

(b) Where the terms are in an unsigned document, the person seeking to rely on them must show that the other party knew, or should have known, that the document was a contractual one which could be expected to contain terms. He must show that everything reasonable has been done to bring the terms to the notice of the other party. Most of the cases concern documents such as tickets, order forms and unsigned receipts.

In *Chapleton* v. *Barry UDC* (1940), the claimant hired a deck chair, and was injured when it collapsed. The ticket which he had received when paying contained a clause excluding liability, but he had put the ticket into his pocket without looking at it. The court decided that he was entitled to assume that a deck chair ticket was merely a receipt without conditions, and his action succeeded.

In *Thompson* v. *LMS Railway Co.* (1930), Mrs Thompson obtained a cheap excursion ticket with the customary wording referring the buyer to conditions in the company's timetables. One such condition excluded liability for injury. The court upheld the company's contention that a rail ticket, particularly a cheaper one, must reasonably be expected to contain terms. The fact that Mrs Thompson was illiterate was disregarded, and she recovered no damages.

In *Roe* v. *R. A. Naylor Ltd* (1918), a 'sold note' containing an exclusion clause was simply placed in front of the business buyer at the time of sale. This document clearly contained terms, and it was held that the buyer was bound by the clause even though he had not read it. As a prudent businessman he should have done, and the seller had done everything reasonable to bring it to his notice.

(c) Any attempt to introduce an exemption clause *after* the contract has been made will be ineffective.

In *Olley* v. *Marlborough Court Ltd* (1949), property was stolen from the claimant during her stay at a hotel. There was a notice in the bedroom that the proprietors accepted no responsibility for articles stolen, but this was held to be ineffective. The claimant only saw it *after* the contract had been made at the reception desk.

In *Thornton* v. *Shoe Lane Parking Ltd* (1971), the claimant made his contract with the car park company when he inserted a coin in the automatic ticket machine (at the latest). The ticket which he received referred to conditions displayed inside the car park, and which he could only see after entry. It was held that he was not bound by the conditions, which purported to exempt the company from liability for injury to customers.

(d) Exceptionally, a court may assume knowledge of an exemption clause from the course of past dealings between the parties. If they have contracted many times, always with the same exemption, it might only be natural to expect it in the present contract.

143

In *Spurling (J.) Ltd* v. *Bradshaw* (1956), Bradshaw deposited some barrels of orange juice with Spurlings, a warehouse firm. The parties had dealt with each other for many years and always the warehouse firm had excluded its liability for 'negligence, wrongful act or default'. On this occasion, the document containing the exclusion was not sent until several days after the contract. Nevertheless, the clause was held to be implied into the contract, because the parties had always previously dealt on this basis. Spurlings, therefore, were not liable when most of the barrels were found to be empty on collection by Bradshaw.

However, the past dealings must always have been on the same basis. If other terms have varied in the past, or are different this time, then the court may refuse to assume that both parties expected an exemption clause this time.

2. *Construing exemption clauses.* Traditionally, the courts have construed exemption clauses *contra proferentem*, that is, in the manner least favourable to the person who put them into the contract. Any ambiguity or loophole in the drafting has been seized upon.

In *Wallis, Son & Wells* v. *Pratt & Haynes* (1911), the buyer of seed found when it grew that it was not what he had ordered. The sellers relied on a clause in the contract excluding all '*warranties*, express or implied, as to growth or description'. This did not protect them, because the term broken was a *condition*, not a warranty.

In *White* v. *John Warrick & Co. Ltd* (1953), the claimant hired a tricycle. The contract provided that '*Nothing in this agreement* shall render the owners liable ...'. The claimant was injured when the saddle tilted forward. It was held that the clause only excluded liability *for breach of contract*; the owners might still be liable for the tort of negligence (Unit 9).

Moreover, the courts have sometimes assumed that a clause was not intended to cover fundamental breach, where one party does something fundamentally different from what he contracted to do (supplying beans instead of peas). However, this is only a presumption and a sufficiently clear clause can cover even the most serious breach.

If the contract is between two businesses with equal bargaining power, the court will not even make the presumption. The clause will be examined in the context of the contract as a whole. Was the price kept low on the understanding that the supplier's liability was limited? Was it assumed that the buyer of the property or service would insure himself against any loss? Was the exemption clause simply one of a set of trading terms upon which both sides were apparently content to do business? If so, then the clause—if it is clear and comprehensive—can be upheld.

In *Photo Production Ltd* v. *Securicor Transport Ltd* (1980), Securicor contracted to guard the claimant's factory where paper was stored. The patrolman deliberately started a fire, and it destroyed the premises. It was held that an exemption clause in the contract protected Securicor. Both parties were established businesses that had reached terms freely. The price of the patrol was modest. Both parties were insured, the claimant against the loss of the building, Securicor against liability. The court was satisfied that both sides had intended Photo Production (or its insurers) to bear the risk.

The courts have also made an important distinction between clauses *excluding* liability and clauses which merely *limit* liability to a particular sum. The courts will be less hostile to mere limitation clauses, especially where (as above) the limitation is reflected in the other terms.

> *Ailsa Craig Fishing Co. Ltd* v. *Malvern Fishing Co. Ltd* (1983) again involved Securicor, which was guarding a quay where ships were berthed. The patrolman went off for the celebrations on New Year's Eve, leaving the vessels unattended. The tide rose and a boat rose with it. Its bow jammed under a quay and it sank. Again the owner was insured against such an incident, and therefore plainly did not envisage Securicor taking the entire responsibility. A clause limiting Securicor's liability to £1000 was therefore upheld.

3. *Privity of contract.* The terms of a contract generally only affect the parties to that contract. Therefore, an exemption clause will normally not protect anyone who is not party to the contract; see *Adler* v. *Dickson* (Unit 16).

Unfair Contract Terms Act 1977

This is the most important piece of legislation affecting exemption clauses. Most of the Act applies only to 'business liability', that is, liability arising from things done or to be done by a person in the course of a business, or from occupation of premises used for business purposes. Certain contracts are excepted from the Act, principally those relating to land, patents and copyright, shares, contracts affecting formation or internal management of companies, and insurance. The Act *can* apply to contracts of employment. The Act deals slightly differently with various situations.

1. *Negligence liability* is covered by section 2. No one acting in the course of a business can, either by contractual terms or by any notice given or displayed, exclude his liability, in contract or tort, for *death or bodily injury* arising from *negligence*. He can exclude or limit liability for mere financial loss or loss of property due to negligence, but only if he can prove that the exemption is reasonable. This will usually be difficult, although it may be possible where two large businesses are concerned; the two *Securicor* cases above show the way in which the courts approach this today (although the Act did not apply to them because both arose from things which happened before 1977).

> In *Smith* v. *Eric S. Bush* (1989), exemption clauses in a *consumer* case were held invalid under section 2(2). Mrs Smith bought a house relying partly on a valuer's favourable report. The report had been prepared for a building society, but Mrs Smith had had to pay towards the cost, and the valuer knew that Mrs Smith would rely on it. The report was inadequate, and chimneys later collapsed. Exemption clauses in the application and report were held invalid unless the valuer could prove them reasonable, which he could not.

2. *Liability under a contract* may also be affected by two further rules in section 3. Where a business contracts on *its own* written standard terms, it cannot exclude or vary its liability for breach of contract unless it can show that the exemption is

reasonable. The same rule applies whenever a business contracts with a *consumer*, whether or not on its standard terms.

3. *Sale of goods contracts* are also governed by section 6, which can apply even to non-business liability. We have seen that the Sale of Goods Act 1979 imposes terms binding on sellers. By section 6, if the buyer is a *consumer*, these obligations cannot be excluded. A buyer is a consumer when he buys, for his private use, goods normally supplied for such use, from a seller selling in the course of a business.

> In *R & B Customs Brokers Ltd* v. *UDT* (1988), it was held that a shipping *company* which, on an isolated occasion, bought a car for one of its directors could be a consumer for this purpose. The purchase had no integral part in the company's business.

If the buyer is not a consumer (for example if he is a trader buying for re-sale) section 6 does allow the seller to exclude or restrict the Sale of Goods Act, sections 13–15, but only if he, the seller, can show that the exemption is reasonable. Section 12 cannot be excluded.

The 1977 Act, Schedule 2, contains guidelines to help determine what is 'reasonable'. Regard may be had to various matters: (a) the relative bargaining strength of the parties; (b) whether the customer is given an inducement such as a price reduction to agree to the terms; (c) whether the customer should have known the existence and extent of the exemption clause, especially in the light of trade customs or past dealings; (d) whether it was reasonable to expect compliance with any condition imposed on the claimant (for example that complaints must be made within *x* days of delivery); and (e) whether the goods were made to the customer's special order.

> In *R. W. Green Ltd* v. *Cade Bros Farms* (1978), a farmer bought seed potatoes from a supplier. The contract provided, *inter alia*, that any complaint must be made within three days of the seed being delivered. The court had no difficulty in holding this part of the term unreasonable, because the defect was one which could not become apparent until the seed had had time to grow.

> In *Mitchell Ltd* v. *Finney Lock Seeds Ltd* (1983) a farmer bought cabbage seed from a supplier. When the cabbage grew, it proved inferior and of the wrong type. The seller relied on clauses in the standard form contract which purported to limit and/or exclude his liability. The House of Lords held these clauses unreasonable (partly because, in the past, the suppliers had negotiated settlements rather than tried to rely on the clauses; therefore, even the suppliers may have had doubts about their reasonableness).

4. *Hire-purchase contracts* too are governed by section 6. We have seen that the Supply of Goods (Implied Terms) Act 1973 imposes obligations on the owner of goods who lets them on hire-purchase. These are basically the same as the seller's obligations under the Sale of Goods Act, and are subject to the same rules regarding exemption.

5. *In other contracts for the supply of goods*, such as hire, or 'work and materials' agreements, the Supply of Goods and Services Act 1982 imposes obligations on the supplier. The 1977 Act, section 7, applies to these. Again, the supplier's statutory obligations as regards the goods cannot be excluded or varied in consumer

transactions. They can be excluded or limited – except normally for the obligations as to title – in non-consumer contracts, but only if the supplier can prove that the exemption is reasonable.

6. *Separate 'guarantees' of goods*, by manufacturers or suppliers, sometimes also contain exemption clauses. Such clauses can be caught by the 1977 Act, section 5. If the goods are of a type normally supplied for private use or consumption, then no term in the guarantee can exclude or restrict the supplier's liability for defects while the goods are in consumer use, if the loss results from the negligence of the manufacturer or a distributor.

Misrepresentation Act 1967

By the Misrepresentation Act, section 3, as amended in 1977, any term excluding or restricting liability for misrepresentation is void unless the person making the false statement proves that the exemption is fair and reasonable having regard to the circumstances which were, or ought reasonably to have been, known to or in the contemplation of the parties when the contract was made. This applies even to non-business liability.

> In *Walker* v. *Boyle* (1982), misrepresentations were made on behalf of the private seller of a house. When the buyer discovered this he rescinded the contract and recovered the £10 500 deposit which he had paid, plus damages under the Misrepresentation Act, section 2(1). An exemption clause in the conditions of sale did not protect the seller, because she could not show that the exemption was reasonable.

Fair Trading Act 1973

This Act empowers the Secretary of State for Trade and Industry to make regulations prohibiting certain undesirable consumer trade practices. He can, for example, prohibit the inclusion in specified consumer transactions of terms or conditions purporting to exclude or limit a party's liability. Under these powers, the Minister could invalidate exemption clauses which at present are unaffected by legislation. He can also impose criminal sanctions: for example, by the Consumer Transactions (Restriction on Statements) Order 1976 it can be criminal for a business seller of goods to use a void exemption clause or notice such as a 'no refunds' notice to consumers. (This was sometimes done by traders to deter consumers who did not know that the notice was ineffective.)

E. The Unfair Terms in Consumer Contracts Regulations 1999

These regulations implement an EC Directive, and replace earlier regulations. They overlap to some extent with the existing UK legislation, but they do not replace it or affect its validity. They apply to a wider variety of terms in a narrower (and different) variety of contracts.

147

The regulations, unlike the Unfair Contract Terms Act (UCTA), apply only to *consumer* contracts. These are contracts between a seller or supplier of goods or services who, in making the contract, is acting for purposes relating to his business, and a consumer who is a *natural* person who is *not* acting for business purposes. A company can never be a consumer under the regulations; nor can an individual or partnership when acting for business purposes. 'Business' includes a trade or profession, and the activities of a Government department or local authority. To date, these regulations have been used almost entirely in small claims, for example against estate agents, hirers of clothing, or issuers of parking tickets.

Certain types of contract are specifically excluded, particularly those relating to employment, the incorporation and organization of companies and partnerships, and rights in family law and succession. However (unlike the UCTA) the regulations do cover private insurance and mortgages of land, both of which have often contained harsh terms.

The other limit on the regulations is that, with one exception, they apply only to terms which 'have not been individually negotiated'. For the most part, these will be the printed terms in standard form contracts, where the terms have been drafted in advance and the consumer has not been able to influence their substance. The regulations do not generally apply to terms which define the main subject matter ('core' obligations) of the contract, or concern the adequacy of the price. If *some* of the terms have been negotiated, the regulations may still apply to the rest of the contract if an overall assessment shows that it is essentially a standard form one.

If the regulations do apply, their provisions are much wider than those of the UCTA. First, a seller or supplier must ensure that any written term of the contract is expressed in plain, intelligible language, and if there is any doubt about the meaning of a written term, the interpretation most favourable to the consumer shall prevail. This applies even to terms which have been negotiated.

More importantly, the regulations provide that a non-negotiated written term which is *unfair* shall not be binding on the consumer. An unfair term is one which 'contrary to the requirement of good faith causes a significant imbalance in the parties' rights and obligations under the contract to the detriment of the consumer'.

An assessment of the unfair nature of a term must take into account the nature of the goods and services for which the contract was made. It must refer to all circumstances at the time when the contract was made, and to all the other terms of the contract or of another contract on which it is dependent. Schedule 3 of the regulations contains an 'indicative and non-exhaustive' list of terms which *may* be regarded as unfair. Many of these are exemption clauses of various kinds, and in some contracts these are already totally void or subject to the requirement of 'reasonableness' under the UCTA. The list also includes other types of clauses, such as some 'penalty' damages clauses; see Units 15 and 21, and *Interfoto Ltd* v. *Stiletto Ltd* earlier (to which the regulations would *not* apply). Clauses which entitle a supplier to alter unilaterally, without a valid reason, either the product/service to be provided or the (other) terms of the contract are further illustrations; also certain 'inertia' provisions where a contract of fixed duration will automatically be extended unless the consumer chooses otherwise, and the deadline for doing so is unreasonably early.

In making an assessment of *good faith*, the regulations require that regard must be had in particular to the strength of the bargaining positions of the parties; whether the consumer had an inducement to agree to the term; whether the goods or services were sold or supplied to the special order of the consumer; and the extent to which the seller or supplier has dealt fairly and equitably with the consumer. (Many of these are similar to the guidelines for 'reasonable' in UCTA; see page 146.)

An unfair term will not be binding on the consumer, but the contract may continue if it is capable of existing without that term. A complaint may also be made to the Director General of Fair Trading who may seek or accept an undertaking from the supplier to discontinue the use of a particular term. A substantial number of exemption clauses have apparently been abandoned by businesses as a result of persuasion by the Director.

The court, on an application by the Director, may grant an injunction on such terms as it thinks fit.

Specimen questions

1. (a) Explain the strict legal distinction between conditions and warranties.
   (b) Jones agreed to hire a specific type of car for a week's holiday and called at the premises of the hire firm to collect it on the morning of his departure. Advise him in each of the following situations:
      (i) The car is an older model with a higher petrol consumption.
      (ii) The luggage capacity of the car is much smaller than the hire firm previously stated.
      (iii) Part of the bodywork of the car is in a very dangerous condition.

2. (a) Under what circumstances will terms be implied into contracts to cover issues for which the parties have made no express provision?
   (b) Penny buys a new word processor from Stephen for use in her office. The word processor was selected from Stephen's catalogue which also contains a clear statement that Stephen accepts no responsibility for errors in description of any of the catalogue items.

      Penny has now discovered that the word processor had been previously sold to another customer and returned to Stephen shortly afterwards as unsuitable for that other customer's needs.

      Advise her as to the grounds on which she may seek a remedy.

3. (a) To what extent have the courts intervened to protect parties to a contract who would otherwise suffer from the presence of an exclusion clause?
   (b) William, a wholesaler, receives an urgent order for certain electrical goods. He therefore agrees to buy these goods from Martin, a manufacturer, who promises delivery in about two weeks' time. During the negotiations, Martin produces a catalogue of his firm's products, which he leaves on William's desk.

William does not look at the catalogue and places it in the waste paper basket after Martin has left.

Martin does not deliver for two months and William loses his order. Martin then produces the goods and explains that labour trouble has upset production. When William refuses to accept delivery, Martin points out a clause in the catalogue that excuses late delivery for any reasonable cause.

Advise William.

4. S. Cleaners Ltd offered 'to clean two garments for the price of one'. A notice was displayed in the shop to this effect but with the addition, in smaller print, of a statement that the customer must agree in return to accept full responsibility if anything should happen to the garments. A similar statement was printed on the back of the tickets, which were handed to customers when they deposited the garments.

Albert brought two jackets for cleaning. Because of poor eyesight he was unable to read the small print on the notice, and he put the ticket in his pocket without reading it.

Some days later when Albert collected the jackets he saw that one had now been badly torn. After wearing the other jacket he contracted a skin disease which was caused by a chemical that the cleaner had used.

Advise Albert.

5. (a) Many contractual clauses purport to exclude liability for injury, loss or damage. Explain the general rules determining the effectiveness of such clauses.

(b) Discuss the effectiveness of the following statements:
(i) a notice in a car park that reads 'No liability is accepted for any cars parked here';
(ii) a sign in a shop window that states 'Goods bought in the sale will not be exchanged'.

6. It is difficult to exclude or limit liability when entering a contract. In what ways has freedom to contract in this respect been restricted by the following:
(a) the Unfair Contract Terms Act 1977;
(b) the Unfair Terms in Consumer Contracts Regulations 1999?

Unit 15. Performance, Breach and Remedies

A. Performance

The number of contracts broken is very small in relation to the number performed, but it is the broken contracts which attract attention. Since most contracts are made with the intention of performance, and most are so performed, this method of discharging the bargain will be discussed first.

The basic rule is that each party must perform completely and precisely what he has bargained to do.

> In *Re Moore & Co. and Landauer & Co.* (1921) the buyer ordered a consignment of canned fruit, to be packed in cases of 30 tins each. The correct amount was delivered, but about half was in cases of 24 tins each. It was held that the buyer was entitled to reject the whole consignment.

This rule is not always so inflexible as it seems. Difficult questions of interpretation sometimes arise as to exactly what the parties *did* promise to do, and the court will try to give a common-sense meaning to the terms agreed.

> In *Peter Darlington Partners Ltd* v. *Gosho Ltd* (1964), the seller agreed to supply a quantity of canary seed on a 'pure basis'. The seed delivered was 98 per cent pure, and evidence was given that this was the highest standard of purity which it was normally possible to obtain in the trade. The seller was held to have performed his obligation.

> In *Reardon Smith Line Ltd* v. *Hansen-Tangen* (1976), the contract involved building a ship. It specified details of the proposed vessel, and referred to 'yard no. 354' as the place for building. In fact a ship was supplied which met all of the requirements, but was built at another yard. The defendants rejected it on this pretext (but in reality because the market had fallen and they no longer wanted a ship). It was held that the rejection was wrongful.

151

The reference to 'yard no. 354' was merely an indication of what was intended, not a term in the contract that the vessel *must* be built there.

The courts will also ignore microscopic deviations, such as a few pounds in a load of thousands of tons.

If one party *has* broken his obligations, it will normally be no defence to him that the breach was not his fault. He has promised to perform his contract, and he will be liable if he does not. Only if some outside cause makes performance physically, legally or commercially *impossible* will he have an excuse for non-performance (Unit 16). The fact that he has taken all reasonable care will be no defence to him.

In *Frost* v. *Aylesbury Dairy Co. Ltd* (1905), the dairy supplied milk infected with typhoid germs, and Mrs Frost died of the disease. It was held that, even if the dairy could prove that it had taken all possible precautions, it was still liable for breach of its implied duty to supply milk which was reasonably fit for drinking.

The consequences of non-performance will be discussed later. If the breach is a minor one, a breach of warranty, the contract will not be discharged. Both parties must go on with it, but the injured party can recover damages. If there has been a more serious breach, a breach of condition, the injured party will have a right to discharge the contract and bring it to an end.

Special rules as to performance apply to an obligation to pay money. It is the duty of the debtor to seek out and tender to the creditor, at a reasonable time of day, payment of the correct amount of money in *legal tender*, without any necessity for the creditor to give change. Legal tender consists of those coins or notes which by law must be accepted in payment of a debt. It comprises bank notes up to any amount; 20p, 50p and £1 pieces up to £10; silver (or cupro-nickel) coins of 10p or less up to £5; and bronze coins up to 20p. A cheque is not legal tender, and the creditor need not take it in payment. If a cheque is taken, it will normally be treated as conditional payment, and the debt will not be discharged until the cheque is honoured. On the other hand, payment by cheque card or credit card does discharge the card-holder. The supplier must recover the money from the card company instead. If the latter becomes insolvent and does not pay, the card-holder is not liable.

If a creditor refuses to take the money when tendered, the debt is not discharged; the debtor must still pay, but the creditor must now come and seek him. If money is sent by post, the risk of loss lies upon the sender unless his creditor has authorized him to use the post. In this latter event, the risk passes to the creditor, provided that the sender takes reasonable precautions for care of the money in transit.

Where a debtor owes several debts to his creditor, and pays a sum insufficient to satisfy them all, it may be important to determine which debts the payment satisfies or reduces. The creditor will prefer to appropriate the payment to the oldest debts, because after six years they may become unenforceable. The rule, however, is that the debtor has a right to appropriate at the time of payment. Only if he does not appropriate then, can the creditor appropriate at any time thereafter. Exceptionally, in the case of current accounts, the rule is that first debts are paid first, for where money is continually paid in and out it would be difficult to carry out specific appropriation with every payment.

B. Breach of contract

Breach of contract can occur in several ways. For example, one party may expressly repudiate his liabilities and refuse to perform his side of the bargain. This can happen either at or before the time when performance was due. If a party renounces his obligations in advance, this is known as *anticipatory* breach. A person can impliedly renounce his obligations by rendering himself incapable of performing them; for example, if he had contracted to sell a specific painting, he would renounce the contract by selling the painting elsewhere. Alternatively, one party may simply fail to perform the contract. He may fail altogether to perform his bargain or he may merely fail to perform one, or some, of his many obligations under the agreement. If the obligation broken was a major part of the contract, there will be *breach of condition*; if only a minor part, there will be *breach of warranty*.

Sometimes the courts have classified a breach according to whether or not it is 'fundamental', but this classification was used mainly in relation to exemption clauses (Unit 14).

Effects of breach

1. Every breach of contract will give an injured party the right to recover damages (see below).
2. If the breach is sufficiently serious, it also gives the injured party a right to avoid the contract and bring it to an end. This right arises if the contract has been repudiated, or if there is breach of condition. It will not arise for breach of warranty.

The physical consequences of breach can be so serious that the injured party has no choice. He may have to treat the contract as ended if, for example, the property is destroyed. Subject to this, however, he need not end the contract unless he wants to. He can either avoid the agreement and no longer perform his side; or he can go on with it and either be content with defective performance from the other (recovering damages for this) or, sometimes, continue to press for performance. If he does wish to end the contract, he must do so reasonably promptly and, as with rescission for misrepresentation (Unit 13), the right is lost if he 'affirms' the agreement.

If a term is so wide that it is not possible to classify it in advance as a condition or a mere warranty, then the right to avoid the contract will depend upon the seriousness of the breach; see *Hong Kong Fir Shipping Co. Ltd* v. *Kawasaki Kisen Kaisha Ltd* (Unit 14).

In practice, particularly in larger contracts, words such as 'condition' and 'warranty' are often used to mean many things. Nevertheless, whatever a term is

153

called, the breach of a major term is treated as a breach of condition, and breach of a minor term as a breach of warranty.

Terms implied by statute are very often classified in advance. For example, the terms implied by sections 13–15 of the Sale of Goods Act are all named in the Act as conditions, and breach entitles the buyer to withdraw from the contract.

Generally, delivery and payment for goods are concurrent obligations, so that unless otherwise agreed payment is due on delivery. Late payment does not normally entitle the seller to avoid, unless the parties have specifically agreed otherwise. On the other hand, a time set for delivery of the goods is very frequently treated as a condition, and lateness entitles the buyer to reject the goods and end the contract. The buyer can, alternatively, waive failure to deliver on time, but impose a new deadline, breach of which will again entitle him to set the contract aside.

> In *Charles Rickards Ltd* v. *Oppenheim* (1950), the buyer ordered a new car body, to be ready in seven months' time. It was not, but the buyer agreed to wait a further three months. When it was still not completed, the buyer imposed a new deadline and indicated that he would cancel the order unless the body was ready within a further four weeks. He was held entitled to do so, and to refuse the car body when it was finally tendered months later.

3. If one party renounces his obligations and commits an anticipatory breach, the injured party may have two possible courses of action. He may treat the contract as at an end and bring an action immediately, either for damages for breach or for reasonable remuneration for the work which he has performed.

> In *Hochster* v. *De La Tour* (1853), the defendant agreed in April to employ the claimant as a courier on a European tour as from 1 June. In May, the defendant repudiated this agreement, and the claimant was held entitled to commence proceedings immediately, before waiting for 1 June.

The claimant may, in fact, be forced to adopt this course if the defendant has made it impossible to go on with the contract, perhaps by destroying the subject-matter. In any event, when the contract ends, the claimant must try to mitigate his loss immediately, for example by seeking another job or a new supplier.

Alternatively, since renunciation does not generally discharge a contract automatically, the injured party can often continue to press for performance until the due date arrives. If this is done, the contract continues to exist, for the benefit and at the risk of both parties, until the final date for performance. If, before that date, performance becomes impossible, this will discharge the contract without the party who renounced it having to pay damages.

> In *Avery* v. *Bowden* (1855), a ship arrived at Odessa for a cargo of wheat and was met by a refusal to load. This renunciation was not accepted and, before the last date for performance arrived, war broke out between England and Russia. This discharged the contract, and the shipowner was unable to recover damages.

C. Damages for breach of contract

Whenever one person has broken a contract, the other can recover damages which are assessed according to the following principles:

1. The basic rule is that the claimant should be *compensated*, but no more than compensated, for loss which he has suffered as a result of the breach. Loss can be financial, damage to property, personal injuries or even distress to the claimant, as where a holiday firm defaults on its obligations; see *Jarvis* v. *Swans Tours Ltd* (1973). Where no loss has been suffered, as where a seller fails to deliver the goods but the buyer is able to purchase elsewhere at no extra cost, the court may award *nominal* damages, a nominal sum, perhaps of £2, to mark the breach.

   Exemplary or *punitive* damages, which exceed the actual loss suffered by an amount intended to punish the offending party, are not normally awarded for breach of contract, although they have been awarded in the past against banks who have dishonoured traders' cheques when the account had sufficient funds to meet them.

2. The claimant, however, cannot be compensated for *all* of the consequences which might logically 'result' from the defendant's breach, otherwise there might be no end to liability. Some loss, therefore, will be too remote.

   > In *Hadley* v. *Baxendale* (1854), a mill owner entrusted a broken crankshaft to a carrier, for delivery to an engineer who would replace it. Delivery was delayed through the fault of the carrier, and the mill stood idle longer than was necessary. The mill owner recovered some damages against the carrier, but the claim for loss of profits was disallowed, because it was not shown that the carrier knew that the mill would have to stand idle.

   The court suggested two tests which still form the basis of the rules covering remoteness of damage. The damage or loss treated as resulting from the breach should only include:

   (a) such damage as may fairly and reasonably be considered as arising naturally, that is, according to the usual course of things, from the breach; and

   (b) such other loss as may reasonably be supposed to have been in the contemplation of both parties at the time they made the contract, so that the defendant in effect accepted responsibility for it.

   The working of these rules can best be illustrated by some of the cases which have arisen.

   > In *Horne* v. *Midland Railway Co.* (1873), Horne had a contract to manufacture boots for the French army at a price higher than the normal market price, provided that he could deliver by a certain date. The boots were consigned to the railway company, which was informed of the importance of the delivery date but not the special price. Delivery was delayed, the boots were rejected and had to be sold elsewhere at below the normal market price. Horne only recovered the difference between his re-sale price and the *market* price. His claim for the difference between the *contract* price and the price on re-sale failed, because the carriers did not know of the original (higher) contract price.

   > In *Victoria Laundry* (*Windsor*) *Ltd* v. *Newman Industries Ltd* (1949), a laundry firm ordered a new boiler which arrived late. The firm was held entitled to recover damages

155

for *normal* loss of profits, because the supplier should have anticipated this. It was not, however, entitled to recover for further losses due to losing an exceptionally profitable contract of which the suppliers did not know.

In *The Heron II* (1969), a shipowner was late in delivering a cargo of sugar to Basrah, and by the time of delivery the market price had fallen. It was held that the loss of profits could be recovered, because this possibility must reasonably have been in the contemplation of the parties.

3. At least when the contract is ended, the injured party must try to *mitigate* or minimize his loss, that is, take all reasonable steps to reduce it. A worker who is wrongly dismissed must attempt to find other work; a seller whose goods are rejected must attempt to get the best price for them elsewhere; a buyer of goods which are not delivered must attempt to buy as cheaply as possible elsewhere. Loss arising from failure to take such steps will not be recovered. On the other hand, only *reasonable* steps need to be taken to mitigate; the buyer, for example, need not tour the globe looking for the cheapest alternative supplier.

4. Damages for breach of contract will not normally be reduced for the claimant's contributory negligence, unlike in tort (see page 101). The only circumstances in which contributory negligence can apply are for breach of a contractual duty of care.

In *Sayers* v. *Harlow UDC* (Unit 10), the claimant had to put money into the door slot to gain access to the public lavatory. She therefore had a contract with the local authority, and could have sued them for breach of this as well as for the tort of negligence. Her damages could have been reduced for her contributory negligence in either case.

The defence will not apply to breach of a *strict* contractual duty, where negligence need not be proved (as in *Frost* v. *Aylesbury Dairy Co. Ltd*, see page 152); and the damages will not be reduced for the claimant's contributory negligence if the defendant has been fraudulent.

5. In some cases, the parties, foreseeing the possibility of breach, make an attempt in the original contract to assess in advance the damages which will be payable on breach. Such provision for *liquidated* damages will be perfectly valid if it is a genuine attempt to pre-estimate the likely loss. If it is not a genuine pre-estimate, however, but an attempt to impose punitive damages where none would otherwise be awarded, then the liquidated damages clause will be void as a *penalty*. The essence of a penalty is that it was inserted *in terrorem*, to frighten the potential defaulter. Such clauses often used to appear in hire-purchase agreements, so that if a hirer returned the goods after paying only one instalment, he might have to bring his payments under the agreement up to half or more of the original hire-purchase price. The courts held such clauses to be void and, where the Consumer Credit Act 1974 applies, such penalties are invalidated by statute.

In *Bridge* v. *Campbell Discount Co. Ltd* (1962), Bridge agreed to take a vehicle on hire-purchase for £482. He paid a deposit of £105 and one instalment of £10, but then repudiated the agreement because he could afford no more. He was sued for a further

£206, under a clause in the agreement requiring him to bring his total payments up to two-thirds of the hire-purchase price of £482 'by way of agreed compensation for depreciation of the vehicle'. Bridge had only had the vehicle for a few weeks, had returned it in good condition, and had already paid £115. The clause was held void as a penalty.

In *Interfoto Ltd* v. *Stiletto Ltd* (Unit 14), the offending clause would probably have been void as a penalty, but this point was not pleaded.

If the buyer or other customer is a natural person acting for non-business purposes, a penalty clause may be caught by The Unfair Terms in Consumer Contracts Regulations 1999 (see page 147). If so, it will not be binding on the consumer.

Contracts for the sale of goods and building contracts sometimes provide that, in the event of late performance, a specified sum shall be payable for each day of delay. Minimum price agreements have sometimes contained similar provisions to apply in the event of breach.

In *Ford Motor Co. Ltd* v. *Armstrong* (1915), a promise to pay an *exorbitant* sum for each car sold below the listed price was held void as a penalty.

Note that in practice the phrase 'penalty clause' is often used to describe all types of provision imposing monetary sanctions for late or defective performance. Nevertheless, whatever the clause is called, the above tests apply: the clause can be valid if it is genuinely related to the claimant's likely losses (i.e. liquidated damages), and it will be void if it imposes an exorbitant penalty.

D. Other remedies for breach

1. *Claims on a quantum meruit.* In some situations a claim for damages may not be the appropriate financial remedy. This may happen where the claimant is prevented from completing his side of the bargain by the defendant's conduct and repudiation. The claimant may have done a lot of work, but not yet earned any fee. He may be entitled to claim on a *quantum meruit* basis (for so much as he deserves) for what he has done.

In *Planché* v. *Colburn* (1831) the claimant was commissioned by a publisher to write a book for £100. After he had done the necessary research and written part of the book, the publisher repudiated the contract. It was held that the claimant could recover £50 on a *quantum meruit*.

A claim on this basis may also be made where work has been done under a void contract. The claimant cannot recover damages for breach, because no contract exists, but he may recover on a *quantum meruit*.

In *Craven-Ellis* v. *Canons Ltd* (1936), the claimant recovered reasonable remuneration for work which he had done as managing director of the company, when it transpired that his appointment was void.

In *British Steel Corporation* v. *Cleveland Bridge & Engineering Co. Ltd* (1984), BSC supplied steel to the defendants while still negotiating terms. Negotiations failed and

157

there was, therefore, no contract. BSC was entitled to a *quantum meruit* payment for what it had supplied and Cleveland had used.

2. A *decree for specific performance* is an equitable remedy which is sometimes granted where damages would not be an adequate remedy. It is an order of the court directing the party in breach to carry out his promises, on pain of penalties for contempt of court. Since it is equitable, it is discretionary (Unit 1). The following principles *normally* apply:

(a) It will not be awarded where damages would be enough and, for this reason, it will rarely be granted in commercial transactions. Monetary compensation will usually enable a disappointed buyer to obtain similar commodities elsewhere. In a sale of goods, the seller will normally only be ordered to hand over the article specifically where it is unique, such as an original painting.

> In *Cohen* v. *Roche* (1927), the court refused to order specific performance of a contract to sell some Hepplewhite chairs which were rare, but not unique. Similar chairs could be bought elsewhere, albeit with difficulty.

On the other hand, each piece of land *is* unique, and the main use of the remedy today is in contracts for the sale of land.

(b) The court must be sure that it can adequately supervise enforcement. Therefore contracts of a personal nature, such as employment, which depend upon good faith which the court cannot ensure, will not be specifically enforced. Similarly building contracts will not be enforced.

> In *Cooperative Insurance Society Ltd* v. *Argyll Stores Ltd* (1997), the tenant of a shop was contractually bound to keep it open until the year 2014. The shop was losing money, and the tenant closed it, admitting liability to pay damages. The court refused specific performance however, because the tenant could not be forced to work.

(c) Specific performance will not be awarded either to or against a minor.

(d) The court may exercise its discretion to refuse specific performance in any other situation where it is not felt just or equitable to grant it.

> In *Malins* v. *Freeman* (1837), the remedy was refused where a bidder foolishly bought property at an auction in the belief that he was bidding for an entirely different lot. It would have been harsh to compel him to take the property; the seller could still sue for damages if he so wished.

3. *An injunction* is an order of the court directing a person *not* to break his contract. It is normally appropriate to enforce a negative provision in the agreement and, being an equitable remedy, is only awarded on the same principles as specific performance. It can, however, be awarded to enforce a negative stipulation in a contract for services or employment.

> In *Warner Brothers Pictures Incorporated* v. *Nelson* (1937), an actress had contracted with the film company not to work as an actress for anyone else during her present

contract. It was held that she could be restrained by injunction from breaking this undertaking.

On the other hand, an injunction will not be granted in contracts of employment if it would operate as an indirect way of specifically enforcing the agreement; thus, Nelson could only be restrained from working elsewhere *as an actress*, otherwise she might be faced with the alternatives of either working for Warner Brothers or starving. An employer, however, may *temporarily* be restrained from dismissing an employee; this is not tantamount to specific performance, because the employer can usually suspend the person on full pay if the employee's presence is an embarrassment.

> In *Hill* v. *C. A. Parsons & Co. Ltd* (1972), the claimant was dismissed with inadequate notice as a result of trade union pressure to maintain a 'closed shop'. The court granted an injunction restraining Parsons Ltd from dismissing Hill until adequate notice had been given.

As will be seen, injunctions are sometimes granted to enforce lawful restraints on trade; see cases such as *Home Counties Dairies Ltd* v. *Skilton* (Unit 17). The remedy may be granted to enforce negative promises in contracts relating to land; for example, a purchaser may be restrained from breaking his contractual promise not to build on the land sold. In exceptional circumstances, injunctions may even be issued to order the seller of goods not to withhold delivery.

> In *Sky Petroleum Ltd* v. *VIP Petroleum Ltd* (1974), the parties made a 10-year agreement in 1970 that VIP would supply all Sky Ltd's petrol requirements. In November 1973 a dispute arose between the parties, and VIP withheld supplies. In the oil crisis then existing, Sky Ltd could not get supplies from any other source (contrast *Cohen* v. *Roche*, page 158). The court granted a temporary injunction restraining VIP from withholding reasonable supplies, even though this was equivalent to a temporary order of specific performance.

Specimen questions

1. (a) It is said that each party to a contract must perform completely that which he had agreed to do. Discuss this statement.
   (b) PCM Ltd buys photocopying machines from the manufacturer, and hires them to firms. Your firm hires such a machine from PCM Ltd for one year. The following problems arise:
     (i) the machine is delivered two hours after the agreed time;
     (ii) the 'stop' button, which should light up when pressed, does not do so, although it does stop the machine;
     (iii) the machine overheats badly when operated.
   PCM Ltd proves that each problem was solely the manufacturer's fault. Discuss whether any of the above problems entitles your firm to any remedies, and if so what, against PCM Ltd.

2. Advise *B* in both of the following situations, explaining the relevant principles of law:
   (a) *B* agrees to buy a second-hand car from *S* for £1000; the profit of *S* from the transaction would be £200. *B* then refuses to go through with the purchase. *S* sells the car to *X* for £1000 but claims £200 loss of profit from *B* on the grounds that *X* would have bought another car from him and he has thereby lost another sale. Would your advice differ if the car had been a new one and *S* had a number of cars of this model for sale?
   (b) *B* agrees to buy a consignment of coffee from *S* for £1000 and then refuses to accept the goods. By this time the market price has fallen to £900. *S* turns down a sale at this price as he feels that the price will rise again. The market price continues to fall and the coffee is eventually sold for £800. *S* claims £200 from *B*.

3. (a) What action is open to the injured party when a contract is repudiated by the other party before the date of performance?
   (b) Under what circumstances is (i) a decree for specific performance, and (ii) an injunction likely to be awarded for a breach of contract?

4. (a) *M* agrees to build an extension to *N*'s factory at a cost of £8000, this sum to be paid upon completion. After *M* has committed work and materials to the project to the extent of £5000, *N* claims that the workmanship is defective and refuses to allow *M* on to the site to complete the work. Advise *M*.
   (b) *P*, a well-known musician, agrees to give a performance at *Q*'s club and promises that he will not give another performance in the same town for one month before or after the date in question. *Q* later hears that *R*, a rival club owner, has engaged *P* for a much larger fee to appear at *R*'s club the following night. Advise *Q*.

5. Better Builders contracts to reconstruct a laundry and to complete the work within eight weeks. The work, in fact, takes ten weeks and the laundry is now claiming damages for the loss of normal profits during the two additional weeks and also for the loss of a particularly valuable contract, which it could not accept because its plant was out of action.
   (a) Advise Better Builders.
   (b) To what extent would your advice differ if the contract had contained a clause under which Better Builders agreed to pay £1200 by way of penalty for each week late in completing the work?

6. (a) Various remedies are available to a person who has suffered following a breach of contract. Some remedies may be claimed as a right, while other remedies depend upon the exercise of discretion by a court.
   Discuss this statement.
   (b) Maurice is offered and accepts a post of cost accountant to begin in three weeks. One week later, he receives a letter from his prospective employer stating that his services will not be required.
   Advise Maurice.

Unit 16. Discharge, Limitation and Privity

A contract may be discharged, that is, come to an end, in four main ways. Two of these, namely performance and discharge as a result of breach, arise directly out of the terms of the original contract, and were discussed in the last unit. The present unit is concerned with methods of discharge which do not necessarily arise out of what was originally agreed, but from extraneous events. These methods of discharge are new agreement and frustration.

Two other matters which affect the right to sue on a contract will also be discussed here, namely the time limits affecting *when* actions must be brought, and the rules of privity affecting *who* can sue or be sued.

A. Discharge by agreement

There are three main ways in which a contract can be discharged by agreement.

1. The parties may have made provision for discharge in their original contract. For example, the parties may have agreed at the outset that the contract should end automatically on some determining event or on the expiration of a fixed time. Thus goods may be hired, premises may be leased, or a person employed for a fixed term. On the expiration of the term, the contract will cease.

   Alternatively, the contract may contain a provision entitling one or both parties to terminate it if they so wish. Thus a contract of employment can normally be brought to an end by either party on reasonable notice to the other (subject only to statutory minimum periods of notice laid down by the Employment Act). Hire-purchase contracts usually give the hirer a contractual right to end the agreement and return the goods at any time; where the Consumer Credit Act 1974 applies, there is also a statutory right to do this.

Discharge in these ways does arise out of the terms of the original agreement.

2. Discharge can also arise, not out of the original agreement, but by reason of a new, extraneous contract. In order that the new agreement may discharge the old one, however, the new contract must be valid; for example, there must be consideration.

Where neither side of the original contract has yet been performed, there will be no difficulty; each side still owes duties, and the consideration for one party waiving his rights is the waiver of rights by the other. Thus the buyer and seller may agree to cancel an order; the seller need no longer supply the goods, and the buyer no longer has to pay.

The position is more complicated where one party has completely performed his original obligations. The agreement for discharge will only be binding if, in return for the release, the other party does or promises something which he is *not* already bound to do, such as paying earlier than he was bound to do or in a different manner.

> In *Re Charge Card Services Ltd* (1986), a garage agreed to accept payment for petrol by a charge card instead of cash. This was held to discharge the customer's obligation to pay cash so that, when the card company became insolvent, the customer did not have to pay again.

In the absence of such new consideration, the agreement for release will not be binding, and the original contract will stand; see *D & C Builders Ltd* v. *Rees* (1966) (Unit 11). For this reason discharge by new agreement is sometimes called discharge by accord (agreement) and satisfaction (consideration).

3. Finally, one party can release the other unilaterally, without consideration, but only if he does so by *deed*.

B. Discharge by frustration

Until the last century, the obligation to perform a contractual duty was absolute. If it became physically impossible for a party to perform his bargain, he nevertheless had to pay damages for breach, and if extraneous events took away the whole purpose of the contract without the fault of either party, the parties still had to continue with the agreement.

> In *Paradine* v. *Jane* (1647), a lessee was evicted during the Civil War. It was held that he still had to pay the rent; the fact that he could not enjoy the property because of events beyond his control was of no concern to the lessor, and was no excuse.

Starting with the case of *Taylor* v. *Caldwell* in 1863 (see below), the courts have developed the doctrine of frustration as an exception to this absolute rule. If some outside event occurs, for which neither party is responsible and which makes total nonsense of the original agreement, then the contract will be discharged by frustration. A radical change in circumstances can sometimes, therefore, be pleaded by a party as a valid excuse for not performing his side of the bargain. This doctrine must be approached with caution, however, because the courts have understandably been reluctant to accept anything but the most fundamental changes as frustrating events. The following are the main examples.

1. *Subsequent physical impossibility.* This will occur where, *after* the contract was made, it becomes physically impossible or impracticable to perform it. (If this was already impossible when the contract was *made*, the agreement would be void from the outset.)

> In *Taylor* v. *Caldwell* (1863), a music hall hired for a series of concerts was burnt down before the date for the first performance. This was held to frustrate the contract, because there was no longer any hall to hire. The hirer, therefore, no longer had to pay.

> In *Robinson* v. *Davison* (1871), a pianist, who was engaged to give a concert on a specified date, became ill and was incapable of appearing. It was held that this frustrated the contract.

2. *Subsequent illegality.* This will occur where, *after* the contract was made, a change in the law or in the circumstances renders it illegal to perform the agreement.

> In *Avery* v. *Bowden* (1855), the contract to load a cargo at Odessa was eventually discharged by the outbreak of the Crimean War, which made it thenceforth an illegal contract of trading with the enemy.

3. *Basis of the contract removed.* The contract may be frustrated where both parties made it on the basis of a future event which does not take place.

> In *Chandler* v. *Webster* (1904), the contract was for the hire of a room in Pall Mall for the day of Edward VII's coronation procession. The rent was over £140, because the procession would pass directly beneath the window. Unfortunately the coronation was postponed when the King became ill. This was held to frustrate the contract.

4. *Frustration of the commercial purpose of the contract.* A change may occur which makes a total nonsense of what was originally agreed, so that what the parties would have to perform bears no relation to what was originally intended. This change must be radical; an event which merely makes it more difficult or expensive for a party to perform the contract will be no excuse. It is rare that a contract will be frustrated on this ground.

> In *Metropolitan Water Board* v. *Dick, Kerr & Co.* (1918), a firm of contractors agreed in 1914 to build a reservoir. In 1916, under wartime emergency powers, the Government ordered the contractor to stop work and sell the plant. This was held to frustrate the contract. Although it might eventually be possible to start work again after the war, the enforced hold-up for an indefinite period made nonsense of the contract.

> On the other hand, in *Tsakiroglou Ltd* v. *Noblee & Thorl G.m.b.H.* (1962), the sellers agreed to deliver groundnuts from Port Sudan to the buyers in Hamburg, and to ship them in November or December 1956. In November 1956, the Suez Canal was closed, and the sellers would now have had to ship the goods round the Cape of Good Hope, a much longer and more expensive journey. It was held that this did *not* frustrate the contract, but merely made it more difficult to perform.

163

If a seller wishes to protect himself against liability to the buyer for delays due to such matters as shortages or non-delivery of raw materials, he should make special provision for this in the contract. If one party makes a promise which he fails to perform, the court is reluctant to allow him to say, in effect, 'Oh, but it's not my fault'.

The effects of frustration

Frustration automatically brings the contract to an end and renders it void. As a general rule, all sums paid by either party in pursuance of the contract before it was discharged are recoverable, and all sums not yet paid cease to be due.

> In the *Fibrosa* case (1943), an English company agreed in 1939 to make some machinery for a Polish buyer at a price of £4800. The buyer paid an initial sum of £1000. When war broke out, Poland was occupied by the German army, and the contract was, therefore, frustrated by subsequent illegality. It was held that the London agent of the Polish buyer had no further liability, and could recover the £1000 already paid.

This was rather harsh to the seller, who had already done considerable work and incurred expense in manufacturing the goods. The Law Reform (Frustrated Contracts) Act 1943, therefore, restated the general rule, but introduced two exceptions to it.

1. If one party has, before the time of discharge, incurred expenses in performing it, the court may in its discretion allow him to keep or recover all or part of sums *already paid or due* under the contract.
2. If one party has, by reason of anything done by the other, obtained a valuable benefit (other than the payment of money), then the other may recover such sum as the court considers just.

The Law Reform (Frustrated Contracts) Act applies to all contracts except (a) contracts for the carriage of goods by sea, (b) contracts of insurance, (c) contracts containing special provisions to meet the case of frustration, and (d) contracts for the sale of specific goods where the agreement is frustrated because the goods perish before risk passes to the buyer. This last category is covered by the Sale of Goods Act 1979, section 7 (Unit 19).

C. Limitation of actions

Contractual obligations are not enforceable for ever. Apart from other considerations, evidence becomes less reliable with the passage of time, and therefore, after a certain period, the law bars any remedy.

The Limitation Act 1980 lays down the general periods within which an action must be brought. These are as follows:

1. Actions based on a *simple* contract will be barred after six years from the date when the cause of action accrued.

2. Where the contract is made by *deed*, actions can be brought up to 12 years from the date when the cause of action accrued.
3. Actions to recover *land* can be brought up to 12 years from the date when the cause of action accrued.

A right of action 'accrues' when breach occurs. Thus, if a loan is made for a fixed time, the right will accrue when this time expires. If no time is agreed it will be when a written demand for payment is made.

If, when the cause of action accrues, the claimant is under a disability by reason of minority or unsoundness of mind, the period will not run until the disability has ended or until his death, whichever comes first. Once the period has started to run, subsequent insanity will have no effect.

If the claimant is the victim of fraud or acts under a mistake or if the defendant deliberately conceals relevant facts, the limitation period will not begin until the true state of affairs is discovered or should reasonably have been discovered.

> In *Lynn* v. *Bamber* (1930), some plum trees were sold in 1921 with an undertaking by the seller that they were of a particular type. Not until they matured in 1928 was it discovered that they were of inferior quality. It was held that an action for damages could still be brought, since the fraudulent misrepresentations by the seller had postponed the operation of the period of limitation.

Provided that the limitation period has not already expired, the period may be extended where the party in breach either acknowledges his liability in writing, signed by him or his agent, or makes part payment in respect of the debt or claim. Time will then begin to run afresh from the date of acknowledgement or part payment. Property obtained by theft may be recovered at any time unless it has passed to a bona fide purchaser who is protected after six years.

Equitable remedies, such as specific performance or an injunction, are not covered by the ordinary limitation periods, but will almost invariably be barred much earlier under general equitable principles. An equitable remedy must be sought reasonably promptly, because 'equity aids the vigilant, not the indolent'. A short delay, of weeks or even days, may bar the remedy; see also *Bernstein* v. *Pamson Motors Ltd* (page 186).

D. Privity of contract

As a general rule, the legal effects of a contract are confined to the contracting parties. At common law an agreement between *A* and *B* cannot confer any legally enforceable benefit on a stranger, cannot impose any obligations on a stranger, and cannot take away the rights of a stranger. Only *A* can sue *B* for breach, and vice versa.

> In *Adler* v. *Dickson* (1955), a passenger on board a ship was injured by the negligence of the master and boatswain. Her ticket from the shipping company provided that 'passengers are carried at passengers' entire risk'. Nevertheless she successfully sued the master and the boatswain; the exclusion clause was in a contract between the passenger and the company, and could not protect employees.

165

This rule is of great importance in English law. A customer who buys a new car from a garage cannot sue the manufacturer for breach of contract, because the customer contracted only with the garage. If the car breaks down and a passenger is injured, the passenger has no contract with either the manufacturer or the garage. The claimant can only sue in tort in these cases, and must, therefore, prove that the defendant has been negligent (see *Donoghue* v. *Stevenson* in Unit 9). Similarly, a shareholder cannot take the benefit of a contract made by the company, because the company is a separate legal person (Unit 7).

There are some situations where the privity rule does not apply. For example, where an agent contracts with a third party on behalf of a principal whose existence he does not disclose, the undisclosed principal may sometimes be entitled to step in and sue or be sued on the contract. If two people contract with the intention of creating a trust in favour of a third person (the 'beneficiary'), the latter is unable to enforce the contract. However, he may be entitled to sue for breach of trust.

Contractual rights may be assigned, in which case someone other than the original parties may sue or be sued. A lease of land, for instance, may create rights and obligations that attach to the land, and bind not only the present landlord and tenant, but also future assignees of the lease. More generally, rights are easier to transfer than obligations, if only because the recipient will not be eager to take on new obligations. The consent of the recipient is therefore normally required for obligations.

In other situations the parties to a contract may effectively change by operation of law. Thus, in the case of bankruptcy, rights and liabilities pass to the trustees in bankruptcy, and in the case of death they pass to the personal representatives.

As regards the *benefit* of a contract, by far the most important exceptions to the privity rule come from statute, particularly the Contracts (Rights of Third Parties) Act 1999. Under this Act, a person who is not a party to a contract (a 'third party') may in his own right enforce a term of the contract if:

(a) the contract expressly provides that he may; or
(b) the term purports to confer a benefit on him.

In both cases the third party may be expressly identified, by name, or as a member of a class, or as answering to a particular description; but the third party need not be in existence when the contract is made. The provision can therefore be for the benefit of present and future members of a particular group or organization; or even for an unborn child. Head (b) does not apply if it appears from the contract that the parties did not intend the term to be enforceable by the third party, and it can therefore very easily be excluded by a simple express statement to this effect in the contract.

If the third party sues to enforce a term against the promisor, he may be met with any defence that the promisor would have had against the promisee (including a valid exemption clause), or by, for example, any arbitration clause.

Another important situation where a third party can take the benefit of a contract made between two others is in connection with liability insurance. The contract is between the insured (policy holder) and his insurance company. The company promises to indemnify the policy holder against possible liability to third parties whom he might injure. As a general rule only the policy holder can demand payment from the insurance company. The third party has no contract with anyone. Where the policy holder has become bankrupt, however, the Third Parties (Rights Against Insurers) Act 1930 allows the third party to claim directly from the insurance company; otherwise the money would go to the policy holder's trustee in bankruptcy, and the third party victim might get nothing. The 1930 Act can apply to motor policies as well as to other liability insurance. There are more important provisions for motor insurance, however, in the Road Traffic Act 1988.

A person driving with the owner's consent may be entitled to cover even though not a party to the insurance agreement and, in respect of compulsory third party risks, the person injured can recover directly from the insurance company under section 149.

The *burden* of a contract can be imposed on a stranger where a restrictive covenant is imposed on land at the time of sale, for example a covenant prohibiting its use as an inn or alehouse; this can bind all future occupiers of the land, even though they are not parties to the original contract of sale.

In *Tulk* v. *Moxhay* (1848), the owner of land which included Leicester Square in London sold the Square itself but retained some land round it. The buyer contracted not to build on the Square, but later sold the land and, after it had passed through several hands, an ultimate purchaser did propose to build. It was held that the original seller could restrain the present purchaser from building even though there was no privity of contract between them. The present purchaser had taken with notice of the restrictive covenant, and equity restrained him from breaking it.

Specimen questions

1. Miller decides to stage a big band concert and engages a number of eminent musicians, paying each of them 10 per cent of the agreed fee at the time the separate contracts are made. Four days before the concert he is informed that four of the musicians will not be appearing. Shaw cannot get a visa to enter the country and Armstrong claims that his fee is not large enough. Dorsey has injured his fingers chopping firewood, while James says that he is incapacitated with a heavy cold. Miller believes that the concert will be a failure and decides to cancel it.
   Advise Miller as to:
   (a) the effect of each incident on the contracts, whether he may recover the advance payment from any of these four musicians, and whether he has any further claim for compensation against any of them;
   (b) his legal position with respect to the other members of the band who are willing to appear, and to the public who have bought tickets for the concert.
2. Wheels Ltd, a bus company, secures a licence to operate a new service and orders 10 new buses for this purpose. It pays 10% of the cost to the manufacturer, Maxibus Ltd, when the contract is made.
   Discuss the legal position in both of the following circumstances, before any of the buses have been delivered.

(a) Wheels Ltd states that the licence has now been withdrawn and that it no longer wishes to buy the buses. Maxibus Ltd replies that materials have been bought and that work on the buses has begun.

(b) Maxibus Ltd states that it cannot complete the contract without increasing the price because of the increased cost of materials. Wheels Ltd replies that it will not pay more and that it will claim for loss of profits and for the cost of a ceremony planned for the opening of the new service.

3. Advise Bernard whether he may begin legal proceedings in 2003 in respect of the following:

(a) He bought a case of wine from Charles in 1996, and when the first bottle was opened in 2000 he discovered that it was of an inferior quality to that ordered.

(b) He sold goods to David in 1995. When pressed for payment in 1998, David admitted the debt and promised to pay but has not done so.

(c) He agreed in writing to buy land from Eric in 2000 and now seeks specific performance of the contract.

(d) He lent money to Fred in 1994 without fixing a date for repayment. The first of many demands for the return of the money was made in 1999.

4. Explain the applicable principles of law and advise Weaver in both of the following cases:

(a) Weaver bought a small textiles factory from Spinner. As part of the agreement, Weaver promised to pay Spinner a weekly pension for life and to continue paying this pension to Mrs Spinner after Spinner's death. Spinner has now died and Weaver wonders whether he is still obliged to pay the pension to the widow.

(b) Merchant owed Weaver £1000 for goods supplied. Merchant said that he was in serious financial difficulties and he offered Weaver £600 in full satisfaction of the debt. Weaver accepted this but has now heard that Merchant's business is flourishing. Weaver enquires whether he may claim the balance of the debt.

5. (a) To what extent is it true to say that only a person who is a party to a contract may sue or be sued in respect of its breach?

(b) A contract for the sale of goods includes a provision that the seller will deliver but only at the purchaser's risk. The goods are entrusted by the seller to a carrier for delivery and are damaged by the carrier's negligence.

Advise the purchaser.

6. (a) Discuss the circumstances in which a contract may be discharged by agreement before all the contractual obligations have been performed.

(b) *L*, a builder, contracted to build two houses for *M* and *N*, each house to cost £60 000. When the houses were finished, *M* said that he could not afford to pay the full price and offered *L* £50 000 in full settlement; *L* accepted this amount. *N* said that he would only pay if *L* landscaped the garden; *L* did this at a cost of £2000.

Discuss whether *L* may now recover £10 000 from *M* and £2000 from *N*.

Unit 17. Contracts and Public Policy

Earlier units have dealt with those agreements which English law will recognize as contracts, and the nature, effect and discharge of such agreements. This unit refers to another aspect of the concept of freedom of contract. From the earliest days of this branch of the law, freedom of contract has been subject to overriding considerations of public policy. Some agreements have been completely *illegal*, and the courts will normally do nothing to help parties who rely on them. Other agreements or terms in agreements, while not being illegal, have been held *void*, so that the courts will give no remedy for breach, but will allow money paid under the contract to be recovered. Various statutes have added to the list of contractual provisions which are illegal or void as contrary to public policy at common law.

A. Contracts that are illegal at common law

1. *An agreement to commit a criminal offence or a tort* is probably the oldest example of an illegal contract. An agreement to do something in a friendly foreign country which will be an offence in that country will also be illegal in England under this head.

   In *Allen* v. *Rescous* (1676), the claimant paid the defendant 20 shillings to assault *X* and evict him. It was held that the claimant was not entitled to recover his money when the defendant failed in this illegal purpose.

   In *Foster* v. *Driscoll* (1929), an English partnership, formed to smuggle whisky into the United States at a time when liquor was prohibited there, was held to be illegal in English law.

169

2. *A contract to defraud the Revenue* will be illegal for similar reasons.

> In *Miller* v. *Karlinski* (1945), an agreement between employer and employees to disguise part of the salary as expenses, so as to evade income tax, was held to be illegal. As a result, the employee was not entitled to reclaim arrears of salary from the employer.

3. *Contracts to corrupt public life*, such as contracts to bribe officials, to sell public offices, or to purchase a title or honour are similarly illegal.

> In *Parkinson* v. *College of Ambulance Ltd* (1925), the secretary of the College, which was a charity, promised that he could obtain a knighthood for the claimant in return for a suitable donation. Parkinson donated £3000 but did not obtain a knighthood. His action for the return of the £3000 failed.

4. *Immoral contracts.* This category is limited to contracts for a sexually immoral purpose, such as a contract between a man and a woman for future cohabitation. Any contract clearly connected with an immoral purpose will be illegal.

> In *Pearce* v. *Brooks* (1866), the owner of a horse-drawn coach could not recover the cost of hire from a prostitute who, to his knowledge, had hired it to attract clients.

A contract to pay money for past illicit cohabitation could not be sued upon since the consideration is past.

5. *Contracts for trading with the enemy.* These include all contracts with a person or firm voluntarily residing in enemy territory in time of war. If war breaks out after the contract was made but before it was performed the contract is frustrated by subsequent illegality; see *Fibrosa* case (Unit 16).

6. *Contracts to impede the course of justice.* These include agreements to prevent or hinder the prosecution of a serious criminal offence, for example by paying the victim not to report the offence or not to cooperate in the prosecution.

    Contracts of maintenance, where a person with no legal interest in the proceedings gives financial assistance to another to enable him to bring or defend the proceedings, and contracts of champerty, where a litigant is assisted in return for a share in the proceeds if he wins, are still sometimes illegal under this head.

Effects of illegality

Illegal contracts are invalid, at least to the extent that a party who knows of the illegality cannot sue the other for breach of the illegal purpose. Money paid for such a purpose is irrecoverable; thus in *Parkinson* v. *College of Ambulance Ltd*, Parkinson could not recover his donation. Any contract so closely connected with the illegality as to be tainted by it may also be invalid; thus the contract of hire in *Pearce* v. *Brooks* and the partnership in *Foster* v. *Driscoll* were illegal. However (as several recent cases have illustrated) there are limits to these rules.

1. Where one party was innocent of the illegality, he will be entitled to sue on the contract, even if the other party could not. This will occur where the contract appears perfectly innocent, but one party is performing it for an illegal purpose without the other's knowledge. For example, in *Pearce* v. *Brooks*, had the owner of

the coach not known the purpose for which his customer was using it, he *would* have been entitled to recover his hire.

2. Where one party repents of the illegal purpose before carrying it out, the court may allow him a remedy if he has a cause of action not based on the illegality. On the other hand, his repentance must be genuine; if he withdraws simply because the other party is in breach, or because it has become impossible to carry out the illegal purpose, then the court will not believe his repentance.

3. If the contract is not inherently illegal, but it is performed in an unlawful manner, an action by the offending party might still succeed if the illegality was not his prime motive.

> In *Howard* v. *Shirlstar Transport Ltd* (1990), a pilot was sent to collect a plane from a foreign airport. He took off without permission from local air traffic control, which made his performance illegal in English Law. However his motive was to protect his own life, which was threatened locally. Therefore he was still entitled to his fee.

4. The ownership of goods and rights to land can pass under a contract which is illegal, so long as the person claiming the property does not base his claim directly on his own illegal conduct.

> In *Tinsley* v. *Milligan* (1993), two women bought a house jointly, but registered the legal title in the name of only one of them (*T*) so as to enable the other (*M*) to make illegal social security claims, which they then shared. *M* later repented and ceased to make dishonest claims. Later still, *T* and *M* quarrelled and *M* claimed partial owner-ship of the house in equity. She was held entitled to it. Her claim was based solely on the fact that she had paid part of the price when the house was bought.

B. Contracts that are illegal by statute

The nature and effects of statutory illegality vary with the terms of the Act concerned. Some statutes expressly declare the whole contract illegal, with the same conse-quences as illegality at common law. An example of this is the Life Assurance Act 1774, under which a contract to insure a life in which the proposer has no 'insurable interest' will be illegal. In spite of its title, the Act also applies to insurance of buildings, and liability insurance. The temptations which might be raised if the proposer were free to insure the life or buildings of a stranger are obvious. A proposer will normally have an insurable interest in his own life, the life of his wife, and the lives of debtors and others whose deaths would financially affect him.

> In *Harse* v. *Pearl Life Assurance Co.* (1904), it was held that the claimant had no insurable interest in the life of his mother, whose life he had insured. The policy was illegal, and the claimant was not entitled to recover the premiums which he had paid.

Some difficulty arises from statutes which, while not expressly making a contract illegal, provide that it shall only be carried out by someone who has a licence to do so. For example, licences are required by those who sell alcoholic drinks, or carry goods by road. Someone who acts without a licence commits a criminal offence, but does this render his contracts illegal? The answer depends on the purpose of the legislation in question. If, in the view of the courts, the Act was designed to forbid contracts of this type by unlicensed dealers, so as to protect the public, then the contract will be illegal. If the purpose of licensing was only to raise revenue or to help in the administration of the trade, contracts will not be affected.

> In *Cope* v. *Rowlands* (1836), an unlicensed broker in the City of London was held not to be entitled to sue for his fees, because the purpose of the licensing requirements was to protect the public against possible shady dealers.

> On the other hand, in *Archbolds (Freightage) Ltd* v. *Spanglett Ltd* (1961), a contract by an unlicensed carrier to carry goods by road was held valid, because the legislation was only designed to help in the administration of road transport.

Similar problems arise where a statute requires that certain contracts be carried out in a particular manner, with penalties in the event of breach.

> In *Anderson Ltd* v. *Daniel* (1924), the seller of artificial fertilizers was required by statute to state in the invoice the percentages of certain ingredients. Failure to do this was held to render the contract illegal, and the seller was unable to recover the price of goods which he had delivered.

> On the other hand, in *Shaw* v. *Groom* (1970), a landlord who let unfurnished premises without a proper rent book did recover arrears of rent. The court took the view that the rent book requirements were not central to the contract as a whole, and that the Act did not intend the landlord to lose more in unpaid arrears than could have been imposed by way of fine.

Finally, some statutes declare certain *terms* of a contract to be illegal, without thereby affecting the rest of the contract. For example, a contract for sale of goods can still be valid even if it contains an exemption clause which is void and criminal under the Fair Trading Act (see page 147). Employment can still be valid even if some of the terms are illegal under the Race Relations and Sex Discrimination Acts.

C. Contracts in restraint of trade

It is a long tradition of the common law that all agreements or provisions in agreements which tend to restrain trade are contrary to public policy and therefore *void* (although not generally illegal). Most restraints are still governed by the rules of common law. Some, such as price-fixing agreements, are also governed by statute (see page 176).

Restraints may take many forms, but the following are the main types:

1. Contracts of employment sometimes provide that the employee, after leaving his present employment, may not compete against his present employer either by setting up in business on his own or by working for a rival firm. Similarly, partnership agreements often limit partners from setting up in business or practice nearby for some years after leaving. Even independent commercial agents may sometimes be restrained from switching to another client.
2. On the sale of a business, the buyer will often require the seller to promise that, in future, he will not carry on a similar business in competition with the buyer.

(Otherwise the seller might set up in business nearby and attract all his old customers away from the buyer.)

3. Retailers sometimes make *solus* or similar agreements with suppliers, under which the retailer promises to sell only that supplier's brand of goods. The main cases have involved agreements between garages and petrol companies.

4. Suppliers of goods and services sometimes agree between themselves to fix prices, restrict output, regulate the methods of supply, or otherwise influence the market for their product. These are dealt with under a separate sub-heading on *Monopolies, cartels, price-fixing agreements*, etc. below.

Except under the fourth head above, the restraint will normally be only one clause in a much wider agreement, such as a contract of employment or a sales agreement. In these circumstances, the bulk of the agreement will not be affected; the only clause in question is the one which attempts to impose the restraint.

The rules relating to covenants in restraint are basically the same for all types. Every restraint is *presumed void* unless it can be proved otherwise. It can be proved valid if it can be shown to be reasonable in the interests of both parties *and* in the interests of the public at large.

Reasonableness between the parties depends upon whether the person for whose benefit the covenant was made had any legitimate interest in imposing it, that is, whether he had anything to lose, such as trade secrets or contact with customers. The restraint must then be measured against this interest. The nature of the restraint, its geographical area, the time for which it is to operate, and all other features must be no more than is reasonable to protect the interest in question.

Reasonableness in the public interest affects restraints which have a wide economic effect, particularly restraints under the third head above. This is less likely to be important in restraints on employment.

The common law rules are supplemented by statutory rules applying to commercial agents (see page 68).

Restraints on employment

In the main, the courts have not been sympathetic to restraints which attempt to restrict the right of a person to earn his living where and with whom he likes. Furthermore, the worker may have been 'persuaded' to agree to the restraint because the employer was in a stronger bargaining position. The following cases will illustrate the rules.

> In *Home Counties Dairies Ltd* v. *Skilton* (1970), a milk roundsman had to agree in his original contract of employment that, for one year after leaving his present job, he would not sell milk to customers of his present employer. The restraint applied both to setting up a rival business himself, and to working for any rival firm. The restriction was held valid, and necessary to protect his employer against potential loss of customers. Skilton was restrained by injunction from breaking his undertaking.

173

In *Forster & Sons Ltd* v. *Suggett* (1918), the works manager of a glass-making company had agreed not to work for any rival firm for five years after leaving his present job. This was held valid, because the manager knew of secret manufacturing processes which would be of value to a rival.

On the other hand, in *Eastham* v. *Newcastle United Football Club* (1964), the Football Association's retain and transfer rules, whereby a player could not transfer to any other club without the consent of his present one, were held invalid as being wider than necessary to protect the clubs. (The retain and transfer rules are more complex today.)

In *Mason* v. *Provident Clothing Co. Ltd* (1913), the clothing company had imposed a term restraining Mason, a collector and canvasser, from working for any similar business within 25 miles of London for three years after leaving. The House of Lords held that the onus was on the company to prove that such a wide restraint was reasonable to protect them, and that they had failed to do this.

Any attempt by an employer to impose restraints by indirect means will be subject to the same tests.

In *Bull* v. *Pitney-Bowes Ltd* (1966), a rule in the pensions scheme of the defendant company provided that employees should lose their pension rights if they left work for a competing company. Bull did leave after 26 years, and went to work for a competitor. It was held that this rule in the pension scheme was void as an attempted restraint on trade.

In *Kores Ltd* v. *Kolok Ltd* (1959), an agreement between two employers that neither would employ anyone who had worked for the other in the last five years was held invalid.

A party who has broken and repudiated the main contract may no longer be allowed to enforce a restraint clause in it.

In *Briggs* v. *Oates* (1990), the employer (a solicitor) *wrongfully* dismissed an employee. It was held that, having broken and repudiated the contract in this way, the solicitor could not at the same time claim the benefit of a restraint clause in it. His ex-employee (a younger solicitor) was therefore free to set up in practice nearby and immediately.

Restraints on the seller of a business

The courts have been much more ready to uphold restraints imposed in these circumstances, because the buyer plainly has an interest to protect and the seller is a free agent. The restriction must, however, be no more than is necessary to protect the business which the buyer has acquired; he cannot validly prevent the seller from competing with other businesses which the buyer already owns elsewhere. The restriction must also be reasonable as to time and area.

'Solus' and similar agreements

In *Esso Petroleum Co. Ltd* v. *Harper's Garage Ltd* (1968), the garage company agreed to sell only Esso petrol for the next four years, and to keep its garages open at all reasonable hours. In return, it received a discount on the price of the petrol. This agreement, although it restricted the garage company's freedom to sell whatever petrol it wished, was held as being reasonable in the interests of both parties and the public at large. An agreement affecting another of Harper's garages, however, tied the garage to sell only Esso for 21 years, in return for a loan of £7000. This was held to be too long a restraint, and therefore, against the public interest and void.

In *Cleveland Petroleum Co. Ltd* v. *Dartstone Ltd* (1969), the position was slightly different. *D* bought the remaining 17 years of a 25-year lease knowing at the time of purchase that it was a 'tied' garage until the end of the lease. Here the restraint was held valid. Unlike Harper's Garage, *D* had not given up a freedom which it had previously had. It had paid for, and got, only a tied garage. The restraint, therefore, was not unreasonable between the parties. (It might in some cases still be held contrary to public policy, but it was not here.)

Interpretation of restraint clauses

1. The court will not alter or re-write the words of a restraint clause. If it is void, it is totally void. The court will not cut down a 25-mile or a 21-year restraint to a more acceptable figure; if this is too wide, the person restrained can ignore it and set up business next door and tomorrow.

2. On the other hand, if the clause restricts several different activities, it may be possible to sever the void restrictions from the valid ones. The court does not alter the restriction; it merely deletes—puts a 'blue pencil' through—*one or more* of the restraints.

   In the *Nordenfelt* case (1894), an inventor and manufacturer of munitions sold his business to a company and agreed not to engage in munitions business, or in any other business liable to compete in any way with that for the time being carried out by the company, in any part of the world for the next 25 years. The House of Lords held that this was really two restrictions. The munitions restraint was valid, notwithstanding its time and extent, because of Nordenfelt's importance as an inventor and the world-wide scope of the business. The second restriction, covering competition with any other activity of the company, was too wide and, therefore, void.

3. The court will sometimes give a common-sense meaning to the words actually used, again without altering them.

   In *Littlewoods Organisation Ltd* v. *Harris* (1978), *H* was employed by Littlewoods. A clause in his contract restrained him from working for GUS (Littlewoods' rival) for 12 months after leaving. Littlewoods only operated a *mail-order* business *in this country*, whereas GUS had many types of business throughout the world. *H* claimed that the restraint was, therefore, void as being wider than necessary to protect Littlewoods. The court held that the restraint had plainly been intended to apply only to mail-order in the UK, and, therefore, issued an injunction against *H* limited to this.

   In *Clarke* v. *Newland* (1991), a doctor in general practice was limited by his contract from 'practising' locally for three years after leaving the partnership. He claimed that this was too wide a restraint because it could prevent him from practising as a local hospital doctor, which would not compete in any way. It was held that the restraint was intended to apply to general practice only, and would be valid to this extent. He could be restrained by injunction from starting a rival general practice.

175

Monopolies, cartels, price-fixing agreements, etc.

For the most part, restraints such as these are governed by statute today, particularly by the Competition Act 1998.

Various *agreements* that distort competition are covered by 'Chapter I' of the 1998 Act (starting with s.2). Agreements between undertakings which (a) may affect trade within (the whole or part of) the UK; and (b) have as their object or effect the prevention, restriction or distortion of competition within the UK, are prohibited and void. This applies, for example, to agreements that fix purchase or selling prices; or that limit or control production, markets, technical development or investment; or which share sources of supply, or markets. A party to such an agreement may apply to the Director General of Fair Trading for guidance as to whether the agreement is valid, and/or for an exemption on the grounds that it contributes to improving production or distribution, or to promoting technical or economic progress, but it may be difficult to obtain an exemption.

'Chapter II' of the Act (starting with s.18) prohibits any conduct on the part of one or more undertakings that amounts to the *abuse of a dominant position* in a market if it might affect trade within the UK. This could include, for example, directly or indirectly imposing unfair purchase or selling prices or other unfair trading conditions; or limiting production, markets or technical development to the prejudice of consumers.

Breach of these prohibitions can ultimately result in a penalty payable to the Director General.

Restrictive trading agreements may also be affected in English law by Article 81 (formerly 85) of the EC Treaty of Rome. This provides that *agreements* between undertakings that may affect trade *between member states*, and that have as their object or effect the prevention, restriction or distortion of competition within the common market are prohibited and void. This applies, for example, to agreements that fix purchase or selling prices – and all of the other matters set out in the Competition Act above. In short, some parts of the Competition Act 1998 mirror very closely the provisions of the EC Treaty, but apply them also to trade *within the UK*. Article 82 (formerly 86) of the EC Treaty prohibits any *abuse of dominant position* within the common market, and again the 1998 Act is modelled very closely on this. Applications for *exemption* from the Treaty provisions go to the EU Commission, but claims that the provisions have been *broken* can be made in the UK courts.

D. Other contracts that are void

Contracts prejudicial to the institution of marriage

The courts will not recognize contracts which interfere with marriage or the proper performances of marital or parental duties. A promise never to marry is deemed to be against public policy and void, though a promise not to marry a particular person or not to marry for a short period of time may be valid.

So far as parental duties are concerned, a parent cannot by contract deprive himself of the custody, control and education of his children, except by certain clearly defined legal procedures such as adoption.

Gaming and wagering contracts

Wagering contracts are void under the Gaming Acts, and no action may be brought to enforce payment of the bet, either directly or indirectly. On the other hand, the contract is not illegal; a partnership formed to carry on a wagering business can be valid, whereas a partnership to smuggle drugs is illegal and void. Wagering contracts, where neither party has an 'interest' in the event concerned other than the amount of the bet, must be distinguished from insurance contracts. If X insures his own goods against theft, this is valid, because X has an insurable interest in the goods; if X insures someone else's goods, the contract will be void, because X's only interest in the goods is the amount of his bet that they will be stolen. (Note that the Life Assurance Act 1774 does not apply to insurance of goods, and so the contract is not illegal.)

Gaming contracts involve the playing of a game of chance for winnings in money or money's worth. They can be valid if they comply with certain statutory requirements, for example that all players have an equal chance.

Clauses excluding certain statutory requirements

Frequently an Act will expressly prohibit and declare void any attempt to contract out of its requirements. Examples include the Employers' Liability (Defective Equipment) Act 1969 (section 2), the Consumer Credit Act 1974 (section 173), the Road Traffic Act 1988 (section 148), and the Employment Rights Act 1996 (section 203).

Specimen questions

1. (a) Outline the types of contract that the courts will not recognize on the grounds that they are illegal or contrary to public policy.
   (b) David has a small business in the town of Barchester for the supply and fitting of tyres. Occasionally, he will obtain and fit other car accessories for his customers. He agrees to sell his business to a company that sells car accessories and has branches in several towns in the region. In the contract of sale, he promises 'not to set up or be employed in any business concerned with tyres or other car accessories within ten miles of Barchester or within five miles of any other branch of the company for a period of five years'.

   Consider whether or not this promise is enforceable.
2. (a) Discuss the principles governing the validity or otherwise of a contract restraining an employee in respect of his future employment and those

177

applicable to a restraint upon the vendor of a business in respect of his future business activities.

  (b) Antonio sold his hairdressing business to Marcel and promised that he would not open a hairdressing shop or solicit customers within ten miles of the business he had sold for a period of three years. Is this promise binding upon Antonio? Give reasons for your answer.

3. Your company is about to market on a large scale a new and inexpensive brand of paint. It is intending to do this principally through existing retail shops, but is prepared to give financial assistance towards the opening of new shops in localities where there would otherwise be no retail outlets.

  Advise the company whether it may, by contract, ensure:

  (a) that retailers stock only this particular brand of paint and none other;
  (b) that the jurisdiction of the courts be excluded from any dispute arising with a retailer.

4. Explain, with reasons, whether the following agreements are valid and enforceable:

  (a) A partnership agreement under which whisky is to be smuggled into a country where its import is forbidden;
  (b) Two life assurance policies effected by a wife on the lives of her husband and her brother, respectively;
  (c) An agreement between two manufacturers fixing a minimum price below which they will not sell their products;
  (d) A promise by a retailer that he will not sell below a price fixed by a manufacturer;
  (e) A contract by a retailer to sell only one manufacturer's goods.

5. (a) Service is the owner of a hotel in Todfield, an industrial town in the north of England, and is negotiating its sale to Buttery. Buttery, who already owns other hotels in other towns, wishes to obtain protection against competition from Service after the sale. He seeks to prevent Service from either opening another hotel or working as an employee in the hotel trade.

  To what extent is he able to do this by inserting a restraint of trade clause in the contract of sale?

  (b) Comment upon the validity or otherwise of the following clause Buttery intends to use:

  'Mr. Service promises not to own, operate or be employed by a hotel or other catering business within ten miles of Todfield or any other town in which Buttery owns a hotel for a period of five years.'

Unit 18. Sale and Supply of Goods: Obligations of Parties

The law affecting contracts for the sale of goods was largely codified by the Sale of Goods Act 1893. This was later amended several times, and has now been replaced by a consolidating Act, the Sale of Goods Act 1979 which, for convenience, will be called simply 'the Act' in this unit and the next. There have been other changes since then, notably in 1994 and 1995. The Act covers the obligations and remedies of the parties, and the transfer of ownership and risk. Other matters, however, such as offer and acceptance, and consideration, are still governed by the ordinary law of contract (Units 11–17).

The contract need not be in writing. The vast majority of *cash* sales are made orally, as where goods are sold over the counter in a shop or pub, or in a restaurant, or where a car is sold for cash. Only where credit is allowed *may* the contract have to be in writing, under the Consumer Credit Act 1974.

The Act covers contracts 'whereby the seller transfers or agrees to transfer the property in goods to the buyer for a money consideration called the price'. This applies both to a '*sale*', where ownership passes immediately to the buyer, and to an '*agreement to sell*', where the parties agree now that ownership ('property') shall pass later.

The Act does not apply to barter or exchange, because there is no 'price' in money, although it does apply to part-exchange. It does not apply to hire, because no ownership passes to the hirer. It does not apply to contracts for 'work (or skill) and materials', where the goods supplied form only a fairly small part of the consideration.

Therefore the Act would not apply to the vaccine provided by a vet as a small part of his treatment of the animals, nor to the filling which a dentist puts into a tooth.

What the consumer principally pays for in each case is the professional service. Even contracts to supply and fit double glazing or central heating may be 'work and materials' contracts rather than sales of goods.

All of the above contracts which are not sales are now governed by the Supply of Goods and Services Act 1982. As regards the materials supplied, this imposes obligations on the supplier almost identical to those in the Sale of Goods Act, sections 12–15 (below).

A. Obligations of the seller

Section 27 sets out the principal obligations of the parties:

> 'It is the duty of the seller to deliver the goods, and of the buyer to accept and pay for them in accordance with the contract of sale.'

What the seller delivers, therefore, must accord with his express or implied obligations under the contract of sale. The Act sets out various implied obligations, as to title, description, quality, quantity, time and place of delivery, etc., some of which the parties are free to vary, some not. These provisions have been modified slightly by the Sale and Supply of Goods Act 1994, but the changes are not great, and pre-1994 cases cited here all still apply. The terms implied by sections 12–15 below are all conditions, except for the warranties in section 12(2)–(5).

Title

By section 12(1) of the Act as amended there is:

> 'an implied term on the part of the seller that in the case of a sale, he has a right to sell the goods, and in the case of an agreement to sell, he will have such a right at the time when the property is to pass'.

If the seller has no right to sell the goods (e.g., because they have been stolen, or he only holds them on hire or hire-purchase), then he will be liable to the buyer for breach of condition. Even an innocent seller, who had himself 'bought' the goods in good faith from or through a villain, can be liable (but see page 197). The buyer can recover the full price which he paid, even if he has had the use of the goods for some time.

> In *Rowland* v. *Divall* (1923), the buyer of a car used it for about three months, but then found that it was stolen and had to return it to the true owner. He was held entitled to recover from the (innocent) seller the full price which he had paid even though, when he had to part with it, the car was probably worth rather less. He had paid to become owner, he had not become owner, and he was, therefore, entitled to the return of his money.

It will be noticed that, if the buyer obtains no title, he will be bound to return the goods to the true owner, or be liable to him for conversion (Unit 10).

Section 12(2) also implies two *warranties* into contracts for sale: that the goods are free from encumbrance (such as a mortgage) not disclosed or made known to the buyer before the contract is made, and that the buyer will enjoy quiet possession of the goods. These overlap with section 12(1), but they can sometimes be useful.

In *Microbeads A.G.* v. *Vinhurst Road Markings Ltd* (1975), shortly *after* the sale, a third party obtained a patent which interfered with the buyer's right to use the machines (i.e. with his quiet possession). There had been no breach of section 12(1), because the seller had had a right to sell. However, the buyer was entitled to recover damages for breach of section 12(2).

Sections 12(3)–(5) do provide limited rights for the seller to contract out of his obligations as to title, if it is made quite clear in the contract that the seller's title may be defective, so that the buyer knows the risk he may be taking. In this event, there is no condition that the seller has a right to sell, only various warranties to the effect, for example, that all *known* encumbrances have been disclosed, and that the buyer's quiet possession will not be disturbed *by the seller*.

Description

Section 13(1) provides that:

'Where there is a contract for the sale of goods by description there is an implied term that the goods shall correspond with the description.'

Goods ordered through a catalogue, or a new car ordered from the manufacturers through a dealer, will always be sold by description, because this is the only way to identify what is required. Even goods seen and specifically chosen by the customer can be sold by description, and a customer is entitled to expect, for example, that goods which he chooses from the shelf in a supermarket will correspond to the description on the tin or packet.

In *Beale* v. *Taylor* (1967), a car was advertised as a 'Herald Convertible, white, 1961'. The buyer saw the vehicle before buying it, but only discovered some time later that, while the rear part had been accurately described, the front half had been part of an earlier model. The seller was held to be in breach of section 13.

The word 'description' covers a wide variety of matters. Statements as to quantity, weight, ingredients and even packing have been held to be part of the description.

In *Re Moore & Co. and Landauer & Co.* (Unit 15), the buyer described in the contract how he wished the consignment of canned fruit to be packed. When the seller supplied fruit which was not packed as stipulated, the buyer was entitled to reject the goods.

We have seen in Unit 15 that compliance with the description must be complete and exact.

In *Arcos* v. *E. & A. Ronaasen & Son* (1933), the contract was for half-inch wooden staves. Some of the staves supplied were as much as nine-sixteenths of an inch thick, and it was held that the buyer was entitled to reject the consignment.

On the other hand, we have seen in cases such as *Peter Darlington Partners Ltd* v. *Gosho Ltd* (Unit 15) that the courts will usually try to give a common-sense meaning

181

to any descriptive terms agreed and that, in any event, microscopic deviations may sometimes be ignored.

Quality

Unlike the obligations imposed by sections 12, 13 and 15, which apply to all sales of goods, section 14 only applies where the seller sells *in the course of a business*. As a general rule, a seller owes no obligation as regards the quality or suitability of his goods, but where section 14 (as amended) applies, there are three important exceptions to this general rule.

1. *Satisfactory quality*. Section 14(2) provides that:

> 'Where the seller sells goods in the course of a business, there is an implied term that the goods supplied under the contract are of satisfactory quality.'

The goods must meet the standard that a reasonable person would regard as satisfactory, taking account of any description of the goods, the price (if relevant) and all the other relevant circumstances. Quality includes the state and condition of the goods, and the following can, in appropriate cases, be aspects of their quality: (a) fitness for all purposes for which goods of that kind are commonly supplied, (b) appearance and finish, (c) freedom from minor defects, (d) safety, and (e) durability. What the buyer can expect, therefore, can depend upon many factors. If he buys cheap goods, he must reasonably expect lower quality than if he pays more. Similarly, older goods sold second hand may be satisfactory as such, even though they would not be reasonable if sold new in that condition.

> In *Bartlett* v. *Sidney Marcus Ltd* (1965), a second-hand car was sold with a defective clutch. The seller had warned of the defect, and the price took account of this. The car was held to be of satisfactory quality, even though repair cost more than the buyer expected.

> In *Rogers* v. *Parish (Scarborough) Ltd* (1987), the vehicle was an expensive new one. Although it was driveable, it did have mechanical and bodywork faults. It was not of satisfactory quality. At that price it should have been usable 'with the appropriate degree of comfort, ease of handling and reliability and, may one add, pride...'.

The above obligations do not apply (a) to matters affecting quality which are specifically drawn to the buyer's attention before the contract is made, or (b) if the buyer examines the goods before the contract is made, as regards matters which that examination ought to reveal, or (c) in the case of a sale by sample, to matters which would have been apparent on a reasonable examination of the sample. Part (b) of this last provision is much misunderstood; there is *no* obligation on the buyer to examine the goods, and if he chooses not to do so, he is entitled to the full protection of section 14(2).

2. *Reasonable fitness for the purpose made known*. Section 14(3) provides that:

> 'Where the seller sells goods in the course of a business and the buyer, expressly or by implication, makes known ... to the seller ... any particular purpose for which the

182

goods are being bought, there is an implied term that the goods supplied are reasonably fit for that purpose, whether or not that is a purpose for which such goods are commonly supplied, except where the circumstances show that the buyer does not rely, or that it is unreasonable for him to rely, on the skill or judgment of the seller...'.

This subsection only applies, therefore, if the buyer has expressly or impliedly made known to the seller the purpose for which he requires the goods. Where the goods only have one or two obvious uses, it will readily be assumed that the buyer has impliedly indicated that he wants them for their normal purpose. Thus, if someone buys food, it will be taken to indicate that he wants it to be reasonably fit for eating.

> In *Grant* v. *Australian Knitting Mills* (1936), a customer bought underpants from a shop. The garment still contained a chemical substance which had not been removed after manufacture, and this caused dermatitis. It was held that the buyer had impliedly made known that he intended to wear the underpants, which were not reasonably fit for that purpose. Furthermore, the garment was not of satisfactory quality.

The goods supplied need only be *reasonably* fit, however, and then only for the purposes made known.

> In *Griffiths* v. *Peter Conway Ltd* (1939), a lady with abnormally sensitive skin suffered dermatitis from contact with her new tweed coat. The garment would not have affected normal skin, and the lady's action against the seller therefore failed. The garment was reasonably fit for normal purposes, and the buyer had not made known her special circumstances.

> In *Slater* v. *Finning Ltd* (1996), marine engineers supplied a new camshaft for the buyer's fishing vessel. Unknown to both sellers and buyers, the vessel had an abnormal tendency to 'torsional resonance'. This damaged the camshaft, which proved unsuitable for *this* vessel (but not for other vessels). The buyer's action failed.

The subsection contains one exception to this implied condition, namely, where the circumstances show that the buyer does not rely, or that it is unreasonable for him to rely, on the seller's skill or judgment. This may apply, for example, where the buyer is an expert in such goods, and gives detailed specifications as to what he requires. On the other hand, even partial reliance on the seller is enough, and several important cases have held that it can be reasonable for one dealer or expert to rely partly on the skill or judgment of another.

Many buyers need credit. Section 14(3) also applies, therefore, where the owner does not sell directly to the buyer, but only indirectly, via a finance house or other consumer credit business. The owner sells the goods for cash to the finance house, which then re-sells the goods on conditional sale or credit sale to the buyer, who pays by instalments (page 214). In this event, the original owner (e.g. the garage selling a car) is called a 'credit-broker' because he introduces the would-be buyer to the finance house. It is sufficient for section 14(3) if the would-be buyer makes known to the original owner or 'credit-broker' (e.g. garage) the purpose for which the goods are being bought.

3. *Terms implied by usage*. Section 14(4) provides that implied terms as to quality or fitness may be annexed by usage.

183

Two final points must be made about section 14 as a whole. First, the section applies to all goods *supplied* under the contract, so that even if the goods sold are in order, there can be breach if packaging is defective.

> In *Geddling* v. *Marsh* (1920), mineral water was sold by the manufacturer to a retailer in bottles which had to be returned to the manufacturer. The buyer was injured when a defective bottle burst. He recovered damages under section 14 because, even though the bottles were not *sold* under the contract, the section applies to all goods supplied.

There will also be breach if dangerous extraneous matter is supplied with the goods sold.

> In *Wilson* v. *Rickett, Cockerell & Co. Ltd* (1954), the claimant ordered 'Coalite' from the seller. The consignment contained a detonator, which exploded when put on the fire. When sued, the seller pleaded that the detonator was included by mistake, was not part of the goods *sold*, and, therefore, was not subject to section 14. The Court of Appeal rejected this defence; the detonator had been *supplied* under the contract, albeit erroneously.

Secondly, compliance with section 14 must be strict.

> In *Frost* v. *Aylesbury Dairy Co. Ltd* (1905), a dairy supplied milk which contained typhoid germs. The dairy showed that it had taken all reasonable care to prevent this. It was held that this was no defence (Unit 15).

Sample

By section 15 (as amended), if goods are sold by sample, there are implied terms that the bulk will correspond with the sample in quality, and that the goods will be free from any defect making their quality unsatisfactory, which would not be apparent on reasonable examination of the sample.

A sale will be by sample if there is an express or implied term to this effect, and such sales are not uncommon, particularly in bulk orders.

> In *Godley* v. *Perry* (1960), a boy bought a plastic catapult from a retail shop. The catapult broke almost immediately, and the boy lost an eye. The retailer had bought his catapults by sample from a wholesaler. The retailer had tested the sample by pulling back the elastic, and no defect was apparent at that stage. It was held that (a) the boy could recover damages from the retailer for breach of sections 14(2) and (3), and (b) the retailer could recover damages from the wholesaler for breach of section 15.

Delivery

The mechanics of delivery (as opposed to *what* is delivered) are covered by a series of sections later in the Act. By section 28, delivery and payment are concurrent obligations, so the seller can retain the goods until payment is tendered. Section 29(1) provides that, in the absence of agreement to the contrary, it is for the buyer to collect the goods from wherever the seller has them, not for the seller to dispatch them to the buyer. Where the seller does agree to dispatch the goods, he must do so within a reasonable time and, in any event, demand or tender of delivery must be at a reasonable time of day. By section 31, the buyer is entitled to delivery of all the goods at once, and need not accept delivery by instalments.

Exclusion of the seller's obligations

Although as a general rule the parties can make whatever bargain they please, we have seen in Unit 14 that any clause purporting to exclude sections 13 to 15 above will be void as against a person buying as a *consumer*; it may be void even against a non-consumer unless the *seller* can show that the exclusion is reasonable under the Unfair Contract Terms Act 1977. Section 12 of the 1979 Act can never be wholly excluded.

On the other hand, the parties are quite free to exclude or vary provisions such as sections 28, 29 and 31 if they so wish.

B. Remedies of the buyer

Where the seller breaks one of his express or implied obligations under the contract, the buyer may have the following remedies.

Damages for breach of contract

Damages can always be claimed as of right, although where no real loss has occurred the amount may be nominal. The measure of damages and the question of remoteness are the same as in contract generally; sections 51 and 53 provide rules very similar to those put forward in *Hadley* v. *Baxendale* (Unit 15), the basic rule being that 'the measure of damages is the estimated loss directly and naturally resulting, in the ordinary course of events, from the seller's breach of contract'. The second rule in *Hadley* v. *Baxendale* is preserved by section 54.

An action for damages may be commenced at any time within the normal limitation period of six years.

Rights to reject the goods and treat the contract as ended

Where breach of an implied term is serious, the buyer has rights to reject the goods and treat the contract as repudiated. Again these rules have been modified by the Sale and Supply of Goods Act 1994. It will be noted that most of the terms implied by sections 12 to 15 are conditions; similarly, the courts have held that late delivery by a seller is a breach that entitles the buyer to reject the goods and end the contract.

These rights derive from equity, and can therefore easily be lost. Section 11(4) provides that, where the contract of sale is non-severable, the rights to reject the goods and treat the contract as repudiated are lost as soon as the buyer has *accepted* the goods. This is based on the ordinary equitable principle that a party who 'affirms' the contract thereby loses his right to rescind it. By section 35, a buyer is deemed to have accepted the goods in the following circumstances:

185

1. When he intimates to the seller that he has accepted them (express acceptance).
2. When the goods have been delivered to the buyer and he does any act in relation to them which is inconsistent with the ownership of the seller (implied acceptance). This can occur when the buyer treats the goods as his, by consuming or re-selling or altering them. Goods cannot be rejected unless they are still there to be returned.

   However where goods are delivered which the buyer has not yet examined, he is not deemed to have accepted them (expressly or impliedly) until he has had a reasonable opportunity of examining them to see whether they conform with the contract or, in the case of sale by sample, conform with the sample. Therefore, if a buyer re-sells goods which were pre-packed so that he could not examine them (e.g. in cans), and then is told by the sub-buyer that they are defective, he can still reject against the original seller, so long as only a reasonable time has elapsed.

   Moreover, a buyer is not deemed to have accepted goods merely because he asks for, or agrees to, their repair by the seller or under an arrangement with him.
3. The buyer is also deemed to have accepted the goods when, after the lapse of a reasonable time, he retains the goods without intimating to the seller that he has rejected them. 'Reasonable time' is a question of fact; it may be very brief for perishable goods, and/or in cash sales.

   > In *Bernstein* v. *Pamson Motors Ltd* (1987), a new car broke down only three weeks after purchase and after only 140 miles. The buyer had lost his right to reject (although he did still get damages). The judge commented that 'there should, whenever possible, be finality in commercial transactions'.

The right to reject may last longer when the goods have not yet been fully paid for (e.g. where credit is allowed), so that the seller cannot yet 'close his ledger'. Moreover *Bernstein v Pamson Motors* has been widely criticized in subsequent cases. The buyer will normally not lose his right to reject, at least until he has had a reasonable time to use and examine the goods.

By section 15A, where breach of sections 13, 14 or 15 is so slight that it would be unreasonable for a *business* buyer (a non-consumer) to reject the goods, then he will not be entitled to do so, but will only be entitled to damages. It is for the seller to show that the breach is so slight and, in any event, the parties are free to exclude this provision.

Partial rejection is specifically allowed. If the buyer has the right to reject goods because of a breach by the seller which affects some or all of them, but nevertheless accepts some of them including all of those unaffected by the breach, he can still reject the rest.

Section 30 covers tender of the wrong quantity:

1. Where the seller delivers too small a quantity, the buyer can either reject the consignment, or he can accept the lesser amount, the price being reduced rateably.
2. Where the seller delivers too large a quantity, the buyer may reject the whole, accept the contract amount and reject the rest, or accept the whole and pay a price increased rateably.

Section 31(2) deals with instalment contracts. It will be recalled that section 11(4) applies only to 'non-severable' contracts. Where the goods are to be delivered by instalments, each to be paid for separately, the contract is treated as severable. In this event, if only one or two of many instalments is defective, each defective delivery can be rejected, wholly or partly, notwithstanding that earlier instalments have been accepted. The rules as to partial acceptance can apply to each instalment; so do the rules limiting rejection by a business buyer on the pretext of a very slight breach (see above). The main difficulty arises over whether one defective instalment entitles the buyer to treat the whole contract as *repudiated*, and refuse all future deliveries, satisfactory or not. The tests to determine this are the relation which the size of the breach bears to the contract as a whole, and the likelihood or otherwise of the breach being repeated.

> In *Munro Ltd* v. *Meyer* (1930), a first delivery of 611 tons of defective bone meal out of a contract to supply 1500 tons did entitle the buyer to refuse further deliveries.

> In *Maple Flock Co.* v. *Universal Furniture Ltd* (1934), a defect in one instalment of rag flock, the 16th out of 20 deliveries made, did not entitle the buyer to treat the contract as ended.

Finally, it should be noted that all of these rules affect only a buyer's rights to reject the goods and end the contract. Where the buyer has lost these rights, *he can still sue the seller for damages* within the six-year limitation period.

Specific performance

Section 52 preserves the remedy of specific performance in contracts for the sale of goods but, as noted elsewhere, this will only be awarded where the article sold is unique, such as an original painting. Mere rarity is not normally enough; see *Cohen* v. *Roche* (Unit 15).

C. Other sanctions against suppliers of goods

Actions in tort

Sections 12 to 15 of the Sale of Goods Act merely imply terms into the contract between the seller and buyer and, therefore, because of privity of contract rules, have serious weaknesses as a means of protecting consumers. Thus, where the goods have passed through several hands, the Sale of Goods Act only gives remedies against the immediate seller, not previous owners or the manufacturer. If the immediate seller is not worth suing, the buyer's only right of action may be in tort if he can, for example, prove negligence by the manufacturer. Similar problems arise when dangerous goods (such as a defective car) injure someone other than the buyer himself; the person injured may not be able to sue on a contract to which he is not a party, and the Sale of Goods Act is, therefore, of no help. Cases such as *Donoghue* v. *Stevenson* and *Steer* v. *Durable Rubber Co. Ltd* (Unit 9) arose in this type of situation. The problems are

187

discussed more fully in Unit 20, including the possible effect of the Contracts (Rights of Third Parties) Act 1999.

Criminal liability of seller

A second problem arises because few buyers have the energy or initiative to pursue claims against the sellers of defective goods. Moreover, many buyers are inhibited by the likely cost of proceedings.

Consumers are protected, therefore, by the criminal law, which prohibits certain practices by sellers. The main provision is section 1 of the Trade Descriptions Act 1968.

> 'Any person who, in the course of a trade or business ... (a) applies a false trade description to any goods; or (b) supplies or offers to supply any goods to which a false trade description is applied; shall ... be guilty of an offence.'

This section has fairly limited scope: it applies only where the sale is in the course of a business, and it covers only false *descriptions*. The section does not prohibit the supply of defective goods, so long as the seller makes no false claims about them. Criminal sanctions as to the *quality* of what is sold only exist over a few types of goods; for example, the Road Traffic Act makes it an offence in some circumstances to sell a vehicle in a dangerous condition, and the Food Safety Act 1990 creates offences for selling unfit or adulterated food.

Administration and enforcement of these criminal controls is by various public officers: trading standards inspectors in the case of trade descriptions, public health inspectors for food, police in the case of vehicles. These controls, therefore, are not dependent upon the initiative of the buyer.

The sanctions are the normal criminal ones of fines and, exceptionally, imprisonment. These do not directly benefit the buyer, but a Magistrates' Court can, under the Powers of Criminal Courts Act as amended, award limited compensation to a person affected by the offence, and such compensation orders are quite frequently made for trade descriptions offences.

Work and materials contracts

In these contracts the buyer pays largely or substantially for the 'service' provided (see page 179). They are governed by the Supply of Goods and Services Act 1982. As regards *what* is provided—the vaccine, the material put into the tooth or the paint put on to a house—sections 2–5 of the 1982 Act impose a strict liability, which is effectively the same as that under the Sale of Goods Act, sections 12–15. The 1994 Sale and Supply of Goods Act makes similar provisions. As regards the service part of the contract—the *way* in which the work is done—liability is not strict. By the 1982 Act, section 13, 'there is an implied term that the supplier will carry out the service with reasonable care and skill'. Sections 2–4 of the 1982 Act are as difficult to exclude as the equivalent Sale of Goods Act sections. Section 13 of the 1982 Act can be excluded or varied more easily (Unit 14).

D. Obligations of the buyer

The buyer must accept the goods and pay for them in accordance with the contract.

Payment

The amount of the price is normally fixed by the contract. Alternatively, it may be determined by the course of earlier dealings between the parties, or may be left to be fixed by a valuer or referee.

The time for payment is on delivery of the goods. A later date or dates may be agreed where credit is allowed. Section 10 provides that, unless otherwise agreed, delay in payment is only a breach of warranty, not condition.

Acceptance

This is largely self-explanatory; a buyer, having ordered goods, breaks his contract if he then refuses to take them. He can only validly reject the goods if the seller is in breach of condition.

By the Consumer Protection (Cancellation of Contracts concluded away from Business Premises) Regulations 1987, made under the European Communities Act, a private 'consumer' has limited protection from 'doorstep' sales. If he buys during an unsolicited visit by a trader, and if his total payments would have exceeded £35, he can cancel the contract within seven days. This is similar to the cancellation rights in credit transactions (Unit 21).

E. Remedies of the seller

Action for the price

Where the ownership of the goods has passed to the buyer, or where a specified date for payment was set and has passed, the seller can sue for the contract price.

Damages for non-acceptance

Moreover, where the buyer refuses to accept or pay for the goods the seller may claim damages, the measure being 'the estimated loss directly and naturally resulting, in the ordinary course of events, from the buyer's breach of contract' (section 50). Where, between the contract and the date of delivery, the market price of such goods has fallen, so that the seller will get less on a re-sale, the damages will, *prima facie*, be the difference between the contract price and the market price at the time when the goods should have been accepted.

189

Unpaid seller's rights over the goods

A common reason for non-payment is because the buyer has no money. In these circumstances, the seller's rights to sue for the price or damages may be worthless, and he will often prefer simply to keep the goods. The Act, therefore, gives him certain rights.

1. Under sections 41 and 39(2), an unpaid seller has a *lien* or *right to withhold delivery* until he is paid. These rights exist while the goods are still in the seller's possession and no credit has been allowed to the buyer. The rights are lost as soon as the seller parts with possession; he has no right to re-take them from the buyer. Note also that the lien gives the seller no right to *re-sell* the goods yet, only to retain them.

2. By section 44, if an unpaid seller has parted with the goods to a carrier, he still has a *right of stoppage in transit* if, during the transit, the buyer *becomes insolvent* (not otherwise). The seller can order the carrier to re-deliver the goods to the seller or his agent, so that the buyer will not get possession.

3. By section 48, if an unpaid seller still has the goods, he will have a *right to re-sell* them in three circumstances: (a) where the goods are perishable; or (b) where the unpaid seller gives notice to the buyer of his intention to re-sell, and the buyer still does not pay or tender the price within a reasonable time; and (c) where, in the contract, the seller expressly reserved a right to re-sell should the buyer default.

   Where re-sale is at a profit, so that the seller gets more than the original contract price, the seller can keep the profit. If an unpaid seller re-sells wrongfully, e.g. without giving reasonable notice, the new buyer still gets a good title but, in this event, the seller must account to the old buyer for any profit as compared with the original contract price.

4. In addition to these statutory rights, some sellers of valuable industrial goods have used 'reservation of title' clauses for further protection.

   > In *Aluminium Industrie Vaassen BV* v. *Romalpa Aluminium Ltd* (1976), AIV sold some aluminium foil to Romalpa. The written contract provided that, notwithstanding delivery, ownership of the foil would only pass to Romalpa when the latter paid what it owed to AIV. This part of the clause was held valid.

However, later cases have made it clear that such a clause cannot normally give a right to retake goods that the buyer has used to make a new object; or to recover goods that have been mixed with other things so as to change the goods; or to take the profits of any resale to a sub-purchaser.

Specimen questions

1. Simple wishes to buy his son a car as a birthday present. He approaches Wheeler, a retailer of car spares, who he knows sells cars for his customers from time to time. Wheeler offers to sell Simple a second-hand car, explains that the brakes require attention and reduces the price to take account of this. He also says that he will take no responsibility for this or any other defect. Simple accepts the offer without

examining the car. If he had done so he would have seen that the tyres were badly worn.

Simple drives away the car but, because of its defects, fails to negotiate a bend in the road. The car strikes a wall and is damaged beyond repair.

Advise Simple of his rights, if any, against Wheeler.

2. A company operating a chain of retail wine shops sells a considerable amount of wine, which is imported in bottles. It is not possible for the company to ensure that the wine will always comply with the label on the bottle or that the wine is free from harmful substances.

Draft a report explaining the legal liability that might arise towards a customer and whether or not this liability might be avoided. (Do not consider the effect of the Trade Descriptions Act 1968 or any other possible criminal liability.)

3. Section 27, Sale of Goods Act 1979, states, 'It is the duty of the seller to deliver the goods, and of the buyer to accept and pay for them, in accordance with the terms of the contract of sale'.

Explain the meaning and effect of this section. In particular, describe the seller's duties in connection with delivery and indicate what constitutes acceptance by the buyer.

4. Advise *H* in the following cases, explaining the relevant principles of law:
   (a) *J* sold *H* 2000 lb of fruit, to be delivered in 10 lb tins. *J* delivered the total quantity in 20 lb tins.
   (b) *J* sold *H* 1000 tins of biscuits. *J* delivered 1500 tins.
   (c) *J* sold *H* 600 blue shirts. *J* delivered 400 blue shirts and 200 brown shirts:

5. Advise the seller of goods as to his remedies in the following situations:
   (a) Two consignments of goods have been sold to Eric. The first consignment has been delivered but Eric refuses to pay on the grounds that the goods are defective. Eric has refused to accept delivery of the second consignment, claiming that these goods may also be defective.
   (b) An agreement has been made to sell goods to Frank. Part of the order has been dispatched when the seller hears of Frank's insolvency. The remaining goods are still in the seller's warehouse.

6. (a) Assess the protection given to purchasers by section 14 of the Sale of Goods Act 1979 under which it is implied that goods shall be both of satisfactory quality and fit for the purpose for which they have been bought.
   (b) *B* Ltd manufactures and distributes its product in glass bottles bought from *G* Ltd and all bottles are normally examined before use. Roger, a retailer, sells a bottle to Charles, a customer. The bottle is slippery because Roger has kept it under damp conditions and Charles drops it as he is leaving the store. The bottle explodes, injuring Charles.

   Discuss the remedies available to Charles.

Unit 19. Sale of Goods: Ownership and Risk

A. Transfer of property between seller and buyer

The purpose of a contract of sale is to transfer ownership of the goods from seller to buyer, and the Act contains rules for determining precisely when this happens. This is important mainly because of the questions of risk; by section 20, any loss, prima facie, falls on the party who is owner at that time. In this unit the words 'property' and 'ownership' mean the same thing.

To determine when ownership passes, it is important first to distinguish between specific and unascertained goods. *Specific* goods normally are 'goods identified and agreed on *at the time a contract of sale is made*'. Thus a buyer may point to a specific car in the showroom as the one which he wants. All sales in self-service shops, and most over-the-counter sales will be of specific goods; in each case the buyer chooses or approves a specific item before agreeing to take it. All goods which are not specific are *unascertained*. If a buyer orders a new car which is yet to be delivered from the manufacturer, it is not yet possible to point to which specific car is to become his. Almost all orders by post (for example from a mail order catalogue firm) will be of unascertained goods, as will many orders in bulk (e.g. 100 tons of wheat).

In a contract for unascertained goods, the subject-matter will, at some stage, be 'appropriated' to the contract. Thus, 100 tons of wheat will, at some stage, be set aside for the buyer. The 100 tons is then said to be *ascertained*. The 100 tons do not become specific goods, however, because they were not identified at the time of the contract: unascertained goods cannot become specific ones under the same sale.

Passing of property in specific goods

Section 17 provides that the property in specific goods passes whenever the parties intend it to pass. They can make their own provision (as in the *Romalpa* case). To ascertain the intention of the parties, 'regard shall be had to the terms of the contract, the conduct of the parties, and the circumstances of the case'. This is the overriding rule, and section 18, below, must always be read subject to it.

Where the parties do not expressly or impliedly indicate when they want ownership to pass, section 18 sets out various rules to ascertain their presumed intention:

> *Rule 1* 'Where there is an unconditional contract for the sale of specific goods, in a deliverable state, the property in the goods passes to the buyer *when the contract is made*, and it is immaterial whether the time of payment or the time of delivery, or both, be postponed.'

In spite of the last words of this rule, the courts are still free under section 17 to hold that, where both payment and delivery are postponed, the parties did not intend ownership to pass yet.

> In *Ward (R.V.) Ltd* v. *Bignall* (1967), the seller unconditionally sold a specific car to the buyer, but retained possession until the buyer could pay for it. In the Court of Appeal, Diplock, L.J. indicated (*obiter*) that he would, if necessary, be willing to treat the car as still belonging to the seller, in spite of the wording of Rule 1. It was arguable that both parties regarded the car as being the seller's until the buyer paid or was allowed to take delivery, and the court *might* assume that this was their real intention.

It should be noted that Rule 1 applies only where the goods are already in a 'deliverable state'; if they are not, then the second rule may apply:

> *Rule 2* 'Where there is a contract for the sale of specific goods and the seller is bound to do something to the goods for the purpose of putting them into a deliverable state, the property does not pass until the thing is done, and the buyer has notice that it has been done.'

Goods are only in a deliverable state 'when they are in such a state that the buyer would under the contract be bound to take delivery of them' (section 61(5)). If, therefore, the seller still has things to do to the goods under the contract, the ownership will not pass yet. For example, if the seller agrees in the contract to fit new tyres to the car, the car will remain in the seller's ownership and at his risk until the tyres are fitted *and* the buyer has notice of this.

The third rule is self-explanatory:

> *Rule 3* 'Where there is a contract for the sale of specific goods in a deliverable state, but the seller is bound to weigh, measure, test, or do some other act or thing with reference to the goods for the purpose of ascertaining the price, the property does not pass until the act or thing is done and the buyer has notice that it has been done.'

The fourth rule covers the situation where a buyer asks for goods, such as a new book or machine, on approval. Note that this rule applies only where the buyer has *agreed* to take the goods on this basis; it does *not* apply where a would-be seller sends unsolicited goods to someone (Unit 12).

> *Rule 4* 'When goods are delivered to the buyer on approval or on sale or return or other similar terms, the property in the goods passes to the buyer:

(a) when he signifies his approval or acceptance or does any other act adopting the transaction (for example, by re-selling the goods);

(b) if he does not signify his approval or acceptance to the seller but retains the goods without giving notice of rejection, then, if a time has been fixed for the return of the goods, on the expiration of that time, and, if no time has been fixed, on the expiration of a reasonable time.' (What is a reasonable time is a question of fact.)

Passing of property in unascertained goods

Section 16 provides that:

'Where there is a contract for the sale of unascertained goods, no property in the goods is transferred to the buyer unless and until the goods are ascertained.'

This is simply a rule of common sense; while goods remain unascertained, it is impossible to point out which car or bag of wheat is to belong to the buyer. It should be noted, however, that the section is phrased negatively; even when the goods are ascertained, they do not necessarily become the buyer's (see the *Romalpa* case again). Passing of property is, prima facie, governed by section 18 again:

Rule 5 'Where there is a contract for the sale of unascertained ... goods by description, and goods of that description and in a deliverable state are unconditionally appropriated to the contract, either by the seller with the assent of the buyer, or by the buyer with the assent of the seller, the property in the goods then passes to the buyer; and the assent may be express or implied, and may be given either before or after the appropriation is made.'

Ownership can only pass, therefore, when goods are 'appropriated' to the contract, that is, set aside or otherwise identified, labelled, etc., with the firm intention that these are the goods covered by the contract. Delivery of the correct amount to a carrier for transport to the buyer will be appropriation for this purpose.

Moreover, ownership does not pass to the buyer unless and until the goods are in a deliverable state.

In *Philip Head & Sons* v. *Showfronts Ltd* (1970), the seller agreed to deliver and lay fitted carpets. A carpet was delivered, but left overnight to be laid next morning. It was held that the carpet was still at the seller's risk, so that when it was stolen overnight, the seller bore the loss.

Ownership in common of a bulk

Section 16 and section 18 rule 5 have been modified slightly by the Sale of Goods (Amendment) Act 1995. This Act applies where there is a contract for a specified quantity of unascertained goods *forming part of a bulk which is identified* either in the contract or by subsequent agreement of the parties (compare *Inglis* v. *Stock*, page 197). In this event, if the buyer has paid the price for some or all of the goods, he becomes an 'owner in common' of the bulk. His 'undivided share' is 'such share as the quantity of goods paid for and due to the buyer out of the bulk bears to the quantity of goods in the bulk at that time'. There are detailed rules concerning the deemed consent of a co-owner to dealings in the bulk goods.

The 1995 Act also extends the definition of specific goods to include an undivided share, specified as a fraction or percentage, of goods identified and agreed on at the time of the contract.

B. Risk

'Risk' can cover a multitude of mishaps, from slight damage to theft or total destruction. The basic rule to determine on whom the loss should fall is in section 20 of the Act:

> 'Unless otherwise agreed, the goods remain at the seller's risk until the property in them is transferred to the buyer, but when the property in them is transferred to the buyer, the goods are at the buyer's risk whether delivery has been made or not.'

The Act also contains more detailed rules. There are three possible times when loss can occur.

1. Loss occurring before the contract is made

This obviously falls on the seller. He may not only lose the goods, but also be liable to the buyer for damages if he contracts to deliver goods and then cannot do so. Where *unascertained* goods are sold, for example, it is up to the seller to find supplies and, if his own stocks turn out to be damaged, stolen or destroyed, this is his misfortune; he must find alternative supplies or face damages for non-delivery.

Where *specific* goods are sold, however, the seller may be protected from liability to the buyer by section 6:

> 'Where there is a contract for the sale of specific goods, and the goods without the knowledge of the seller have perished at the time when the contract is made, the contract is void.'

This section has limited scope; it applies only where the goods have *perished*, that is, ceased to exist either physically or commercially, and it applies only where this has happened without the seller's knowledge. (A seller who tries to sell goods which he knows have perished will be guilty of fraud.) Goods can 'perish' without being totally destroyed.

> In *Asfar & Co. Ltd* v. *Blundell* (1896), a cargo of dates which had sunk in the harbour and, when raised two days later, was 'simply a mass of pulpy matter impregnated with sewage and in a state of fermentation', was held to have 'perished' although still physically in existence.

> In *Barrow, Lane & Ballard Ltd* v. *Phillips & Co. Ltd* (1929), the sellers sold 700 *specific* bags of Chinese nuts. Unknown to the sellers, 109 bags had already been stolen. It was held that the specific consignment of 700 bags had perished, because a substantial part of it had gone.

195

Section 6 is based on the common law rules of mistake, and on cases such as *Couturier* v. *Hastie* (Unit 13). If the contract is void, the seller still bears the loss, but has no liability to the buyer.

2. Loss occurring between contract and the passing of property

Property will pass immediately on making the contract only when section 18, Rule 1 applies. Loss occurring after the contract but before ownership passes will be subject to rules similar to those discussed above; prima facie the loss falls on the seller and, moreover, the buyer may recover damages for non-delivery if the seller does not get other supplies.

Where *specific* goods are sold, however, section 7 may protect the seller against liability to the buyer:

> 'Where there is an agreement to sell specific goods and subsequently the goods, without any fault on the part of the seller or buyer, perish before the risk passes to the buyer, the agreement is avoided.'

This is based on the common law rules of frustration and, like section 6, applies only where specific goods have 'perished'. Where the specific goods are only slightly damaged, section 7 may not apply, and the seller may face liability to the buyer, even though the damage was not the seller's fault.

When section 7 applies, the Law Reform (Frustrated Contracts) Act 1943 does not; all moneys payable, therefore, cease to be due, and all moneys paid under the contract must be returned. If the seller has incurred expenses under the contract, he can neither recover these from the buyer, nor keep part of any deposit which the buyer may have paid.

3. Loss occurring after the passing of property

Under section 20, this falls on the buyer, even if the goods are still in the seller's possession.

> In *Tarling* v. *Baxter* (1827), a farmer sold a haystack, which remained on his farm, to be collected in the spring. Before collection, the stack was destroyed. It was held that, on the facts, ownership had passed to the buyer and, therefore, he bore the loss.

There are, however, two provisos. First, section 20(2) provides that where delivery has been delayed through the fault of either seller or buyer, the goods are at the risk of the party at fault as regards any loss which might not have occurred but for the delay.

> In *Demby Hamilton & Co. Ltd* v. *Barden* (1949), the seller agreed to send 30 tons of apple juice by weekly consignments to the buyer. The buyer delayed taking delivery of some of the juice which, as a result, went bad. The buyer was still held liable to pay, because the delay was his fault.

Secondly, by section 20(3), 'nothing in this section affects the duties or liabilities of either seller or buyer as a bailee of the goods of the other party'. Thus, if the seller remains in possession after ownership has passed to the buyer, the seller must take reasonable care of the goods and may be liable if he does not do so.

Finally, section 20 applies only in the absence of contrary agreement, and the parties can always agree that the risk is to pass before the ownership, or vice versa.

> In *Inglis* v. *Stock* (1885), the buyer bought a specified quantity of sugar, forming an unascertained part of a larger cargo. The contract validly provided that risk should pass when the cargo was put aboard ship.

C. Transfer of title by a non-owner

As a general rule, only the owner of goods or his agent can validly sell them. This is often expressed in the phrase *nemo dat quod non habet* (no one can give what he does not have), and the rule is embodied in section 21:

> '... where goods are sold by a person who is not their owner, and who does not sell them under the authority or with the consent of the owner, the buyer acquires no better title to the goods than the seller had. ...'

When the buyer obtains no title, he must return the goods on demand to the true owner, or face an action for the tort of conversion. In turn, the buyer can recover damages from the seller for breach of section 12 of the Act, but by this time the seller may have absconded.

This rule can, therefore, be hard on buyers, who often have no means of knowing whether the seller is the true owner. The issue is often between an innocent true owner and an innocent ultimate buyer, both of whom are victims of a rogue who has departed. There are other situations discussed below where the *nemo dat* rule would be harsh to buyers, and a number of exceptions to the general rule have, therefore, developed.

Sale by an agent

An agent acting within his actual authority can pass a good title to his principal's goods. Even if the agent exceeds his actual authority, he may still pass a good title if he is acting within his implied or apparent (ostensible) authority, so that the buyer has no reason to suspect that the agent has no right to sell.

The Factors Act 1889 puts these rules into statutory form as regards *mercantile agents*. A mercantile agent is one having, in the course of his business as an independent agent (*not* merely as an employee of the principal), authority to sell goods or otherwise deal with them. Section 2(1) of the Factors Act provides that:

> 'Where a mercantile agent is, with the consent of the owner, in possession of goods or of the documents of title to the goods, any sale, pledge or other disposition of the goods, made by him when acting in the ordinary course of business of a mercantile agent, shall ... be as valid as if he were expressly authorized by the owner of the goods to make the same, provided that the person taking under the disposition acts in good faith, and that he has

197

not at the time of the disposition notice that the person making the disposition has not authority to make the same.'

> In *Folkes* v. *King* (1923), an agent had authority to sell his principal's car for not less that £575. In breach of these instructions, he sold for only £340. The buyer obtained a good title, because the agent was clearly in possession with authority to sell, and the buyer had no reason to suspect the limitation which the principal had imposed.

The section applies only where the person who sells was in possession *as agent to sell*. If a car is left with a garage for repairs, and wrongly sold by the garage, the Factors Act will not apply, because the garage was not in possession as agent to sell. The agent must, moreover, have obtained possession with the owner's consent, although consent induced by fraud can be enough.

Sale by the mercantile agent must be in the ordinary course of business, and the buyer must take in good faith. These requirements are often connected, because if there are unusual features surrounding the sale, so that it is not in the ordinary course of business, then the buyer should be suspicious and, if he makes no enquiries, his good faith is in doubt. The owner of a car can, therefore, protect himself when entrusting the vehicle to a dealer for sale, by retaining the registration document. If the dealer sells a second-hand car without the registration document, this should make the buyer enquire further, and the buyer will get no title under the Factors Act if the dealer exceeds his authority.

Estoppel

Section 21 of the Sale of Goods Act itself provides an exception to the *nemo dat* rule, where 'the owner of the goods is by his conduct precluded from denying the seller's authority to sell'. This may occur where the owner deliberately gives someone else the appearance of having a right to deal with the goods.

> In *Eastern Distributors Ltd* v. *Goldring* (1957), a car owner gave a dealer documents which made the dealer appear to be the owner, as part of a scheme to enable the car owner to borrow money without adequate security. The scheme fell through, but the dealer went ahead and sold the car to a finance company. It was held that the finance company obtained a good title because, although the dealer had no right to sell, the owner's conduct estopped him from asserting this.

Sale under voidable title (section 23)

We have seen in Unit 13 that if a buyer obtains goods under a contract which is voidable (e.g., for misrepresentation or breach of condition), he can pass on a good title to someone who buys from him in good faith without notice of the defect in title, provided that the re-sale takes place before the original contract is rescinded (see cases such as *Lewis* v. *Averay* (1972)). On the other hand, if the original contract is *void* (e.g., for mistake), no title can pass under section 23, although other exceptions to the *nemo dat* rule might apply in some circumstances.

198

Re-sale by seller in possession (section 24)

Where a person who has sold goods remains in possession of them, or of documents of title to them, any re-sale by him to a buyer who takes the goods in good faith without notice of the previous sale will give a good title to the new buyer as soon as the latter *takes physical delivery* of the goods or documents of title. The old buyer is left to sue the seller for damages for non-delivery. A similar rule applies if the seller in possession pledges (pawns) the goods or disposes of them in any other way.

Re-sale by buyer in possession with the consent of the seller (section 25)

Where a person who has bought or agreed to buy goods obtains possession of the goods or documents of title *with the seller's consent*, any sale and delivery by the buyer to a person who takes in good faith, without notice of any rights of the original seller to the goods, shall have 'the same effect as if the person making the delivery ... were a mercantile agent in possession ... with the consent of the owner'. The rule also applies if the buyer pledges the goods or disposes of them in any other way.

This section has very limited effect. It applies only where the original buyer re-sells *in the ordinary course of business*, as if he were a mercantile agent, or at least where the circumstances are such that the ultimate buyer could assume that he was buying from a mercantile agent or dealer.

> In *Newtons of Wembley Ltd* v. *Williams* (1965), a rogue bought the seller's car with a cheque which was dishonoured. Meanwhile the rogue had taken the car to Warren Street, which was an established street market for second-hand cars, and sold it to an innocent buyer for cash. It was held that the buyer obtained a good title, because the rogue was a buyer in possession with the consent of the owner and, although the rogue was not himself a mercantile agent, he had sold the car in a place where car dealers ordinarily did business.

The first buyer must have obtained possession with the consent of the seller, who must in effect have entrusted the goods to him. Consent induced by fraud can be enough, but *National Employers Insurance* v. *Jones* (1988) confirms that section 25 will not protect the subsequent buyer of goods which have been *stolen*, i.e., taken from the owner *without* his consent.

Motor vehicles on hire-purchase

Under the Hire-Purchase Act 1964, Part III, if a *vehicle* on hire-purchase is sold by the hirer to a *private* purchaser, who takes in good faith and without notice of the hire-purchase agreement, a good title will pass. A 'private' purchaser is one who is not a 'trade' purchaser (e.g., a garage) or a 'finance' purchaser (e.g. a hire-purchase company). If the hirer sells to a garage, the garage gets no title under these provisions. Moreover, a garage which buys and re-sells a vehicle in these circumstances commits the tort of conversion against the true owner. On the other hand, although the garage is not protected, an innocent private purchaser from the garage does get a good title; and once the goods have become the private purchaser's property, the title is cured, so

199

that a *subsequent* trade or finance purchaser does get a good title. If the first private purchaser did not take in good faith, however, then Part III does not apply.

Finally, the first private person to take the vehicle may acquire it on hire-purchase, and then be told before completing his payments that he has no right to it because an earlier seller had only had it on hire-purchase. Nevertheless, the present hire-purchaser is protected so long as he was in good faith when he *made* his contract.

Sale under common law or statutory powers

Various powers of sale by non-owners exist at common law or under statute. A pledgee has common law powers to sell unredeemed goods pawned or pledged with him. Innkeepers, and bailees such as shoe repairers, may have statutory powers to sell their customers' goods to satisfy unpaid charges, and landlords can in some circumstances sell tenants' goods for arrears of rent. An unpaid seller of goods may have power to re-sell under section 48(2) of the Act (see page 190).

Sale under a court order

The High Court has wide powers to order the sale of goods which are affected by some dispute, and which are perishable or likely to deteriorate if kept, or which it is desirable to sell immediately for any other reason.

Summary

A further exception, the very old 'market overt' rule, was fairly recently abolished by the Sale of Goods (Amendment) Act 1994. The comments by Denning L.J. in *Pearson* v. *Rose and Young* (1950) sum up the problems behind this and the remaining exceptions to the *nemo dat* rule.

> 'In the early days of the common law the governing principle of our law of property was that no person could give a better title than he himself had got, but the needs of commerce have led to a progressive modification of this principle so as to protect innocent purchasers.... The cases show how difficult it is to strike the right balance between the claims of true owners and the claims of innocent purchasers.'

Specimen questions

1. A furniture dealer agreed to sell two pieces of furniture to *B*:
   (a) an antique commode, which *B* had chosen in the shop; the dealer agreed to replace one of the handles before delivery; and
   (b) a new bureau of a standard design, as soon as the dealer could obtain one from the manufacturer; the dealer again agreed to fix new handles to match those on the antique commode.

When both pieces of furniture were in the shop, with the handles fitted, and ready for collection by *B*, the dealer's shop and furniture were accidentally destroyed by fire. Explain whether *B* still has to pay for the furniture.

2. In April, *B* agreed to buy 1000 rare 'Dutch Uncle' tulip bulbs from *S* Ltd. *B* paid a deposit of 5% of the price, and agreed to pay the balance on 1 September when the bulbs were to be delivered. In July, all the 'Dutch Uncles' in the world were destroyed by a fungus disease. Advise *B*:

   (a) whether he still has to pay for the bulbs; and

   (b) alternatively, whether he can get back his 5% deposit.

   Would it make any difference whether or not *B* had chosen the specific bulbs which he wanted from *S* Ltd's stock?

3. Advise *BTV* Ltd, which retails television sets, on its legal position in respect of each of the following transactions:

   (a) A set was sold to *L* but not removed from the store. It was subsequently sold and delivered to another customer.

   (b) A set was delivered to *M* on approval for a 10 days' free trial. *M* has now retained the set for one month.

   (c) A particular set was sold to *N* but received slight damage during the course of delivery. *N* thereupon refused to accept delivery.

4. *B* buys goods from a second-hand shop owned by *S*. *B* uses the goods for a month, but then is told that they had been taken unlawfully from the stock of a firm that was bankrupt.

   (a) Does *B* have to give the goods back to representatives of the bankrupt firm?

   (b) Has *B* any remedy against *S*?

   Explain your answers.

5. *B* orders 900 packets of goods from a seller, *S*. They are to be delivered in three equal monthly instalments, one month apart.

   (a) 200 packets in the first instalment are mouldy. Explain what remedies *B* might have against *S*.

   (b) Can *B* refuse to take the other two instalments because he is afraid that they might be mouldy too? Explain your answer.

Unit 20. Product Liability

In the last couple of centuries, manufactured goods have become more numerous, more complicated, and more dangerous. Two hundred years ago there were no motor vehicles, no electrically powered goods, and few manufactured chemicals or drugs. It is generally accepted today that the producers of such things should have some responsibility for the safety of what they produce. The question which has occupied the courts and the legislature is, 'How much responsibility?'

The first three parts of this unit, headings A–C, discuss some of the ways in which the courts have used the rules of common law, of contract and tort, to deal with product liability. Heading D deals with some of the legislative rules which have been added.

A. Producer's liability for breach of contract

When the producer sells his goods, he makes a contract with his buyer. The Sale of Goods Acts 1979–94 imply certain terms into that contract, in particular that the goods will correspond with any description which he has applied to them (section 13), that the goods will be of satisfactory quality (section 14(2)), that the goods will be reasonably fit for any purpose which the buyer has expressly or impliedly made known to him (section 14(3)), and, if appropriate, that the bulk will correspond in quality with any sample (section 15); see Unit 18, where these terms are discussed in more detail. If the producer is in breach, the buyer is entitled to damages and/or, possibly, to reject the goods. The producer's liability is strict, and the buyer does not have to prove that the defect was the seller's fault; see Frost v. *Aylesbury Dairy* (Unit 15). It would be no defence, therefore, for the seller to prove that the defect in the finished product was due to a faulty component which, in all innocence, he had bought from someone else. Moreover, the buyer can recover damages not only for personal injury or for harm to other property caused by the faulty product, but also for purely financial loss, as in *Victoria Laundry (Windsor) Ltd* v. *Newman Industries Ltd* (Unit 15).

The problem, however, is that it is not usually the first buyer who is harmed. In the first place, the eventual consumer does not usually buy his goods directly from the manufacturer. He buys from a local shop or chemist or garage. Between the manufacturer and the shop, the goods may have been bought and re-sold by several distributors or wholesalers. In this event, the consumer has no contract with the manufacturer/producer, and the Sale of Goods Acts need a contract before they can apply. Secondly, faulty goods can easily harm the consumer's family or friends, as in *Donoghue* v. *Stevenson* (Unit 9). They can even, as in the case of defective motor cars, injure complete strangers. These people have no contract with anyone. The problem, therefore, is one of privity of contract (Unit 16).

Nevertheless, the producer of goods may sometimes find himself liable for breach of contract even where the goods do not directly harm his immediate buyer. First, there may be a chain of actions which comes back to him. Let us assume that the goods prove defective and injure the eventual consumer. The consumer can sue the retailer from whom he bought the goods. The retailer will be liable if, for example, the goods were not of satisfactory quality, and the fact that this was not the retailer's fault is immaterial. The retailer can then sue his own supplier, and so on back to the producer. If possible, the court may try to hear all of the actions in the chain at the same time, so as to save time and expense. *Godley* v. *Perry* in Unit 18 (the plastic catapult case) is a partial example, but there are many more complicated ones.

> In *Young & Marten Ltd* v. *McManus Childs Ltd* (1969), the buyers of houses found that the roof tiles were faulty, and successfully claimed compensation from the builder. He in turn recovered damages from the subcontractor who had supplied the tiles and laid the roofs. The court commented that the subcontractor could then normally have sued his own supplier, who could in turn have sued the manufacturer—but these last two possible actions were now barred by the Limitation Act (see Unit 16).

However, such a 'chain' can only help the eventual buyer. It does not help a friend or stranger who did not buy the goods from anyone, as in *Donoghue* v. *Stevenson*. Moreover, the chain can easily be broken, so as to give accidental protection to the producer.

> In *Muirhead* v. *Industrial Tank Specialities Ltd* (1985) (Unit 9), the immediate seller was insolvent and not worth suing. The possible chain of contract actions therefore did not even start. The producer had to be sued (unsuccessfully) in tort.

> In *Lambert* v. *Lewis* (1982), a motor dealer kept inadequate stock records, and did not know which of several wholesalers had supplied him with a defective coupling. Any chain of contract actions would therefore have stopped with him, and not got back to the original producer.

Similarly, a valid exemption clause by one supplier in the chain may protect him, and therefore break the chain; and even the passage of time may stop the chain from running further, as in *Young & Marten* v. *McManus Childs*, on page 203.

A second way in which a producer may find himself liable to the eventual consumer for breach of contract is through some 'collateral' contract. One possibility is a valid manufacturer's guarantee, by which the manufacturer makes promises about repairs or replacements to the eventual user. This guarantee will only be binding on the manufacturer if it can be shown that the eventual user gave consideration for it (Unit 11). It may be shown, for example, that the eventual user knew of the guarantee when he bought the goods, and that this influenced his decision to buy. Another possibility is that the manufacturer/producer may have made separate promises to the eventual user.

> In *Shanklin Pier Ltd* v. *Detel Products Ltd* (1951), a paint manufacturer approached the pier company and promised that its paint would stand up well to sea-water. The pier, therefore, instructed contractors who were painting the pier to use this paint. The contractors bought from a wholesaler. The paint proved inadequate. The pier company recovered damages directly from the manufacturer for breach of a collateral contract. The manufacturers had promised, in effect, that 'in consideration of you, the pier, telling the contractor to use my paint, I promise that it will be suitable'.

Very exceptionally, even a producer's advertisement can create a collateral contract between him and the eventual user.

> *Carlill* v. *Carbolic Smoke Ball Co.* (Unit 12) is a product liability case. Mrs Carlill bought the smoke ball *from a shop* in reliance on the promises in the manufacturer's advertisement. She recovered damages for breach of contract from the manufacturer when the smoke ball did not, as had been promised, prevent 'flu.

This is a very unusual case however, if only because most advertisements by manufacturers do not contain promises which would be taken seriously. Not all aftershave lotions or lagers have the qualities claimed for them.

It should again be emphasized here that the 'collateral contract' idea will not help those who have given no consideration for the producer's promises. It will therefore help neither friends and family of the eventual buyer, nor strangers injured by dangerous goods.

The Contracts (Rights of Third Parties) Act 1999 is unlikely to help consumers very much. The Act provides that a third party (the consumer in this case) may in his own right enforce a contract if the contract *expressly* provides that he may. A producer or retailer might be unlikely to make such a provision. Alternatively, the third party can enforce a term that purports to confer a benefit on him – but not if it appears that the parties did not intend this. To avoid any uncertainty, a retailer can always make it clear (on the label?) that he accepts no responsibility to a user other than to his immediate buyer.

B. Producer's liability for the tort of negligence

At common law, a producer of goods owes duties of care not only to the person who buys from and pays him, but also to others to whom he should reasonably foresee the possibility of harm. As we have seen, *Donoghue* v. *Stevenson* itself, once the leading case on the tort of negligence, is a product liability case (Unit 9).

This duty of care is not the same as the strict liability which can arise under a contract. A producer is only liable for the tort of negligence if he has been negligent. This can take many forms. There may be faults in design or in the manufacturing process, or inadequate testing and quality control. There may be negligence in failing to warn users of concealed dangers, or even in failing to recall goods which have already been sold but which turn out to have hitherto unsuspected faults. The level of care required can be high.

In *Vacwell Engineering Ltd* v. *BDH Chemicals Ltd* (1971), BDH supplied glass ampoules of a chemical which would explode violently on contact with water. An ampoule broke, killing a scientist who worked with Vacwell. The labels on the ampoules warned that the chemical could give off a harmful vapour, but gave no warning that it could explode. Indeed, this danger was not mentioned in recent scientific literature, only in some very old journals, and BDH were probably unaware of it. Nevertheless they were liable for negligence: as experts, they *should* have known and warned of the danger.

In *Walton* v. *British Leyland Ltd* (1978), car manufacturers discovered that, because of a design defect, the wheel-bearings on their new vehicle might fail. Some such cars had already been sold. The manufacturers considered recalling them all so as to remedy the defect, but decided against this because the publicity might harm future sales. Franchised dealers were advised to remedy the defect when cars came in to be serviced, but this was all. Later, Mrs Walton, a passenger, was injured when a wheel flew off. The manufacturers were liable for negligence because, on the facts, they had not taken reasonable care.

In *Winward* v. *TVR Engineering Ltd* (1987), Weber made carburettors which were sold to Ford and incorporated in Ford engines. In turn, TVR bought Ford engines for TVR sports cars. Because of a faulty carburettor, one of the cars caught fire and injured Mrs Winward. There was no history of such fires, and TVR claimed that they had bought the engine from a top manufacturer, and were entitled to rely on the latter's expertise. It was held that TVR had still been negligent, in that they themselves should have checked the engine too.

The victim's difficulties can sometimes be ones of proof. The victim is usually not an expert, and he does not know what the producer did or did not do. Since the producer is the only one who does—or should—know what went wrong, the courts may reverse the burden of proof and require the producer to prove that he was *not* negligent. This is the concept of *res ipsa loquitur*; see *Steer* v. *Durable Rubber Co. Ltd* (Unit 9). As we have seen, the producer's burden may then be difficult to discharge.

Finally, the victim must have suffered some harm as a result of the defective goods. Most of the successful claims have involved physical injury to the person or, in the case of drugs and chemicals, illness or disability. Damages can also be recovered for other property damaged by the defective product and for financial loss immediately connected with this. Damages for the tort of negligence cannot generally be

205

recovered, however, for purely economic loss. This can be important when the eventual user of the product is a business.

> In *Muirhead Ltd* v. *Industrial Tank Specialities Ltd* (Unit 9), the products were pumps for a sea-water tank. The claimant, a fish merchant, did not recover damages for the future profits which he might have made had the pumps not been defective.

Exceptionally, the damages awarded against a producer may be reduced if he can show that the victim had been negligent in his use of the product and that this contributory negligence was a partial cause of the mishap (Unit 10).

C. Liability in contract and tort compared

We have seen that a producer of goods can be liable to his immediate buyer for breach of contract, and that this liability can sometimes be extended to subsequent buyers by 'chain' actions. To anyone else, the producer can only be liable, at common law, in tort. The two types of liability have differences.

1. Liability for breach of contract demands that there is a contract to be broken. The doctrine of privity of contract restricts contractual duties and rights to the immediate buyer, who is not, usually, the eventual user. The duties of care for the tort of negligence extend much more widely.
2. Liability for breach of contract can be strict, and a producer can be liable even if the default was not his fault. This does not apply to the tort of negligence.
3. Purely financial loss (e.g., loss of future profits by a business buyer harmed by a defective product) can readily be recovered for breach of contract, but only in rare and exceptional cases for the tort of negligence; see *Muirhead* v. *ITS* again. For this reason if for no other, the *business* victim of a defective product may prefer to sue his immediate seller for breach of contract rather than the producer in tort.
4. Contributory negligence by the eventual user may be a partial defence to an action in tort, and cause the damages to be reduced. It can also be a partial defence in an action for breach of a contractual duty of care. However it will be no defence to an action for breach of a strict contractual duty.
5. The limitation period for breach of contract is six years, but for personal injuries in tort only three years.
6. Contract and tort have one important similarity, however, in that they are both available to *business* as well as private users of a product. The Consumer Protection Act, Part I, which follows, generally protects only the *private* consumer.

D. The Consumer Protection Act 1987

Part I

The 1987 Act, Part I, was passed as a result of a Directive of the Council of the European Communities in 1985. It adds to, but does not replace, the common law rules described above. This can be important, because the scope of the Act is limited. In particular, liability under Part I only arises if the product is of a type ordinarily intended for *private* use, and in fact intended by the victim for his private use or consumption. It would not, for example, apply to the business consumer in *Muirhead* v. *Industrial Tank Specialities Ltd*, earlier. Secondly, Part I only applies to certain types of loss, mainly death, personal injury, and loss of or damage to property exceeding £275. Thirdly, Part I contains certain defences which are not quite the same as those available in contract and in tort (see above). There may sometimes, therefore, be good reasons for suing at common law rather than, or as well as, under the Act.

Part I imposes civil liability (damages to the victim), and the usual person who can be liable is the *producer* who manufactured or processed the defective product. The Act also applies to a person who, by putting his name on a product, or using his trade or other distinguishing mark, holds himself out to be the producer. This could cover, for example, a large company which buys identical goods from several producers, but re-sells them as if they were its own product. A business which imports goods from outside the Common Market can also be liable, thus avoiding the possible need to sue a producer on the other side of the world. Finally, even a mere supplier of goods can be liable under Part I if a victim who cannot reasonably identify the producer asks his supplier to identify a producer, and the supplier neither does this nor names his own supplier (compare *Lambert* v. *Lewis*, page 203).

The producer, etc., can be liable if the product is *defective*, that is, if its safety to persons or to other property is not such as people generally are entitled to expect. This can vary according to, for example, what might reasonably be expected to be done with the product, the way in which it is sold, and any instructions or warnings as regards use. The time to judge these matters is when the product was supplied, and a thing is not treated as unsafe merely because something safer was produced at a later date.

The types of loss covered are limited to death or personal injury, or any loss of or damage to other property (including land). Small claims for property are not allowed, however, and the loss of or damage to property must exceed £275. Damages cannot be recovered for the fact that the product itself is worth less than it should have been. Financial loss unconnected with death, injury or damage to property cannot be recovered under Part I, and in all of these respects the Act can be compared and contrasted with the rules of contract and tort above.

Anyone physically injured by a dangerous product can claim, not just the eventual buyer, and to this extent liability is similar to that in tort. As regards property damage there are further limits and, in effect, claims are limited to loss of private rather than business property.

The victim does not have to prove that the producer was negligent, but Part I does contain a number of defences. The burden of proving these is on the defendant (the producer), and the Act does therefore start from a position similar to *res ipsa loquitur* above. Some of the defences are fairly straightforward: that the person proceeded against did not supply the product; or that he did not supply it in the course of his business or with a view to profit; or that the product was not defective when it was supplied. It is also a defence if the defect was attributable to compliance with any European Community obligation or any enactment. More controversial is the 'state of the art' defence in section 4(1) (e): it is a defence to show:

> 'that the state of scientific and technical knowledge at the relevant time was not such that a producer of products of the same description as the product in question might be expected to have discovered the defect if it had existed in his products while they were under his control'.

This might give a defence to the producer of, for example, a new drug which was later found to have unfortunate side-effects of which the producer could not reasonably have known when he produced it. The onus of proving this would be on the producer, and it might be hard to prove. But there are those who argue that the producer and seller of something potentially dangerous should take *full* responsibility if things go wrong, irrespective of fault, and would prefer to see this defence removed. It is also interesting to compare this with the decisions in pre-Act cases such as *Vacwell Engineering* v. *BDH Chemicals*, page 205.

When a product such as a valve later becomes part of a larger article, such as a TV set, it is a defence for the producer of the valve to show that any subsequent failure was wholly attributable to the design of the TV set; the valve had simply been used for an inappropriate purpose. There is a similar defence for the producer who makes a part in compliance with instructions given to him by the maker of the larger product.

A partial defence, which might reduce the damages, could be the contributory negligence of the person suffering harm from the offending product. One thing which will not be a defence, however, is an exemption clause; by section 7:

> 'The liability of a person by virtue of this Part ... shall not be limited or excluded by any contract term, by any notice or by any other provision.'

Part II

Part II of the 1987 Act replaces the Consumer Safety Acts. Certain types of goods must comply with specific safety regulations which have been made from time to time, particularly the General Product Safety Regulations 1994, to cover potentially dangerous consumer goods such as electrical appliances, oil heaters, children's clothing and toys. Breach of any of these sets of regulations is a criminal offence. By section 41 of the Act, breach is also civilly actionable for damages if someone is injured or killed.

Specimen questions

1. *B* buys a new electrical hair drier from a local shop. After two days, the hair drier breaks down, and *B* takes it back to the shop. The shop expresses its regret and advises *B* to contact the manufacturer. (The shop deals with many electrical

products and has no particular expertise on hair driers.) Advise *B* as to what remedies he can seek, and against whom.

2. (a) For the purposes of the Consumer Protection Act 1987, who is treated as a 'producer' of goods?
   (b) To what extent is he strictly liable for defects in his products?
   (c) Has he any possible defences?

3. *M* manufactures goods in Britain using parts imported from the Far East. He sells the goods to *S*, a shop, which in turn re-sells to the public. Unknown to *M* and *S*, one of the imported parts has a hidden flaw. As a result, one of the goods breaks down, injuring *B* who had bought it from *S*. It also injures *B*'s wife. Discuss whether *B* or his wife can recover damages from *S* or *M*.

4. *W* manufactures and markets electrical goods. A new model of electric fire is introduced and, after a number have been sold, is found to have a fault in the wiring, which could prove to be dangerous.

   To what extent may *W* then be liable:
   (a) for breach of contract;
   (b) under the tort of negligence;
   (c) under the Consumer Protection Act 1987?

5. Sparks buys old radios, reconditions them and then re-sells them at a cheap price. He always attaches a note stating that they are second-hand and that they are bought at the purchaser's risk with no liability on Sparks's part. Some are sold to traders and others directly to the public.

   In repairing a number of sets, Sparks uses some faulty wiring with the following results:
   (a) Watt, who bought a set from a trader, receives an electric shock.
   (b) Volt, who bought a set from Sparks, suffers damage to furniture when the radio causes a fire.
   (c) Ampere, Volt's wife, is burned when she attempts to put out the fire.
       Discuss whether Sparks may be liable to Watt, Volt or Ampere.

Unit 21. Credit and Security

Money may be lent and credit may be given in many ways, and on many different terms. A specified sum may be lent for a fixed term at a stated rate of interest. The whole sum may be repayable on a fixed date, or the loan may be repayable by instalments. The creditor may allow the borrower to draw varying sums on a current account up to a stated limit, as on a bank overdraft. The borrower may have a credit card which he can use to pay bills, on an arrangement that he will repay the lender (often a company controlled by his bank) in due course. Some credit is for a specific purpose, as where the supplier of goods allows his customer to pay for them by instalments, or where a building society lends money to a house buyer in return for a mortgage on a house. In other instances there may be no arrangement between lender and borrower as to how the money is to be used, as where a company issues debentures to the public.

Frequently the lender will require some *security*. We shall see later how property such as goods and land can be used in various ways as security. Other forms of property too, such as shares, can be mortgaged or charged.

The legal problems and rules can vary according to many things. The nature of the borrower may be important: the Companies Act applies to borrowing by companies, which is discussed in Unit 24. The Consumer Credit Act applies only to borrowing by *non*-corporate bodies. The rules can vary according to the amount owed: the Consumer Credit Act applies only where the credit does not exceed £25 000. Differences also arise according to who is the lender: an individual may lend money to a corporation (by opening a savings account at a building society, for instance), or a corporation may lend to an individual (a finance company letting a car on hire-purchase). This unit deals with some of the possibilities.

210

For as long as loans have existed, some creditors have abused their stronger bargaining position to impose harsh and unfair burdens on debtors, and many of the rules discussed below are attempts to prevent such injustices. On the other hand, all creditors, including large creditors, need protection against debtors who will not pay. Furthermore, many investors – a term which can include lenders—have needed protection against businesses offering financial advice and management. The Financial Services Act 1986 contains controls over some such investment businesses.

A. Consumer credit

The Consumer Credit Act 1974 applies to personal credit agreements by which the creditor provides the debtor with *credit not exceeding £25 000*. Credit is 'personal' when the borrower is an individual or partnership, not a corporate body. The purpose for which the money is required is immaterial; a loan for an individual's business is still 'personal'. The 'credit' is the amount *borrowed*, not necessarily the amount to be repaid. Therefore, if someone borrows £24 000 but, with interest, has to pay back £27 000, the agreement is within the Act. The interest is a 'charge for credit'. There are, therefore, two limits on the operation of the Act: (a) as to the amount borrowed; and (b) as to the nature of the borrower.

Some agreements are 'exempt' from most provisions of the Act. The following are the main examples:

1. Loans by building societies, local authorities, and many other corporate bodies, if the loan is secured by a mortgage of land.
2. Fixed sum loans to finance the purchase of goods, services or land, if the credit is repayable by four or fewer instalments; but hire-purchase and conditional sale agreements are *not* exempt, however many instalments are payable (see later).
3. 'Running account' credits, where no specific sum is borrowed, but credit up to a certain amount is allowed. These can be exempt if the whole credit *for a period* is to be repaid by a single payment. Some credit card accounts, and accounts with the local greengrocer where the bill comes in and is payable, say, monthly, can be exempt under (2) and/or (3).

The 'extortionate bargain' provisions (see page 213) can apply even to exempt agreements and to personal credit outside the financial limits.

Controls over lenders and advertising

Any person wishing to carry on consumer credit business must first obtain a licence from the Director-General of Fair Trading, who must be satisfied that the applicant is a fit person to engage in such activities. This can apply not only to potential creditors, but also to credit brokers such as retailers who have arrangements to introduce customers requiring credit to a particular finance company. Regulations govern the ways in which a licensee must conduct his business. Loans by unlicensed creditors are criminal offences, and are enforceable against the borrower only at the Director's discretion.

The Department of Trade and Industry has made regulations controlling advertisements by credit dealers, to ensure that a fair picture is given as to the nature of the credit offered, and the true rate of interest, etc. There are similar controls over quotations by dealers as to the terms on which they offer credit. Canvassing people elsewhere than on business premises to persuade them to borrow, sending unsolicited credit tokens (credit cards), and activities persuading minors to borrow are prohibited. Breach is usually a criminal offence.

Information

In *commercial* consumer credit agreements, i.e., where the creditor acts in the course of his business, the Act aims to ensure that a prospective debtor knows what he is letting himself in for.

Before the agreement is made, the creditor must give written details of terms such as the charge for credit e.g., the annual percentage rate of interest (APR).

The agreement itself must be in writing, signed by the debtor personally and by or on behalf of the creditor. Signature of a form in blank, leaving it to an agent or the creditor to fill in the blanks, is not enough. Regulations cover the type, size, and in some instances colour of the print, and the document must give details of the debtor's rights as well as his duties (see later). If these requirements are not met, the agreement is unenforceable against the debtor without a court order, and the court has powers to vary the terms of the loan and/or refuse to allow the creditor to recover arrears.

Copies of the agreement must be given to the debtor. He must always receive, immediately, a copy of the form which he signs. If the form then has to be sent away for completion by the creditor, the debtor must also be given a copy of the completed agreement within seven days of its completion, so that he can check that no alterations have been made since his signature. Non-compliance can similarly render the agreement unenforceable without a court order.

Later, while a fixed-sum credit is being repaid, a debtor is entitled to information about how much he has currently paid and still owes, and to further copies of the agreement.

Rash or hasty agreements

A prospective debtor can withdraw his offer at any time before the creditor accepts it. Therefore, if the debtor's proposal has to be sent away to the creditor, the debtor has a short interval in which to think again. He can withdraw his offer by informing either the lender, or any agent of the lender (such as the garage or other retailer in a hire-purchase 'triangular' transaction; see page 214). The offer may also end for other reasons, as in *Financings* v. *Stimson* (Unit 12).

If a credit agreement has been induced by the creditor's misrepresentations, the debtor has a reasonable time in which to rescind the contract (see Unit 13).

If a commercial consumer credit agreement, within the 1974 Act, is signed by the debtor when not on the trade premises of the creditor or any dealer with whom the debtor originally negotiated, the debtor has a statutory *right of cancellation*. This gives a 'cooling off' period, and particularly protects people who are persuaded by door-step salesmen to sign credit or hire-purchase agreements at home. In cancellable transactions, the debtor must receive a copy of the agreement as soon as he signs, and a second statutory copy must be sent to him *by post* within seven days of its completion. He then has until the end of the fifth day following receipt of his second statutory copy in which to cancel the agreement. Cancellation must be in writing, but posting it is sufficient. Both copies of the agreement must inform him of his right to cancel.

Terms of the agreement and enforcement by the creditor

Various provisions in the Consumer Credit Act protect the debtor during the credit period. For example, the *debtor* under a regulated agreement is entitled *at any time* to pay off what he owes, on giving notice to the creditor that he intends to do so. He may also be entitled to a rebate of interest if the creditor is getting his money earlier than originally contracted for.

Second, before the *creditor* can terminate the agreement or take other action for the debtor's breach, he must serve a 'notice of default'. This must specify the alleged breach, give at least seven days in which to remedy it or pay compensation, and explain the consequences of failure to comply. If the debtor complies with the notice, 'the breach shall be treated as if it had never occurred'. Similar seven day notices must be served if the creditor wishes to enforce any of his rights in the agreement, even if there has been no breach.

Only if the debtor fails to comply with a notice of default can the creditor ask the court for an enforcement order, and even at this stage the court can give the debtor additional time to pay or grant other relief.

Third, if at any time a court finds a personal credit bargain to be *extortionate*, it may re-open the agreement so as to do justice between the parties. This can be done under sections 137–140, either in proceedings brought by the debtor or as a defence to an action by the creditor. A bargain is extortionate if it requires the debtor, or any relative of his, to make payments which are exorbitant or grossly contravene 'ordinary principles of fair dealing'. The court can have regard to (i) interest rates prevailing at the time, (ii) the debtor's age, experience, business capacity and health, and whether he was under any financial pressure at the time, and (iii) the degree of risk accepted by the creditor, his relationship with the debtor, and whether a 'colourable' (i.e., inflated) cash price was quoted for goods or services so as to make the interest rates seem less.

The court has power to set aside the whole or part of the debtor's obligations, to require the creditor to repay all or part of what the debtor has paid, and/or to alter the terms of the credit agreement.

In *Barcabe Ltd* v. *Edwards* (1983), a low-paid man with four children had answered an advertisement, and been persuaded to borrow £400 at interest totalling 100 per cent per year. There was no evidence that he had defaulted on earlier debts, or otherwise was a bad security risk. The court reduced the interest to 40 per cent.

B. Goods as security

Conditional sale and hire-purchase

When customers seek goods they often need credit, which can be given in various ways. If a seller allows payment by instalments, and makes no provision for when ownership is to pass, the contract is a *credit sale*. Ownership in the goods will pass as soon as the buyer takes possession, and the seller has no right to re-take if the buyer defaults. Some sellers, therefore, use the goods as security, by stipulating that ownership is not to pass to the buyer until he satisfies some condition (usually payment of the last instalment). This is a *conditional sale*. The goods remain the seller's, and he can reclaim possession until the condition is met. Alternatively, the supplier may simply hire the goods to the customer but, on payment of a specified number of hire 'instalments', the hirer will have the option to buy the goods for a nominal sum of, say, £1. This is *hire-purchase*.

Frequently, the garage or retailer supplying the goods will prefer payment immediately and will, therefore, have arrangements with a finance house. In one common 'triangular' transaction of this sort, the dealer will have a stock of the finance company's hire-purchase forms. If the customer wants credit, the dealer asks him to fill in his part of such a form which constitutes an offer, addressed to the finance house, to take the goods on hire-purchase *from the finance house*. The dealer forwards this form together with his own offer to sell the goods for cash to the finance house. If the latter accepts both offers, it pays the dealer the cash price, becomes owner of the goods, and lets them on hire-purchase to the customer, the hire-purchase price being (much) higher than the cash price. The customer collects the goods from the dealer, and the finance house rarely sees them.

Hire-purchase and conditional sales to individuals or partnerships are governed by the Consumer Credit Act within the financial limits. Notice again that, for the Consumer Credit Act, it is the amount of *credit* which matters. If someone acquires a car on hire-purchase for £30 000 but pays a £5000 deposit, the amount of credit is only £25 000 and, therefore, within the Act.

Some of the protections given by the 1974 Act have already been described. The controls over lenders, information to debtors, rash 'door-step' agreements, and harsh terms apply to hire-purchase and conditional sale in the same way as to other agreements under the Act. There are additional protections.

1. By section 99, a hire-purchaser or buyer on conditional sale can *terminate* the agreement at any time. He must give notice to the creditor, return the goods, and pay off any arrears of instalments currently due. He is then no longer liable to complete his payments under the agreement. This right to terminate the agreement

and surrender the goods is in addition to his right, discussed earlier, to pay off the whole balance early (in which case he keeps the goods).

2. The Act protects against harsh 'minimum payment' clauses. If the hirer terminates the contract early and returns goods which have drastically depreciated, the creditor might suffer loss. Many agreements, therefore, required the debtor to bring his payments up to, say, 75% of the hire-purchase price if the agreement ended early. Such clauses were often in reality more attempts to penalize the debtor than to compensate the creditor and, even at common law, could probably be struck out as in *Bridge* v. *Campbell Discount Ltd* (Unit 15), whether or not the hirer was in breach.

When the 1974 Act applies, section 100 imposes statutory limits on minimum payment clauses. If there is such a clause, the payment must not exceed the amount, if any, by which one-half of the total price exceeds the aggregate of the sums paid and due immediately before termination. If the creditor's actual loss is less than this, the court may order payment of his actual loss only. On the other hand, if the debtor has not taken reasonable care of the goods, the debtor's payment can be increased to over half if need be, to compensate the creditor.

3. Hire-purchasers and conditional sale buyers are also protected against 'snatch-back'. At common law, if the hirer or buyer was late with *any* instalment, the creditor could rescind the agreement and take back the goods. This could cause injustice.

> In *Cramer* v. *Giles* (1883), the hirer took a piano at a hire-purchase price of 60 guineas. After paying more than 50 guineas (probably more than the piano's cash value), the hirer was late with his last two instalments. He tendered payment shortly afterwards, but this was refused. Instead, the creditor sued for return of the piano, and was held entitled to it, leaving the hirer with nothing for the instalments which he had paid.

Many creditors did not trouble to sue, but simply took the goods back summarily at the slightest default. The contract often gave the creditor right of entry to the hirer's premises for the purpose. This process sometimes gave the creditor a considerable profit.

If the Act applies, it protects the hirer against this. We have seen that a creditor must give at least seven days' notice of default before taking any steps against the debtor. Moreover, a creditor must not now enter any premises to take back the goods without first obtaining a court order. Even more importantly, by section 90, when one-third of the hire-purchase or conditional sale price has been paid, the goods become 'protected goods', and must not be taken back without a court order unless the debtor himself ended the agreement. If the debtor pays the whole balance of the price before the court order, the goods become his. Even if he does not do this, the court can give him additional time to pay.

If a creditor does take back protected goods without a court order, the agreement and the debtor's liabilities end, and the latter can recover *all* that he has previously paid.

215

In *Capital Finance Ltd* v. *Bray* (1964), a finance company took back, without a court order, a car which Bray had on hire-purchase. The car was protected goods and, when the company realized its mistake, it returned the car immediately. Bray used it for several months, refusing all requests for payment. Eventually, the company sued for possession, and this was granted. The company could not, however, recover payment for Bray's use of the car after its return to him. Moreover, Bray recovered everything which he had paid.

A creditor can only recover protected goods without a court order if the debtor voluntarily returns them, or if the debtor has abandoned them.

4. Finally, finance houses and other suppliers of goods on hire-purchase owe obligations as regards title to the goods, description, fitness, and quality under the Supply of Goods (Implied Terms) Act 1973 (as amended in 1994). This applies to all hire-purchase, irrespective of the amount borrowed or the nature of the borrower. The obligations implied are almost identical to those imposed on the seller by the Sale of Goods Act, with the same limits on exclusion. Where a triangular transaction takes place, the finance company is liable for representations or promises made by the dealer.

Other uses of goods as security

When credit is needed in order to buy goods, another means by which the seller can protect himself is by a 'retention of title' (*Romalpa*) clause (Unit 18). This is sometimes used where the buyer is a large company.

If someone who *already owns* goods wishes to use them as security, different problems arise. First he can *transfer ownership* to the creditor, but retain possession. The creditor will undertake to re-transfer ownership when the loan is repaid. In practice this 'mortgage' of goods will be in writing, to provide the proof needed to prevent an unscrupulous borrower from abusing his retention of the goods. If the borrower is an individual, such a document is known as a *bill of sale*. It must be in a form laid down by statute, and the bill must be registered at the Central Office of the Supreme Court.

Alternatively, the borrower can *transfer possession* of the goods to the lender while retaining ownership, the reverse of the situation with a bill of sale. This is known as *pawn* or *pledge*. The goods are redeemed by repayment and, in the event of default, the lender may sell the goods either after lapse of an agreed time or, if no time has been agreed, by giving reasonable notice to the borrower of intention to sell. There are again statutory protections, imposed now under the Consumer Credit Act.

Goods may also be subject to a *lien* when the creditor has a right to *retain possession* until a debt has been discharged. Thus a garage may retain a car as security for the cost of repairs carried out, and a hotel or dry cleaners may hold a customer's goods until the bill is paid.

C. Land as security

Mortgages

The most common method of using land as security is the mortgage. The borrower (*mortgagor*) transfers an interest in the land to the lender (*mortgagee*), and the lender may realize his interest if the loan is not repaid. The most familiar example is a loan from a building society to buy a house. The loan is repaid by the purchaser, with interest, by periodic repayments.

A legal mortgage may be created today in two ways. The first is to grant a legal estate to the mortgagee in the form of a very long lease, with a proviso that the lease shall come to an end on repayment of the loan. If the property is leasehold, then a sub-lease is granted for a slightly shorter period than the original lease. The mortgagee does not take possession of the property; this remains with the mortgagor, who retains his legal estate.

An alternative and more usual method is by the execution of a deed, which declares that a legal charge has been created. This is a more simple method, applicable to both freehold and leasehold, introduced by the Law of Property Act 1925. The mortgagee has the same protection as if a lease had been created.

Legal mortgages normally take priority according to the date of creation. The problem of priority may arise when a mortgagor defaults after raising several loans on the security of his land to a total amount which exceeds the current value of the land.

If the mortgagor defaults, the lender has various remedies. He may sue for the money due. He may take possession of the land, either personally or by appointing a receiver, and recoup himself from any income arising from the management of the property. He may ask the court for a foreclosure order which transfers the land to him if the mortgagor does not repay within a specified time. The most usual action is to exercise the mortgagee's power of sale, and recoup himself from the proceeds of the sale; any surplus must ultimately be returned to the borrower.

From early times, the courts have protected mortgagors from harsh and unconscionable terms. For example, they have not permitted terms which make it impossible for the borrower to redeem his mortgage for an *unreasonable* time.

> In *Fairclough* v. *Swan Brewery Co. Ltd* (1912), a 20-year lease was mortgaged on terms which made redemption impossible until six weeks before the 20 years expired. These terms were held void, and the borrower could redeem earlier.

Similarly, the courts have sometimes held terms to be void if they give collateral advantages to the lender, but only if the advantages are unreasonable. A loan by a brewery making the mortgaged property a 'tied' public house until redemption could well be reasonable. Too long a restraint, however, might be void as an unlawful restraint of trade, as in *Esso Petroleum* v. *Harper's Garage* (Unit 17).

If the mortgagor is an individual or partnership, the 'extortionate bargain' provisions of the Consumer Credit Act can apply to it now, with the consequences described earlier. Apart from this, however, the Act does not apply to loans secured

217

by mortgages of land if the lender is a building society, local authority or other body which gives loans to buy land.

Equitable liens

Equitable liens, unlike legal ones, are not merely rights to *keep* possession of property, but can exist over property in the possession of someone else. One example is that the vendor of land has an equitable lien over the property sold, even after the buyer takes possession, as security for any unpaid part of the purchase price.

Examination questions

1. Rash enters into a loan agreement under which he agrees to borrow £2000, and repay the creditor by 24 monthly instalments of £130 each. Soon after making the agreement, he has second thoughts and wishes to escape from this liability.
   Advise him.
2. A buyer takes goods on conditional sale from a dealer for £30 000, paying a deposit of one-third and agreeing to pay the balance by monthly instalments over two years. After two months, the buyer defaults in paying instalments. Advise the dealer as to his rights, if any, to recover possession of the goods, including the consequences of failure to observe any legal requirements.
3. A salesman in Dealer Ltd's shop, talking to a customer, describes a washing machine in the showroom as being 'in perfect condition'. The customer agrees to take the machine, but wants credit. Dealer Ltd has an arrangement with a finance company, under which Dealer Ltd sells the machine for cash to the finance company, which then lets it on hire-purchase to the customer. The machine proves seriously defective, and the customer wishes to know whether he has any remedies against either the finance company or Dealer Ltd.
   Advise him.
4. Explain briefly the meaning of:
   (a) bill of sale;
   (b) credit sale;
   (c) 'triangular transaction';
   (d) equitable lien;
   (e) protected goods.
5. Eric and Freda enter into a partnership for the supply of motor vehicles for which hire-purchase will be directly provided.
   (a) To what extent are they liable for any defects in the vehicles supplied on hire-purchase?
   (b) What are their remedies against the vehicles if their customers default on payments?
   (c) If one of them make a contract without the knowledge or consent of the other, are they both liable on it?

Unit 22. Business Associations

Businesses can be of all sorts and sizes, ranging from self-employed, individual tradesmen to massive, multi-national, billion pound enterprises. Units 22–25 will describe some of the more important types of business *association*, where a number of human beings combine to further a common business interest. As mentioned in Unit 7, business associations may or may not become corporate bodies. The earlier parts of this Unit deal with some unincorporated business associations. Sections C and D introduce, in more detail, the nature and characteristics of registered companies.

A. Partnerships

The Partnership Act 1890, section 1, defines a partnership as 'the relation which subsists between persons carrying on a business in common with a view to profit'. As will be seen, this can include a wide variety of enterprises, both in nature and in size.

Formation

When a partnership is created, the parties often draw up a deed or 'articles' of partnership. This usually covers such matters as the provision of capital, management, and the sharing of profits. The Partnership Act provides for these matters, but only in the absence of agreement to the contrary by the partners. This contrasts sharply with the provisions of the Companies Acts, with which companies *must* comply (see Unit 23).

219

In some instances, partnerships are not formal or long term. They may be created informally, or even inadvertently. If *X* and *Y* cooperate in a once-only business venture, being paid jointly to remove rubbish from Lord *Z*'s back garden, then *X* and *Y* are partners under the Act, although the thought may never have occurred to them. It is similar with many very small or part-time businesses.

Difficulties do sometimes arise as to whether there is a partnership, and the Act contains rules to help determine this. First, the persons involved must be in *business*. Therefore, by section 2, the mere fact that two or more people are co-owners of property does not of *itself* render them partners, even if the property brings in income such as rent or dividends. Similarly, the sharing of *gross* returns (not profits) does not of itself create a partnership. Secondly, they must be carrying on the business 'in common'. If both carry on the business, then they are partners under section 1. If someone shares in the profits *without* taking part in the business, then section 2 applies. As a general rule anyone sharing profits is *presumed* a partner, but this can be rebutted. For example, repayment of a loan or debt out of profits, or at a rate varying with profits, does not necessarily make the creditor a partner, nor is the seller of a business who is being paid off out of the buyer's profits necessarily still a partner. The section also provides that paying an employee or agent at a rate varying with the profits does not necessarily make him a partner.

Someone who merely receives a *fixed* salary without sharing profits will normally *not* be a partner even if the firm calls him a 'salaried partner'; but this can be varied by the partnership deed if, for example, he is given rights to share capital on a winding-up (see section 39).

In forming a partnership, the ordinary rules of contract apply. It is voidable if induced by misrepresentation. It is void if formed for an illegal purpose: see *Foster* v. *Driscoll* (Unit 17). By the rules of capacity, a company, being a person, can be a partner (see *Stevenson Ltd* v. *Cartonnagen-Industrie*, later). A minor can be a partner, but can repudiate before or within a reasonable time after majority. He is not liable for partnership debts, but cannot be credited with profits without also being debited with losses.

By the Companies Act 1985, section 716, an unlimited partnership must not normally have more than 20 members. A partnership is, therefore, often at a disadvantage when raising large amounts of capital. It is a suitable form of business organization where close cooperation between members is required, and where minimal formality is sought. Moreover, even wealthy partnerships need not publish their accounts.

Solicitors and accountants, who cannot practise as companies, have long been exempt from the 20 partner limit. In any event, it is thought that many such firms, particularly larger ones, will in future seek to practise as LLPs under the Limited Liability Partnerships Act 2000, which imposes no upper limit on the number of members; see page 228.

Partners are known collectively as a 'firm', and the name under which they carry on business is the 'firm name'. They can, within limits, choose whatever name they think fit, subject only to the Business Names Act 1985. This Act, like the Companies Act, consolidates earlier legislation, and provides that wherever a firm carries on business in a name which does not consist of the surnames of all partners, with or without 'permitted additions' such as first names, initials, phrases such as 'and Sons' or, where two or more partners have the same surname, the addition of an 's' at the end of that surname ('Smiths'), then it is subject to limits.

It must not, for example, use a firm name which suggests Government or local authority connections, is offensive, or falsely suggests connection with another business. Other important checks are that a partnership must not use 'limited' or 'public limited company' as the last words of its name, although it can use 'company' or an abbreviation thereof. In any event, the true surnames of all partners must appear on letters (although there are exceptions for firms with more than 20 partners), and must be displayed in a prominent place to which customers have access at the firm's business premises. Non-compliance with any of the above provisions is a criminal offence.

Relations between the partners and outsiders

Four main issues arise under this heading.

When can the acts of one partner render the whole firm liable?

By the Partnership Act, section 5, the rules are those of agency. The firm is bound by anything which an individual partner was *expressly* authorized to do. The firm may also be bound if the partner does something for '*carrying on in the usual way business of the kind carried on by the firm*', so that there is nothing to make the outsider suspicious. The partner has *implied* authority, and the firm is bound even if he has exceeded his actual authority. It follows, however, that the firm will not be bound if the outsider either knows that a partner has no authority, or does not know or believe him to be a partner (see also Unit 7).

The key question as regards the unauthorized acts of a partner is what sort of thing *is* it 'usual' for an individual partner to do? This depends largely upon what sort of business it is, but the following can normally be assumed to be within a partner's powers, so long as his actions are not so unusual as to raise suspicions: selling the firm's goods; buying goods normally bought by the firm; giving receipts for debts; engaging and dismissing employees; signing ordinary cheques. In trading partnerships, as opposed to professional ones, it may also be usual for one partner to borrow money on the firm's behalf.

> In *Mercantile Credit Ltd* v. *Garrod* (1962), *G* and *P* were partners in a garage business concerned with *repairing* cars and letting lock-up garages. They had expressly agreed *not* to *sell* cars. Nevertheless *P*, without *G*'s knowledge, sold a car to *M Ltd* for £700. It then transpired that *P* had had no title to the car, so *M Ltd* demanded back the £700. When *P* did not pay, *G* was held liable as his partner. There was nothing to make *M Ltd* suspect that *P* and *G* had restricted their authority to repairing contracts. Therefore both of the partners were liable.

221

An outsider can doubly protect himself by contacting the other partners to see whether they do in fact agree with what the one partner proposes.

When is the firm liable for wrongs, such as torts, committed by one partner?

By section 10, where one partner commits an act which is wrong in itself, as opposed to being outside his authority, the firm will be civilly liable for any harm caused, and criminally for any penalty incurred if either:

(a) the act was done with the actual authority of his fellow partners; or
(b) the act was within his 'usual' authority, in the ordinary course of the firm's business.

> In *Hamlyn* v. *Houston & Co.* (1903), it was held to be quite 'usual' for a partner to obtain information about a rival business. His firm was therefore held liable when, without actual authority, he used bribery for this purpose.

Section 11 applies where a partner misapplies money or property received for, or in the custody of, the firm. The problem can arise in two ways. First, a *partner* may receive money or property *for* the firm, and misapply it before it reaches the firm. Here, the firm is liable if it was within the actual or 'usual' authority of that partner to receive the property. Secondly, the *firm* may already have custody of someone else's money or property, and a partner then takes it from the firm. In this case, so long as the money or property was in the firm's custody in the ordinary course of its business, the firm and all of its partners are liable.

When is an individual partner personally liable for the firm's debts and liabilities?

Partners in *ordinary* partnerships do not have limited liability. By section 9, they are jointly liable on the firm's contracts. Each partner is liable for the full amount due, but can apply to the court to have the others joined as co-defendants. In practice, claimants usually sue the firm in the firm's name, but can then enforce the full judgment against any partner. By section 12, partners are liable jointly and severally for torts committed by or on behalf of the firm. Again, each can be made liable for the full amount. (In all these situations contrast the Limited Liability Partnerships Act 2000.)

New partners are not liable for things done or debts incurred before they became partners. A *retiring partner* remains liable for debts incurred *before* his retirement, but can be discharged if a contract of 'novation' is made between himself, the other partners, and the creditor. He may also be liable for debts incurred *after* he leaves. Someone dealing with a firm after a change in its constitution is entitled to treat all apparent members of the old firm as still being members until he has notice of the change. The retiring partner should, therefore, protect himself by notifying all existing customers and suppliers of his retirement, so that he no longer appears to them to be a partner. He should also advertise his retirement in the *London Gazette*, which serves as notice to those who have not previously dealt with the firm. In any event, he is not liable to those who have not previously dealt with the firm, and who did not even know that he had been a partner.

> In *Tower Cabinet Co. Ltd* v. *Ingram* (1949), Ingram and *C* traded as partners under the name 'Merry's' until 1947. Ingram then left, but *C* carried on under the old name. In 1948, *C* ordered furniture from *T Ltd*, and failed to pay. *T Ltd* obtained judgment against Merry's and tried to enforce this against Ingram. Ingram was held not liable, because *T* Ltd had never dealt with Merry's while he was a partner, and only knew of his existence because, at a late stage, *C* had used some *old* notepaper showing Ingram's name. Discovery at this late stage did not make Ingram an 'apparent member'. (Nevertheless he would have saved himself much trouble had he destroyed *all* of the old headed notepaper before leaving.)

The estate of a partner who dies or becomes bankrupt is not liable for partnership debts incurred after the death or bankruptcy.

When is a person who is not a partner liable for the debts of the firm?
We have seen that a retiring partner can sometimes be liable for debts incurred after he left. By section 14, others may also be liable. A non-partner can be liable for the debt if he has by his words, spoken or written, or by his conduct, represented himself to be a partner and, as a result, an outsider has given credit to the firm. Similarly, a non-partner can be liable if he has *allowed* himself to be 'held out' as being a partner, but only if the creditor can show that he has *relied* on this misapprehension.

> In *Nationwide Building Society* v. *Lewis* (1998), Lewis, a sole solicitor, engaged *W* as a 'salaried partner'. *W*'s name appeared as a partner on the firm's notepaper, but he received no share of the profits. Nationwide sued the firm for negligence by Lewis, but Lewis was by this time bankrupt. Nationwide therefore wished to sue *W*. It was held on appeal that (a) *W* was really an employee, not a partner; and (b) Nationwide had dealt solely with Lewis, and could not show that it had relied in any way on *W*'s apparent status. Therefore *W* was not liable.

> In *Tower Cabinet* v. *Ingram*, Ingram was not liable under section 14 because he had not *allowed* the use of the old headed paper.

Relations of partners to each other

This is basically a matter for agreement between the partners. Section 24, however, sets out rules which apply in the absence of express or implied agreement to the contrary.

1. All partners are entitled to share equally in capital and profits, and must contribute equally to losses.
2. The firm must indemnify partners in respect of expenses and personal liabilities incurred in the ordinary and proper conduct of the business, or in anything necessarily done to preserve the firm's business or property.
3. A partner is entitled to interest on payments or loans which he makes to the firm beyond his agreed capital.

4. He is not, however, entitled to interest on his capital before ascertainment of profits.
5. Every partner may take part in managing the firm's business.
6. No partner is entitled to remuneration (such as salary) for acting in the partnership business. (This is often varied.)
7. No new partner may be introduced without the consent of all the existing partners. (This is sometimes expressly varied in practice, so as to give a partner the right to introduce a son or daughter.)
8. Ordinary management decisions can be by a majority, but any change in the *nature* of the business must be unanimous.
9. The records and accounts must be kept at the main place of business, and be open to all partners, or their proper agents such as accountants, to inspect and copy.
10. By section 25, no majority can expel a partner unless a power to do so has been conferred by express agreement between the partners.

Partners owe statutory duties of good faith to each other.

1. Section 28 imposes a statutory duty to account: 'Partners are bound to render true accounts and full information of all things affecting the partnership to any partner or his legal representative'.
2. Section 29 deals with secret or unauthorized profits: 'Every partner must account to the firm for any benefit derived by him without the consent of the other partners from any transaction concerning the partnership property, name or business connection'.

> In *Pathirana* v. *Pathirana* (1967), *R* and *A* were partners in a petrol service station. *A* gave *R* three months' notice that he intended to leave. Without waiting, R almost immediately took full control, and pocketed the entire profits. *A* was held entitled to his own share of profits for the rest of the notice period.

3. Section 30 imposes a duty not to compete with the firm: 'If a partner, without the consent of the other partners, carries on any business of the same nature as and competing with that of the firm, he must account for and pay over to the firm all profits made by him in that business'.

Dissolution of a partnership

Partnerships may be dissolved in various ways. For example, a partnership for a fixed term, or for a single venture or undertaking, *expires* automatically when the term or undertaking ends. If the partners continue working together after this, it is a new partnership.

If the partnership was for an indefinite period, as is more usual, it can be ended by any partner giving *notice* to *all* of the others. Notice can be oral unless the original partnership was created by deed, in which case notice must be written.

Death or bankruptcy of any partner automatically dissolves the entire partnership, unless otherwise provided. This can be inconvenient, so partnership agreements often exclude this rule and provide, for example, that the partnership shall continue, and that the others shall buy the deceased or bankrupt's share at a valuation.

If a court makes a *charging order* over any partner's share as a result of his private debts, the other partners may dissolve the firm.

A partnership is automatically dissolved by any event which makes it *illegal* to carry on the business, or for the members to carry it on in partnership.

> In *Stevenson Ltd* v. *Cartonnagen-Industrie* (1918), the outbreak of war in 1914 automatically ended the partnership between a British company and a German firm.

Any partner may apply for a *court order* to dissolve the partnership if any of the following conditions apply.

1. If any partner becomes a patient under the Mental Health Acts, or is shown to be permanently of unsound mind: application can be either on behalf of the mentally ill partner, or by the others.
2. If a partner other than the one applying becomes in any other way incapable of performing his partnership contract.
3. If a partner, other than the one suing, is guilty of such conduct as, in view of the nature of the business, is calculated to affect it prejudicially; an order might be made under this head if, for example, a solicitor, accountant or other professional partner was convicted of dishonesty, either within or outside the business.
4. If a partner, other than the one suing, wilfully or persistently breaks the partnership agreement, or otherwise so conducts himself that it is not reasonably practicable for the others to carry on business with him: examples might include persistent absence or laziness, or simply unpleasantness.
5. If the partnership business can *only* be carried on at a loss: merely making a loss *at present* is not necessarily enough.
6. If circumstances have arisen which, in the court's opinion, render it just and equitable that the partnership be dissolved.

> In *Ebrahimi* v. *Westbourne Galleries Ltd* (1972), *E* and *N* had been equal members for many years in a successful partnership. They then formed a company to run the business, with themselves as the sole shareholders and directors. Later, as a favour, *E* allowed *N* to introduce *N*'s son into the business, and *E* voluntarily transferred some of his shares to the son. *N* and his son then combined deliberately to force *E* out. The court granted *E*'s application to wind up (dissolve) the company, under provisions of the Companies Act very similar to those of the Partnership Act.

Finally, like any other contract, a partnership can be *rescinded* within a reasonable time of formation if it was induced by fraud or misrepresentation.

If a partnership is dissolved for any of the above reasons, the authority, rights and duties of the partners continue, but only for the purpose of winding up. Any partner may publicize the dissolution, and the others must concur.

By section 39, partnership property must be applied in payment of the firm's debts and liabilities. Any surplus must then be paid to the individual partners as, in effect, repayment of capital. Any partner can insist on this and, if necessary, ask the court to supervise it.

In settling accounts between the partners, the rules in section 44 apply unless otherwise agreed. Losses, including deficiencies in capital, must be paid (a) out of profits, (b) then out of capital, and (c) lastly, if necessary, by the partners themselves in the proportions in which they were entitled to share profits. If there are no outstanding losses, assets are to be applied (a) in paying trade and other creditors, (b) then in repaying to partners any loans which they have made to the firm, (c) then in repaying to each partner what he has contributed in capital, and finally (d) anything left goes to the partners in the proportions in which they were entitled to profits.

When there ought to be a final settlement and it does not take place, for example if a partner dies or retires and the remaining partners carry on without settling with him or his estate, then the outgoing partner may claim either such share of profits made after he left as are attributable to his share of the assets, or interest on the amount of his share; see *Pathirana* v. *Pathirana* again.

In practice, partnership agreements often expressly exclude this part of the Act. For example the agreement may provide that the partnership shall not end on the death or retirement of one partner, but that the remaining partners shall buy the interest of the out-going partner at a valuation.

B. Problems of unlimited liability

Some partnerships today are enormous enterprises, especially professional partnerships such as solicitors and, more particularly, accountants. Members of these professions are prohibited, by statute, from practising as limited companies. Therefore, the Companies Act 1985, section 716, which imposes a general maximum of 20 on the number of partners in a firm, makes specific exception for these professions. They can have as many partners as they wish. Some firms of solicitors have well over 100 partners. Some accountancy firms are much bigger, and have many hundreds, even thousands, of partners. In both cases, the firms practise internationally, have many thousands of employees, and vast assets. They act for even larger enterprises, such as the vast multi-national limited companies and groups.

In the context, with unlimited liability, the potential personal liability of partners can be daunting.

> In *Barings p.l.c.* v. *Coopers & Lybrand* (1996), a limited company was given leave to sue an unlimited partnership (and some others) for about £1 *billion* for alleged negligence.

> In *ADT Ltd* v. *BDO Binder Hamlyn* (1995), a firm of chartered accountants was held liable for damages of £65 million for negligence.

Strictly, a successful claimant could demand the whole of this amount from any one of the partners (see Partnership Act section 12). Not surprisingly, large professional firms have become interested in some means of escape.

The Limited Partnerships Act 1907 is not much help. It has for a long time allowed firms where 'limited partners' each contribute a stated amount of capital, and then have no further liability for the firm's debts. However, the following rules apply:

- At least one partner must still have unlimited liability.
- A limited partner must not take any part in the firm's management, and if he does so he loses his limited liability. He may examine the firm's books and the state and prospects of the business, and advise the unlimited partner(s), but he cannot take an active rôle.
- A limited partner's death, bankruptcy or mental illness will not dissolve the partnership.
- Unlike ordinary firms, limited partnerships must register details of the firm, the business and the partners with the Registrar of Companies, who issues a certificate of registration. They therefore have some of the administrative burden and costs which are associated with limited companies.

The restrictions on the activities of limited partners make the 1907 structure unsuitable for many types of firm, especially professional partnerships which depend for their existence on the active availability of professional partners. Limited partnerships are uncommon.

Insurance against liability is a partial solution to the risk problem for most professional firms, and for some professions, such as solicitors, insurance is compulsory. This does not necessarily solve all of the problems however. Insurance provisions are not always sufficiently wide to cover the wrong in question, or sufficiently large to cover the loss. *Binder Hamlyn's* indemnity insurance apparently covered only £31 million of their liability in the above case. Moreover, insurance cover at this level can itself be very expensive.

An exemption clause in the contract between a professional partnership and its client (excluding or limiting the partnership's liability for negligence etc.) is unlikely to be effective. For many activities, such clauses are prohibited: for example, by the Companies Act 1985, section 310, any provision which tries to exempt an auditor from liability for negligence, default, breach of duty or trust is void (see Unit 23). Even if an exemption clause is possible, it will normally be *presumed* invalid under the Unfair Contract Terms Act 1977, in which case it will only be valid if the partnership can prove that it is reasonable (see Unit 14). Moreover, because of the privity of contract rules (Unit 16), it will normally only protect the firm against liability to its client, not against liability to others (as in the above cases).

Contribution between partners normally eases the burden for each individual partner. *As against outsiders*, the whole of any debt is recoverable against any one partner, under the joint and several liability rule in the Partnership Act, section 12. But *as between themselves*, partners must normally all contribute to losses, equally, if section 24 applies. Any one partner who has to pay can usually, therefore, demand contribution from his fellow partners. Action is normally against the firm rather than against one partner, and the largest firms have several hundred partners. Even so, in cases such as those above, the loss for each partner personally can still be enormous. In smaller cases, where there are only a few partners, the offending partner(s) may well be insolvent or have absconded, leaving the remaining one or two liable for the whole loss.

The Limited Liability Partnerships Act 2000

This Act is a more radical response to the problems of unlimited liability. Since April 2001 it has been possible to create a new form of legal entity to be known as a limited liability partnership (LLP). This has the following features.

- There is no limit on the number of partners. (Moreover, as in an ordinary partnership, a company can be a partner.)
- An LLP is a corporate body with separate legal personality, like a company. Contracts are made with the LLP, and it is the LLP that can sue or be sued. The property of the body belongs to the LLP, not to the members, and the LLP will continue in existence notwithstanding the death or retirement of a partner, or any other change in membership.
- Above all, the members have limited liability. If the firm cannot pay all of its debts, the individual partners normally have no further liability from their own resources.

In return for some of these benefits, the LLP also has some of the burdens often associated with separate legal personality. In particular, it must be publicly formed and supervised, in this case by the Registrar of Companies.

- It is formed by registration. Two or more applicants must send a signed registration document and a statement of compliance to the Registrar. The document must give the proposed name of the LLP, its registered office, and the names and addresses of initial members. The applicants must be associated 'for carrying on a lawful business with a view to profit', but they have no need to state the specific 'objects' of the business (compare with companies, see page 239). The Registrar must examine applications and he can reject misleading business names for example, but when he is satisfied he will issue a certificate of incorporation, which is conclusive evidence that the LLP is formed.
- After the LLP is incorporated, the Registrar continues to exercise some controls. He will keep a register of members, and must be notified of changes. An annual return and audited annual accounts must be sent to him. A firm may, either at the outset or later, specify some partners as 'designated members', with specific responsibility for these matters. Otherwise (for example, in small firms) all partners will be treated as designated. Only limited functions are carried out by designated members, and they are not like the directors of a company.

All of these requirements are much less complex and onerous than those for companies. Moreover, the internal requirements are much simpler. There need not be a board of directors. There are no statutory rules for types of meeting and resolution. In a large firm, the partners may have a written agreement between themselves about some of these matters, but such an agreement is a matter for the partners themselves, and it is private (unlike the Articles of Association of a company).

It seems likely that many LLPs will be formed by professional firms, particularly larger ones who deal in vast amounts of money. Solicitors and accountants will be allowed to practise in this form.

C. Types of registered company

Classification by limitation of liability

An unlimited company is a corporate body with the benefits arising from separate legal personality when membership changes. However when the company is wound up, if its assets are insufficient to meet its liabilities, all members are liable without limit for the company's debts and liquidation costs. If the present members cannot pay, then ex-members who left within the last twelve months are liable for debts incurred while they were members. Unlimited companies have no statutory obligation to have their accounts audited or to make annual returns to the Registrar of Companies. This advantage does not apply, however, if the unlimited company is a subsidiary of, or a holding company in, a limited one; otherwise the exemption could be used to evade the disclosure requirements of the Companies Acts.

An unlimited company may or may not have shares. It can convert into a limited company by following all of the requirements for forming such companies (see Unit 23). A limited company can change to unlimited if the Registrar of Companies is sent an assent form signed by *all* members, a statutory declaration by the directors that these are all of the members, and a new memorandum and articles.

Unlimited companies are rare because of the risks.

A company limited by guarantee is one where each member, on joining, guarantees that if the company is wound up while he is a member or within a year afterwards, and it is insolvent, then he will contribute up to a certain amount (usually small) towards the payment of its debts and liquidation costs. There is no statutory minimum guarantee, and it may be only £1. (In practice, therefore, any large creditor may demand a further *personal* guarantee from leading members.)

Because the liability of members is limited, guarantee companies are subject to the Companies Acts' requirements for annual returns and audit. They cannot now be created with shares, although such companies created before 1985 still exist. Guarantee companies are not very common and are used mainly for non-business bodies.

Companies limited by shares are the vast majority. Each member holds one or more 'shares', for which he pays the company. Large companies issue many billions of shares. Payment can sometimes be by instalments, and some shares, therefore, are 'partly paid' (see Unit 24). A shareholder's liability to the company is normally limited to such part of the issue price as is not yet paid. The great majority of shares are fully paid up, and such shareholders therefore have no liability at all for the company's debts; see *Salomon* v. *Salomon & Co Ltd* (page 232).

Most shares can be sold or transferred from one holder to another, and this takes place regularly. The rest of this Unit, and Units 23–25, deal predominantly with companies limited by shares.

Public and private companies

A public limited company created now must be limited by shares, and must meet the following requirements of the Companies Act 1985: its memorandum of association must specifically state that the company is to be public; its name must end with 'public limited company' or the initials 'p.l.c.'; its memorandum must take the form specified in regulations under the Act; and it must have a nominal share capital of at least the authorized minimum, currently £50 000 (see Unit 23).

A private company is one which does not satisfy all of these requirements. It must not, therefore, offer its shares for sale to the public. A private company can turn itself into a public one and vice versa (see later), but most companies are formed as and remain private.

Differences between public and private companies are, in some instances, only discussed later, but for convenience they are summarised here.

1. A public limited company's name must end with these words, or 'p.l.c.' (or Welsh equivalents in Wales).
2. Private companies need have no minimum nominal share capital.
3. A private company can start business as soon as it receives its certificate of incorporation from the Registrar. A public company must also fulfil the requirements for a further certificate under section 117; see Unit 23.
4. A private company only needs one director. A public company must have at least two.
5. A private company can be a 'one-man company' with only a single shareholder (see later). A public company must have at least two shareholders.
6. A private company can be unlimited or created limited by guarantee. A public company can not.
7. The administrative exemptions for 'small' and 'medium-sized' companies (see below) can only apply to private companies.
8. A private company must not offer its shares for sale to the public.

'Small', 'medium-sized' and 'dormant' companies

In return for the privilege of limited liability, companies are required to send detailed annual reports and professionally audited accounts to the Registrar of Companies. These are then open to public inspection (see Unit 23). Parts of this administrative burden are felt inappropriate for smaller private companies, which therefore have some exemptions.

A 'small' company is one with an annual turnover not exceeding £2.8 million, total balance sheet assets not exceeding £1.4 million, and/or no more than 50 employees on average. Any two of these requirements will do. It must still submit annual audited accounts with a shortened balance sheet, but it need not submit a profit and loss account, directors' report, details of dividends or directors' emoluments. If sales are less than £350 000, it need only send a 'compilation report', which is less than a full audit. If sales are less than £90 000 it need not have its accounts audited at all.

A 'medium-sized' company has (any two of) an annual turnover not exceeding £11.2 million, total balance sheet assets not exceeding £5.6 million, and/or not more than 250 employees on average. It has all of the normal obligations, except that it need only submit a shortened profit and loss account.

A 'dormant' company is one which is not doing business at all. It need only submit a modified balance sheet, and it need not have its accounts audited.

Single-member private companies

These were introduced by the Companies (Single Member Private Companies) Regulations 1992. Only one shareholder is required. He/it may hold very many shares or, sometimes, only one. Such companies are likely either to be very small businesses, or wholly-owned subsidiaries (sometimes very large) of another company. They have to comply in full with the audit and annual return requirements unless they qualify as 'small' or 'medium-sized' (above). There are special rules for the 'meetings of shareholders' requirements of the Companies Act: no notice of meeting is needed; nor are minutes; the quorum is one; he/it can pass a (100%) written resolution to dispense with an annual general meeting; but the company must still keep a record of resolutions passed. Companies can reduce their membership to one without re-registering, but the Companies Register must clearly show that there is now only one member.

Single-member companies must still have two *officers*, a director and a secretary. Neither need be a shareholder.

Some other classifications

'Holding' and 'subsidiary' companies exist where one company controls another. 'Control' exists where a 'holding' company has shares in its subsidiary, and controls the composition of the subsidiary's board of directors; or holds more than half of the subsidiary's share capital. Where the subsidiary itself has similar powers over another company, the latter is also a subsidiary of the holding company. In general, a subsidiary must not hold shares in any of its holding or 'parent' companies (Companies Act, section 23), but if a company takes-over a company which *already* holds shares in its new parent, the subsidiary can continue to hold these.

Although in law each company in a 'group' is a separate person, they usually operate as one enterprise, and for some purposes the law recognizes this. Often the arrangements are very complex, and may involve companies or their equivalents in many parts of the world.

A *'quoted'* company is a public company whose shares (and/or debentures, see Unit 24) are dealt with on a recognized Stock Exchange. This may be desirable in order to increase the saleability and value of the company's shares, but by no means all public companies are 'quoted' or 'listed'. If a company wishes its shares to be dealt with in this way, it must apply to the Exchange and satisfy it that legal requirements and the requirements *of the Exchange* have been satisfied as to matters such as the total value of shares, disclosure, and the Exchange's standards of 'corporate governance' (see Unit 25).

D. Features of companies

Separate legal personality

As we have noted already, a company of any type has a separate legal personality from its members. The cases discussed below show how fundamental this rule can be. As regards companies limited by shares, the leading case is also the leading one on limited liability.

> In *Salomon* v. *Salomon & Co. Ltd* (1897), Salomon, who manufactured boots, formed a company in which he and six members of his family held one share each. He then transferred his business to the company, which 'paid' him by issuing him a further 20 000 shares plus secured debentures (loan certificates) for a further £10 000. This made him (legally) a secured creditor of the company as well as its main shareholder. The company became insolvent. Salomon's shares became worthless, but he himself was not liable for the company's debts. He and the company were separate persons, and the debts were the company's, not his. Moreover, his secured debentures entitled him to some of the company's remaining assets even though trade creditors remained unpaid.

> In *Macaura* v. *Northern Assurance Co. Ltd* (1925), Macaura formed a company with himself as the main shareholder. He then insured *himself* against damage to *the company's* property. When the company's property was damaged by fire, the loss was the company's, not his, and his insurance claim failed.

'Lifting the veil of incorporation'

In a variety of ways, some shareholders have tried to use the separate legal personality rule to veil their own wrongdoing or to escape their own obligations. Both the courts and the legislature, therefore, have been prepared *exceptionally* to 'lift the veil', and impose liability on the human beings behind the corporate screen. The importance of limited liability for members of a large enterprise has been emphasized earlier, and *inability* to pay debts has not been regarded as 'wrongdoing' for this purpose; but there can sometimes be a very narrow line between preserving the economically vital privilege of limited liability, and preventing abuse of its separate personality basis.

The courts themselves have sometimes taken the initiative:

1. If the company is set up as a 'cloak or sham' with the dishonest purpose of evading the promoter/shareholder's existing obligations, the court may exceptionally give an equitable remedy against both the company and the shareholder.

   > In *Gilford Motor Co. Ltd* v. *Horne* (1933), an ex-employee personally could have been prevented by a valid restraint of trade clause (see Unit 17) from approaching his ex-employer's customers. He therefore formed a company which, he claimed, could not be so restrained. The court issued an injunction against both him and the new company.

   > In *Jones* v. *Lipman* (1962), Lipman contracted to sell land to Jones, but then changed his mind. He therefore set up a company to which he sold the land. He knew that he would be liable to Jones for damages, but he hoped that 'his' company, as a separate person, would be able to keep the land. The court ordered both him and the company to transfer the land as originally agreed.

   There can be other 'sham' company situations, as in *Catamaran Cruisers Ltd* v. *Williams* (1994) (see page 294).

2. Where *tax fraud* is alleged, involving *criminal* conduct, the courts have sometimes refused to allow companies to be used to disguise or misrepresent the true facts.

   > In *Re H* (1996), two companies in which the defendants owned all of the shares were used for the fraudulent evasion of excise duty. The 'veil' was lifted by the court, and property owned by the companies was treated as owned by the defendants themselves.

3. *'Groups'*, with various holding and subsidiary companies, have given rise to particular difficulties. As a general rule, the courts have treated each company in the group as separate: one company is not liable for another's debts, and this generally extends to other liabilities.

   > In *Adams* v. *Cape Industries plc* (1991), a company in the USA was alleged to be liable for injuries caused by asbestos dust, but the US company was insolvent. The claimants therefore sued its UK parent, Cape. The action failed. The Court of Appeal held that Cape was entitled to the protection of the separate legal personality and limited liability rules. The subsidiary was a separate company, not Cape's agent (even though Cape supplied it with asbestos); and the group should not be regarded as a single economic unit for this purpose.

4. In wartime, or other national emergencies where sanctions are imposed, the courts have sometimes raised the 'veil' and looked at the shareholders to reveal a company's nationality.

   > In *Daimler Co. Ltd* v. *Continental Tyre and Rubber (GB) Ltd* (1916), although Continental was registered in Britain, almost all of the shares were German owned. It was held to be German.

Legislation provides other instances.

1. By the Companies Act 1985, section 24, if a *public* company (which can *not* be one-man, see earlier) carries on business without at least two members and does so for more than six months, a member who continues the business thereafter, knowing that he is the only member, is liable jointly and severally with the company for debts incurred while he does so. This can apply to a wholly-owned (public)

233

subsidiary and its (sole-shareholder) holding company. Some holding companies therefore ensure that at least one share is held by someone else.

2. 'Groups' of companies have also had legislative recognition.
   (a) Under the EEC Treaty, Articles 81 and 82, a group has sometimes been recognized by the European Court of Justice as a 'single economic unit' *for the purposes of the EC anti-competition rules*. This does not affect separate legal personality for the rest of English law; see *Adams* v. *Cape Industries* above.
   (b) Taxation legislation sometimes recognizes the reality of a group *for tax purposes*. Losses by one of the companies can sometimes be set off against profits of another.
   (c) The Companies Act itself applies 'disclosure' rules realistically, and groups of companies generally have to produce group accounts.

3. Various legislative provisions (discussed in Unit 25) can make *directors or managers* who are guilty of misconduct personally liable for the company's acts. These people are not necessarily shareholders, and their liability does not arise *from membership*. (Nevertheless, they often will have shares.)

Ultra vires and companies

A company's powers are set out in the 'objects clause' of its memorandum of association (see Unit 23). This clause was partly to protect shareholders, who invested their money on the understanding that the company would only do the things specified, and it was sometimes used on behalf of shareholders when the company was wound up, to escape from contracts which the directors had made. This did not occur often, partly because most objects clauses are drafted very widely; and since 1989 the objects can be simply 'to carry on business as a general commercial company'.

Most objects are more restrictive than this, but even for these companies the *ultra vires* rule has effectively been abolished as between companies and outsiders. By the Companies Act 1985, section 35, as amended in 1989, 'The validity of an act done by a company shall not be called into question on the ground of lack of capacity by reason of anything in the company's memorandum'. A party to a transaction with the company is not bound to enquire whether it is permitted by the company's memorandum, and the company can be bound even if the outsider knew that the proposed transaction was *ultra vires* the objects clause. There are limited exceptions for companies which are charities. Subject to this, contracts which exceed the objects are not void.

The other problem is substantially one of agency. The authority to act for a company rests basically in the board of directors, and the objects clause may limit this actual authority. However, by the Companies Act, section 35A, 'In favour of a person dealing with the company in good faith, the power of the board of directors to bind the company or authorize others to do so, shall be deemed to be free of any limitation under the company's constitution'. For this purpose, the 'constitution' includes not only the objects and the rest of the memorandum and articles, but also resolutions and agreements between members. An outsider is presumed to act in good faith unless the contrary is proved. He is not to be regarded as in bad faith by reason only of knowing that an act is beyond the directors' powers under the company's constitution, but collusion in breach of fiduciary duties (Unit 23) could show bad faith. The outsider is not bound to enquire as to the company's capacity or as to the authority of its directors.

Limits on the power of a company and of its directors can still have consequences *within the company* (not directly affecting outsiders).

1. Any shareholder can seek a court injunction to prevent a *proposed* ultra vires or unauthorized transaction; but this cannot affect a contract already made. Moreover, the proposed unauthorized act can be ratified by special resolution (75% majority) of shareholders.
2. If directors do exceed their powers, they can be personally liable (like other disobedient agents) to the company for any loss which it suffers as a result. Even here, however, a special resolution can absolve the directors.

There are special rules for transactions between a company and its own director(s). These are not really outsiders, and the protection in section 35A for 'a person dealing with the company' does not apply to directors themselves, members of close family, or directors/family in a holding company. Unauthorized transactions with such people are not void, but are *voidable* at the instance of the company. Moreover, whether or not the company rescinds the contract, any director of the company who authorized the transaction is liable to account to the company for any gain which he makes, and indemnify the company for any loss which it makes. A person other than a director of the company can escape such liability, but only if he shows that at the time of the transaction he did not know that the directors were exceeding their powers.

E. Advantages and disadvantages of companies

The main advantages have been discussed already. They are:

1. separate legal personality: see particularly Unit 7 and Part D above; moreover a company can sue and be sued in its own name, without having to involve shareholders;
2. limited liability, discussed above;
3. perpetual succession to its property; ownership of the property does not change on the (billions of) occasions when shares change hands. Partnerships and other unincorporated bodies can, however, get a degree of perpetual succession by vesting their property in trustees (see Unit 7).
   (Note also the extent to which all of the above advantages can now be enjoyed by Limited Liability Partnerships; see particularly on page 228.)

The main disadvantages are:

1. the cost and complexity of formation, although this is not vast;

2. the continuing administrative burden of keeping records, having annual audits and making annual returns to the Registrar of Companies (see Unit 23). Note, however, the exemptions for 'small' companies earlier;

3. the lack of privacy involved in access to the Registrar's records and (some of) those at the company's registered office (Unit 23).

Specimen questions

1. Discuss whether the following are partners within the Partnership Act 1890:
   (a) the committee of a tennis club;
   (b) Mr A and his son B who take turns in driving Mr A's van to deliver vegetables from a market garden to retail grocers' shops;
   (c) C and D, who organize a jumble sale for charity;
   (d) E who runs a business, and F who has lent him money to expand it.

2. An ordinary partnership is insolvent, with debts of £500 000, all incurred during the last year. To what extent are the following liable to the creditors:
   (a) the senior partner, who retired from active participation two years ago, but was still entitled to 5% of profits under the partnership agreement;
   (b) a partner who is himself insolvent;
   (c) a partner who is solvent, and was entitled to 20% of profits under the partnership agreement;
   (d) a 'salaried partner', who received a salary but no share in the profits (his name appeared in the list of partners on letter heads)?

3. (a) Bright is a partner in a firm of accountants. Without consulting the others, he orders a word processor, although the price exceeds the figure for which agreement of all partners is required by the partnership agreement. He appoints a new clerk without consulting his fellow partners. Explain whether these contracts are binding on the firm, and Bright's legal position.
   (b) Bright becomes a part-time financial consultant with a local company without telling his fellow partners. Discuss the legal position.

4. 'Some shareholders have tried to use the separate legal personality rule to veil their own wrongdoing or to escape their own obligations.'
   (a) Explain this statement.
   (b) Describe the main ways in which this 'veil of incorporation' can be lifted so as to make shareholders personally liable.

5. Five people are in partnership as a cleaning firm. They are thinking of forming a limited company. Advise them on the advantages and disadvantages of operating as a limited company rather than as a partnership.

Unit 23. Companies: Formation and Public Controls

A. Promotion

Those who form a company are called its 'promoters'. They include those who acquire property for the company and/or transfer a business (often their own) to the company; also those who choose the first directors; open the company's bank account(s); design the financial structure, its shares and borrowing; and arrange for the registration documents to be prepared and sent to the Registrar of Companies (see below). Another task of promoters will normally be to choose and instruct the company's professional advisers, such as accountants and solicitors. The advisers themselves, however, normally act independently, and are not promoters.

Strict duties of good faith and care are owed by promoters to the new company. They must also exercise such skill as they have professed. There must also be full disclosure to any independent directors and shareholders of all financial matters connected with the promotion. Promoters may, for example, make a personal profit from connected transactions but, if so, this must be disclosed in full to the new company.

> In *Gluckstein* v. *Barnes* (1900), the promoters formed a company and transferred property to it, making a profit of £60 000 for themselves. They only disclosed £40 000 of this to the new shareholders. The new company (or rather its liquidator because it soon failed) was entitled to the remaining £20 000 from all or *any* of the promoters (their liability is joint and several, like that of ordinary partners, Unit 22).

The above rules will cause no problem when the promoters and the first shareholders and directors are the same persons, as will often be the case when an existing small business turns itself into a company. But if new shareholders and/or directors are also brought in (to provide extra money for example), these new participants become vulnerable to any breach of the above duties by the promoters. Even here, however, it must be emphasized that the duties of promoters are owed *to the company*, and if the promoters themselves have a controlling interest in the new company, then it is unlikely to sue. Individual new shareholders have no direct right of action (see *Foss* v. *Harbottle* page 283) although they may have rights under the minority protection rules in the Companies Act, section 459. These topics are discussed in Unit 25.

If promoters are liable, a number of remedies are possible: they may be made to account for improper profits and/or pay damages; and, where appropriate, contracts with the promoters may be rescinded by the new company. If the company becomes insolvent, an offending promoter may be disqualified from acting as a promoter for a limited time in the future (Insolvency Act 1986, section 212).

Promoters may want to make other pre-incorporation contracts in starting or transferring a business and starting a new company. These are discussed in Part D of this unit.

B. Registration

The main task of promoters is to prepare the registration documents and to lodge these, with fees, with the Registrar of Companies.

1. The memorandum of association

This, in effect, defines the company and what it can do. It must contain five compulsory provisions, and may contain more.

The company's name must be stated. Choice rests with the promoters, but the Registrar exercises some constraints. The name *must* end with 'public limited company' or the initials 'p.l.c.' or, for a private company, 'limited' or 'ltd'. These words or abbreviations *must* not appear at the beginning or in the middle of a name. The Registrar *must* refuse a name which is the same as that of an existing registered company, limited liability partnership or industrial and provident society. He must also refuse a name which, in his opinion, is a criminal offence or offensive.

Certain other names may only be used with appropriate consents, including that of the Secretary of State (for Trade and Industry). These include names which suggest that the company has connections with the government or a local authority, or which contain any word or expression specified in Company and Business Names Regulations made under the Act (words like 'National', 'Royal', 'Stock Exchange').

Members can later change the name by special resolution, subject to the above limits. The Secretary of State can *order* a change if, for example, the name is too *similar* to an existing registered name, or if misleading information has been given to obtain registration with a particular name.

Promoters must also beware of trade marks and/or the tort of passing off, which can entitle another business to restrain use of a name too like its own or that of its *products*, irrespective of what the Registrar has approved.

The registered office will be stated. Strictly, only the (British) *country* need be given in the memorandum: England and Wales; specifically Wales (in which case words like 'limited' can be expressed in Welsh); or Scotland (where the general law is slightly different). The actual address must be given with the particulars of directors (form G.10, later), but in practice is usually given in the memorandum too. The registered office is the company's *legal* home for many purposes, including receipt of writs and other documents, and keeping of registers (see later). It need not be at or near the company's place of business. The address may later be changed by ordinary resolution of members, of which the Registrar is notified.

The 'objects clause' states the purpose for which the company is formed, and the powers which it is to have (often at great length). Historically, its purpose was to protect members and creditors by limiting the purposes for which their investment could be used. Its importance has been greatly reduced by changes, derived from EC law, removing much of the effect of the *ultra vires* rule as regards outsiders; see the 1985 Act, section 35 (page 234). Moreover, a company's stated objects can now be simply 'to carry on business as a general commercial company', allowing it to carry on any trade or business whatsoever; see Companies Act 1989, section 110. Most existing companies still keep their original objects, however, and even most new companies do not use these 'general commercial' objects.

Existing objects may be altered by special resolution of shareholders (75% of votes cast at a general meeting). A private company can also use a written resolution (100% of all shareholders) without a meeting.

The liability clause simply states that the members have limited liability.

The capital clause must state the company's *nominal* capital, and how this is to be divided into shares of a fixed nominal amount. This is the capital which the company is *authorized* to issue; it need not issue all of its shares (see Unit 24). A p.l.c. must have a nominal/authorized capital of at least £50 000.

The capital clause does not necessarily represent the *amount* of money which a company can raise, because shares are often issued at a 'premium', for more than their nominal value. They must not be issued at a discount. The capital clause may be changed later by special resolution, for example so as to increase the number of shares which a company can issue if it wishes to expand. A private company can reduce its number of shares to one.

The 'association clause' which ends the memorandum is a request by the 'subscribers', whose names and addresses appear at the end, to be formed into a company. A public company must have at least two subscribers. Each must take at least one share, and the memorandum must state how many he does take. Since 1992, a private company need only have one subscriber. Each subscriber must sign, and the signatures must be witnessed.

Other clauses may sometimes be necessary within the memorandum. If the company is to be a public limited company, then a clause in its memorandum must expressly say so. If a company does not wish to have its own articles of association, then it must expressly provide in its memorandum that it is adopting Table A.

2. Articles of association

These will usually be submitted. They regulate the internal management, and the rights and duties of shareholders vis-à-vis the company and each other. They deal with matters such as transfer of shares, meetings, voting and other rights of shareholders, dividends, and the directors' powers of management. A printed copy must be signed by the subscribers, and the signatures must be witnessed.

A company need not, in fact, submit any articles. It can state in its memorandum that it will adopt Table A, a model set of articles in regulations made under the Companies Act 1985 (or, before 1985, set out in Schedules to earlier Companies Acts). There have been slight changes, and a company which adopts Table A keeps the version existing when it was formed. In any event, Table A always applies except in so far as it is expressly or impliedly overruled by actual articles. The articles may later be altered by special resolution of shareholders or by written resolution (see later).

3. Particulars of directors and company secretary (Form G.10)

This must be filed with the memorandum, with the witnessed signatures of the subscribers. It must name the first directors with their signed and witnessed consents to act, and give prescribed particulars about them (such as other directorships). It must name the first company secretary, with due consent to act. A director can also serve as company secretary, but not if he is a sole director; there must always be two *officers*, even in a company with only one shareholder. The statement must also give the *address* of the registered office.

4. Statutory declaration

A statutory declaration that the requirements of the Act have been satisfied must be made by a person named above as a director or company secretary, or by a solicitor engaged in forming the company. This must be filed with the Registrar, and may be accepted by him as sufficient evidence of compliance.

5. Registration fee

A small registration fee must be paid.

The certificate of incorporation

When he is satisfied that the statutory requirements have been met, the Registrar issues a certificate of incorporation, which is the company's 'birth certificate'. The company comes into existence on the date given in the certificate, and the registered number given there must thenceforth be used in all of the company's official documents and business letters.

240

The certificate of incorporation prevents any later claim that the registration procedure was defective. The certificate is conclusive evidence of all matters which it states, such as the date of the company's incorporation and its status as a public or private company.

Re-registration

A private company can be re-registered as a public one at a later date, and vice versa. A special resolution of shareholders is needed or, in the case of a private company, a written resolution (see Unit 25). Appropriate changes must be made to the memorandum and articles. Application to the Registrar must be signed by a director or the company secretary, and accompanied by the new memorandum and articles, audited accounts, and a statutory declaration of compliance with the Act, as above. In the case of a change to a public company, the capital requirements must be met, and there are controls over payment for shares other than by money. A private company can also re-register as unlimited and vice versa.

Pre-formed 'off-the-shelf' companies

Many businesses wishing to incorporate choose to buy ready-made 'off-the-shelf' companies rather than go through the full registration procedure themselves. These are companies which have already been formed by firms specialising in such activity. The existing dormant company is then taken over by the new owners. The promotion firm sells the shares to the new owners, changes the objects clause, and holds meetings of directors and/or shareholders to appoint the new directors and, in particular, a new company secretary. The procedure is fairly quick and cheap. However, the off-the-peg documents are standardized and, particularly the articles, may be unsatisfactory and need to be changed. Moreover, the shareholders may often want a new name and registered office.

In view of the number of changes that may have to be made, it is often questionable whether an off-the-shelf company is necessarily quicker and cheaper than a specially formed one.

C. The company's 'constitution'

The memorandum and articles effectively form the company's constitution. Subject to legislative provisions, they define a shareholder's rights and duties vis-à-vis both the company and fellow shareholders. By the 1985 Act, section 14, the memorandum and articles, when registered, bind the company and its members as if they were a contract between them, containing a covenant by each member to observe its provisions. Members have rights in the company, mainly to attend meetings and vote on resolutions (often vitally important); they also have duties to the company, mainly to pay the company when their shares are issued (see Unit 24). Those who become shareholders later are equally bound by this contract: they have the same rights, and they may still have duties to the company if the shares are not yet 'fully paid'. Members also have rights and duties as regards each other (see Unit 25).

Alteration of the memorandum

The compulsory clauses in the memorandum can be changed by special resolution of shareholders (75% of votes in a meeting) or, for private companies, by written resolution of all shareholders without need for a meeting. The registered office can be changed by ordinary (or written) resolution. If other clauses are put in the memorandum (for example to protect preference shares, see Unit 24), these can be changed by special or written resolution under the 1985 Act, section 17. In all cases, the Registrar must be informed.

There is additional protection for the *objects* clause in that, even if a special resolution has been passed, the holders of 15% of the share capital can apply to the *court* to reverse it and keep the former objects. Application must be within 21 days of the resolution, and if the application is not granted the court *may* order the *company* to buy back the shares of the dissenters. Alternatively, some of the other shareholders may agree to buy the shares for themselves.

Alteration of the articles

Articles may later be altered (even with retrospective effect) by special (or written) resolution of shareholders under the 1985 Act, section 9, but there are limits on this power. The alteration must not clash with the memorandum, which prevails if there is conflict. The change must not contravene any provision of the Companies Acts or other legislation, or any court order under, for example, sections 459–61; (see Unit 25). It must not oblige existing shareholders to provide more capital without their written consent; or take away the rights of any class of shareholders without a special resolution of members of that class; or otherwise discriminate between members. The resolution must not be illegal, and it must be made in good faith for the benefit of all shareholders and the company as a whole.

D. Commencement of business

Pre-incorporation contracts

A company cannot make valid contracts before it is incorporated. The company simply does not exist yet. The contract is void, and neither the company nor the other contracting party can sue on it.

Nor can the company ratify a contract made before incorporation so as to validate it; see Unit 7.

In *Kelner* v. *Baxter* (1866), three promoters bought goods in their own names, but as 'agents' for the unformed company. The company, when formed, could not ratify the transaction later.

In *Newborne* v. *Sensolid Ltd* (1953), the promoters made a 'contract' in the name of the unformed company. Again, the company could not be bound at the time, and could not ratify later.

By the Companies Act 1985, section 36C (see 1989 Act, section 130), a contract which purports to be made by or on behalf of a company at a time when the company has not been formed has effect as one made with the person purporting to act for the company or as agent for it, and he is personally liable on the contract. He can probably also sue on it. The Act makes section 36C 'subject to any agreement to the contrary', and a promoter can seek a clause exempting him from personal liability, but only if the other parties agree.

Promoters will incur costs and liabilities before incorporation. There will be the legal and other costs of forming the company. There will also be the more substantial costs of starting a business or transferring an existing business to the new company. The promoters will want to avoid personal liability, and they may want the expenses to be those of the company for tax purposes. The costs of starting or transferring the business can usually be allocated to the company simply by incorporating early, before the costs are incurred. Alternatively, the promoters may make a pre-incorporation contract in their own names, and expressly provide in the agreement that the contract is to be for the benefit of the company. In this case the Contracts (Rights of Third Parties) Act 1999 will apply, even though the contract is not formed yet. After incorporation, the company can then sue and be sued in its own name. For some types of contract such as buying property, the promoters may take only an option or other non-binding arrangement, which the company can later decide to make binding if it so wishes; however, the other side might not wish to proceed on this basis.

After incorporation

A company registered as private can do business as soon as it is incorporated. Neither the directors nor the shareholders have personal liability thenceforth.

A *public* company, however, must not do business or borrow money until it has satisfied the further requirements of the 1985 Act, section 117. It must satisfy the Registrar that shares with a nominal value of £50 000 have actually been *allotted*, with at least one quarter of the nominal value of each allotted share and the whole of any premium paid up (see Unit 24). A director or the company secretary must sign and file a statutory declaration (a) that the nominal value of the allotted capital is not less than the authorized minimum; (b) as to the amount paid up on the allotted capital; (c) as to the company's preliminary expenses, and by whom these have been paid or are payable; and (d) as to any payments by the company to its promoters. These rules aim to ensure that a public company starts business with at least some capital.

If he is satisfied, the Registrar issues a section 117 certificate, after which the company, its directors and members can operate normally. If a public company does do business or borrow money before its section 117 certificate, the contracts are binding; but if the company fails to comply with its obligations under the contract within 21 days, the directors personally become jointly and severally liable if the company defaults.

E. Company records and information

Companies have the privileges of separate legal personality and limited liability. In return, the human beings behind companies have to accept disclosure regarding membership, management, debts and financial position generally. This renders it more difficult to commit wrongdoing anonymously and, hopefully, helps to prevent misconduct. It aims to protect members, creditors, and those dealing with the company.

As a first stage, the company is required to collect and keep a lot of information about itself. It must then make most of this available to *shareholders*: through access to documents and registers; through its annual accounts and reports; and through general meetings. Information must also be sent to the *Registrar of Companies*, in particular an annual return and copies of the annual accounts. *Public* access to company information must be given partly by the company itself, and partly through the Registrar.

Information to be kept by a company

A company must keep its memorandum and articles, the documents which form its constitution. It must also keep *registers*

1. of shareholders, indexed, with addresses, dates of becoming and ceasing to be members, and numbers of shares held;
2. of directors and company secretaries, with addresses and, for directors, information about other directorships;
3. of directors' interests in shares and debentures of the company and of any holding or subsidiary company; also shareholdings by directors' spouses or infant children;
4. of secured debentures, including mortgages or other charges on the company's property (even if there are none at present); also a copy of the instrument creating each charge.

Minutes of general meetings of shareholders must be kept, and copies of directors' service contracts.

Under the 1985 Act Part VII, a company must also keep proper *accounting records*. By section 221, a company must maintain current accounting records which disclose the company's financial position at any time with reasonable accuracy, and enable the directors to prepare the statutory annual accounts properly. The current accounts must have entries from day to day of all sums received and spent, and matters in respect of which each receipt or payment takes place; and a record of the company's assets and liabilities. A private company must retain its accounts for three years, a public company for six. The accounts and registers can be kept on computer so long as a print-out is possible.

A company must also prepare *annual accounts*, which must be presented to a general meeting of shareholders, and include a directors' report and auditors' report; see below.

All of this material will normally be kept at the company's registered office, but it may be kept elsewhere so long as the Registrar of Companies is told where it is.

Current information for shareholders

A shareholder is entitled to examine the memorandum and articles, and to receive one copy free of charge each year. He also has access to the above registers, minutes and copies of directors' contracts. Any shareholder or debenture holder is entitled to be furnished with, on demand and without charge, a copy of its last *annual* accounts. However only the *officers* (directors and company secretary) have a right to inspect the current accounts.

The annual accounts

For most shareholders, the main sources of information are the company's statutory annual accounts, and the statutory directors' and auditors' reports which must accompany them.

Each company should choose an 'accounting reference date'. If it does not, then the date will be the last day of the month one year after incorporation. This then determines the company's 'accounting reference period' and 'financial year'. For each financial year the company must produce annual accounts and reports, and circulate these to shareholders and debenture holders.

The accounts must comprise a *profit and loss account*, giving a true and fair view of the profit and loss, and a *balance sheet*, giving 'a true and fair view of the state of affairs of the company as at the end of the financial year'. There are detailed rules for the form and content of these accounts, but the 'true and fair' rule overrides everything else, and if need be the normal format can be varied.

In 'groups' of companies, each company must prepare its own accounts. The directors of the senior 'parent' company must also prepare *group accounts*, giving a true and fair view of the state of the group as a whole.

The accounts must give limited information about the 'emoluments' of directors. Total amounts for the directors as a whole must be given; also total pensions to ex-directors, and total severance payments. If these aggregate sums exceed a specified amount, particulars must also be given of the highest payments, and how many directors are paid within each of a series of bands.

245

There are detailed provisions for the accounts to be approved by the board of directors. The balance sheet must be signed by a director on behalf of the board, and his name must appear on copies sent to members.

The directors' report must give a fair review of the business of the company (and subsidiaries if any) during the financial year, and at the end of it. The amount (if any) which the directors recommend as dividend to shareholders must be stated, as must amounts (if any) which they propose to carry to reserves (see Unit 24). The report must also state (a) names of all directors during the year, (b) their shareholdings and personal interests in company contracts, (c) changes in the value of the company's fixed assets, (d) any purchases by the company of its own shares, (e) any political and charitable donations, and (f) the profitability of each business, if more than one.

The auditors' report (see later) must state whether, in the opinion of the auditors, the balance sheet, profit and loss account, and any group accounts give a 'true and fair' view. If the auditors do not consider the directors' report to be consistent with the accounts, their report must say so.

General meeting of shareholders

By the 1985 Act, section 241, the directors must, for each financial year, lay before the company in a general meeting copies of that year's accounts and reports. Copies must have been sent to share and debenture holders at least 21 days before the meeting, which will normally be the annual general meeting. All shareholders may attend. For a public company, the meeting must be within seven months after the accounting reference date; for a private company, within ten months.

Exemptions

All of this can be an expensive administrative burden, and various exemptions therefore exist. Public companies which are 'listed' on a Stock Exchange may give members the choice of receiving only a summary financial statement; but any member can still demand the full accounts and reports if so required.

More importantly, 'small' and 'medium-sized' *private* companies have a number of important exemptions, increasing for the smallest companies (see page 231).

A private company can also pass an 'elective' resolution (by 100% of those entitled to vote) *not* to hold a general meeting or lay accounts before it. It can also suspend the need to reappoint auditors each year. However, in spite of the resolution, any member can still demand these things in any year; and an auditor has power to demand that the accounts etc. be laid before a general meeting (see later).

Information held by the Registrar of Companies

The Registrar acquires a lot of information about a company from the registration documents themselves at the outset (see earlier). He retains this, particularly the memorandum and articles.

246

In addition, the company must each year send an '*annual return*' which, to a substantial extent, operates simply to update the Registrar's existing information. Details required include confirming (a) the type of company; (b) changes of registered office; (c) principal business activities (a VAT number may suffice); (d) any changes regarding directors, company secretary, places where registers are kept, issued share capital, list of members; (e) notice of any 'elective' resolution by a private company.

More importantly in some ways, the accounts and reports 'laid before' the company's general meeting each year must also be sent to the Registrar. The balance sheet must be signed by a director, and the auditors must sign their report.

Most of the Registrar's information is then publicly available through him; see below.

Public information from the company itself

The registered name of a company must be shown conspicuously and in easily legible letters outside every office and place of its business. The name must similarly appear in all business letters, notices and official publications, invoices, receipts and letters of credit. It must appear legibly on all bills of exchange, promissory notes, endorsements, cheques, and orders for money or goods purporting to be signed by or on behalf of the company. If the company has a seal, which many larger companies still do although it is no longer essential, the name must appear legibly on it.

Breach of any of these requirements is a criminal offence by the company and/or officers or persons acting on its behalf. Furthermore, by section 394(4), if an officer of a company or a person on its behalf signs a bill of exchange etc., or order for money or goods, in which the company's name is not properly mentioned, he is personally liable on the document if the company defaults. This can be applied strictly, and officers have several times been personally liable when 'limited' or 'Ltd' was omitted from the company's name on a cheque or other document.

> See also *Hendon* v. *Adelman* (1973), where the name 'L & R Agencies' appeared as 'LR Agencies' on a cheque. Directors who had signed the cheque were personally liable when the company defaulted.

Registration particulars, principally the country of registration, the registered number, and the registered office address, must also be shown legibly in all letters and order forms. A company need not show the name of any director in letter headings or order forms; but if it does show one then it must show all.

Documents and records must be available at the registered office or, if they are not kept there, at the place made known to the Registrar. These are the memorandum and articles, and the registers of shareholders, directors and secretary, directors' interests, and charges (secured debentures) mentioned earlier. These must be accessible for members, creditors *and the public* for at least two hours per day in business time. Other material, such as directors' service contracts and minutes of general meetings, is not publicly available, although it is to members.

Public information from the Registrar of Companies

The Registrar must advertise in the London Gazette (a formal paper for public announcements) that he has received certain information about a company. Only the fact of receipt is advertised, not the content of documents: the fact that a memorandum and articles have been received; that a certificate of incorporation has been issued; that annual accounts have been received, or notice of changes of directors or registered office; or that a declaration has been filed for a public company to start business. Receipt of documents to do with winding up or liquidation must also be advertised.

Those proposing to deal with a company may well, then, conduct a *company search*, by reference to the index of company names and the company's registered number. The company's file can be obtained on microfiche, and should disclose:

1. memorandum and articles;
2. particulars of directors and company secretary (see earlier);
3. subsequent changes in directors, secretary, registered office;
4. accounting reference date;
5. last annual accounts and reports;
6. special, extraordinary and elective resolutions;
7. recent increases in capital and/or share issues;
8. existing and recent charges on company's property.

In some instances, the company need only inform the Registrar of changes within a stated time limit (usually 15 days), and therefore the Registrar's information may not always be totally up-to-date. Nevertheless, a company search can be a considerable safeguard.

F. Auditors

It is essential for the 'information' provisions in the Acts that the information should be true. One problem is that the annual accounts and reports are prepared by the directors, the very people whose performance will be judged by them. To meet this 'moral hazard', the Acts require that the accounts be checked by professionally qualified independent auditors. The auditors' report must accompany the accounts and directors' reports to shareholders, and be sent to the Registrar. It must also be available to the public in the same way. Only very small companies, and dormant ones, do not need to have auditors; see Unit 22.

Conduct of the audit

The main *duties* of the auditors are auditing the accounts and reporting to members. In exercising both of these duties, auditors must show professional standards of care, skill, competence and integrity. They must confirm the true financial state of the company at the time of the audit, and check the completeness and accuracy of the

248

accounts. They must be familiar with the memorandum and articles, because breach of these can be one form of impropriety.

An auditor need not specially *look for* misconduct; he is a 'watchdog, not a bloodhound'. But if he does see any inaccuracy or impropriety, he must then investigate fully. He can believe without question statements made to him by directors, company secretaries or managers; but if anything does or ought to make him suspicious he must enquire further. He need not do a full stocktaking of the company's assets, but probably he should do sample checks.

An auditor has wide *powers* under the Act in order to carry out his duties. He must have access to the company's accounts, books and vouchers at all times. He can require such information from the company's officers etc. as he deems necessary for the audit. In groups of companies, an auditor of the parent company can require help from the auditors of subsidiaries, who must give such information and explanations as may reasonably be needed. An auditor is entitled to attend general meetings of shareholders in the company being audited, and to be heard on business of the meeting which concerns him as auditor. He must receive the same notice as shareholders of meetings to be held. In a private company which has elected not to hold a general meeting, auditors have amended but similar powers, including the right to insist that a general meeting actually be held if there is any written resolution which concerns the audit. In all cases, any officer etc. of the company who knowingly or recklessly makes an oral or written statement to the auditors which is false, misleading or deceptive in a material particular commits a criminal offence.

The *auditors' report* must be signed by them and delivered to the company secretary. He must send a copy to all members with the accounts, and have the report 'laid before' the general meeting. He must then send a signed copy to the Registrar with the accounts. The report will be fairly short unless there is something wrong, in which case there are detailed provisions for auditors to give only qualified approval, or even an adverse report.

Appointment and qualifications of auditors

An auditor has been compared to a watchdog, but this raises a further problem. Who guards the guardian? There are therefore detailed limits on who can validly act as an auditor. He must first be a member of a Recognized Qualifying Body, and he must then be 'registered' as a member of a Recognized Supervisory Body. In Britain, the qualification and supervisory functions are performed basically by the professional accountancy bodies, although some overseas qualifications may also be recognized. Supervision includes monitoring the continuing competence, professional integrity and independence of members, and the supervisory bodies must investigate complaints.

Partnership firms may be appointed as auditors. If so, any partner qualified at the time of appointment may act, and even a partner who joins the firm later can do the work provided that the firm's membership stays basically the same. A corporate body may be an auditor, but there are strict rules as to control of the corporation, and who actually does the work.

Persons too closely connected with the company to be audited are obviously disqualified from auditing it: any officer or employee of the company, or his partner or employee; officers, employees etc. of any holding or subsidiary company; and those 'connected' by matters such as close financial interests in the company or a parent or subsidiary company, the interests of close family being included.

The first auditors are usually appointed by the directors before the first general meeting at which accounts are laid. This general meeting must then appoint the auditors until the next such meeting. If no such appointment is made, the Department of Trade and Industry must be informed within one week, and it will then appoint. A private company which elects not to hold general meetings can also suspend the need to reappoint auditors each year. In this case, the auditors hold office indefinitely, until dismissal or resignation.

Vacation of office

Auditors may lose office if the shareholders in the general meeting simply decide not to re-appoint them, and appoint new ones. In any event, the shareholders can remove any auditor at any time by ordinary resolution in any general meeting. Removal is effective even if it breaks the auditor's contract with the company, but in this case the auditor might be entitled to damages. Notice of any change must be given to the Registrar within fourteen days. In an 'elective' private company, any member may send a proposal to the registered office asking that the auditors be changed, in which case the directors must call a general meeting within 28 days.

Because of the 'watchdog' rôle of auditors, attempts to remove them might be for nefarious reasons. They therefore have special rights and duties. In each of the above situations, 28 days' special notice must be given to the company of the proposal to remove or not re-appoint. The company must immediately send a copy to the auditors. They then *may* make written representations to the company and (unless these are defamatory) the company must send them to members before the meeting; otherwise the auditors can have the representations read to the meeting. The auditors can also be heard at the meeting.

Moreover, whenever an auditor ceases to hold office, he *must* also make a statement to the company under section 394; see below.

Resignation by the auditors is the other way in which their office may be vacated. If an auditor chooses to resign, he must give notice to the registered office. This must be accompanied, under the 1985 Act section 394, by a statement of connected circumstances which he considers should be brought to the attention of share and debenture holders; or that he considers that there are no such circumstances. If the auditor has stated circumstances, a copy must be sent to members and the Registrar. The auditor *may* with his notice require that the directors call an extraordinary general meeting of members, in which case he has similar rights to be heard, etc. to those above. Notice of the change of auditor must be given to the Registrar.

Liability of auditors

To the company

An auditor has a contract with the company, and will normally be paid fees fixed by the general meeting or by the directors. If he fails to show proper standards, he can therefore be sued by the company for damages, which will typically be any loss suffered by the company.

If the company is wound up, an auditor guilty of misfeasance or breach of duty may alternatively be liable under the Insolvency Act 1986, section 212. The court can order that he repay, restore or contribute to the company's assets.

To shareholders

The auditors owe no actionable duty to shareholders, even though individuals or groups may have lost heavily by relying on badly audited accounts. The duty of auditors is to the *company* not its members (another example of separate legal personality). The holders of a majority of shares may, however, ensure that the company sues.

To outsiders

People proposing to deal with the company, buy shares in it or lend it money can all lose financially if its accounts are negligently audited. However none of these has a contract with the auditors and, for reasons discussed more fully in Unit 9, they cannot as a general rule recover damages from them.

> In *Caparo Industries plc* v. *Dickman* (1990), the auditors of Fidelity Ltd were alleged to have been negligent, as a result of which the company's accounts were misleading. Caparo plc already owned some shares in Fidelity and, relying on the accounts, bought more in a successful take-over bid. Caparo suffered financial loss, and sued the auditors for damages. The action failed. As mentioned above, auditors owe no actionable duty of care to individual shareholders, of which there could be millions. Still less do they owe a duty to *potential shareholders*, of which there might be even more.

There is no liability to outsiders, then, purely from the statutory annual audit. The auditors will only be liable if, in addition to the statutory audit, they have prepared a special audit or made special promises specifically for only one or two people.

> In *ADT Ltd* v. *Binder Hamlyn* (1995), ADT wished to take over a company, and Binder Hamlyn were the 'target' company's auditors. At a special meeting with ADT, Binder Hamlyn expressly said, without reservation, that the target company's annual accounts were reliable. This proved inaccurate, and the auditors were held liable in tort.

> In *Barings plc* v. *Coopers & Lybrand* (1996), the auditors of a subsidiary of Barings plc are alleged to have been negligent in auditing the subsidiary company's accounts (so as not to disclose the Nick Leeson transactions). The subsidiary's auditors knew that the accounts which they audited would eventually be relied upon by Barings in preparing group accounts, but their contract was with the subsidiary, not with Barings. The Court of Appeal has held that it is arguable that the subsidiary's auditors owed a duty of care in tort to Barings.

251

Attempted exemptions

By the 1985 Act, section 310, any provision in the articles, in any contract with the company, or elsewhere, which tries to exempt a director, company secretary *or auditor* from liability for negligence, default, or breach of duty or trust, is *void*. Any provision to indemnify him, by paying the damages for example, is also void. A provision allowing the company to pay the legal costs *if the director, secretary or auditor is held not liable* can be valid.

Specimen questions

1. (a) Explain the nature of, and differences between, public and private companies.
   (b) What, legally, is a 'small' company? Explain the importance of this classification (see also Unit 22).
2. 'An objects clause is much less important today than it was hitherto.' Explain the nature of an objects clause, and discuss this view (see also Unit 22).
3. *X*, *Y* and *Z* are trading in partnership. They decide to form a limited company. They are told that certain documents must be filed by the promoters. They ask you:
   (a) Who are the promoters?
   (b) Where must the documents be filed?
   (c) What are these documents and, in summary, what must each contain?
   (d) What are the advantages and disadvantages of buying an 'off-the-shelf', already registered company?
   Advise them.
4. *X*, *Y* and *Z* also ask you:
   (a) What restrictions are there on the name that they can register under and/or trade under?
   (b) When can they begin to operate in the company's name?
   (c) What will be the consequences if they do so too soon?
   Advise them.
5. (a) What registers must a company keep?
   (b) Who is responsible for this task?
   (c) Those proposing to deal with a company sometimes conduct a 'company search'. Explain this, and say what it can reveal.

Unit 24. Financial Structure of Companies

A. Meaning of 'capital'

Whatever a company's objects, it will almost certainly need money. If its objects include running a business, it will probably need other assets such as goods and land. In order to obtain these assets, the company must persuade people and other bodies to invest in it. Broadly, 'capital' represents what has been invested in the company, and the relationship between the company and its investors.

In companies limited by shares, the basic way of attracting investment is through the sale by the company of its *shares*. The initial shareholders must pay the company (in cash or other assets) for the shares issued to them; similarly when the company subsequently issues shares. In return, the shareholders become members of the company, and the amount contributed by shareholders to the company's resources is the '*share capital*'.

In its memorandum, a company must state its *nominal capital*. This is the face value of the total number of shares which the company has, at present, authorized itself to issue. The nominal (or 'authorized') capital may, for example, be £60 000, divided into 120 000 shares of 50p each. This does not necessarily mean that all of these shares have been allotted and issued yet; only that the company *may* issue them. (Strictly, a share is 'allotted' when the applicant is informed that the company has accepted his bid for it, and 'issued' when the requisite entry is made in the register of members.)

The real value of a share may be more than its nominal value. For example, if a company's assets are worth more than the nominal value of its shares, then its shares may reflect this. If potential shareholders pay the company £5 for each 50p share, the new shares are said to be allotted at a 'premium' of £4.50. A share must not, however, be issued at a 'discount', at a price *less* than its nominal value.

A company need not demand that a share be *paid for* immediately. It can allot a 50p share for 25p now, with a right to call for the other 25p later. Such shares are, as yet, 'partly paid'. More often today the price is fully payable on allotment.

For the company, its *allotted* or *issued* capital is the total nominal value of the shares that have actually been allotted/issued. The *called-up* capital is the nominal amount that the company has called for from the holders of shares (fully or partly paid) that it has allotted. The *uncalled* capital is the nominal amount that the company has not yet called for on shares that are only partly paid. The *paid-up* capital is the total nominal amount actually paid by shareholders.

When shares are issued for more than their nominal value, the excess is a share premium, which must be recorded in a share premium account, separately from the nominal value of the shares.

Once issued, shares can be transferred by the holder. For example, if the business prospers, the shares may increase in real value, and a member may wish to sell his shares to someone else (at a profit to *himself*, not the company). The company's capital is maintained; the shares are simply held by someone new.

Another way in which a company can raise finance is by borrowing it. A document issued by a company and evidencing a loan to it is called a *debenture*. Debenture holders are not members of the company, although they can acquire rights to influence management. Money borrowed is usually called '*loan capital*'.

In the case of both shares and debentures, the company as a separate person owes duties to those who have invested in it.

B. Shares

The nature of shares

A share confers membership, and the rights and duties in relation to the company and fellow members that go with this. These come from the memorandum and articles under the 1985 Act, section 14 (Unit 23), and from the terms on which the share was issued. The main rights are to attend meetings and/or to vote on resolutions, and to receive such dividends out of profits as the company may declare. If the company is wound up, there is also a right to share in residual assets, if any, when debts and liabilities have been paid.

A shareholder as such has no part in day-to-day management. This is the responsibility of the directors. In a small private company where the main shareholders and the directors are the same persons, this may not matter. In larger companies, small shareholders will usually be quite content to leave management to the directors if all is going well; otherwise, the holders of a majority of shares can usually remove directors if need be.

Different types of share can be created, and the nature of a holder's rights can depend upon the terms on which his share was issued.

Types of share

Ordinary shares are the most common. They are entitled to a dividend, if and when the company declares one from profits (usually once or twice per year, see page 262). They normally give rights to attend meetings, and carry one vote per share. Sometimes, shares are issued without voting rights, although they do still participate in dividends; holders do, therefore, have a return on their investment, but cannot directly limit the control by other shareholders over the company. If non-voting shares are issued in a *listed* public company, the Exchange will require that they be identified as non-voting when traded. Exceptionally, the articles may allow shares with multiple votes.

> In *Bushell v. Faith* (1970), a director held one third of the ordinary shares. The articles, however, provided that on any resolution *to remove that director, his* shares should then carry three votes each. This was held valid, even though it defeated an attempt to sack him.

Preference shares are entitled to a fixed rate of dividend before anything becomes available for ordinary shareholders. However, even preference shares can only be paid out of profits: no profits, no dividend. Moreover, the preference only applies to dividends. Unless the articles provide otherwise, preference shareholders receive no preferential repayment of capital on a winding up. Normally, the articles give no voting rights to preference shareholders.

Different varieties of preference shares exist. For example, shares are 'participating' if, in addition to the preferential dividend, holders are also entitled to any ordinary dividend declared. Preference shares are presumed to be non-participating. They are 'cumulative' if, should the preference dividend not be paid in one year, it is carried forward, so that in future all arrears are paid before anyone else gets a dividend. Unless otherwise provided, they *are* presumed cumulative.

Deferred shares are normally not entitled to any dividend at all until preference shareholders are paid in full, and then ordinary shares receive at least a specified amount or percentage dividend. Exact rights are set by the articles and the terms of issue. Deferred shares (or 'management' or 'founders' shares) are uncommon now.

Redeemable shares can be issued, if authorized by the articles. Either the shareholder or the company can be empowered by the terms of issue to insist that the shares be bought back by the company, and both ordinary and preference shares can be redeemable. Normally, redemption must be either out of profits, or from the proceeds of a new share issue made for the purpose. Private companies can sometimes use further sources. Redeemable shares are an exception to the general rule that a company must not reduce its share capital, and they are mentioned again later under 'capital maintenance'.

Scrip is a term used for 'bonus' shares issued to existing holders when certain reserve funds are turned into capital. It also describes extra shares which some companies offer to existing holders instead of a money dividend.

If a company has different classes of shares, any later attempt to vary class rights is strictly controlled (see Unit 25).

Allotment and issue of shares

The *subscribers* of the memorandum will be the first shareholders. Each must take at least one share, and may take many more.

Subsequently, the *directors* will usually be responsible for allotting and issuing shares. They may be given authority by the articles; the present Table A does not do so, but a special article can be added. Alternatively, the directors may be authorized by ordinary resolution of members in a meeting, or by a written resolution in a private company. The resolution must be registered with the Registrar of Companies.

The authority given to directors has limits.

1. A share issue must not take total holdings beyond the current nominal capital; but the shareholders can also raise the nominal capital by ordinary or written resolution.
2. A *public* company, by section 101, must not allot a share unless at least one-quarter of the share's nominal value, and the whole of any premium on it, have been received. Moreover, under section 117, the company must not commence business or borrow money until such shares with a nominal value of at least £50 000 have been allotted (see Unit 23).
3. *Private* companies must not offer their shares for public sale. An attempt to do so would be a criminal offence by the directors. The articles of a private company sometimes give existing members the right to buy the shares of a member who leaves.
4. By the 1985 Act, section 89, for both public and private companies, if it is proposed to offer new shares for *cash* to *specific* buyers, the existing members must first be given pre-emption rights in proportion to their existing holdings. They must have at least 21 days' notice, and this can give some protection to their existing rights in the company. This can, however, be excluded by the articles or by a special resolution. Alternatively, the articles may give pre-emption rights if shares are offered other than for cash, for example in exchange for other assets.
5. The authority of directors may be restricted by the company itself. The articles or resolution might only authorize them to issue ordinary shares, not preference, for example. The authorization *must* impose a maximum number or amount which they may issue; also, when the authority expires, normally after five years. These limits may be extended by another, duly registered, resolution. Authorization by written resolution in a private company need have no time limit.
6. Above all, there is a general equitable rule that directors must exercise their powers to issue shares, like their other powers, for the benefit of the company as a whole. They must not, for instance, act mainly to protect or increase their own interests.

> In *Piercy v. Mills Ltd* (1920), the directors issued voting shares to themselves and their supporters, not because the company needed the extra capital, but solely to prevent the election of rival directors. The issue was held void.

> In *Howard Smith Ltd v. Ampol Petroleum Ltd* (1973), the directors of *M Ltd* issued 4.5 million new shares to Smith Ltd, so as to change the balance of power in *M Ltd.*

After the issue, the previous majority shareholder, Ampol, would no longer have a majority. The issue was set aside.

When new shares are allotted, appropriate entries must be made in the company's registers, and a return made to the Registrar of Companies within one month (see Unit 23). A share certificate may be sent to the holder within two months. This is only prima facie evidence of ownership of the shares which it covers; the document of title is the register of members. Share certificates need no longer be sent unless requested.

Finding buyers

A private company must find buyers for its shares by private contracts with specific buyers, and there may be pre-emption rights. A public company has more possibilities. It may 'place' shares with specific buyers, usually with help from agents such as issuing houses, banks or stockbrokers. Sometimes the shares may be bought by the issuing house itself with a view to its finding specific buyers from itself. If the company wishes to offer the shares for public sale, it might seek to have its shares 'listed' or 'quoted' on a Stock Exchange. If the company then gets long-term admission to the official list of the Exchange, the share is referred to as a 'listed' security; otherwise it is 'unlisted'. Again the shares may be sold to an issuing house which then issues an 'offer for sale' to the public (not a placing with specific buyers).

When a public company offers (or 'places') shares, it must publish detailed information about itself, its officers and agents, so as to protect potential investors and lessen the risk of fraud. For listed shares, the rules are administered by the Council of the Stock Exchange, both before it will admit the shares to the Exchange and subsequently while the shares remain listed. Listing particulars must be sent to the Registrar of Companies on or before publication. For unlisted shares, the rules are administered by the Department of Trade and Industry. Particulars must be set out in a 'prospectus', again published to potential investors, and registered.

In all cases, non-disclosure or (more seriously) falsehood is a criminal offence, and the company, directors and agents may be fined or (where appropriate) imprisoned. Buyers may be entitled to damages in civil proceedings, and the share issue could even be rescinded. A Stock Exchange could suspend the listing.

A potential buyer, having had access to the prospectus or listing particulars, applies to the company for the number of shares sought. He might be unsuccessful or only partly successful if, for example, more shares are sought than are available. The terms of issue normally make provision for this.

Payment for shares

In a public company, if less than the statutory minimum amount is actually paid (one quarter of the nominal value and the whole of any premium), the share is still validly issued, but the buyer is liable to interest on the deficit. The company and officers responsible commit criminal offences. If shares are issued at a discount, similarly, they

257

can still be valid, but the holders are liable to interest on any short-fall, and the issuers commit criminal offences.

A private company can issue shares before actually receiving any payment at all, but the nominal value must become payable.

Payment for shares is not necessarily in money. When an existing unincorporated firm is turned into a company, the present owners transfer their assets, including goodwill of the business, to the company in return for their shares. This is a fairly common situation; (see *Salomon v. Salomon & Co Ltd*, Unit 22, for example). In takeovers and mergers between existing firms and companies there can be more complex arrangements.

If shares in a public company are to be paid for other than in money, the non-money consideration must be independently valued. A valuer's report must be sent to the company, and a copy to the proposed buyer, less than six months before the allotment. Certain things must not be accepted by a public company in payment for its shares: any undertaking for the future which might be performed more than five years after the allotment; and a promise that any person will do work in the future. If such promises are accepted, the promisor remains bound by the promise, but must also pay the cash price of the shares.

In a private company, the value of assets used in payment for shares is subjectively agreed. A court would not intervene unless, perhaps, the real value was less than the nominal value of the shares, so that they were being issued at a discount, or unless there was fraud.

Where a person is acquiring or has acquired shares in a company, it is not lawful for the company or any of its subsidiaries to give financial assistance (such as a gift, loan or guarantee) for the purpose of the acquisition; see section 151, page 261.

C. Maintenance of capital

The general rule

A company's share capital must be 'maintained' and, as a *general* rule, shareholders must not be repaid until the company is wound up. There are many exceptions to this general principle, but even today issued share capital can only be reduced under strict safeguards.

The principle has two main purposes: it offers some protection to creditors, in that shareholders must not generally withdraw their investments while creditors remain unpaid; and it protects shareholders against others who might withdraw leaving the rest (them) to face the creditors.

This does *not* mean that money invested by shareholders must specifically be set aside. This would be contrary to the whole concept of venture capital. Once it receives payment for its shares, the company can use all of the money and other assets in whatever way it thinks best for the enterprise; but *not* normally to repay shareholders before creditors. The principle works in various ways.

1. There are rules to ensure that payment for shares actually *reaches* the company. Shares must not be issued at a discount; and the rules in sections 101 and 117 above aim to ensure that a *public* company receives at least one quarter of the nominal value and the whole of any premium at the outset.

2. Dividends must not be paid to shareholders except out of current profits or, sometimes, from profits specifically set aside from earlier years (see page 262).

3. By section 143, a company must not buy or otherwise acquire its own shares, except under strict control (see below).

4. If shares in a company are acquired by its nominee, they must be treated as held by the nominee on his/its own account, with the company itself having no beneficial interest.

5. In general, a subsidiary must not have shares in its holding company (section 23). However, if the subsidiary already owned shares in the parent company before being taken-over, it can continue to do so.

6. Perhaps most importantly now, by section 142, where the net *assets* of a public company fall to half or less of its called-up share *capital*, the directors must convene an extraordinary general meeting of members, to consider what steps should be taken to deal with the situation. The meeting must be called within 28 days of any director discovering the facts, and it must take place within 56 days of the discovery. The 'steps' can include decisions to remove directors. This section is intended to protect against fall in the *real* value of a company's capital.

Share premium account

Any premium received on shares must be recorded separately from the nominal value of the shares. The premium must appear in a separate 'share premium account'. For capital maintenance, this must then be treated in almost the same way as (other) capital. However, it can be reduced by being converted into new bonus shares, as a scrip issue to existing members without further payment by them. This is not a reduction in the company's issued capital, because the new shares replace the amount taken from the share premium account as capital of the company. The same rules apply to a 'capital redemption reserve' (see below).

Preliminary expenses of forming the company can be set off against a share premium account.

Permissible reductions in share capital

The nominal share capital can be reduced at any time as regards shares not yet issued. By ordinary (or written) resolution, the members can resolve to reduce the amount of unissued capital which the company is *authorized* to issue. The resolution must be notified to the Registrar within one month.

Redeemable shares

By the 1985 Act, section 159, a company can issue shares which, by their terms of issue, are 'redeemable'. The articles must authorize this, and Table A does so.

Usually either the holder or the company can opt to redeem, but the articles must limit the redemption period and specify the redemption terms, or allow the directors to do this by the terms of issue. Not all of a company's shares can be redeemable. Moreover, only fully-paid-up shares can be redeemed. The company must repay immediately on redemption. A premium can be charged and become repayable.

In a *public* company, the redemption payment must come either from distributable profits, or from the proceeds of a new share issue (in which case there is no reduction of capital). New shares will usually be issued before redemption, and for this purpose a company is allowed temporarily to exceed its nominal capital. If repayment is from profits then, by section 170, the amount by which capital is reduced must be transferred from profits to a 'capital redemption reserve' which, like the share premium account above, is treated as capital.

In a *private* company, the above rules apply but, in addition, there may be a 'permissible capital payment' ('p.c.p.') from other sources if the articles permit (Table A does). All distributable profits must be used first, plus the proceeds of any share issue *if* one is made. Subject to this, the directors can acquire the money elsewhere, for example by borrowing it. Before a p.c.p., the directors must make a statutory declaration that the company can pay its debts both now and during the coming year. This must be supported by an auditors' report. The scheme must be approved by a special resolution (75% of votes cast) at a general meeting, or a 100% written resolution. Holders of shares to be redeemed cannot use the votes given by those shares. The resolution must be advertised in the London Gazette, and there are detailed provisions for members *or creditors* to apply to cancel the scheme before the repayment.

The Registrar of Companies must be notified within 28 days of any reduction in issued capital resulting from redemption.

A company which wrongfully refuses to redeem on demand is liable for breach of contract. A holder cannot recover damages, but he can seek a court order for specific performance (see page 158) if the company could have redeemed from profits. He can also prevent the use of these profits for dividends, and may even petition for winding-up the company.

Purchase by a company of its own shares
Under section 162, the articles (including Table A) can give a *company* powers to buy out non-redeemable shares (but no shareholder can demand this). The rules are very similar to those for redeemable shares. In particular, for a public company, the buy-back must be from a new share issue or from profits. For a private company, there may also be a p.c.p.

A *listed* public company can authorize itself to buy a limited number of its own shares on the *market*, within a limited time of up to 18 months. This ordinary resolution must be sent to the Registrar.

Otherwise, for an 'off-the-market' buy, the company must pass a special resolution (or a written one in a private company). The proposed contract must be available

15 days before the resolution for members to inspect; otherwise the resolution is invalid.

If the shares are bought from profits, the proceeds must go to a capital redemption reserve, as above. The shares themselves are cancelled, and the Registrar must be notified.

Reduction with confirmation by the court

Section 135 allows shareholders to reduce issued share capital in a scheme which is approved by the court. The company may, for example, extinguish or reduce liability on shares not fully paid-up; or cancel paid-up capital which is lost or not represented by assets; or pay off paid-up capital which exceeds the company's wants.

The articles must authorize this, and Table A does. A special (or written) resolution must then be passed. Creditors can object if shareholders are repaid or unpaid capital is released, and in this event the creditors must normally be repaid or given security. The interests of different classes of shareholders must be balanced. The court must also consider potential future investors.

Reduction by order of the court

Various sections of the 1985 Act empower a court to *order* a company to buy all or some of a member's shares. For example:

1. If a company alters its memorandum, a 15% minority can object to the court, which *may* order the company to buy the objectors' shares.
2. Where a public company resolves to change to a private one, the holders of 5% in nominal value, or of any class, or 50 members, can apply to the court to cancel the change; whereupon the court *may* order the company to buy the objectors' shares.
3. If any (one) member alleges that the company's affairs are being conducted in a manner unfairly prejudicial to himself or others, he can apply to the court under section 459, which again *may* order the purchase of an objector's shares.

In all cases, the shares will be cancelled, and alterations made to the memorandum and (possibly) articles. The Registrar must be notified.

Financial assistance by a company to buy its own shares

As a general rule, this is unlawful, under the 1985 Act section 151. However there are now many exceptions. The following are some examples.

1. By section 153(1), help can be given if it is merely 'an incidental part of some larger purpose of the company', and given in good faith in the interests of the company. For example, the company can buy an asset knowing that the seller will use the proceeds to buy shares in the company; but only if the company genuinely needs or wants the asset. In a company like a bank, which regularly lends money, a loan to a customer who then uses the money to buy shares in the bank can be lawful.

2. In an employees' share scheme, a company can lend money to its employees (but not if they are also directors) to help them buy shares in itself or a holding company; see section 153(4).

3. In *private* companies there is almost complete exemption, so long as the net assets of the company are not reduced (see section 155). The help can therefore come from profits, or from a *loan* to the buyers. There must be a special or written resolution of members, and an audited statutory declaration, by the directors, of the company's solvency, the nature of the business, the form of help given and identity of the recipients. There are detailed rules for objection by at least 10% of shares.

   If the major shareholder of a company wanted to close the business down, the managers might be able to use these provisions to buy the majority shares, and keep the company alive.

D. Dividends

One reward for shareholders is that the company may pay periodic monetary dividends on the shares. By the 1985 Act, section 263, these must only be paid out of 'profits available' for the purpose. Anything else would be an unlawful reduction in capital. 'Profits available' are the company's 'accumulated, realized profits, so far as not utilized by distribution or capitalisation, less accumulated realized losses'. The existence of available profits must be shown by the relevant accounts, normally the latest audited annual accounts (see Unit 23). Profits in earlier years can be accumulated for future years, but so must realized losses.

The 'realized profits' are (i) trading profits, plus (ii) realized capital profits from actual disposal of fixed assets. Unrealized capital appreciation, such as an assumed increase in the value of the company's land, can *not* be included; nor can 'capitalized' profits which have already been used to redeem or buy the company's own shares or to issue bonus shares.

The 'realized losses' are (i) trading losses, and (ii) realized capital losses on the actual disposal of an asset (unless provision has already been made for this depreciation). Provision *can* be made for unrealized depreciation of assets like vehicles and machinery.

The *procedures* for declaring and paying dividends are governed largely by the articles. Where Table A applies, the initial decision is made by the directors, who *may* (if profits are sufficient) recommend a dividend. This recommendation is then put to members, who can vote themselves a dividend by ordinary resolution in a general meeting, or by written resolution in a private company. The amount may be up to, but not exceeding, the amount recommended by the directors. Any preference shareholders must normally be paid the preferential amount in full before money becomes available for ordinary dividends. Some preference shares may then also be 'participating' (see earlier).

The members may declare more than one dividend in a year. Table A allows directors to recommend 'interim' dividends in addition to the annual 'final dividend'. Payments will take place on the date(s) resolved by the members. Dividends must be paid in money unless the articles provide otherwise; Table A allows members to resolve that they be given the option to take shares in the company instead of money.

Table A can be altered in various ways. For example, articles may provide that all decisions on dividends be left to the directors, without the need for a members' resolution. This does not, however, affect the rule that the *source* must be a profit from which a dividend can be declared.

Section 277 covers dividends paid unlawfully. Where a distribution, or part of one, is made unlawfully and, at the time of the distribution the member knows or has reasonable grounds for believing that it is made wrongfully, he is liable to repay the whole or the unlawful part to the company. If the distribution was not made in cash, he must pay the cash value of the unlawful part. The directors who recommend an unlawful dividend may also be liable to the company.

E. Loan capital

Initially, companies acquire money (and other assets) through issuing shares, and they can issue more shares later if need be, even in instances where they have to raise the company's nominal/authorised capital as a first step. Profitable companies can then retain most of their profits for re-investment, rather than distributing them as dividends.

Companies may also raise money by borrowing it, and this can have advantages: if the company is doing well, the existing shareholders may not want to dilute their prospects by introducing new members; and if the company is not doing well, it may need extra money when it has few profits to retain, and its shares are not attractive to potential new buyers.

The disadvantages of borrowing are obvious, in that the debt will have to be repaid as and when agreed, whether or not this suits the company. Moreover, interest on loans must be paid, whereas dividends need not be declared. But at least interest on debts is an expense which can reduce tax, whereas any dividends are paid *after* tax (see later).

The *power* to borrow is usually given *expressly* in the company's objects. In any event, a trading company has *implied* power to borrow for the purposes of the business.

The power is *exercised* under the articles. It can be exercisable by the members by ordinary or written resolution, normally without limit. Borrowing powers are also, almost invariably, exercisable by the directors, although in this case it is more common to impose a limit; indeed, for 'listed' public companies, a maximum limit must be imposed.

Any document issued by a company as evidence of a loan to it is called a *debenture*. (A company may be able to borrow without the lender seeking documentary evidence, but this is very unlikely, particularly for large loans.)

Unsecured debentures

Debentures need not be secured by any charge on the company's property. For example, in a very small company, a creditor such as the bank might seek a personal guarantee from a director or major shareholder, and this could be secured by a mortgage of the director's own house. This, of course, is not a charge on the *company's* assets. Moreover, if the house is jointly owned by husband and wife, the transaction might prove to be voidable by the spouse under the *Barclays Bank* v. *O'Brien* series of cases today (see Unit 13). Therefore, some charge given by a company over its own assets will make lenders more likely to lend, particularly over a long term.

Debentures secured by a fixed charge

The company can declare a fixed charge on a specific item of its property. A mortgage of one of the company's buildings is a debenture of this kind; so is a charge on a specific piece of machinery. A charge on the company's present and future book debts may be fixed if it prevents the company from using the debts without the chargee's consent.

> In *Re Keenan Bros Ltd* (1986) (an Irish case), the bank loaned money to the company in return for an undertaking by the company to pay all money which it received for book debts into specified accounts with the bank. It could then only be withdrawn with the bank's consent. The charge was held to be fixed.

The disadvantage of a fixed charge for the borrower is that it ties up the assets charged, which cannot now be dealt with without the creditor's consent.

Debentures secured by a floating charge

A company can also give a lender a 'floating' charge, which is an equitable charge on some or all of the present and future property of the company. In *Re Yorkshire Woolcombers Association Ltd* (1903), Romer L.J. said that a floating charge has three features.

1. It is a charge on a class of assets of a company, present and future.
2. This class is, in the ordinary course of the company's business, changing from time to time.
3. By the charge it is contemplated that, until the charge holders take steps to enforce it, the company may carry on business in the normal way so far as concerns the assets charged.

The charge will normally relate, therefore, to assets which are changing constantly, such as the company's stock-in-trade. The company must be left free to deal with the assets as it pleases in the course of its business (contrast *Re Keenan Ltd*, above). The charge only becomes attached to any item if and when the charge 'crystallizes', whereupon it becomes a fixed charge on all current items which it covers. A charge crystallizes when:

(a) the company passes a voluntary winding-up resolution;
(b) the court petitions for winding-up;
(c) a receiver is appointed by the court;
(d) a receiver is appointed by creditors under any powers given by their debentures;
(e) anything else occurs which, under the terms of the debenture, will cause the charge to crystallize; for example, the company defaults in paying interest.

Floating charges can be advantageous both for the creditors and the debtor company, in that they give the creditor some security without inhibiting the activities of the company (unless one of the danger signals in the above list shows itself). For private traders and unincorporated associations, floating charges are rendered impracticable by the Bills of Sale Acts 1878 and 1882 (which do not apply to company borrowers).

However, a floating charge can have some weaknesses. For example, rapidly changing assets like stock-in-trade can quickly reduce in value as security. There can also be difficulties regarding priority of charges if the company is wound-up (see later).

Registration of charges

Registers must be kept of charges on a company's property. These provisions of the 1985 Act help to protect those dealing with the company, as a check on its financial soundness, and to establish the priority of claims over company property if it becomes insolvent.

The Registrar of Companies keeps the main register of company charges, and this is open to public inspection (often as part of a company search, see page 248). When a company creates a charge over its property, fixed or floating, it must send particulars to the Registrar within 21 days of execution of the charge document. Registration may also be effected by someone else 'interested' in the charge, and the creditor will often carry out the task; but responsibility lies with the company, whose officers are criminally liable if no-one registers in time. If the company acquires property which is already subject to a charge, it must similarly register within 21 days of acquisition.

Registration must give particulars of the charge (such as date of creation, amount secured, property charged, identity of creditor/persons entitled), and be sent with the document by which the charge is created. The Registrar records the prescribed particulars, returns the document, and gives a signed or sealed certificate of registration showing the amount secured. This is conclusive evidence of registration, and gives constructive notice of the charge to those dealing with the company.

265

In the event of non-registration, section 395 renders the charge void against any creditor of the company, and the liquidator if it is wound-up. This does not affect the debt secured except that it now becomes immediately repayable.

If the charge has been properly registered, the Registrar will make appropriate amendments to the register when the debt is repaid or the property released from the charge. The company can receive a copy memorandum. If the creditor has to take steps to enforce the charge, he must give notice of this to the Registrar within 7 days, and the Registrar must enter this fact on the register.

Part IV of the Companies Act 1989 made several changes to these rules, but it was provided that Part IV could only be brought into force by statutory instrument. This has not been done, and it is unlikely now.

The company itself must keep a copy of every instrument creating a registrable charge at its registered office (1985 Act, section 406). It must also keep at its registered office a register of charges, fixed and floating (section 407). The copy instruments and the register must be available for inspection by members and creditors without fee, and by others for a nominal fee. Default by an officer of the company is a criminal offence. The court may also compel inspection.

H.M. Land Registry keeps a further register of mortgages and charges over a company's *land*. An unregistered mortgage is void against a subsequent buyer or mortgagee of the land. There are special rules where a floating charge includes the company's land. A buyer of land from the company will search the register, and usually insist that any mortgage be redeemed before he buys.

Priority of charges

Questions of priority can arise if there are several charges affecting a company's property. In particular, there may be competing claims if a company is insolvent when wound-up.

1. A fixed charge over specific property has priority over a floating one, even if the floating charge was made earlier and properly registered. The fixed charge has first claim *on this property*.
2. The terms of issue of a floating charge therefore often contain a 'negative pledge' clause, by which the company undertakes not to create any other charge ranking in priority to, or equally with, the floating charge over the things which the floating charge could cover. This gives the floating charge priority over any fixed chargee who has notice *of the clause* when he/it takes its charge. In order to ensure notice, the *terms* of the negative pledge clause must expressly be registered with the floating charge.
3. Floating charges rank between themselves in order of *creation* if they are all registered within their 21 day time limits. If a floating charge is registered late, however, it ranks after any other floating charge *registered* before it. If neither of two floating charges is registered in time, both can register late, and the first one to do so takes priority.

4. Where one floating charge covers the whole of a company's property, and a later floating charge covers only some of the assets, the latter charge takes priority over those assets, unless the later chargee has notice of a negative pledge clause in the earlier charge.

5. When a company is wound up, a number of other claimants can take priority over a floating chargee.

    (a) A landlord from whom the company leases land can take possession of company goods as distress for arrears of rent, sometimes even after a floating charge has crystallized over these goods.

    (b) Preferential creditors, such as the Crown for arrears of VAT, or ex-employees for arrears of wages, can have priority even over a floating charge which has crystallized before the company was dissolved.

    (c) A creditor can have priority if he has obtained a court judgment against the company and, to enforce the judgment, had goods seized and sold by the sheriff, or actually enforced a garnishee order on money in the company's bank accounts.

    (d) Where the company is acquiring goods on hire-purchase, the goods still belong to the hire-purchase firm until the price is paid in full. The goods do not belong to the debtor company, and are therefore not subject to its charges.

    (e) An unpaid seller of goods to the company may insist on a 'retention of title' ('*Romalpa*') clause in the sale contract. By this, even if the debtor company is allowed to take possession of the goods, they may remain the property of the seller until full payment. Again, therefore, they are not subject to charges by the debtor company; see also Unit 18.

6. A floating charge in favour of a 'connected' person, such as a director or shadow director, or his associate such as spouse, close relative, partner etc., will be invalid if it was created within two years of the effective start of the winding-up. The debt remains due, but the creditor is unsecured. A floating charge in favour of anyone else will be void insofar as it is made to secure a pre-existing debt, if it was created within one year of the start of winding up, and the company was insolvent immediately after creation of the charge; see Insolvency Act 1986, section 245.

Debenture stock

A public company can seek loan capital from public subscription. It can issue a prospectus inviting offers from the public for a series of debentures, usually for only a small amount each. The process is similar to that for the issue of shares. A private company cannot issue debentures for public subscription.

Usually, the public company will issue debentures through a financial institution such as a bank, which will initially buy them, and administer re-sale to the eventual buyers. Sometimes the bank will retain legal title, but sell equitable ownership under a trust deed (see below). Buyers will receive a debenture or debenture stock certificate, and can usually sell on their investment to other holders if they wish to do so, as with shares. A company will normally keep a register of debenture holders at its registered office, although strictly this is only required for debentures which are secured.

267

Debentures are often long-term, and may even be perpetual in that the company is not *bound* to repay the loan until the company is wound up, although it may reserve the *right* to redeem earlier. The terms of issue usually give holders the right to interest payments, often twice a year, which must be paid whether or not the company is making a profit.

Debentures for public subscription are usually issued under a *trust deed*, under which legal title is held (or retained) by trustees, or a trust corporation such as a bank, for the duration of the loan, on behalf of the holders who are the equitable/beneficial owners. This has several advantages, arising from the probable huge numbers of debenture holders, who would find it impossible to act together quickly. For the company, it is easier to deal with a single trustee or a small number. For the holders, the trustee(s) can act quickly on their behalf, for example by appointing a receiver should the company default in paying interest. Any security given by the debenture can be enforced quickly by the trustee(s) if the need should arise. If the company wishes its debentures to be quoted/listed on a Stock Exchange, the Exchange will require a trust deed, with a trust corporation as one of the trustees or the sole trustee.

The trust deed will generally specify the terms of issue of the debentures, including the amount of each, and also the date and terms for redemption. If the debentures are secured, the deed will set out the conditions which will entitle the trustees to enforce the security.

Remedies of debenture holders

On default of the company, a debenture holder may have the following remedies, at common law, by statute, and/or by the terms of issue.

1. He can simply sue for the amount due.
2. The terms of issue usually give the unpaid creditor the right to have any property charged sold. The terms normally give him the right to appoint a receiver to carry out the sale. Any surplus is paid to the company.
3. As well as powers expressly given, the unpaid debenture holder has various statutory powers to have a receiver appointed to dispose of property charged.
4. If the assets charged are virtually the whole business, there may be power to appoint an 'administrative receiver', to take over management from the directors, but to keep the business alive for the time being.
5. A petition for winding up the company may result from any of this.

An ordinary receiver is usually appointed under a fixed charge on a specific asset. An administrative receiver is more likely when a floating charge on all of the company's assets crystallizes. There can sometimes be an administrative receiver and an ordinary receiver at the same time. If so, the administrative receiver can ask for a court order allowing him to take the place of the ordinary receiver, particularly if this will help him to sell off the whole business as a going concern (and therefore at a better price). The court will allow the property subject to a fixed charge to be sold, but only if the proceeds of sale, or the market value if greater, is used to pay off the fixed chargee.

F. Shares and debentures compared

1. A shareholder is a member of the company, and has the rights given by the 1985 Act, section 14. In particular, he has rights to attend meetings and vote on resolutions. A debenture holder is not a member.
2. Directors and members *may* choose to declare a dividend to shareholders, but this can only come from company profits. Debenture interest *must* be paid, whether or not the company has profits.
3. A company is taxed on its profits. The interest on debentures is deducted from income in order to ascertain profits, and therefore before tax is assessed. Dividends are paid from profits after they have been assessed for tax.
4. It is easier for a company to borrow money than to issue new shares. A trading company has implied power to borrow, and the articles usually give the directors express authority to exercise this power.
5. A debenture can be issued at a discount; a share must not be.
6. It is easier for the company to get rid of a debenture than a share. Even 'perpetual' debentures usually give the company the option to repay early, and other debentures *must* be repaid when due. On the other hand, it is difficult for a company to buy back its own shares; see the maintenance of capital rules earlier.
7. On a winding-up, debenture holders (creditors) must be repaid before shareholders get anything.
8. As investments, shares may fluctuate substantially in value, according to the market's view of things like the company's possible profits and/or growth. Debentures for fixed loans, are likely to be more stable.

Specimen questions

1. Explain each of the following terms:
   (a) share capital;
   (b) nominal capital;
   (c) issued capital;
   (d) uncalled capital;
   (e) loan capital.
2. Explain each of the following:
   (a) ordinary shares;
   (b) non-participating cumulative preference shares;
   (c) redeemable shares;
   (d) share premium account;
   (e) bonus shares.
3. (a) In what circumstances can a company buy its own shares?
   (b) Can a company give financial assistance to a buyer of its shares to help him make the purchase?
   Explain your answer in each case.

4. (a) What is a debenture?
   (b) Distinguish between fixed and floating charges.
   (c) What records must be kept, and by whom, of charges on a company's property?

5. (a) Compare and contrast shares and debentures.
   (b) If a large company is seeking more money, discuss the advantages and disadvantages of issuing shares and issuing debentures.

Unit 25. Companies: Membership and Management

A. Members

We have seen that there are three ways in which someone can become a shareholder: the subscribers of the memorandum must each take at least one share; new shares may later be issued by the company; or a shareholder may acquire shares from another holder.

The position of shareholders is set out in the 1985 Act, section 14; see Unit 23. Their rights are based primarily on the company's memorandum and articles, and on the terms of issue of their shares.

Company meetings

Much of the constitutional work of companies is done through meetings of members. There are two types of general meeting.

An annual general meeting ('a.g.m.') must be held initially within 18 months of incorporation, and thereafter at least once in every calendar year, with not more than 15 months between any two meetings. At least 21 days' notice in writing of an impending a.g.m. must be given to members, directors and the auditors. The meeting should be called by the directors. If they do not, any member can ask the DTI to call it and, if so, the Department can give instructions on how the meeting should be conducted, and can even provide for a quorum of one.

The *ordinary business* of an a.g.m. is considering the accounts, receiving the directors' and auditors' reports, deciding upon any dividend, and electing directors. No notice of ordinary business need be given in the notice calling an a.g.m. Anything else at the meeting is *special business*, of which express notice must be given to members. The directors can propose special business and, by the 1985 Act, section 376, members holding 5% of the voting rights can insist that an item be put on the agenda and that their views be circularized before the meeting.

An extraordinary general meeting is any general meeting other than the a.g.m. All business there is special. It can be called in various ways.

1. The directors usually have power under the articles (including Table A). They must give at least 14 days' notice to members holding voting shares, and state the purpose of the meeting sufficiently for them to decide whether to attend.
2. By s.368, a minority of shareholders can require that the directors call an e.g.m., notwithstanding anything in the articles. The requisitionists must together hold at least 10% of such of the paid-up share capital as carries voting rights at general meetings. Those requiring the meeting must say why they want it on a signed requisition to the registered office. There are then complex and detailed rules to prevent the directors from unduly delaying calling and holding the meeting. (The articles can provide additional protection for members, but not less than the statutory ones.)
3. By s.370, two or more members holding at least one-tenth of the issued share capital can themselves call an e.g.m., but this only applies 'in so far as the articles of the company do not make other provision in that behalf'. Table A in fact makes more generous provisions than s.370 in one situation: 'If there are not within the UK sufficient directors to call a general meeting, any (one) director or any member of the company may call a general meeting' (which could cover some instances where directors have absconded).
4. By section 371, the court can order that an e.g.m. be held if it is otherwise impracticable to call or conduct one properly. Any director *or member* can apply, or the court can take the initiative itself.

> In *Re El Sombrero Ltd* (1958), the company had three members. The majority shareholder wanted a meeting, but the quorum was two, and the other two would not attend. The court ordered a 'meeting' of the one member, who then used his voting power to sack the other two as directors.

5. An auditor who resigns can require that the directors call an e.g.m. (see Unit 23). (Incidentally, an auditor is entitled to *attend any* general meeting, and to receive notices, and to be heard.)
6. By s.142, the directors must call an e.g.m. if the value of the capital in a p.l.c. is threatened by a serious loss of assets. This applies where the net assets of the p.l.c. fall to less than half of its called-up share capital, and the e.g.m. must consider what steps should be taken to deal with the situation. There are again provisions to ensure that the meeting is called and held reasonably promptly (see Unit 24).

A general meeting called without proper notice can still be valid if (a) for an a.g.m., all members entitled to attend and vote agree, and (b) for an e.g.m., it is agreed by a majority in number of those entitled to vote and having at least 95% of the shares; a private company can reduce this to 90% by elective resolution. This 'short notice' procedure can allow an e.g.m. immediately after a board meeting of directors in small companies where the directors themselves are almost the only members and hold almost all of the shares.

Resolutions

Irrespective of the type of business, there are three main types of resolution at company meetings. *Ordinary resolutions* can be passed by a simple majority of those voting. Table A, if it applies, gives a casting vote to the chairman. It should be emphasized that the rule is one vote per share, not one per person. Someone holding most of the voting shares can therefore dictate what will be passed. Sometimes the articles and terms of issue can give weighted voting rights, as in *Bushell* v. *Faith* (Unit 24). Secondly, some powers of shareholders can only be exercised by *extraordinary resolution*. This must be passed by a three-quarters majority of votes cast. Notice of intention to move such a resolution must be given to members when the meeting is called. It is needed for various decisions connected with winding-up, and the articles may require it elsewhere. Thirdly, some things such as altering the objects or the articles must be done by *special resolution*. Again, a three-quarters majority is needed. Furthermore, at least 21 days' notice must be given to members, even if it is moved at an e.g.m. for which only 14 days' notice is otherwise required.

Besides these provisions for notice to be given *by* the company to its members, special notice of 28 days must be given *to* the company of members' (ordinary) resolutions to dismiss directors or auditors. The company must then notify members of the text when it calls the a.g.m. or e.g.m. at which it is moved.

Most powers of shareholders can also be exercised without a meeting today, by a *written resolution* signed by all members *entitled* to vote (100%). Signatures need not all be on the same piece of paper, and separate printed copies of a resolution can be sent to members for signature and return. This will only be practicable for companies with few members, since any abstention defeats the resolution. They can only be used by private companies. A copy of the proposed resolution must be sent to the auditor at or before the time it is supplied to a member for signature (but this does not apply to those very small companies that do not have an auditor; see Unit 22). Written resolutions cannot be used to remove directors or auditors, since this would prejudice their right to put their case to members.

A *private* company can pass an *elective resolution* (again 100%) to dispense with holding an a.g.m. and, for example, laying accounts and reports before it; also the need to reappoint auditors each year. The written resolution procedure can be used. However, any member can still demand an a.g.m., etc., and an auditor can demand that accounts and reports be laid. An elective resolution can be reversed by an ordinary one.

Minutes must be kept of resolutions passed at meetings. If they are signed by the chairman of this or the next meeting, they are presumed correct. The articles sometimes provide that they are conclusive, and cannot be challenged at all. Copies must be kept at the registered office, and be available to members and auditors without charge. There must also be a record of written resolutions. All special, extraordinary and elective resolutions must be filed with the Registrar of Companies within 15 days. Ordinary resolutions need not be filed, other than in some special cases such as resolutions to increase nominal capital.

Class rights and their variation

We have seen that, under the company's constitution and the terms of issue, there can be many different classes of share, such as ordinary and the different varieties of preference. There are many cases on what can amount to a class, and on what can amount to a variation on the rights of that class.

> In *Re United Provident Assurance Co Ltd* (1910), a group of members within a class who had paid up a different amount on their shares were held to be a separate class.

> In *Re Northern Engineering Industries plc* (1994), the company wanted to pay off all of its preference shares. The articles expressly provided that this would be a variation of class rights, which could only be done with the appropriate consent of members of the class.

Class meetings can be authorized by the articles to discuss matters affecting only the class concerned. The rules relating to resolutions etc. above can apply broadly to class meetings.

Variation of class rights is subject to complex special safeguards. By the 1985 Act, section 125(2), the rights of any class can normally only be varied (a) with the written consent of the holders of three-quarters of the issued shares of that class, or (b) by an extraordinary resolution at a separate meeting of members of that class. Any further requirements imposed by the memorandum, articles and/or terms of issue must also be satisfied. If rights are attached to a class by the memorandum, and no provision is made for variation, they can normally only be varied if all of the members of the company agree.

If the requirements of section 125(2) above have been met, the holders of 15 per cent of the issued shares of the class, who did not vote for the alteration, can still apply to the court to have the change set aside. This must be done within 21 days of the vote. The court may approve or refuse a variation, but not change it. One dissentient can act on behalf of the others with their written consent.

Duties of shareholders

Unlike directors, shareholders as such owe no general duties of good faith, care or skill to the company. Generally, they can exercise their powers and rights for whatever motive they think fit. There are, however, limits on this freedom. In altering the articles, for example, it is well established that members must act in good faith for the benefit of the company.

> In *Brown* v. *British Abrasive Wheel Co Ltd* (1919), the holders of 98% of the issued shares promised to provide more capital, but only if they could make a compulsory purchase of the remaining shares. An alteration of the articles was needed to allow this. It was held that

the proposed change was invalid. It was not for the benefit of the whole company, only of the majority.

There can be more general restraints on the absolute freedom of voting power; see *Clemens* v. *Clemens Bros Ltd* (page 284).

Even an outsider such as a creditor can sometimes limit the freedom of a shareholder to vote as he wishes.

In *Standard Chartered Bank* v. *Walker* (1992), a company was in difficulty, and would have to be wound up unless the members agreed to a 'rescue package' devised by its creditors. A minority shareholder was in a position to frustrate this, and intended to do so. The creditors obtained an injunction stopping him from using his votes in a general meeting in a way which would probably destroy the company. The creditors had charges over the shares, which would become worthless if the company ended. A secured creditor is entitled to prevent the deliberate destruction of his security.

Transfer of shares

By section 22, a member of a company is a person 'whose name is entered in its register of members', and proof of ownership depends on this. The register can be in writing or on a computer. A member will also normally receive a share certificate within two months of its allotment or transfer to him. It need not be under seal, but the articles often still do require this.

The procedure for transferring shares is set out in the Stock Transfer Act 1963, as amended. In a sale, the share certificate and a stock transfer form are delivered to the transferee in return for payment. The transferee pays any stamp duty, and sends the certificate and form to the company secretary. He alters the register, and ownership passes then. The company must send a new certificate to the transferee within two months. Where only part of a holding is transferred, the procedure is slightly more complex, and the transferor sends the documents to the company secretary.

For some of the shares which are listed on a Stock Exchange, a computerized system of selling exists. Members can hold shares as a computer record and without a certificate if they choose to do so. The can also hold their shares through a nominee company. These arrangements are suitable in the main only for those who deal often in shares.

Restrictions on the right to transfer shares can be imposed by the articles, particularly in private companies. *Pre-emption* clauses provide that existing members must be given first refusal before shares can be transferred to outsiders. *Refusal* clauses go further, and allow directors to refuse a transfer without giving any reason; this power must be exercised within a reasonable time, in good faith, and in the interests of the company as a whole.

A mortgage of shares is possible as security for a loan. In a *legal mortgage*, the member transfers legal ownership of the shares to the lender, with a separate contract for re-transfer when the loan is repaid. To prevent a creditor from selling elsewhere, the debtor can obtain a 'stop notice' from the court, requiring the creditor to give

275

14 days' warning of any projected re-sale. An *equitable mortgage* usually occurs when the debtor simply deposits the share certificate(s) with the lender.

On death of a member, his shares are transmitted to his personal representatives ('PRs') under the will or on intestacy. The PRs can register as members, and vote on resolutions, but they must in due course dispose of the shares under the terms of the will or the intestacy rules. Alternatively, PRs can dispose of shares directly to the deceased's beneficiaries, without ever themselves becoming members.

B. Directors

By the 1985 Act section 282, each public company must have at least two directors, and each private company at least one. Every company must also have a company secretary (see later), and a sole director cannot also be the secretary. Even a one-member company must therefore have at least two officers. The number of directors normally depends upon the articles. Table A provides for a minimum of two, and no maximum. Initial numbers can usually be changed by ordinary resolution.

'Executive' directors are ones who play an active part in managing the company. They may have specific tasks such as finance director or sales director. A *'managing director'* takes executive responsibility for the enterprise as a whole. For agency purposes, a director can be treated as managing director if he fulfils this function, whether or not he has formally been appointed; see *Freeman & Lockyer* v. *Buckhurst Park Properties Ltd*, later. The chairman of a board of directors will often have executive functions, although not always. He will not necessarily be the managing director.

In theory, a company need not have any executive directors at all. The executive work could all be delegated to employees, but this would be most unusual.

Non-executive directors are those who only exercise their basic functions, such as attending board meetings, advising with due diligence and in good faith, and taking a constructive part in making decisions. Their prestige and business experience may also be valuable to the company.

Appointment of directors

The first directors are named in Form G.10, which is filed when the company is formed. They may also be named in the articles. Later directors are usually appointed by ordinary or written resolution of members. The articles may allow the board to appoint temporary or additional directors, for example to fill a vacancy until the next a.g.m. Sometimes, the articles allow a director who knows that he will be absent to appoint his own 'alternate'. Table A allows this, so long as the rest of the board accepts the nominee. The nominating director can remove his alternate in due course.

Life directors can be appointed to hold office indefinitely if the articles so permit. Nevertheless, a life director can still be removed under section 303, later.

A *'shadow director'* is 'a person in accordance with whose directions or instructions the directors of a company are accustomed to act'; see section 741(2). He is treated as being a director without ever having formally been appointed. A 'director' includes any person occupying the position of director. If someone is in fact in charge, wholly or partly, he cannot escape responsibility. Most of the provisions of the Companies Acts and the Insolvency Act can apply equally to shadow directors: their names should be registered as directors; their contracts must be available to members; the disqualification rules apply; so do the limits and controls over directors' powers (see later). However, a person is not deemed a shadow director by reason only that the directors act on advice given by him in a professional capacity; nor is a parent *company* by reason only that its subsidiary acts on its instructions.

Retirement of directors

The articles may require retirement by *rotation*. If Table A applies, all must retire at the first a.g.m., but can apply for re-election. One third must retire in each future year, but again can be re-elected. Directors holding shares can vote for themselves. If no new directors are proposed, retiring ones are re-elected unless members resolve otherwise. Many small private companies simply remove the 'rotation' provisions from their articles.

The articles (including Table A) may allow a director to retire by *written notice*. No fixed time is set, but the director's service contract, if any, may require written notice.

By the 1985 Act section 293, an upper *age limit* of 70 applies to directors of public companies and of private companies which are subsidiaries of a public one. The director must retire at the end of the a.g.m. following his 70th birthday. However, the articles can exclude or vary this section. Moreover, a director may be appointed, or have his appointment confirmed, by special resolution of which special notice, giving his age, has been served. A would-be new director over 70 must give notice of his age when he applies. The section does not apply at all to most private companies.

Removal

By section 303, the members can remove a director at any time by *ordinary* resolution at a general meeting. Special notice of the resolution must be given to the company at least 28 days before the meeting, and this must immediately be sent to the director(s) challenged. The director can make written representations to the company which must, on demand, circulate them to members before the meeting. In any event, he can speak at the meeting, and use his own votes on the resolution.

Most formal and procedural attempts to avoid section 303 will fail. It cannot be excluded by the memorandum and articles, and a director appointed 'for life' can still be removed. The directors have no duty to put a removal resolution expressly on the agenda at a general meeting, but they *must* do so at an a.g.m. if this is demanded by holders of 5% of the shares, and at an e.g.m. by 10%.

The main limit on the section is that a director can vote for himself, and if he holds most of the shares, therefore, the removal resolution will fail. The articles can also provide weighted voting rights, at least in small 'family' companies; see *Bushell* v. *Faith* (page 255).

A practical difficulty might be the director's service contract, if any. It cannot override section 303, but it could provide for very expensive compensation to the director.

Disqualification of directors

We have seen the 70-year *age disqualification* in public companies, and that this can easily be circumvented.

There is no general *qualification share* requirement for directors. They need have no shares at all. However, if the *articles* require a minimum, which often occurs, then section 291 requires a director to have the shares within two months; otherwise he is disqualified.

The *articles* may make further disqualification provisions. For example, Table A reg. 81 deals with absence from board meetings, and can also disqualify a director who becomes bankrupt or a mental patient.

The Company Directors Disqualification Act 1986 empowers the *court* to disqualify a person from acting as a director or being concerned in the management of *any* company. Within limits, the court has discretion over how long a disqualification to impose, usually with a maximum of 15 years. The following are some types of misconduct that may be involved:

- a serious criminal offence connected with promoting, forming, managing or liquidating a company;
- the crime of fraudulent trading (see also page 287);
- wrongful trading (see also page 287);
- persistent default in filing returns, documents or accounts with the Registrar of Companies (only up to 5 years disqualification in this case);
- For an insolvent company, the Secretary of State for Trade and Industry may apply to the court for a disqualification order if it appears to him to be in the public interest as a result of information supplied by a liquidator, etc. If the court is satisfied that a person acted as a director while the company became insolvent, and that his conduct makes him unfit to be concerned with the management of a company, it must disqualify him for between 2 and 15 years. Unfitness can include dishonesty, recklessness or gross incompetence.
- Even if the company is not insolvent, the Secretary of State can apply in the public interest following a report by inspectors, or production of books, etc., or search of premises.

By the 1986 Act s.11, it is a criminal offence for an undischarged bankrupt to take part in the management of a company, or to *act* as a director or liquidator (although he can still nominally remain a director).

A criminal offence is committed by anyone disqualified by a *statutory* provision who continues to act as a director. If he takes part in management while banned or while personally bankrupt, he is personally liable for company debts while he does so. Indirect participation as a management consultant can be enough. A legitimate director who knowingly acts on the instructions of someone disqualified can also be personally liable.

However, as against outsiders, the acts of a disqualified director who has ostensible authority may still bind the company under the rules of agency (see page 286).

Registers of directors and their interests

The Registrar of Companies must receive particulars of the first directors on Form G.10, and of any change within 14 days.

The company itself must keep a public record at its registered office. For each director it must show name, address, nationality, business occupation, and date of birth in companies subject to the age limit. It must list other directorships during the last five years except in holding or subsidiary companies. For a corporate director, it must give name and registered or principal office.

The company must also keep a register of directors' (and shadow directors') interests in its shares and debentures: things like ownership of, charges over, options to buy. Interests of a director's spouse and infant children must be included unless he/she/they are also directors.

Copies of any director's service contract or terms of employment must be available to *members*, usually at the registered office.

Powers of directors

There are some things in a company which can only be done by a resolution of shareholders, such as change of name, objects, nominal capital or articles. Moreover, members can give directions to the board by special resolution. Subject to this, however, the directors have wide powers, which depend on the articles. Table A reg. 70 provides that 'the business of the company shall be managed by the directors, who may exercise all the powers of the company'.

Directors' powers must generally be exercised as a *board*, which operates at meetings. These can be called by the company secretary at the request of any director. The board can agree without a meeting if each member signs a written resolution. The articles usually fix a quorum for meetings, and power to elect a chairman. Decisions are taken by a majority, often with the chairman having a casting vote. Generally each member has one vote, regardless of his shareholding. Minutes must be kept, available to directors but not shareholders.

Individual directors as such have no actual authority to act on behalf of the company, unless the board has expressly or impliedly delegated this power; see the note on executive directors earlier.

Directors may also have service (employment) contracts with the company, and these can often radically affect their relations with the company.

Statutory controls over the powers of directors

Most of these statutory provisions arise where there is a potential conflict between the personal interests of the director, and the interests of the company.

By the 1985 Act section 317, it is the duty of a director who is in any way, whether directly or indirectly, interested in a contract or proposed contract with the company to *declare* the nature of his interest at a meeting of the directors. This also applies to contracts with persons 'connected with' the director, such as spouse, infant children, and associated companies in which the director and/or his family have a one-fifth share interest.

By section 319, directors' service contracts for over 5 years, which cannot be ended earlier by the company, must be approved by an ordinary resolution of members. If Table A applies, a director must not vote on his own contract. A copy must be kept at the registered office. A contract which is not approved may be ended by the company on reasonable notice.

By section 320, a company must have the approval of shareholders, by ordinary resolution, before any contract for valuable property with any of its directors (or a shadow or connected person). The 'requisite value' is currently £100 000, or over 10% of the company's assets, with a £2000 minimum. If the approval is not obtained, the contract is voidable by the company. The director must account for any profits, and other directors who authorized the transaction must indemnify the company against losses.

Sections 330–347 impose detailed and complex constraints on loans and credit to directors. For example, a loan over £5000 to its director in a public company is generally unlawful, but there are exceptions, particularly to help a director to meet expenditure which he incurs for the purposes of the company, or to enable him to perform his duties properly.

Duties of directors

The duties which a director owes to his company are similar to the duties owed by partners to each other (Unit 22), and by an agent to his principal (Unit 7).

1. Directors must show reasonable diligence, care and skill. More work will normally be required from executive directors, and more skill from those with professional expertise, but all of the duties do apply to non-executive directors. A director must show the general standards objectively to be expected from someone in his position, and subjectively to be expected from his own skill, knowledge and experience.

   In *Re City Equitable Fire Insurance Co.* (1925), a managing director was able to defraud his own company partly because non-executive directors were careless in not checking suspicious entries in the annual accounts. This was a breach of their duties.

   In *Dorchester Finance Co. Ltd* v. *Stebbing* (1977), there were three directors. Effectively, only one of them managed the company: he called no board meetings; the other two rarely visited the business; they even signed blank cheques for him. The two had broken their duties. They had not acted as conscientious directors, and they had not made available their professional accountancy skills.

2. A director must not make a secret profit from his position. If he does, he must account to the company for his wrongful gain.

> In *Boston Deep Sea Fishing and Ice Co.* v. *Ansell* (1888), a director received an undisclosed commission from the builders of a new boat for his company, and undisclosed bonuses from a company supplying ice. After he had been dismissed as a director, and had his service contract ended, he had to account for the money.

> In *Regal (Hastings) Ltd* v. *Gulliver* (1942), the company (in effect) bought and sold some cinemas at a profit. Some directors, who had invested their own money in the project, shared in the profit without disclosure to or consent from the other shareholders. They had to account for their profits, which were only made because of knowledge and opportunities arising from their position as directors. (They could have protected themselves by full disclosure to other shareholders, and by obtaining their consent, preferably in advance.)

3. A director must not allow an *undisclosed* conflict of interest.

> In *Cook* v. *Deeks* (1916), the directors of a construction company negotiated a contract in the usual way, as if they were making it for the company. Then, however, they made the contract in their own names, and took the profit. They ultimately had to account to the company for the profit.

4. Directors must exercise their powers for the *company's* benefit, not for their own or for any other ulterior motive. This has often arisen when new shares are issued: see *Piercy* v. *Mills Ltd* and *Howard Smith Ltd* v. *Ampol Petroleum Ltd* in Unit 24. The tests of a director's motives probably include the following: (i) is the transaction reasonably incidental to the business; (ii) is it done for the benefit and prosperity of the company; and (iii) is it done in good faith?

> In *Rolled Steel Products Ltd* v. *British Steel Corporation* (1986), Rolled Steel guaranteed repayment of a loan which *BSC* had made to someone else. Rolled Steel gained no benefit from either the loan or the guarantee. Its directors had therefore acted improperly, and the guarantee was invalid.

It should be emphasized that these duties are owed by directors to the *company*, which means basically that they must act for the benefit of the shareholders as a whole. As to who can *enforce* these duties, see later; a majority of share votes is needed in most cases.

By section 309, the interests of the company's *employees* must also be considered by directors. However, this does not give any right to the employees. It is a fiduciary duty owed to the company, and simply means that the interests of employees (as opposed to *only* those of shareholders) are an appropriate matter for the directors to consider when making decisions. The interests of employees of other companies in the same group are not included.

281

Exemption provisions for directors, etc.

By section 310, any provision, whether in the articles, or any contract with the company, or otherwise, for exempting a director from liability for negligence, default, breach of duty or of trust, is *void*; similarly a provision which seeks to indemnify him by, for example, paying his damages. The section applies equally to company secretaries and auditors. However, a provision to pay the costs of an officer who is held *not* liable or guilty can be valid.

'Corporate Governance'

The Cadbury report on 'Financial Aspects of Corporate Governance' has affected 'listed' public companies since June 1993. It sets out a 'code of best practice'. These rules only determine whether a public company meets the 'listing requirements' of the Stock Exchange, and therefore only affect a small minority of companies directly. However, the rules are intended to have a wider influential effect. The main theme is that there should be no undue and unchecked concentration of power at the top: 'There should be a clearly accepted division of responsibilities at the head of a company, which will ensure a balance of power and authority, such that no one individual has unfettered powers of decision. Where the chairman is also the chief executive, it is essential that there should be a strong and independent element on the board with a recognized senior member'. Emphasis is then placed on the need for *independent* non-executive directors of sufficient calibre, as a proper restraint on executive power and as a source of independent advice. Some attempt is made to control the service contracts and pay of executive directors, and also to help the effectiveness of the audit. Subsequent reports by Greenbury and Hampel largely developed these themes. In 1998, a Combined Code of Corporate Governance was introduced from the Stock Exchange, based on all of these reports.

C. The company secretary

Every company must have at least one company secretary. The first must be named in Form G.10 at the outset. Later appointments are normally by the directors under the articles; see Table A, reg. 99. A director can be company secretary, but not if he is a sole director; there must be at least two officers. A corporate body can be secretary, and there can be joint secretaries. The company must keep brief details with its public register of directors: basically name and residential or corporate address.

In a public company, the directors must take all reasonable steps to ensure that the secretary has the requisite knowledge and experience. For example, he must normally have recent appropriate experience as a company secretary, or be a professionally qualified accountant or lawyer. The secretaries of private companies need no qualifications or experience.

The company secretary is its chief administrative officer. He attends all meetings of shareholders and board meetings of directors. He takes and keeps minutes, and issues the various notices required by the Acts. He has responsibility for the many registers which a company must keep, and administers the annual and other returns to the Registrar. He is responsible to the board for ensuring that board procedures are followed, and that applicable rules are followed.

In many companies, the secretary will deal with outsiders in exercising his functions, and he may acquire usual authority to make contracts which are binding on the company; see *Panorama Developments Ltd* v. *Fidelis Furnishing Fabrics Ltd* (Unit 7).

Removal of the secretary will normally be by the board; see Table A, reg. 99 again. The Combined Code recommends that it be a matter for the *whole* board.

D. Protection of minority shareholders

Majority rule

Directors, officers and others owe their duties *to the company*, not to individual shareholders; see *Percival* v. *Wright* (1902). Therefore, it is the company which must sue them if they break their duties, and if the company decides not to sue then no further action can be taken. The company will not sue if the majority of votes in a general meeting resolves not to do so. Therefore, if the directors have the support of the majority of votes (or if they *have* the majority of votes), the wrong can be condoned.

> In *Foss* v. *Harbottle* (1843), two directors sold their own land to the company, allegedly for more than its true value. Some shareholders tried to sue the directors, but the court would not hear the action. It was up to the *company* to decide whether to sue.

The rule in *Foss* v. *Harbottle* does not, however, allow the majority to get away with everything, and minority shareholders do have important protection.

'Derivative' actions

In exceptional circumstances, a minority shareholder can seek a remedy *for the company* for a wrong done or proposed to be done to the company. The shareholder's right to sue 'derives' from a right of the company, which the majority is not allowing it to exercise.

1. Under the Companies Acts, even one shareholder can restrain a future *ultra vires* act by the directors, so long as this does not break a contract which the company has already made. The proposal to act, however, can proceed if it is ratified by a *special* resolution of members.
2. A minority shareholder can restrain the directors by injunction from a proposed act which would amount to a criminal offence by the company.
3. The court will not permit a 'fraud on the minority'. 'Fraud' is used loosely here as meaning grossly inequitable conduct, not necessarily criminal. A minority share-holder with no other remedy may sue for redress *to the company* in situations

where directors use their powers intentionally, dishonestly, or even only negligently in a manner which benefits themselves personally at the company's expense.

> In *Cook* v. *Deeks* (see page 281), the directors were made to account to the company notwithstanding that, as majority shareholders, they had passed a resolution declaring that the company had no interest in the contract.

> In *Daniels* v. *Daniels* (1978), it was alleged that the directors and majority shareholders had sold land belonging to the company to one member of the board for less than its value. It was sold by the company in 1970 for £4250, and resold by the director in 1974 for £120 000. It was held that, even though no dishonesty was alleged, a minority shareholder could sue for an order that the directors pay damages and account to the company for breach of their duties to it.

4. A minority shareholder may also be allowed to sue if the majority shareholders who control a company exercise their powers over *internal* management inequitably, for example by changing the company's constitution or membership for improper reasons.

> In *Clemens* v. *Clemens Bros Ltd* (1976), the defendant used her majority holding to pass resolutions issuing new shares, with the effect and apparent motive of increasing her own control and reducing the claimant's holding to below 25%. The majority shareholder *as such* owed a duty in a small company to use her power primarily for the benefit of the company, not herself. The court therefore set aside the resolution.

> In *Brown* v. *British Abrasive Wheel Co.* (1919), a proposal to alter the articles was held invalid in an action by a minority shareholder. The articles should be altered for the benefit of the company, not because the majority wanted to buy out the minority compulsorily.

5. If the directors try to do something which requires a special or extraordinary resolution without first obtaining such a resolution, a *simple* majority cannot ratify. To allow this would destroy the whole protection given to minorities by special and extraordinary resolutions, namely that a 26% minority can defeat them.

Wrongs to members personally

Sometimes the directors may commit a wrong to the member personally rather than to the company. By the 1985 Act, section 14, the memorandum and articles are a contract between the members. If the directors refuse a member his rights under the articles, the member has a right of action which is not affected by the *Foss* v. *Harbottle* rule.

> In *Pender* v. *Lushington* (1877), the chairman wrongly refused to accept a shareholder's votes, which would have defeated an amendment to a resolution. Refusal infringed the member's voting rights under the articles, and the injunction which he sought against the directors was granted.

Unfairly prejudicial conduct: section 459

The main protection to minority shareholders today is the 1985 Act, section 459. Any shareholder may petition the court for relief on the ground that the company's affairs are being conducted in a manner which is unfairly prejudicial to the interests of its members generally, or to some part of its members, including himself. Examples might be the issue of shares to directors on unduly favourable terms; or directors' salaries so exorbitant that they deprive shareholders of a dividend; or unfair removal from the board of directors.

> In *Re H. R. Harmer Ltd* (1958), the main shareholder and director was father of the other two directors, and effectively ignored them. He overruled board decisions. His domineering attitude angered employees. He was ordered to obey board decisions in future, and not to intervene in the company otherwise.

> In *Re a Company* (1986), take-over bids were made for the company. The directors recommended a bid by a company in which they had an interest. They ignored a more lucrative bid. This was held to be unfairly prejudicial to the minority shareholders.

The court may 'make such order as it thinks fit for giving relief'. The order may regulate conduct of the company's affairs in future; or restrain the company from doing the offending acts; or require it to do things omitted; or authorize civil proceedings in the name of the company; or require the company or other members to buy the petitioner's shares at a fair price or valuation.

Petition for winding up the company

By the Insolvency Act 1986, section 122(1)(g), any member can petition the court for an order that 'it is just and equitable that the company should be wound up'; see *Ebrahimi* v. *Westbourne Galleries Ltd* in Unit 22.

> In *Re Yenidje Tobacco Co. Ltd* (1916), the court ordered winding up when a company's directors, who were the sole shareholders, quarrelled and could no longer work together, even though the company was profitable.

In these cases the company was a small one, in its operation (if not in law) like a partnership. The court might be less likely to wind up a large and complex organisation. Moreover, petitions under section 459 give much greater powers to keep a company alive today.

Other statutory protection

Many other statutory rights are given to minorities of various sizes. For example, 5% can demand the inclusion of a resolution at the a.g.m.; 10% can demand an e.g.m.; 15% of the votes of a particular class can petition against variation of the rights of the class, and the change must be approved by 75% of the class.

E. The company and outsiders

Liability of the company

As we have seen, this depends largely upon agency (see Unit 7). A shareholder as such, even a majority shareholder, has no implied authority to make contracts for the company. Nor has an individual director as such (see below). Basically it is the board of directors, acting as a board, which has authority, and this was discussed at the end of Unit 22. By section 35A, 'In favour of a person dealing with the company in good faith, the power of the board of directors to bind the company or authorize others to do so, shall be deemed to be free of any limitation under the company's constitution'. An outsider is presumed to act in good faith, and he is not bound to enquire as to the authority of the directors. The words 'or authorize others to do so' apply to the situation where, as is usual, the board delegates some of its powers, and authorizes others to act for the company.

The 'indoor management' rule for companies can apply more widely than section 35A. An outsider who has no means of checking is entitled to assume that all of the internal procedures and steps to be taken within a company have been properly carried out. It would not matter, for instance, if the board meeting which acted was inquorate.

> In *Royal British Bank Ltd* v. *Turquand* (1856), the company borrowed from a bank. The two directors who negotiated the loan only had the right to do so if first authorized by an ordinary resolution of members. No such resolution had been passed. Nevertheless the company was bound because the bank, which had no means of checking, was entitled to assume that the ordinary resolution had been passed.

By section 285, the acts of a director or manager shall be valid notwithstanding any defect which may later be discovered in his appointment or qualification. This is limited, and does not cover either persons who act as executive directors without ever having been appointed at all, or who, having been duly appointed, exceed their actual authority.

An *executive* director or officer, such as a managing director, acquires certain implied powers from his position. An outsider can safely assume, in the absence of suspicious circumstances, that the executive acting within his 'usual' functions can bind the company; see *Panorama Developments Ltd* v. *Fidelis Furnishing Fabrics* (1971), which involved a company secretary (see Unit 7).

If a company has previously honoured contracts made by someone on its behalf, or has otherwise 'held him out' as having authority, it may later be estopped from denying this. The company may be bound by future unauthorized contracts which he makes.

> In *Freeman and Lockyer* v. *Buckhurst Park Properties Ltd* (1964), the board of *B Ltd* had allowed one of its number, *K*, to act as if he were managing director, although he had never been appointed to that position. The board had previously honoured contracts made by *K*, but now claimed not to be bound by the contract which he made with the claimants. It was held that (a) *B Ltd* was estopped from denying that *K* had the usual powers of a managing director, and (b) it was within those powers to make this contract. *B Ltd* was bound.

Personal liability of directors

As a general rule, outsiders cannot hold the directors personally liable. However, there are exceptions, both while the company is still operating and, to a greater extent, when it is wound up. For example:

1. Under the Insolvency Act 1986, section 216, a person who was a director in the last 12 months' life of an insolvent company must not without court permission trade for the next five years in a name too similar to that of the insolvent company. If he does so, he can be personally liable for the new ('phoenix') company's debts.
2. Under the Company Directors Disqualification Act 1986, if someone who has been disqualified by the court from acting as a director disobeys the court order, he can be personally liable for debts which the company incurs while he is wrongly involved in its management.
3. An undischarged bankrupt must not act as a director without leave of the court which adjudged him bankrupt. If he does so, he can be personally liable.
4. The Companies Act 1985 may make directors personally liable. By section 117, the directors of a public company can be liable to outsiders if the company trades without a certificate that the required shares have been allotted. By section 349, if an officer or someone on the company's behalf signs a document or cheque on which its name is not correctly stated, he is personally liable if the company defaults.
5. Exceptionally, a director may be personally liable for torts committed by the company, particularly if he had extensive control over the company's conduct in connection with the wrongful activity.

    In *Evans & Sons Ltd* v. *Spritebrand* (1985), it was held that a director personally, as well as the company, could be liable for the company's breach of copyright.

6. If a director makes a contract without power to do so, so that the company is not liable, the outsider can sue the director personally for breach of warranty of authority (Unit 7). This is rare today, because by section 35A the company almost always will be liable.
7. *Fraudulent trading* occurs if any business of a company is carried on with intent to defraud creditors of the company, or creditors of any other person, or for any other fraudulent purpose. Everyone who was knowingly a party to carrying on the business in this way is guilty of a criminal offence under the Companies Act. The court may also disqualify him from acting as a director for up to 15 years.

    By the Insolvency Act 1986 s.213, if the company is being *wound up* (solvent or not), the liquidator can apply to the court that any director, or anyone else, knowingly a party to carrying on the business in this way, is liable to make such contributions to the company's assets as the court thinks proper. The difficulty can lie in proving fraud (dishonesty), as opposed to mere negligence or folly.
8. If a company is *insolvent* when wound up, the Insolvency Act, section 214, provides the further concept of *wrongful trading* under which directors can be liable even if there is no fraud. When a company has financial difficulties, and a

287

director knows or ought to conclude that it has no reasonable prospect of recovery, he should take immediate steps to minimize the loss to creditors, for example by applying for immediate winding up. A director who wrongfully carries on trading can be ordered to contribute personally to the company's assets on an eventual insolvent liquidation. 'Shadow directors' such as dominant managers can also be liable.

> In *Re Produce Marketing Consortium Ltd* (1989), two directors foolishly continued to operate after being warned by the auditors that the company was insolvent. When the company was wound up shortly afterwards, they were ordered to pay £75 000 with interest towards its debts.

The directors of very small companies may face practical difficulties if their company seeks credit, in that a lender may be unwilling to give credit unless the directors personally guarantee repayment. If the lender seeks a mortgage of a director's own home as security, this can cause further problems; see cases like *Barclays Bank* v. *O'Brien* in Unit 13.

Personal liability of shareholders

As we have seen, shareholders as such generally have no liability for the company's debts. This 'limited liability' rule is fundamental to company law but, even here, there are a few situations where the 'veil of incorporation' can be lifted (see Unit 22).

Criminal offence by companies

Many statutes impose potential criminal liability on companies. Almost always, the Act which creates the criminal offence also contains some such provision as, 'where an offence under this Act which has been committed by a body corporate is proved to have been committed with the consent and connivance of, or to be attributable to any neglect on the part of, any director, manager, secretary or similar officer of the body corporate, or any person who was purporting to act in any such capacity, he as well as the body corporate shall be guilty of that offence ...'. Directors can be imprisoned for serious offences.

F. Winding up

Voluntary winding up

Under the Insolvency Act 1986, the shareholders can resolve at any time to wind up the company, even if it is solvent. The job of winding up is carried out by a *liquidator* (unlike a partnership, which is dissolved by the members themselves). The liquidator's tasks are to settle lists of contributories (shareholders); to collect the company's assets; pay off its creditors; and to pay the surplus, if any, to the contributories.

A members' voluntary winding up takes place if the directors have made a statutory declaration that they have made a full enquiry into the company's affairs, and believe that it will be able to pay its debts in full within not more than 12 months after the start of the winding up. Within at most five weeks after this, the members will pass a special resolution that the company be wound up, and this is the formal start. The directors' statutory declaration must be filed with the Registrar of Companies within 15 days after this. The liquidator is appointed by the members, and is responsible to them.

A creditors' voluntary winding up occurs where the directors are unable to make the statutory declaration of solvency when wishing to wind up. Members will pass an extraordinary resolution that the company cannot continue in business because of its liabilities, usually at an e.g.m. A meeting of creditors must be called, and they will normally appoint a liquidator who will be responsible to them. If, in a members' voluntary winding up, the liquidator forms the opinion that the company will *not* be able to pay its debts in full in accordance with the solvency declaration, *he* must summon a meeting of creditors, and the nature of the winding up changes accordingly.

Compulsory winding up

A petition may be presented to the court by the company itself, the DTI or, most commonly, by a creditor, asking that the company be wound up by the court. There are various grounds on which such a petition may be granted, the most common being that the company cannot pay its debts. The 'just and equitable' ground mentioned earlier is another example, though much less common. If the petition is granted, a liquidator is appointed by the court, normally on application by the creditors, although the Official Receiver acts until this is done.

Distribution of assets

Having realised the assets, the liquidator pays debts in the following order:

1. Costs of the winding up.
2. Preferential debts equally: some examples are PAYE and NIC deductions which were or should have been made in the 12 months before winding up started; VAT for the previous six months; arrears of wages and salaries to (ex)employees for the previous four months, up to a statutory maximum.
3. Debts secured by a floating charge.
4. Unsecured creditors.
5. Some deferred debts, such as sums due to shareholders for dividends declared but not yet paid.

All liabilities in a higher category must be paid in full before any payment can be made to a lower category.

None of the above affect creditors with a properly registered fixed charge. They can simply pay themselves out of their security. If the security proves inadequate, they can prove as unsecured creditors for the rest.

If anything is left after all of this, it is divided amongst shareholders equally as a repayment of capital.

Specimen questions

1. Explain the following terms:
   (a) annual general meeting and extraordinary general meeting;
   (b) ordinary business and special business;
   (c) ordinary, special and extraordinary resolutions;
   (d) written resolutions and elective resolutions.
2. In a medium-sized public company, there are six directors, three executive and three non-executive. X, one of the executive directors, is chairman of the board and a dominant personality. He acts as managing director although he has never been appointed as such. Y and Z, the other executives, seem to spend much of their time quarrelling with each other. The non-executives seem to do very little, and one often misses board meetings. The company is not very profitable, but the directors have voted themselves large increases in fees and salaries.

    Some shareholders are unhappy with the position and seek your advice. They do not wish to sell their shares in spite of poor dividends. A clause in the articles appoints X as a director for life, and exempts him from any wrongdoing by the board.
3. Is it true that shareholders can exercise their votes at meetings in whatever way they like?
4. In what circumstances can directors of a company that is still operating be personally liable for debts of the company?
5. (a) Distinguish briefly between a members' voluntary winding up, a creditors' voluntary winding up, and a compulsory winding up.
   (b) In what order do the company's debts rank when it is wound up?

Unit 26. The Employment Relationship

A. The nature of employment

The employment relationship arises when one person (the employee, worker or servant) supplies skill and labour to another (the employer) in return for payment. The arrangement must be close and continuing, to distinguish it from situations where an independent contractor contracts only for a particular job, whereupon he leaves and sells his services elsewhere. Employment can be for a fixed or indefinite period, long or short, or merely until a particular piece of work is completed; but in all cases the parties are more closely bound than, say, a householder and the plumber engaged as an independent contractor to repair the sink.

A person can be both employed by, and have other legal relations with, his employer. For example, since a company has separate legal personality, it can employ some of its own directors, so that the latter are both directors and employees.

> In *Boulting* v. *ACTAT* (1963), the Boulting brothers, who were managing directors of a film company, also had employment contracts. As 'employees' they were, therefore, held eligible for trade union membership.

On the other hand, where an executive director is also a dominant shareholder, the courts have sometimes more recently been reluctant to treat him as an employee for employment law purposes.

> In *Buchan* v. *Secretary of State for Employment* (1997), *B* was an executive director and dominant shareholder in a company which became insolvent. He claimed to have had a contract of employment with the company and, in this capacity, he claimed arrears of wages, a redundancy payment, and wages in lieu of notice from the National Insurance

Fund. The Employment Appeal Tribunal rejected this claim. On the facts, *B* effectively controlled his own employment and dismissal, and was not genuinely an employee for *this* purpose.

In spite of the corporate form, the courts today will often recognize reality when the arrangement is effectively one human being running his own business. Certainly this could be so if the 'employer' were a single-shareholder company.

Partnerships have no separate legal personality, and someone who shares in profits so as to be a partner is not an employee, even if he also has a salary. On the other hand, someone who is *called* a 'salaried partner' but receives no share in profits *may* only be an employee, and not a partner at all; see *Nationwide Building Society* v. *Lewis* (Unit 22).

Employees are often also agents for the employer if, as commonly occurs, they deal with third parties on behalf of the employer. Thus a salesman may be both employee and agent.

Employment is a contract, and the express and implied terms of this contract are still the basis of the relationship between employer and employee. On the other hand, for social, economic and political reasons, there has been increasing governmental intervention in employment since the early nineteenth century. As will be seen, many of the rights and duties of the parties are imposed by legislation today, and to regard employment *solely* as a contract would be very misleading. There is also a strong European influence today, following numerous EC directives and decisions of the European Court of Justice, particularly in the fields of discrimination, equal pay, and occupational safety.

B. Employees and independent contractors

Tests to distinguish employees from contractors

For various purposes, mentioned later, the courts have had to distinguish between employees and independent contractors, and the following tests used by the judges help to explain the nature of employment.

1. *The control test.* This relatively simple test was evolved in the nineteenth century: a contract of employment exists when the employer has control over the manner in which the employee does his work. The employee can be told not only *what* to do, but also *how* to do it. In contrast, the independent contractor is paid for the completed job, and *how* he does it is his concern.

   This test, by itself, is not satisfactory today. The size of many organizations and the complex skills involved make detailed control impossible. A partial solution is to substitute 'right of control', but even this is unsatisfactory. It is unrealistic, for example, to suggest that a health authority should control how its doctors treat their patients.

Gradually the single 'control' test evolved into a *series* of tests indicating control. The courts would look at matters such as (a) the power to select the employee; (b) the right to control the method of doing the work; and (c) rights of suspension and dismissal. The notion of a series of matters developed into the two tests mainly used today, the 'integration' test, and the 'multiple' or 'economic reality' test.

2. *The organization or 'integration' test.* In *Stevenson, Jordan and Harrison Ltd* v. *Macdonald and Evans* (1952), Denning, L.J. said:

> 'It is often easy to recognize a contract of service when you see it, but difficult to say wherein the distinction lies.' After giving a number of examples, he continued, 'Under a contract of service, a man is employed as part of a business, and his work is done as an integral part of the business: whereas under a contract for services, his work, although done for the business, is not integrated into it but is only accessory to it.'

This statement summarizes the 'organization' or 'integration' test. If a man is an integral part of an organization, he is an employee; if he performs work for the organization but remains outside it, he is an independent contractor. The test is particularly helpful in determining the position of professional people where there is obviously no right of control over the method of performance.

> In *Cassidy* v. *Ministry of Health* (1951), a patient suffered injury to his hand as a result of the negligence of full-time medical staff at a hospital. The hospital authority was held vicariously liable for the acts of these members of staff. (There would have been no vicarious liability had the medical staff been held to be independent contractors.)

> The test was also applied in *Whittaker* v. *Ministry of Pensions and National Insurance* (1967), where a social security benefit claim for a broken wrist depended on the existence of a contract of employment. The claimant worked in a circus as a trapeze artiste but was also required to spend time as an usherette. It was held that her work was an integral part of the circus and a contract of employment existed.

3. *The 'multiple' or 'economic reality' test.* Although both the right of control and the extent of integration are relevant, neither provides the complete answer. In recent years the courts have taken a wider view and tried to consider *all* factors. These have included powers to appoint, suspend and dismiss; the method of payment, and whether deductions are made for PAYE income tax and national insurance; whether the worker has received sick pay; the nature of the work and the degree of independence as to hours of work; whether the worker provides tools and equipment, and/or works at his own premises; and the general 'economic reality' of the relationship. What they call themselves ('employee' or 'contractor') may be evidence, particularly if there is a written contract, but even this is not conclusive.

> In *Ready Mixed Concrete Ltd.* v. *Ministry of Pensions and National Insurance* (1968), the company engaged owner-drivers to deliver concrete and arranged for them to buy their lorries from the company on hire-purchase. The lorries were in the company's

colours and drivers had to wear the company's uniforms. Payment was on a piecework basis subject to a guaranteed minimum. The drivers were responsible for maintaining the lorries and buying the fuel. It was held that, in spite of some control, the lack of integration into the business and the other circumstances meant that, for social security purposes, the drivers were independent contractors, not employees.

In *Hitchcock* v. *Post Office* (1980), a sub-postmaster who used his shop as a sub-post office was held to be self-employed, even though he had to carry out the Post Office's instructions and advise the head postmaster if he was absent for three days or more. However, he could delegate his duties to assistants, and he bore the risk of profit or loss.

In *Ferguson* v. *John Dawson & Partners Ltd* (1976), labour-only subcontractors in the building industry (see page 295) were held to be employees for safety purposes, irrespective of what they were called. For these purposes the court was more concerned with reality than with the labels.

In *Catamaran Cruisers Ltd* v. *Williams* (1994), *W* worked for Catamaran. To avoid tax, *W* formed a company, Unicorn Ltd, in which he held the shares. Catamaran then sub-contracted *W*'s job to Unicorn Ltd, which was paid *W*'s *gross* salary. *W* still did the work. When Catamaran later ended its contract with Unicorn, *W* claimed that he personally had been unfairly dismissed. The Employment Appeal Tribunal ('EAT') held that *W* could make this claim. Unicorn Ltd was a subterfuge. *W* was under the same conditions of service and disciplinary procedure as (other) Catamaran employees, and had been offered sick pay and holiday pay after Unicorn was formed. (The actual dismissal, however, was not unfair.)

In *Hall (Inspector of Taxes)* v. *Lorimer* (1994), a TV vision worker left his full-time job and began to work freelance for various TV companies on short-term contracts of one or two days. He used the companies' premises and equipment, but was paid fees and registered for VAT. The Court of Appeal upheld his claim to be self-employed for tax purposes.

For part-time or casual workers, 'mutuality of obligations', particularly during any off periods, has sometimes been emphasized.

In *Nethermere (St Neots) Ltd* v. *Gardiner* (1984), the claimants were 'outworkers' who made clothes in their own time at home, and were paid weekly per piece. However, they had regularly expected and received some work, albeit not always of the same amount, for some time. There were assumed to be mutual obligations, and they were held to be employees.

In *Carmichael* v. *National Power plc* (1999), the claimants took 'employment' on a 'casual as required basis' as tour guides at a power station. There was no indication of when and how often work would be available. The sickness, holiday and pension provisions for ordinary staff did not apply. They worked on invitation when they were available and when they chose to work, and no sanctions were imposed if either of them was not available. The House of Lords held that they were not employees, at least during the times when they were not actually working, because there were no clear mutual obligations during these times.

The importance of the distinction

It is important to determine whether or not a contract of employment exists for the following reasons:

1. An employer is normally liable vicariously for torts committed by his employees in the course of employment, but not for torts by independent contractors (Unit 8). In limited circumstances an employee's acts may even involve the employer in criminal liability, as for example under the Health and Safety at Work etc. Act 1974.
2. An employee has statutory protection not given to independent contractors, for example minimum periods of notice, compensation for redundancy, and remedies for unfair dismissal, under the Employment Rights Act 1996.
3. Social security provisions for statutory sick and maternity pay, jobseeker's allowance, disablement benefit, etc., differ for employees and independent contractors.
4. An employer must deduct income tax from wages and salaries of employees under the Income and Corporation Taxes Act 1988, Schedule E (PAYE). An independent contractor pays his own income tax under Schedule D and may claim more generous allowances.
5. If the employer's business fails and he is insolvent, an employee has certain preferential rights over other creditors in respect of unpaid wages and redundancy payments.
6. The terms of a contract of employment include implied rights and duties of both employers and employees. These do not apply to the same extent to independent contractors (Unit 27).

Labour-only sub-contracting

For many years now, some businesses which formerly *employed* workmen have engaged 'labour-only subcontractors' instead. The employer provides the materials, and hires the workmen, either individually or as members of a gang, as independent contractors for the job in hand. This is particularly common in the building industry, where gangs of craftsmen are hired as contractors for the bricklaying or joinery work on a particular site. In this context, sub-contracting was popularly called 'the lump'.

The practice has several advantages to the employer. He does not need to keep a large workforce to meet fluctuating demand; he can avoid administrative complications such as deducting income tax and national insurance contributions from wages or paying statutory sick pay; and the workmen cannot claim employment protection rights such as redundancy payments. The employer's duties regarding safety are now similar for both employees and subcontractors, but he may still escape vicarious liability for the torts of subcontractors. The subcontractors themselves sometimes unlawfully evaded income tax and national insurance contributions altogether, but various Finance Acts since 1971 have controlled this. At present, legislation requires construction 'employers' to deduct tax at source from 'lump' subcontractors.

295

C. Formation

The general principles of contract apply to the formation of employment contracts. There must be agreement on the essential terms. Consideration is principally the undertaking to work in return for the undertaking to pay the agreed wage or salary. Capacity to contract is important here chiefly in relation to minors and, as discussed in Unit 13, a minor can be bound. On the other hand, children must attend school full-time until the statutory leaving age, and part-time employment of school children can be strictly controlled by regulations under the Employment of Children Act 1973. Children are encouraged to gain work experience during their final year of compulsory schooling, under the Education (Work Experience) Act 1973.

Mistake, misrepresentation, duress or undue influence can vitiate a contract of employment. On the other hand, a worker seeking a job need not disclose past misdeeds unless asked, even criminal convictions, because the relationship is not one *uberrimae fidei*. Sometimes he need not disclose the truth even if asked, but this is exceptional.

> In *Property Guards Ltd* v. *Taylor* (1982), two applicants for jobs as security guards were asked if they had any previous convictions. They had both been convicted of offences involving dishonesty many years ago, but these convictions were 'spent' under the Rehabilitation of Offenders Act 1974. They, therefore, answered, 'No'. When the employer discovered the truth and dismissed them, the dismissal was held unfair.

Failure to disclose may be relevant if this is a contributory cause of an accident.

> In *Cork* v. *Kirby MacLean Ltd* (1952), the plaintiff suffered injury partly because of breach of statutory duty by his employer and partly because of a fall due to an epileptic fit. The damages were reduced by half for his contributory negligence in not informing the employer that he suffered from epilepsy.

If an employer subsequently discovers a continuing problem such as an illness, this might affect the employee's position, not because of failure to disclose it initially, but because the problem is still there.

> In *O'Brien* v. *Prudential Assurance Co. Ltd* (1979), a job applicant did not disclose his history of mental illness. He was dismissed when the employer later discovered the facts. This was held to be fair, not because of the non-disclosure but because further medical reports showed that the employee could still be ill in a way which prejudiced his job.

Finally, certain terms in contracts of employment may be illegal or void as contrary to public policy. Terms in unreasonable restraint of trade have already been considered in Unit 17. Terms by which an employee purports to surrender statutory rights such as redundancy payment or compensation for unfair dismissal are void by statute except in certain fixed-term contracts. Terms that contravene race relations or sex discrimination legislation are void and, in some instances, illegal; likewise, terms that contravene the Employment Rights Act, Part II (Unit 27).

Written notification of terms

This is now governed by the Employment Rights Act 1996. Not later than two months after the beginning of the employment the employer must give each employee a written statement, in one document, which must:

(a) identify the parties;
(b) specify the date when the employment began; and
(c) give the date on which the employee's period of 'continuous employment' began (taking into account any employment with a previous employer, which counts towards that period).

The document must also give particulars of:

(a) the scale or rate of remuneration, or the method of calculating it;
(b) the intervals at which remuneration is paid;
(c) any terms and conditions relating to hours of work;
(d) any terms and conditions relating to holidays and holiday pay;
(e) the title of the job, or a brief description of the work;
(f) the place of work or, if the employee is required or permitted to work at various places, an indication of that fact and of the address of the employer.

Certain other information may be given 'in instalments', and not necessarily all in one document:

1. any terms or conditions relating to incapacity for work and sick pay, and (normally) pension rights;
2. the length of notice that the employer must give, and is entitled to receive, to end the employment;
3. if the employment is not intended to be permanent, how long it is expected to last, or when any fixed term will end;
4. if the employee is required to work outside the UK for more than one month, details of time, currency, and return provisions;
5. a note of any disciplinary and grievance provisions; but if there are less than 20 employees when the employment began, the note need only specify how and to whom the employee can apply for redress.

Notice of any change by the employer in any of the above particulars must be given in writing to the employee at least one month before the proposed change.

If the employer neglects to give any of the above particulars, the matter may be referred to an employment tribunal, which can try to discover and record what seems to have been intended. However a tribunal will not try to invent its own terms.

It is important to note that the statutory statement and particulars above do not form the contract itself. (In any event, they need not be given until well after the employment has actually begun.) At the most, they will be strong evidence of the terms agreed.

Itemized pay statements

By the Employment Rights Act 1996, if the employer has at least 20 employees, all of them have an absolute right to an itemized pay statement, in writing, on or before each payment of wages or salary. The statement must show:

1. the gross amount of wages or salary;
2. the amounts and purposes of all deductions from the gross amount;
3. the net amount of wages or salary payable; and
4. where different parts of the net amount are paid in different ways, the amount and method of each part-payment.

D. Sources of terms

As suggested earlier, the rights and duties of parties come from a number of sources. Some terms are expressly agreed, in writing or orally; other terms may be implied; other rights and duties are imposed by statute. It should be remembered that a contract of employment need not be, and rarely is, a single written document. We have seen that written *notice* must be given of certain terms, but where the terms come from is a different matter.

Express terms

Some terms will be expressly negotiated between the parties, either orally or, for example, in correspondence, when the employee is offered and accepts the job. Details of the terms agreed may be set out in a number of places: the employer's staff handbook, for example; in many instances, the terms of a collective agreement form an important part of the contract (see page 299). Even obligations displayed on notices at the place of work may be incorporated.

> In *Dal* v. *A.S. Orr* (1980), the Employment Appeal Tribunal (EAT) held that a statement in the employees' handbook, saying 'the Company reserves the right to alter the shift system together with the hours of work to meet production requirements', was contractual, and that the employees were bound.

Sometimes the parties may set out the main terms in one document which is signed by the parties when the job offer is accepted and the contract made, but this mainly occurs in senior managerial appointments. Such contracts are often described as 'service agreements'. The statutory statement earlier *may* become a written contract if the parties *call* it the contract and expressly *sign it as such*.

Implied terms

In a contract of employment, there are implied common law duties on both employer and employee, which apply in the absence of any express term to the contrary. These will be dealt with in Units 27 and 28. Terms may also be implied from long and well-known usage in the trade or industry concerned, provided that they are not inconsistent with any express written terms.

In *Stubbs* v. *Trower, Still and Keeling* (1987) the court implied that an articled clerk's contract would terminate if he did not pass The Law Society's qualifying examinations.

Statutory terms

Important examples of these appear in the Employment Rights Act 1996, and are examined in Unit 27.

Collective agreements

Collective agreements are made between an individual employer or an employers' association on the one hand, and a trade union on the other. An individual employee will not normally be party to such an agreement and, because of the rules of privity of contract, the terms are not directly binding upon him. Nevertheless, collective agreements do govern the terms of employment of many workers today. The reason is that the terms of the collective agreement have become incorporated as terms of the *individual* contract.

1. There may be express incorporation, in which event no problem arises. Thus it may be expressly agreed that the worker shall be paid at the prevailing union rates. The worker will receive notice of this in the statement given him under the Employment Rights Act 1996.
2. Where there is no express reference to the collective terms, there may be implied incorporation if, for example, the parties have known of and constantly observed the terms of collective bargains over a reasonably long time.

In *National Coal Board* v. *Galley* (1958), the contracts of employment of colliery deputies contained a clause expressly incorporating national and county agreements currently in force. These agreements provided for work on such days in each week as the employer might reasonably require. Furthermore, the deputies had worked in accordance with these agreements for some time past. Following a dispute, some deputies refused to work on Saturdays, and the National Coal Board successfully sued them for breach of contract. It was held that the collective agreements formed part of the individual contracts of employment.

In *Gray, Dunn and Co. Ltd* v. *Edwards* (1980), the employer negotiated a detailed agreement with a recognized union over a disciplinary code of practice. The Court of Appeal held that the employer was entitled to assume that all members of the union had agreed to be bound by the code as part of their employment contracts.

299

Transfer of undertakings

When a business or undertaking changes hands, the terms of employment of those working there *may* be affected. This is a complex subject, which is much influenced by EC law. There are many possibilities.

By far the simplest in the UK is where the undertaking is owned by a limited company, and transfer comprises simply the transfer of a strategic number of shares in the company. In this event, the employer is the same separate legal personality throughout, and the contracts of employment are not affected. A significant number of transfers, takeovers, etc. of undertakings take this form.

However, where the seller and the buyer of a business are different persons (including different companies), then at the very least, the terms of the employment now come from a different source. Protection is given to employees by several pieces of legislation, notably the Employment Rights Act 1996 s.218, and the Transfer of Undertakings (Protection of Employment) Regulations 1981 (TUPE), which are based on an EC directive. The continuity of employment, which is important in qualifying for many aspects of employment protection, is normally preserved; see page 320. The terms of the employment are also preserved: by TUPE the new owner of the business takes over rights and obligations as employer, and the contracts of employment of the employees. He/she/it is also obliged to comply with any collective agreement that had been negotiated with the transferor. Dismissal connected with the transfer is automatically unfair unless the employer can show an economic, technical or organizational reason for it (in which case the ex-employee may be able to claim compensation for redundancy). An employee can always object to being transferred, and choose to leave the business, but in this case he will lose any right to payment for unfair dismissal or redundancy.

Variation of terms

From time to time, either party may wish to vary the terms of employment. If both accept the changed conditions, there is no difficulty. This happens frequently when, for example, new wages or salaries are agreed.

Difficulties can arise, however, when one party does not accept the proposed change. In the strict law of contract, terms cannot be changed unilaterally, and a party who tries to impose new terms will be in breach. If an employ*ee* decides unilaterally that his existing duties should be altered, and refuses to carry out his contract then (if the breach is sufficiently serious) the employer can rescind the contract and dismiss the employee. If an employ*er* tries to impose *abnormal* changes without agreement then the employee can leave and claim damages; he is said to have suffered 'constructive dismissal'.

Further problems can arise if an employee does not leave, but carries on under the new terms and conditions. This might be treated as an implied acceptance of the new terms. However, providing that the employee indicates immediately that he does not accept the change and is working under protest, then he will still have a right at common law to treat the contract as ended, and/or claim damages if there is a quantifiable loss.

> In *Rigby* v. *Ferodo Ltd* (1988), an employer in financial difficulty unilaterally reduced his employees' wages by 5 per cent. The plaintiff employee did not agree to this, but carried on working under protest. He was held entitled to damages, based on the 5 per cent withheld, for as long as he continued to work there. (The employee could have rescinded his contract and treated himself as dismissed, but he had validly chosen not to do so. The employer could now dismiss him, but only after giving the proper notice, and subject to the unfair dismissal provisions discussed in Unit 28.)

> In *Marriott* v. *Oxford and District Co-operative Society Ltd* (1970), the plaintiff was told that, because of a reduction in the size of his department, he would lose his status as a foreman and his wages would be reduced. After protest, he continued to work for three or four weeks under the new conditions while seeking another job. It was held that working on in these circumstances did not 'affirm' the change or bar his right to treat the contract as repudiated. He could still treat himself as dismissed, and was therefore entitled to a redundancy payment.

Although the above is all based on the law of contract, the courts, and more particularly the employment tribunals, do recognize that employment is not a static relationship, and that employers and employees must frequently accept change. Many changes in working practice by employers will not be regarded as so abnormal as to amount to constructive dismissal.

If a variation of terms *does* amount to a dismissal, there may then be a statutory claim that the dismissal was *unfair*. This is a very different issue, which is discussed in Unit 28.

Specimen questions

1. *T* is engaged as an instructor by a driving school. The school finds the pupils, supplies and maintains the instruction car, and pays for the petrol. *T* has undertaken not to work for any other driving school while still engaged here. However, he is not paid a wage, only commission on the fees which he brings in. How many pupils he takes and how many hours he works are up to him. There are no directions as to how, where or when he teaches.

   Discuss whether he is an employee or an independent contractor. What other questions might you ask him if he sought your advice on the matter?

2. (a) What tests are applicable to determine whether or not a contract of service exists?

   (b) Better Builders Ltd are building a number of houses and sub-contract the work of roofing to Tidy Tilers Ltd. While employees of Tidy Tilers Ltd are carrying out this work under the supervision of a foreman employed by Better Builders Ltd, a tile falls upon the head of Charles who is walking along the highway. Advise Charles regarding his possible claim for compensation.

3. Your employer, a construction company, has secured a valuable contract to build a new factory. On previous projects of a similar nature, trouble has been

experienced with the electrical installations. Instead of sub-contracting this part of the work as in the past, your employer is considering the employment of a sufficient number of electricians to do the work. Draft a report explaining the legal implications of such a decision.

4. Advise your company regarding both of the following situations:
   (a) An accounts clerk served a term of imprisonment for stealing money from a former employer. He is now employed by your company and his criminal record has just been discovered.
   (b) A labourer falls over a packing case that has been carelessly left in a dark passage by another worker. It is felt that the labourer's injuries were caused partly by his poor eyesight, about which the labourer said nothing until after the accident.

5. (a) An employee of your company claims that he is being underpaid. What sources would you examine to ascertain the validity of this claim?
   (b) Your company decides that it would be less costly to close the factory for a third week's annual holiday and to maintain production by working an extra three-quarters of an hour on each Monday evening throughout the remainder of the year. Advise on the legal considerations affecting the means by which this proposed change in the terms of employment could be introduced.

6. Alan takes over a business which employs a number of salesmen. He initially continues their employment but now wishes to change their conditions of working. He intends to supply them with goods and then to pay them by a commission on sales instead of by a weekly wage. The salesmen will provide their own cars, bought, if necessary, with a loan from Alan.
   (a) To what extent and in what way may these changes be introduced?
   (b) What would be the legal consequences of the change in status from employee to independent contractor?

Unit 27. Terms of Employment

Unit 26 dealt with the nature of employment, how the terms are agreed, where they are to be found, and the statutory provisions aimed to ensure that employees know the terms. This unit aims to set out what some of the normal terms *are*, and to describe the rights and duties of the parties.

A. Wages

The amount of the wage

We have seen that the amount may be fixed by negotiation, may depend upon a collective bargain, may be implied from the custom or practice of the trade, or stem from a combination of these. Exceptionally, in the absence of any agreement, there is an obligation to pay a reasonable amount.

To a limited extent, there is Government intervention. The Equal Pay Act, which aims to ensure equal pay for men and women doing the same work, will be discussed later, as will 'guarantee payments' for employees where no work is provided. The main statutory provision today, however, is the National Minimum Wage Act 1998, which entitles most 'workers' to a minimum rate of pay. The term 'workers' can include many who are self-employed, as well as full-time and part-time employees. The main exceptions are set out in the Act and in regulations made under it. In particular, workers under the age of 18 are excluded entirely, as are many apprentices under 26. Some other young workers are protected only to a limited extent.

A minimum hourly rate of payment (changed each year) is the basic protection. For systems such as 'piece-work' – often at home – the parties must make a 'fair estimate' of the time taken to do given work.

The minimum wage is a contractual right, and provisions such as the Unfair Contract Terms Act 1977 can apply. Moreover, a worker is protected from any detriment for trying to secure his minimum wage entitlement.

Wages during illness

Any question of entitlement to wages during illness will normally be answered in the particulars given to employees under the Employment Rights Act 1996, section 1 (Unit 26). Even if no notice is given, an employment tribunal can decide what the provision ought to be, having regard to the circumstances and what the parties appear to have assumed. Each case today will depend upon its own facts.

> In *Mears* v. *Safecar Security Ltd* (1982), *M* was engaged as a security guard. A few months later he became ill and was absent for a long time. His particulars under section 1 did not mention whether he was entitled to wages during illness, but he was told by his workmates that he would not be paid and he did not claim at the time. When he did apply later, the Court of Appeal held that he was not entitled.

> In *Orman* v. *Saville Sportswear Ltd* (1960), the production manager in a skirt factory was paid a basic rate of about £30 per week, plus a production bonus which was normally another £20. When he was absent ill, the firm paid him his basic £30. There was no express provision in the contract of employment, and it was held in the circumstances that the manager was entitled not only to his basic rate, but also to the bonus which he could reasonably have expected.

By the 1996 Act an employee is entitled to be paid wages during up to 26 weeks of suspension from work by his employer on medical grounds when suspension is required by statute or recommended by statutory code of practice; and a woman is entitled to payment during maternity leave (see later).

In addition to any wages to which an employee is entitled under his contract, he will usually be entitled during absence through illness to receive statutory sick pay from his employer for up to 28 weeks, before receiving a social security allowance from the Government.

Method of payment

Legislation has been necessary in the past to protect the wages of workers from doubtful practices by unscrupulous employers. These included payment of wages in the form of goods (or truck), requirements that wages be spent at the employer's shop, and excessive deductions for bad work or for minor benefits provided by the employer.

For *manual* workers, most of these practices were rendered illegal by the Truck Acts 1831–1940, which generally required the payment of wages in notes and coins. These Acts were repealed and replaced by the Wages Act 1986, partly to lessen the dangers of moving cash. This has in turn been replaced by the Employment Rights Act 1996, Part II. The Act applies to all 'workers', whether manual or not, and for all employees cashless pay, by cheque or credit transfer, is generally now permissible without prior written consent.

The 1996 Act (like the Acts before it) contains detailed provisions regarding deductions from pay. Statutory deductions for income tax (PAYE) and national insurance contributions are allowed. Other deductions can generally be agreed either by a term in the contract of employment, or by the advance written consent of the employee. There can, for example, be payment out of wages into a pension scheme, or for overalls or outdoor clothing. There can also be agreed deductions for bad timekeeping or workmanship.

Special provision is made for retail workers, who include staff and cashiers dealing with the public in places like hotels, restaurants, shops, garages and petrol stations, banks and buses. These employees were not fully protected by earlier legislation. Their contracts sometimes made them liable for all stock losses and cash shortages during their shift, whether or not it was their fault. This could be harsh: in one case in 1986 a petrol station attendant, liable for non-payment by drivers, found in one week that his pay after deductions was nil. The Act provides, therefore, that not only must there be no deductions unless agreed in the worker's contract or by prior written consent, but also that such deductions for retail workers must not exceed 10% of gross pay for the payment period (week or month). However if the amount missing exceeds this 10%, the employer may collect the balance on the following pay dates, providing that the 10% limit is not breached then. The limit does not apply if the deduction is to recover overpayment of wages.

Fragmented employment, often with small firms, has always made collective bargaining difficult for retail workers. Some such employees may benefit from the general minimum wage rates which now exist.

The 1996 Act can apply to an imposed reduction in wages in the same way as to deductions.

> In *Bruce* v. *Wiggins Teape (Stationery) Ltd* (1994), the company paid its night-shift workers at double the overtime rate. It decided, for business reasons, to reduce this to only the ordinary overtime rate, without the agreement of the employees concerned. The EAT held that this contravened the Wages Act. (Such a reduction might also amount to constructive dismissal; see page 300.)

Complaint of unauthorized deductions or reductions must be made to an employment tribunal, normally within three months, and the tribunal can order the employer to reimburse the worker.

B. General duties of employers

Duties of employers are, for the most part, rights of employees. In addition to payment of wages, employers have various common law obligations to employees, which constitute implied terms in the contract of employment in the absence of express agreement to the contrary.

Duty to provide work

This duty can apply in many instances today, particularly when it is vital for the employee actually to have the work.

> In *Collier* v. *Sunday Referee Publishing Co. Ltd* (1940), the chief sub-editor of the *Sunday Referee* was engaged on a long-term contract. Before this expired, the *Sunday Referee* was transferred to another proprietor. Collier was still paid his salary, but was no longer provided with work. He was awarded damages for breach of contract, because the lack of opportunity to exercise his skills and build his reputation could prejudice his future career. (Similar reasoning might apply to an actor, for example.)

> In *Turner* v. *Goldsmith* (1891), a commercial traveller had been paid solely on a commission basis. When he was deprived of work, therefore, he could no longer earn anything. He was held entitled to damages.

> In *Breach* v. *Epsylon Industries Ltd* (1976), it was suggested that a senior engineer, who would need to keep up to date with rapid technical change, was entitled to be given work to enable him to do so.

A connected problem is whether employees are entitled to be paid while laid off or on short time. To remove doubt, some collective agreements specifically guarantee a minimum wage in these situations, for hourly-paid as well as for piece-workers. This is now supplemented for some employees by the Employment Rights Act, section 28, which provides for 'guarantee payments' on days when an employee is not provided with work because (a) the business does not need his services on that day or (b) any other occurrence affects normal working. This right is limited, however, to a maximum of five days in any period of three months

Reasonable management

Employers today owe an implied contractual duty to behave reasonably and responsibly towards their employees. It is suggested that there are implied duties of mutual respect. Arbitrary and inconsiderate action by the employer can amount to breach of contract. If sufficiently serious, this can be another form of implied or 'constructive' dismissal.

> In *Donovan* v. *Invicta Airways Ltd* (1970), a pilot was, three times in rapid succession, put under pressure by management to take abnormal risks on flights. On two occasions, there were passengers aboard. He refused each time. Relations with management deteriorated, and he left the company. Although the decision to leave was his, he was held to have been dismissed, and received £900 damages for breach of contract.

> In *Isle of Wight Tourist Board* v. *Coombes* (1976), a director of the Board, when speaking to another employee, described his personal secretary as an 'intolerable bitch on a Monday morning'. When his secretary learned of this she resigned. It was held that she had been constructively dismissed, because such a comment destroyed the confidence and trust which should exist between the director and his secretary.

> In *Cox* v. *Philips Industries Ltd* (1976), C sent a reasonable and moderate protest to his superiors about his salary. Soon afterwards he was demoted, although there was no suggestion of incompetence. Thenceforth his duties were vague, and nobody told him what

he was supposed to do. He became depressed and ill. His employer was held to have broken the contract by treating him in this way.

In *United Bank* v. *Akhtar* (1989), the employer's contract required A to work anywhere in Britain. He worked in Leeds, and had a house there. On 5 June he was told to transfer to Birmingham on 8 June. He asked for more time in order to sell his house and because his wife was ill. This was refused. He therefore asked to take 24 days' holiday which was due to him. This was ignored. When he did not report to Birmingham, his pay was stopped as from 5 June. He 'resigned', but was held to have been constructively dismissed because of the unreasonable way in which his employers had applied the mobility clause.

What amounts to breach varies with circumstances and the nature of the job.

In *Wares* v. *Caithness Leather Products Ltd* (1974), an employer who abusively reprimanded a woman employee, in foul language, was held to have broken the contract. Such language would not necessarily be breach of contract on a building site.

If a worker reasonably and necessarily incurs liabilities and expenses in the performance of his duties, he can normally claim reimbursement from his employer.

Duty to provide a reasonably safe system of work

The employer owes a common law duty, both as an implied term in the contract, and for the tort of negligence, to take reasonable care for the safety of his employees, and to comply with all statutory safety provisions. In many ways, this can be regarded as part of the more general duty of reasonable management.

In *British Aircraft Corporation* v. *Austin* (1978), Mrs Austin was required to wear safety goggles, but found that those provided by her employer were quite unsuitable. She complained vehemently, but received no response. She 'resigned' and was held to have been constructively dismissed.

Duty to idemnify

If a worker reasonably and necessarily incurs liabilities and expenses in the performance of his duties, he may claim reimbursement from his employer. It is submitted that this duty has limited application and should be narrowly construed.

Statements in references

As a *general* rule, employers have *no* duty to give a testimonial or reference for an employee by answering enquiries from another employer who is considering whether to engage him. There are some situations today, however, where there *is* such a duty: in particular, where the employment is of a kind where it is normal for a new employer to seek a reference; and where, when the employee took his old job, it would be assumed from the outset that a reference would be given when he left. In these circumstances, a right to a reference (although not necessarily a favourable one) may be an implied term in the contract of employment.

Any employer who does give a reference, either voluntarily or under a duty, must be careful and honest. If the reference is falsely unfavourable, the employee may be entitled to damages for negligence (Unit 9) or even (exceptionally) defamation (Unit 10).

In *Spring* v. *Guardian Assurance plc* (1994), Spring sold life assurance policies. He had to leave his old job following a take-over. He tried to obtain similar work from another company which, under the self-regulatory rules of the insurance 'industry', had a *duty* to seek a reference from the ex-employer, which had a corresponding duty to give one. The reference given was described as 'the kiss of death to Spring's career in insurance'. He did not get the work which he sought, and could not obtain other insurance work. The House of Lords held that the ex-employer owed a duty to Spring to give a reference, and to take reasonable care when giving it; in particular, to ensure that the facts given and the factual basis of any opinions were accurate.

The giver of a negligently or deliberately inaccurate reference, even a falsely favourable one, may also be liable to the new employer if quantifiable loss to the latter can be shown to result. An employer who falsely gives a good reference in the hope of getting rid of an employee might run internal risks as well.

In *Haspell* v. *Rostron & Johnson Ltd* (1976), the employer who gave a favourable reference was estopped from relying on inconsistent allegations when he later tried to justify dismissing the employee.

C. Special statutory rights of employees

In recent years, legislation has given increasing rights to employees. Some rights apply generally, such as those to written notification of terms and itemized pay statements (Unit 26), and to minimum periods of notice (Unit 28). Other rights apply only to particular types of employee, or in special situations.

Women employees

The Sex Discrimination Act 1975 renders it unlawful for employers to discriminate on grounds of sex in advertising a post ('foreman', 'salesgirl'), engaging employees, or in the terms offered. It is also unlawful to discriminate in promotion, training, transfer, or other benefits, facilities or services; or in selection for dismissal, short-time or other detriments. Discrimination as to membership of trade unions or other bodies which can affect employment prospects is also covered.

These provisions mainly protect women, but equally apply to discrimination against men, or against any person on grounds that he or she is married. The rules are discussed for convenience mainly in terms of discrimination against women. A person discriminates against a woman if, because she is a woman:

1. he treats her less favourably than he would a man ('direct' discrimination); or
2. he applies some requirements or condition which men are more likely to meet than

women (for example, 'must have a beard') unless he can show that the job really demands this special requirement ('indirect' discrimination).

Discrimination is only permissible, therefore, if being a man (or woman) is a genuine occupational qualification for the job. For example:

1. Some jobs demand authentic male characteristics (for example, actor rather than actress). Physical courage, hardiness, and even strength are not regarded as exclusively male qualities, however, so that discrimination against female steel erectors, pilots, welders or labourers can be unlawful.

    In *Shields* v. *Coomes Ltd* (1979), male counter-hands in betting shops were paid more than women doing the same work, allegedly because it was the men who would have to deal with trouble or violence. This was held to be discrimination because the men had no special training, there was no evidence of past violence, and properly trained women could deal with violence equally well, sometimes better. The Court of Appeal upheld this finding.

   On the other hand some jobs might more effectively be carried out by a man because of the relationships involved: boys' club leader in a tough district, or negotiating in a country where sex equality is not accepted, for example. In such instances, discrimination might be justified.

2. Decency or privacy might require selection, for example because of physical contact (trainer at a football club?), or living together (lighthouse keepers?).

    In *Wylie* v. *Dee & Co (Menswear) Ltd* (1978), an employer refused to employ a woman as sales assistant in a menswear shop. This was held to be unlawful discrimination. It could not be justified on decency grounds, because customers could change in a private cubicle. Contact for measurement and fitting was rarely required, and could be carried out by one of the seven male assistants if so wished.

    Similarly in *Etam plc* v. *Rowan* (1989), a man who was refused employment in a shop which sold ladies' clothing successfully claimed discrimination.

3. Women of child-bearing age can be prohibited from working with certain materials which could harm an unborn child. There are also constraints on pregnant women working on aircraft and ships, and from returning to work in a factory within four weeks after childbirth.

There are special provisions for ministers of religion, police and prison officers. Some provisions relating to death or retirement are excluded but, following the Sex Discrimination Act 1986, an employer must have a common retirement *age* for his male and female employees. As regards retirement *pensions* there are still different qualifying ages for state provision. However, *private* occupational pension schemes which have different qualifying ages for men and women were held to be discriminatory by the European Court of Justice in *Barber* v. *Guardian Royal Exchange Assurance* (1990). The net result of all this will ultimately be to entitle more women to continue in work after 60, but to postpone their entitlement to occupational pensions.

Minor distinctions can be ignored.

> In *Peake* v. *Automotive Products Ltd* (1977), men and women worked the day shift on equal pay. A male employee alleged discrimination because women were allowed to leave five minutes earlier than men to avoid a rush at the factory gates. The Court of Appeal treated this as too trivial to be unlawful. It was chivalrous and safer.

> However, in *Jeremiah* v. *Ministry of Defence* (1979) chivalry was held immaterial, as was safety unless there were dangers solely to women. Men were sometimes required to work with dusty and unpleasant dyes. Women were not. The Court of Appeal held this to be discrimination which, unlike in *Peake's* case, was not trivial. Even the men's extra pay for this work was no excuse; one cannot buy the right to discriminate.

The Equal Opportunities Commission was set up in 1975 to keep this Act and the Equal Pay Act (below) under review and to promote equal opportunity. It has wide powers of investigation. If satisfied that there is discrimination, it may issue a non-discrimination notice after giving the employer the chance to defend himself, with a right of appeal to an industrial tribunal. If the notice is contravened within five years, the Commission may seek a County Court injunction against the employer.

Subject to this, complaints are normally heard by employment tribunals. Any person may complain, within a normal limitation period of three months. A conciliation officer of the Advisory, Conciliation and Arbitration Service (ACAS) will first try to promote a settlement. If this fails, it is for the employer to justify any differences. Unless he does so, the tribunal may (a) declare the rights of the complainant, (b) order the employer to pay compensation (without any ceiling), and (c) recommend that the employer remedy the cause of complaint, under the potential sanction of increased compensation. Compensation for hurt feelings can be included.

> In *Gubala* v. *Crompton Parkinson Ltd* (1977), Mrs Gubala was selected for redundancy ahead of a male colleague. Their length of service was similar, and the employer admitted being influenced by the fact that the man was older and had a house and mortgage, whereas Mrs Gubala's husband worked. She was offered a job at a lower grade which was 'women's work'. She refused, and was compensated for unfair dismissal plus £400 for unlawful discrimination, including recompense for hurt feelings.

Equal pay is governed by similar legislation. By the EC Treaty, Article 141 (formerly Article 119), member states must 'ensure and subsequently maintain the application of the principle that men and women should receive equal pay for equal work'. This became binding in this country in 1973. At that time there already was an Equal Pay Act 1970, but it was not yet in force. The 1970 Act was amended and brought into force with the Sex Discrimination Act 1975.

However, the story did not end there. In several cases, claimants who were unsuccessful under the Equal Pay Act successfully applied to the European Court of Justice under the Treaty and a *Directive* of 1975 which supplemented it.

> In *Macarthy's* v. *Smith* (1981), a male stockroom manager was paid £60 per week. He left and, after four months, was replaced by Mrs Smith, who was paid only £50 per week. Her claim under the Equal Pay Act failed, because the Act applied only to differences in pay for

like work *at the same time*. However, the European Court held that Article 119 had been broken. This binds the English courts and, for this reason, Mrs Smith's claim finally succeeded.

Eventually, in *Commission of the European Communities* v. *United Kingdom* (1982), the European Commission successfully sued the UK Government in the European Court for a declaration that the Equal Pay Act did not yet comply with Article 119. The Government, therefore, amended the Act again, as from the beginning of 1984.

The Equal Pay Act provides that the contracts of women employees shall contain an 'equality clause', under which the woman's terms of employment shall be no less favourable than those of a man in the same employment doing 'like work' or 'work rated as equivalent'. The job is 'like work' with a man's if it is the same or broadly similar. It is 'rated as equivalent' if a job evaluation study has given equal value to the woman's and a man's job with the employer, at the same establishment or, where common terms are applied, elsewhere in Britain. A woman who believes that her value to the business is equivalent to that of a male 'comparator' can make a claim. The job's value is assessed in terms of the demands made on the worker under headings such as effort, skill and decision. The equality clause also allows a woman to claim that her job is of 'equal value' *before* a job evaluation study has been made. In this event, the tribunal itself may ask an independent expert to prepare a report.

> In *Hayward* v. *Cammell Laird Ltd* (1988), the House of Lords held that if the work of a female cook was rated of equal value to that of a thermal heating engineer, a joiner and a painter, then she was entitled to equal terms as to pay and overtime. This was so even if she had better terms as to sickness benefits and holidays. The proper comparison was between one term (as to pay) in her contract, and the equivalent term (as to pay) in the men's contracts.

Complaints are heard by employment tribunals as under the Sex Discrimination Act, except that the times for making claims are different. Equal pay claims can be made at any time during the employment or up to six months after leaving. An award can include arrears of wages or damages, but only for times within two years before the start of proceedings. Despite its name, the Equal Pay Act can also cover terms as to holidays and sickness pay, so long as like is compared with like. The woman's entitlement to holiday must be compared with the equivalent entitlement in an equivalent man's contract.

The Employment Rights Acts 1996 and 1999 give women certain minimum rights in the event of pregnancy and childbirth. An employer may extend these rights but not reduce them.

- By the 1996 Act s.99, it is unfair to dismiss a woman simply or mainly because of pregnancy or giving birth, or because of exercising any of her statutory rights such as maternity leave. No qualifying period of employment is needed for this protection.
- Section 55 gives the right to reasonable time during working hours, with pay, for ante-natal care on medical advice.

- There are detailed provisions for maternity leave. Ordinary entitlement is for at least 18 weeks, starting not earlier than 11 weeks before the expected birth. No qualifying period of employment is needed. Employees who have worked for the employer for at least a year at the eleven-week date can claim additional leave, to return up to 29 weeks after the birth.
- The employee will be entitled to statutory maternity pay from her employer.
- A woman who is subjected by her employer to any detriment because of her pregnancy, or because she exercised her right to maternity leave, can claim compensation from an employment tribunal.

Race relations

Under the Race Relations Act 1976, it is unlawful for an employer to discriminate against employees on grounds of colour, race, ethnic or national origins. This covers advertisements, recruitment, terms, promotion and dismissal. The Commission for Racial Equality keeps the Act under review and works to promote good race relations. It can investigate, and issue non-discrimination notices enforceable in the same way as those of the Equal Opportunities Commission.

Apart from this, complaints of racial discrimination in employment are heard by employment tribunals. A conciliation officer engaged by ACAS can try to promote a settlement but, subject to this, tribunals have the same powers as under the sex discrimination legislation above.

The Commission has issued a code of practice aimed at the elimination of racial discrimination and directed at promoting equal opportunities in employment. Although this is not legally binding on employers, it must be admitted as evidence in proceedings where breach of the Act is alleged (see Unit 2).

Disabled persons

The Disability Discrimination Act 1995 makes it unlawful to treat a disabled person less fairly than others in the field of employment without a justifiable reason. An employment tribunal can order compensation for non-compliance.

Trade union membership

Under the Trade Union and Labour Relations (Consolidation) Act 1992, it is unlawful to discriminate against an employee because he *joins* an *independent* trade union, takes part in its activities, or because he *refuses* to join a union, independent or not. An independent union is one not controlled by the employer. Dismissal for any of these reasons is unfair, and the person has three months in which to claim reinstatement, re-engagement and/or compensation through an employment tribunal. This is dealt with in detail in Unit 28. Three matters can perhaps be mentioned here. First, the person can, within seven days, apply to an employment tribunal for *temporary* reinstatement or re-engagement, pending hearing of the unfair dismissal case. Second, if action *short* of dismissal is taken against the employee on the above grounds, he can complain to a tribunal within three months, and compensation can be awarded. Third, these rights are available from the outset, without any qualifying period with this employer.

Sometimes there may be a 'closed shop' or 'union membership' agreement between an employer and one or more unions, under which the employer agrees to employ only members of the union or unions concerned. Although such agreements are still lawful, they are now less common than hitherto.

Time off work

The Employment Rights Act and the Trade Union and Labour Relations (Consolidation) Act 1992 allow time off for various purposes.

1. The 1992 Act, section 168, entitles an *official* of a recognized trade union to take time off during working hours, without loss of pay, for certain union duties such as collective bargaining with the employer, and also for training in industrial relations which is relevant to those duties.
2. Section 170 entitles a *member* of a recognized trade union to reasonable time off, with no right to pay, to take part in activities of the union, and activities where he is acting as a representative of the union.
3. By the Employment Rights Act 1996, section 50, employers must allow reasonable leave, not necessarily paid, for service as a magistrate, or as a member of a local authority, health or water authority, or statutory tribunal, or for other specified public duties.
4. By section 52, when an employee is given redundancy notice he must, if he has been continuously employed for two years, be given reasonable paid leave (with a two-day minimum) during the notice period, to look for new work or to arrange for retraining.
5. Section 55 can entitle pregnant employees to reasonable time off for antenatal care.
6. Under various Acts, people working with dangerous materials such as radioactive substances or lead may be temporarily suspended from work on medical grounds. By section 64, such an employee must normally get full pay for up to 26 weeks, unless he unreasonably refuses his employer's offer of suitable alternative work, or disregards his employer's requirements imposed with a view to making his services available. Someone totally incapable of work because of disease or disablement is not entitled, but should qualify for social security benefits. Section 64 applies after one month's continuous employment.
7. Safety representatives must be allowed reasonable paid leave for training.
8. Employee representatives in connection with proposed redundancies are entitled to reasonable time off with pay for these functions.

Working time

The Working Time Regulations 1998 were enacted as a result of an EU Directive, and are partly to do with health and safety. They impose a normal maximum working week, but with many exceptions. They also provide for normal weekly/fortnightly 'days off' for adult workers, with longer for workers under 18, and there are minimum 'rest break' provisions, which are more generous for those under 18. There are detailed provisions for night work. Workers are also entitled to at least four weeks of paid holiday each year, but the 'bank holidays' can count towards this in Britain.

D. Duties of employees

As well as rights, employees obviously have duties, and *serious* breach by an employee may justify his dismissal. The following are some examples.

To take reasonable care

The worker must take reasonable care in exercising his duties. He must take reasonable care of his employer's property, and be careful that his conduct does not harm fellow workers or outsiders so as to impose vicarious liability on his employer. The degree of care expected may vary with the employee's job and the responsibility entrusted to him. Negligence may entitle the employer to dismiss the employee, and also to be reimbursed by him.

In *Janata Bank* v. *Ahmed* (1981), a bank manager was dismissed for carrying out his duties negligently. The bank was also awarded damages of £34 640 against him. (See also *Lister* v. *Romford Ice and Cold Storage Co.*, Unit 8).

In *Taylor* v. *Alidair Ltd* (1978), a pilot made such a bad landing that his passengers and the crew were rightly alarmed. His dismissal without prior warnings was held here to be fair.

Skill

An employee must show such skill as he has professed, and can realistically be expected of him in his job.

In *Harmer* v. *Cornelius* (1858), a man engaged as a scene painter proved incapable of painting scenes, and was lawfully dismissed without notice.

In *Tayside Regional Council* v. *McIntosh* (1982), a vehicle mechanic was disqualified from driving and, because this was vital to his job, he was dismissed. This was held to be fair, even though no express term of his employment had been broken.

In *Burrows* v. *Ace Caravan Co. Ltd* (1972), Burrows was promoted but then dismissed with notice for incompetence in his new post. This was held unfair, because he had received no proper training or instruction in the new post.

Duties of obedience and responsibility

An employee is expected to do everything reasonable to comply with instructions, and to show a responsible attitude to situations at work.

In *Laws* v. *London Chronicle Ltd* (1959), the claimant was at a meeting between her immediate superior and the managing director. The meeting was stormy. Her superior walked out, telling her to follow. The managing director told her to stay. She chose to go, whereupon the managing director dismissed her summarily. The dismissal was wrongful; isolated disobedience in this situation did not repudiate her obligations.

In *Cresswell* v. *Board of Inland Revenue* (1984), an Inland Revenue employee claimed that computerization was such a huge change that it amounted to breach of his existing contract of employment. This claim failed.

In *Walmsley* v. *UDEC Refrigeration Ltd* (1972), a manager whose area of responsibility included Wexford in Eire refused to visit the town on grounds that he feared the IRA. His dismissal was held to be fair, because there was no evidence of risk to him there.

In *Martin* v. *Yorkshire Imperial Metals* (1978), the workman operated an automatic lathe. A lever was designed to occupy his left hand while the machine was working so as to reduce the risk of accident. He tied down the lever and, when this was discovered, he was dismissed. Dismissal was held to be fair.

Honesty and loyalty

Dishonesty in the employment is obviously a breach of the employee's duties. The seriousness varies.

In *Reading* v. *Attorney General* (1951), an Army sergeant serving in Egypt used to accompany lorries which were smuggling liquor. Because he was wearing uniform, the lorries were not searched. It was held that the 'profits' accruing to him from this enterprise (some £20 000) belonged to the Crown.

In *Sinclair* v. *Neighbour* (1967), the manager of a betting shop borrowed money from the till, replacing it with an IOU. He did not ask permission, and knew that such a request would have been refused. The money was repaid next day, but the employer found out and dismissed the manager. Dismissal was held justified.

Even misconduct in the employee's own time may be unacceptable, depending partly on the nature of the job.

In *Richardson* v. *City of Bradford* (1975), a senior meat inspector was convicted of theft from his rugby club. His employer, the Council, tried to find other work for him where honesty was not so vital but, unable to do so, dismissed him. This was held to be fair.

Equally, an accountant convicted of fraud unconnected with his employment might, in some cases, legitimately be dismissed.

An employee indulging in 'moonlighting' (working in his own time either for himself or another employer without his main employer's consent) may break his contract if the other work damages that of his employer. A remedy may also be granted against the other employer.

In *Hivac Ltd* v. *Park Royal Scientific Instruments Ltd* (1946), Hivac Ltd made valves for hearing aids. Some of their workers began to work on Sundays for a nearby competing business. This was breach of contract by them. An injunction was also granted against the other firm.

A conflict of interest may even arise without misconduct on anyone's part.

In *Foot* v. *Eastern Counties Timber Co. Ltd* (1972), the dismissal of a cashier who married her employer's business competitor was held to be fair.

Equally, a worker must not deliberately disclose trade secrets or confidential information that he has acquired during his employment.

The worker owes other duties of good faith similar to those owed by an agent to his principal (Unit 7). In particular, he must account for any unauthorized benefit which accrues to him by reason of his position or employment. Thus he must not accept a bribe or secret commission although, where it is customary to do so, he may retain a 'tip' and, possibly, a Christmas present.

Innovations during employment

If a worker makes an invention then, as a general rule, the patent rights and other benefits belong to him. This may be so even if he makes the invention in the course of his employment. By the Patents Acts 1977, the invention belongs to the employer in two circumstances only: (a) if the invention arose from normal duties, or from some special job, which might reasonably be *expected* to produce an invention; or (b) if the employee had a *special obligation* at the time to further the employer's undertaking.

Even if the invention is lawfully patented by the employer, the employee can still apply to the Patents Court for a fair share of the moneys derived from a patent which proves to be of 'outstanding benefit' to the employer. In short, the 1977 Act tries to ensure that employees have a fair reward (and incentive) for inventions. If the employee himself owns and patents the invention, he can sell it freely. If he sells or licenses it to his employer, he can still claim statutory compensation later if it transpires that he sold it too cheaply.

On the other hand, *copyright* of written work produced in the course of employment normally belongs to the employer, see the Copyright, Designs and Patents Act 1988, although the parties can vary this by agreement. Even if the work was not produced during employment, the employer may restrain publication of information which may be considered the employer's property.

In *Stevenson, Jordan and Harrison Ltd* v. *Macdonald and Evans* (1952), an accountant 'sold' to publishers the copyright of his manuscript on business management. Part of the book was based upon public lectures which he had given, and part was derived from a particular assignment which he had carried out for his employer. It was held that the employer could only restrain publication of the latter part.

Duties of ex-workers

Some duties may continue even after the employment has ended. If there is an enforceable restraint clause in his contract of employment, for example, a worker may be restrained from future employment within the time and distance limits imposed. The principles governing validity of restraint clauses were considered in Unit 17.

The duty of secrecy may also continue even in the absence of a specific clause in the contract, although it may be prudent for an employer to insert such a clause. An ex-worker may be restrained from using confidential information obtained during the employment, but not the general knowledge or skill which he then acquired.

> In *Printers and Finishers Ltd* v. *Holloway* (1964), an injunction was granted against the use by a former works manager of secret documents which he had copied while in employment. On the other hand, he was not restrained from using more general information which he had retained in his mind regarding his former employer's business.

> In *Faccenda Chicken Ltd* v. *Fowler* (1986), the claimant's sales manager left and later set up his own competing business. Other employees of the claimant also left and joined Fowler. The claimant alleged that his ex-employees were now using their confidential knowledge of his sales and prices against him. The Court of Appeal held that the information was not confidential, being widely known among the claimant's sales staff and other employees. The action therefore failed.

Specimen questions

1. (a) Perhaps the most important obligation placed upon an employer is the payment of wages. What legal rules may be applied to determine the amount of the wage to be paid?
   (b) To what extent must an employer pay wages:
      (i) during the absence of an employee through illness;
      (ii) when he is unable to provide work?

2. (a) Outline the common law duties owed by an employer to his employee in the absence of any specific provisions in the contract of service.
   (b) Robert is a representative employed to sell washing machines. In each week he earns about £290 of which £150 is his basic wage and the remainder is commission on sales. The employer cuts back production in order to retool for a new model and informs Robert that his supply of machines, and hence his commission, will be halved. Robert claims that not only will his present earnings be reduced considerably but that he will lose his contacts and the chance of increasing his commission when production becomes normal again. Advise Robert.

3. Outline the duties owed by a worker to his employer in the absence of any agreement to the contrary in the contract of employment.

4. *C Ltd* is engaged in a highly competitive business where continued success depends largely upon research into new and improved products. To protect the results of this research, advise *C Ltd* on its rights:

(i) to inventions made by employees;

(ii) to prevent employees passing on confidential information to competitors;

(iii) to prevent employees working for competitors at weekends.

5. (a) Explain how the illness of an employee may affect his employment.

    (b) Wheeler is employed by a retail store and part of his duties involves the delivery of goods by bicycle. One evening he breaks his leg playing football and the following day, when his employer hears of this, he is dismissed. Advise Wheeler.

Unit 28. Notice and Dismissal

A. Qualifying periods of continuous employment

Most of the statutory rights in this unit, particularly rights to notice and remedies for unfair dismissal, are only available for workers who have been *continuously employed* by their employer for a qualifying period. The phrase 'continuously employed' is, therefore, extremely important and, for all of these purposes, the period is computed according to the Employment Rights Act 1996, Part XIV.

Weeks of employment

Continuous employment is built up from week to week and, today, part-time employment is enough. Even a series of one-day contracts with one employer can suffice. By the Employment Rights Act 1996, section 212, any week during the whole or part of which an employee's relations with his employer are governed by a contract of employment counts in computing the employee's period of employment. (The former sixteen- and eight-hours-per-week limits have been removed.)

Generally, any week in which this continuity is broken means that the worker has to start afresh to accumulate qualifying weeks. The Act does, however, make special provision for gaps in the following circumstances.

1. Up to 26 weeks during which the employee is incapable of work due to sickness or injury do not interrupt the continuity, and count in building up the requisite qualifying periods. However, absence for more than 26 weeks can break the continuity. (Moreover, long absence from work can sometimes justify the employer in treating the employment as ended; see page 323).

2. Up to 26 weeks of absence wholly or partly because of pregnancy or childbirth similarly do not interrupt continuity and count towards qualifying periods. A woman who is entitled to exercise her statutory 'maternity rights' (see page 311) can become entitled to longer leave on the same basis.
3. Absence due to a temporary stoppage other than a strike, or absence in such circumstances that the worker is considered by arrangement or custom to be still employed (e.g. sabbatical leave), similarly counts for continuity and qualifying periods, in these cases without the 26-week limit.
4. Where an employee successfully claims to have been unfairly dismissed, and he is reinstated, continuity of employment is preserved and includes the time between dismissal and reinstatement.

Stoppage due to a strike will not affect the continuity of employment, but time spent on strike does not, unlike the above weeks, count towards the qualifying periods.

Change of employer

Continuous employment must all be with the same employer. There can easily be changes which are outside the control of employees, however, and so the 1996 Act section 218 gives some protection.

1. Section 218(2) provides that if a trade, business or undertaking is transferred from one owner to another, the period with the old owner still counts with the new owner, so long as the new owner takes over and carries on the business as a going concern. This is supplemented by the Transfer of Undertakings (Protection of Employment) Regulations 1981 ('TUPE'), which were made in compliance with an EC Directive. The new owner, in effect, takes on the rights and obligations of existing workers (if they consent), so that the employments do not end. 'Undertaking' can include a non-commercial enterprise such as a charity or public authority.
2. If on the death of an employer the employee is taken into the employment of the deceased's personal representatives or trustees, the death does not break the continuity of employment.
3. In an ordinary partnership, if there is a change in the partners who employ a person, the change does not break the continuity.
4. If an employee moves—or is moved—from his present employer to an 'associated employer', the move does not break the continuity. This can be important where employees are moved from one company to an associated company in the same 'group', and to this extent it provides an exception to the separate legal personality of the companies.
5. Similar provisions cover situations (such as privatisations or local government changes) where by or under an Act of Parliament a new corporate employer is substituted for the previous one.

6. Similar provisions are made for education employees whose 'employer' changes because the status of the school changes, and trainees in the health service who have to gain experience with a number of different health service employers.
7. Note that a simple takeover of shares in a company does not interrupt the contracts of employees. The company has a separate legal personality (Unit 7), (as does a Limited Liability Partnership; see Unit 22), and employees are still employed by the same company, albeit controlled by different shareholders or members.

Presumption of continuity

A period of employment is presumed continuous for the purposes of unfair dismissal and redundancy payments unless the employer can prove otherwise.

B. Termination by notice

A contract for a fixed term or a particular piece of work normally ends automatically on the expiration of the time or completion of the work. If, as is more usual, employment is for an indefinite period, either party may end it by giving notice to the other (possibly quite amicably), and the length of notice required is frequently an express term in the contract. Even in a fixed period contract, there may be a term entitling one or both parties to terminate earlier by notice. If there is no prior agreement on the notice period, *reasonable* notice must be given.

At common law, what is reasonable notice will depend upon such matters as trade practice, the length of service, periods by which wages or salary are calculated, and the seniority of the position held. As a general rule, the more important the post, the longer would be the period; see *Hill* v. *C. A. Parsons & Co. Ltd* (Unit 15).

These common law rules are subject to statutory *minimum* periods of notice set out in the Employment Rights Act. Where there has been continuous employment for one month, the *worker* then has a right to at least one week's notice. After two years' employment he/she is entitled to at least two weeks and, thenceforth, at least one week's notice for each year of continuous employment up to a maximum statutory entitlement of 12 weeks. The *employer* has a corresponding right to at least one week's notice from the worker after continuous employment of one month, but there is no sliding scale thereafter; however long the employment, one week is the maximum *statutory* notice which the worker need give.

The statutory periods do not apply if an employer 'sacks' an employee summarily for *serious* misconduct; see page 330.

It should be noted again that these periods are statutory *minima*. The individual contract of employment can expressly or impliedly provide for longer periods of notice, but never less. On the other hand at any time, for example on leaving or dismissal, either party can waive his right to notice. Moreover, since an employer may have no general duty to provide work, it may be sufficient for him to tender wages in lieu of notice and/or require the employee to serve out his notice at home ('garden leave'). This may occur if the employer no longer wants the employee on his premises, but has no grounds for summary dismissal.

The Act contains detailed provisions safeguarding rights of a worker during notice. Basically, he is entitled to be paid at the normal rate.

It should be emphasized that, even if proper notice is given, an employee may still be entitled to redundancy payment or statutory compensation for unfair dismissal.

C. Unfair dismissal

At common law an employer could sack an employee at any time, without giving reasons, provided that appropriate notice was given. Only dismissal *without* adequate notice could be wrongful, and then the burden of proving that the dismissal was wrongful rested upon the complainant.

The new concept of unfair dismissal was introduced after 1971, and is now governed by the Employment Rights Act 1996, Part X.

Qualifying period of continuous employment

Generally, an employee is protected from unfair dismissal only after employment for a qualifying period of one year. All continuous employment from the age of 16 counts. A worker dismissed without notice after 51 weeks may be covered, because the week's statutory notice which he should have received is added to his actual service.

Workers dismissed merely because of statutory medical suspension from work on occupational safety grounds are covered after only one month's qualifying employment.

For some types of dismissal, employees are protected from the outset, without any qualifying period at all: in particular, if dismissal is for one of the automatically unfair reasons set out on pages 324–5.

Dismissal

A person complaining of unfair dismissal must obviously have been dismissed. He is treated as dismissed if:

1. the contract under which he is employed is terminated by the employer, with or without notice; or
2. he is employed for a fixed term which expires without being renewed; or
3. the *employee* leaves voluntarily, with or without notice, in circumstances such that he is entitled to do so because of the employer's misconduct.

An employee who is given notice of dismissal, but leaves voluntarily with proper notice (perhaps to start another job) before the employer's notice expires, is still treated as dismissed for the reasons given for the employer's notice.

As we have seen in Unit 27, dismissal need not be express. There can be 'constructive' dismissal if, for example, the employer unilaterally and fundamentally alters the terms of employment, or commits a major breach of the obligations which he owes as employer (see page 306 and cases such as *United Bank* v. *Akhtar*).

> See also *Cresswell* v. *Board of Inland Revenue* (1984), where the employer computerized the working system. The employees claimed that the need for new skills changed the nature of the job, and amounted to constructive dismissal. Their claim failed.

Refusal to re-engage a worker after a lock-out or to allow a woman to exercise her statutory right to return after pregnancy can be dismissal, although there are exceptions. Unfair selection for redundancy can also be unfair dismissal.

If employment ends because the contract is frustrated, however, there is no dismissal (Unit 16). The contract ends by operation of law, and the employer does not have to justify its non-continuance. Frustration will occur if the employer can show, and the onus is on him, that the employment has been ended by some outside cause or event, substantially outside the control of the parties. Much may depend on the nature of the contract and the length of any enforced absence.

> In *Morgan* v. *Manser* (1948), military conscription for an indefinite period was held to frustrate the employee's contract as manager of a variety performer.

> In *Shepherd & Co. Ltd* v. *Jerrom* (1986), an apprentice was sentenced to Borstal training for a criminal offence, and he served six months of detention. The Court of Appeal said that this *could* have frustrated his four-year service contract; but this was not the case when there was a term in the written contract of employment that entitled the employer to dismiss the apprentice for misconduct.

Illness may or may not frustrate the contract. The tests generally used today are from the case of *Egg Stores (Stamford Hill) Ltd* v. *Leibovici* (1976). It depends upon matters such as the length of the absentee's previous employment; the expected length of his future employment; the nature of the job; the nature, length and effect of the illness; need for a replacement; risk to the employer of the replacement qualifying for unfair dismissal or redundancy rights; whether the absentee still receives wages; whether the employer has given the impression that he still regards the worker as employed; and whether a reasonable employer could be expected to wait any longer. Illness may *eventually* frustrate the contract; but *when*?

> In *Storey* v. *Fulham Steel Works Co.* (1907), the five-year contract of a works manager was not frustrated by an absence of four months after he had worked for two years.

> In *Hart* v. *A. R. Marshall Ltd* (1977), a 'key' worker, one of two service fitters who worked weekly night shifts alternately, was away ill for nearly two years, during which time his employer had to make other arrangements to cover his shift. His contract was held to have been frustrated, so that it was not dismissal when his employer refused to re-engage him.

In *Notcutt* v. *Universal Equipment Co. Ltd* (1986), a skilled employee had a serious heart attack and after several months it became apparent that he would never be able to resume his job. The Court of Appeal held that his contract had been frustrated, and that he was not entitled to the 12 weeks' pay in lieu of dismissal notice which he claimed.

Similarly, if both employer and employee freely agree to end the contract, there is no dismissal. However the courts often view such agreements with suspicion, and if pressure has been exerted by the employer then the 'agreement' may be invalid against the employee.

Reasons for dismissal

An employer who dismisses a worker with one year or more of service must, within 14 days of a request by the worker, give him a written statement of the reasons. This is then admissible as evidence in any proceedings. If an employer unreasonably refuses, or gives inadequate or untrue reasons, the worker can complain to an employment tribunal which (a) may declare what it considers to be the true reasons, and (b) must order the employer to pay the worker a sum equal to two weeks' wages.

If the employer discovers further reasons after giving notice, then these may be admissible in any internal appeal which the employer allows. They may also be admissible in later tribunal proceedings, but only if they were discovered either before the dismissal took effect or before any internal appeal was ended. Anything discovered after this is not admissible in tribunal proceedings; see *Devis & Sons* v. *Atkins* (1977), page 331.

Automatically unfair dismissal

1. By the Trade Union and Labour Relations (Consolidation) Act 1992, section 152, it is automatically unfair, and no 'qualifying period' of employment is required, in effect to sack a worker merely for being a union member. Equally it is unfair to sack him for *refusing* to join a union.
2. By the Employment Rights Act 1996 section 99, dismissal is automatically unfair if it was because of the employee's pregnancy, or during her maternity leave because she has given birth, or after and because she has taken maternity leave. If a woman is unable under health and safety legislation to do her normal job during pregnancy or just after childbirth, and the employer is unable to find her suitable alternative work, she must be given leave with pay. Dismissal in breach of this is unfair. Again, no qualifying period of employment is needed.
3. Section 100 contains detailed provisions making it unfair to dismiss employees for acting properly in connection with health and safety risks and dangers, mainly at the place of employment.
4. Section 102 renders it unfair to dismiss an employee who is also a trustee of an occupational pension scheme for the way in which he carries out this task. Section 103 provides similarly for employees who are representatives over proposed redundancies (see Unit 29).
5. By section 104, dismissal is unfair if the principal reason for it was that the employee (a) brought proceedings against the employer to enforce a relevant

statutory right, or (b) alleged that the employer had infringed a relevant statutory right (see page 308).
6. By section 105, dismissal is unfair if the employee is declared redundant while others in a similar position are retained, and this selective dismissal is for one of the above unfair reasons.

Dismissal for other reasons

By the 1996 Act, section 98, all other reasons are *presumed* unfair, but the employer can prove otherwise if two requirements are satisfied. First, the employer must show that the reason, or the principal reason, for dismissal:

1. is related to the capability (e.g., relevant aptitude, skill, health, etc.) of the worker for the employment in question; or
2. is related to the conduct of the employee; or
3. was that the employee was redundant; or
4. was that the employee could not continue to work in the position which he held without contravention, either on his part or his employer's, of a restriction or duty imposed by statute; or
5. was some other substantial reason justifying the dismissal of a worker in the position which he held (see *Foot* v. *Eastern Counties Timber Co. Ltd*, page 316).

Secondly, the tribunal must go on to decide whether, in the circumstances, having regard to equity and the substantial merits of the case, the employer acted reasonably in dismissing the worker. Since 1980, the *onus* is no longer on the employer to *prove* reasonableness. The tribunal now decides for itself. It looks at the *manner* of the dismissal, and for this purpose the codes of practice issued by ACAS are relevant, particularly one entitled 'Disciplinary Practice and Procedures in Employment'. The codes are designed to contain 'such practical guidance as would be helpful for the purpose of promoting good industrial relations', and recommend, for example, that an employee should normally be given a warning before dismissal for misconduct (although not necessarily for things like theft or violence at work). The tribunal must also ask itself whether dismissal was a reasonable option for the employer on the facts of the case (but *not* whether the members of the tribunal would have made the same decision themselves).

Unless the above requirements are satisfied, the dismissal is unfair. An ex-employee who claims under section 98 must first, of course, have served the one-year qualifying period of continuous employment.

If an employee is told in writing on entering the employment that the job is temporary, to fill a gap during (a) the absence of a woman for pregnancy, or (b) statutory suspension of an employee due to occupational illness, then dismissal of the temporary worker on return of the woman or the suspended employee will normally be fair. Claims by temporary workers may not arise often today, because they may not serve the one-year qualifying period. However, even a temporary worker is protected against the types of dismissal which are *automatically* unfair.

325

In *Webb* v. *Emo Air Cargo Ltd* (1994), an employee was absent on maternity leave. Her temporary replacement herself became pregnant, and was dismissed for this reason. The House of Lords (after reference to the European Court of Justice) held that the dismissal was unfair.

Special situations

In some situations, special directions are given to the tribunal. First, if a Minister of the Crown certifies that dismissal was to safeguard the national interest, the tribunal shall dismiss the complaint.

If an employer dismisses and refuses to re-engage *all* of the workers involved in an official strike, lock-out or other industrial action, the tribunal 'shall not determine whether the dismissal was fair or unfair'.

The tribunal can act only if (a) *some* are singled out for dismissal, or (b) *some* are re-engaged *within three months* of their dismissal, and others are not. In these cases, dismissal is *presumed* unfair under the 1996 Act, section 98, but the employer can rebut this presumption under the above rules.

In *Highland Fabricators Ltd* v. *McLaughlin* (1984), there had been a strike after which all of the participants, except the applicant, were soon re-engaged. The applicant was, however, offered back his job before three months had elapsed. *By the end of this time*, therefore, none had been singled out, and the tribunal had no jurisdiction to hear the applicant's claim.

These 'no picking and choosing' protections only apply to official strikes and industrial action. An *unofficial* striker who is sacked therefore has no redress – even if he complains of being unfairly singled out under (a) or (b) above. (A strike can only be official if it is backed by a union which has observed the proper balloting and other procedures, or if none of the strikers is in a trade union.)

Complaint to an employment tribunal

Complaint of unfair dismissal must normally be presented to an employment tribunal before the end of three months beginning with the effective date of termination. The tribunal can extend this period if satisfied that it was not reasonably practicable to present the claim in time.

The tribunal sends a copy of the papers to the ex-employer, who has 14 days in which to send back his defence. If the complaint seems arguable, copies of the papers are then sent to a conciliation officer designated by ACAS. He may (*must* if requested by either party) try to negotiate a settlement. In particular, he can be required to promote reinstatement or re-engagement of the employee, or to try to negotiate agreed compensation.

If no conciliation is attempted, or if it fails, then the tribunal has power to *order* the employer to reinstate (give back the job to) or re-engage (give a comparable job to) the employee, if this would be practicable and just, having regard, for example, to the employee's past conduct. If a reinstatement or re-engagement order is disobeyed, an additional award of compensation can be made.

Subject to this, the tribunal must award compensation to a worker unfairly dismissed. The amount is calculated in several stages.

1. First, the complainant is entitled to a *basic award*, calculated by length of service in the same way as a redundancy payment (Unit 29). The tribunal can make deductions from this amount (a) where the employee's own conduct contributed to the dismissal; (b) where he has unreasonably refused reinstatement; and (c) where the employee also receives a redundancy payment or compensation under the Sex Discrimination or Race Relations Act, which is set off against compensation for dismissal.
2. In addition to the basic award, the tribunal may make a *compensatory award*, assessed in a similar way to damages for breach of contract at common law. As at common law, the complainant must try reasonably to mitigate his loss, for example by seeking other work.
3. If an employee has been unfairly sacked or selected for redundancy because of trade union membership or activity, or because he is *not* a trade union member, the tribunal can order reinstatement or re-engagement as described above. If the ex-employee requested this order and the employer now disobeys it, the tribunal can make a *special award*. The special award can be reduced (a) for complainants over 64, at the rate of one-twelfth for each month after that age, (b) where the complainant's own conduct before dismissal made a reduction just and equitable, or (c) where the complainant unreasonably refused or prevented reinstatement or re-engagement.

   The above orders and the special award have been particularly relevant since 1988, when dismissal for not being a trade union member is automatically unfair. Sometimes, moreover, the *union* (not the employer) may be ordered to pay a special award (see below).
4. In other cases, *not* concerned with trade unions, where a reinstatement or re-engagement order is disobeyed by the employer, the tribunal can make an *additional award* on top of the basic and compensatory awards. An additional award is between 13 and 26 weeks' pay unless the employer can show that compliance was impracticable. If failure to reinstate, etc., is due to race or sex discrimination, a *higher additional award* of 26–52 weeks' pay can be made.

Generally, the award is made against the employer who dismissed the worker. However, by the 1992 Act, section 160, an employer who dismissed someone for non-membership of a union, and did so because of industrial pressure by the trade union, can have the union joined as party to the proceedings. The tribunal can then order the union to pay the whole or part of any award which would otherwise have been payable by the employer. The employee too can ask that the union be brought into the proceedings and made liable.

A worker unreasonably expelled or excluded from a trade union can obtain a declaration to that effect from an employment tribunal. If the union still excludes him, then the tribunal can order the union to pay further in compensation.

Appeals from employment tribunals lie to the Employment Appeal Tribunal and thence, on a point of law, to the Court of Appeal and House of Lords (Unit 4).

Exclusions from the Acts

1. Employees over the normal retiring age for the job are not covered by the above provisions. By section 109, the retiring age for this purpose is the one agreed in the contract of employment, if this is the same for men and women; or in any other case, 65. However, dismissal for an automatically unfair reason under sections 99–105 is still actionable after these normal retiring ages.
2. Certain classes of employee are excluded: share fishermen; police officers; and those ordinarily employed outside Great Britain. The Acts do govern Crown employees, including members of the armed forces.
3. Unfair dismissal provisions do not apply on the expiration of a fixed-term contract for *one* year or more if, before the term expires, the employee has agreed in writing to exclude any claim in respect of such rights in relation to that contract. The exclusion may be in the contract itself or in a separate document.

   > In *Dixon* v. *BBC* (1979), the Court of Appeal held that a contract for a stated period is still a fixed-term contract even if it could be ended by either party giving notice within the term.

4. Where employers, unions and employees in a firm or industry have agreed their own dismissal procedures, the Secretary of State may, if satisfied that the agreement is as beneficial as the Acts, designate the agreement as applying instead of the unfair dismissal provisions above.
5. Subject to the two previous points, any attempt to 'contract out' of the unfair dismissal provisions is void. It is possible to make a 'compromise' agreement to settle a claim before it comes before the tribunal, but this is subject to complex safeguards to ensure, for example, that the complainant has had proper legal advice.

D. Wrongful dismissal

The common law action for *damages* for *wrongful* dismissal has not been replaced by the statutory concept of unfair dismissal. The latter has largely supplanted the former in practice, particularly because dismissal can be unfair even after proper notice, and proceedings before a tribunal are quicker and less formal than the ordinary courts. Moreover, from 1994, tribunals have power to award damages for breach of contract, without the need for any qualifying period of continuous employment. Nevertheless, particularly for long fixed-term contracts, it may still be more lucrative to succeed in the common law courts, where there is no ceiling on the potential amount of compensation (see below).

Dismissal with proper notice is never wrongful at common law but, if adequate notice is not given, this can be breach of contract by the employer unless he has the right to dismiss the worker summarily because of serious breach of contract by the latter.

If notice is not given, dismissal can apparently be 'wrongful' (at common law) without being 'unfair' (by statute), in that it would be fair to dismiss the employee, but wrongful to do so without notice.

> In *Treganowan* v. *Robert Knee & Co. Ltd* (1975), the complainant was dismissed without notice because she allegedly boasted about her sex life, thereby making the atmosphere at work difficult. She was held to have been fairly dismissed; but the tribunal said, *obiter*, that since about six weeks' notice should have been given, the dismissal would have been wrongful at common law, because her conduct was not sufficient to justify instant dismissal. The tribunal, however, had no power to award damages for breach of contract, and felt that in this case the manner of the dismissal, as opposed to the reasons, did not render it unfair by statute.

If dismissal is wrongful at common law, the employee may have the following remedies:

1. He can recover damages, which are normally based on the wages which would have been payable had proper notice been given. Other regular earnings may be included, such as bonuses, tips and commission, and there may be compensation for loss of pension rights. Where the employment is for a long fixed term, not terminable earlier by notice, damages may be based on the remuneration due if the employment had run its full term, subject only to the employee's duty to mitigate his loss. The sum can, therefore, be substantial.

   The first £30 000 of damages are based on the net salary, after deduction of income tax and social security contributions. Damages over £30 000 are based on gross salary which the employee would have received, but are then taxed in the hands of the employee.

2. In some circumstances, where a claim for damages is inappropriate because, for example, the claimant has worked under a contract which proved void, he can claim compensation on a *quantum meruit* basis, for so much as he deserves (Unit 15).

3. The personal nature of employment means that the remedies of injunction and specific performance will not normally be granted. Very exceptionally, the court may feel that damages would be inadequate, and make a declaratory judgment that the dismissal was wrongful; in this event, an injunction might be issued to delay dismissal until proper notice is given, or the proper procedure followed; see *Hill* v. *C. A. Parsons & Co. Ltd* (Unit 15).

The employer too has a right of action if the worker leaves without good reason or adequate notice. In practice, such actions are rare. The court will not compel a worker to continue his employment, but an injunction may be granted to restrain him from working elsewhere if the contract contains a valid restraint clause (Unit 17).

Apart from the differences between wrongful and unfair dismissal already mentioned, such as the need for qualifying employment under statute but not at common law, the relevance of proper notice, and the different remedies, there are other important distinctions. The Lord Chancellor's order which gave jurisdiction to tribunals over wrongful dismissal claims also imposed a ceiling on the total amount which a tribunal can award in damages. Finally, the limitation period for breach of contract actions is normally six years, as contrasted with three months for unfair dismissal claims.

E. Grounds for dismissal

The following are some common grounds for dismissal, which can perhaps be related to the reasons for dismissal given in the 1996 Act, section 98 (see page 325). They can also be relevant to claims for wrongful dismissal at common law.

Misconduct

Most 'misconduct' involves breach of the requirements of 'capability' and (reasonable) 'conduct' in section 98. *Serious* breach of any of the duties of employees set out in Unit 27, Head D, will normally suffice, and the cases cited there are relevant here.

A difficult situation occurs where an employee is dismissed for possibly inadequate reasons, but the employer *subsequently discovers more serious misconduct*. To what extent can these subsequent discoveries be used?

At common law, misconduct discovered after the employment had ended would not necessarily invalidate any severance *agreement*. For example, in *Bell* v. *Lever Bros.* (Unit 13), the misdeeds which the employer later discovered did not entitle him to recover the £30 000 which he had paid to Bell in consideration of the latter leaving before his employment contract had expired. On the other hand, such evidence would be admissible if an ex-employee claimed damages for wrongful dismissal at common law.

> In *Boston Deep Sea Fishing and Ice Co.* v. *Ansell* (1888), a director was dismissed from his employment contract for inadequate reasons, but it was later discovered that he had been pocketing large undisclosed commissions. It was held that this retrospectively justified his dismissal.

In claims for *statutory* compensation, for unfair dismissal, discoveries made after the employment ends are *not* generally admissible in considering whether or not the dismissal was fair. This is different from the common law, but the difference is not very important for three possible reasons. First, there will often be an interval between the employer giving notice and the employment ending, and discoveries during this period are admissible. Second, if the employer has his own internal appeals system, which the employee uses, the employment is not treated as irrevocably having ended until the internal appeal is over. Therefore evidence discovered during the appeal can be used at any tribunal hearing later. Third, evidence discovered at *any* time before the tribunal hearing can be used in assessing the *amount* of any statutory awards, and there have been cases where although the dismissal was held unfair, a nil or nominal award was made.

In *Devis & Sons Ltd* v. *Atkins* (1977), Atkins was dismissed, mainly because of disobedience. Evidence was later discovered which allegedly also showed that he had been dishonest. Nevertheless he claimed unfair dismissal, and the House of Lords held that this later evidence should not be considered in deciding whether or not his dismissal was fair. On the other hand it *could* be taken into account in deciding *how much* compensation to award.

Redundancy

This is discussed in detail in Unit 29. Dismissal for redundancy is normally fair, but it can become unfair in some situations.

1. There may be no genuine redundancy. For example an employee may be declared redundant but upon examination the employer is unable to convince the tribunal that the employee's rôle had ceased or diminished.
2. There may have been no consultation by the employer with the individual or his representatives.

    In *Polkey* v. *A.E. Dayton Services Ltd* (1987), a van driver was made redundant following reorganization of the business. There was no consultation with him. The House of Lords said that individual consultation was a cornerstone of good industrial relations, and held the dismissal unfair.

3. The selection for redundancy may be in contravention of a customary arrangement or agreed procedure, without any special reasons for such contravention; or be for an automatically unfair reason.

Dismissal to avoid contravention of an enactment

If continuation of the employment would become unlawful because of some enactment affecting either the employer or the employee, then dismissal may be fair. This may occur if, for example, someone employed as a driver loses his licence. However, the employer may still have acted unreasonably if it would have been possible to continue the employment without any illegality. For example, a salesman who is expected to use a car but is not employed primarily as a driver, might be able to use public transport while he is disqualified.

Some other substantial reason

This, under section 98, is sometimes described as the 'dustbin' justification for dismissal. Reorganization dismissals (see Variation of terms in Unit 26) often fall into this category.

Specimen questions

1. (a) Various statutory rights of employees depend upon completion of a qualifying period of continuous employment. What is meant by 'continuous employment'?

(b) Emma works for a firm as a cleaner for 1 hour per day. She has been employed in her present job for the past two years. During the first year of this employment she was absent for 26 weeks on maternity leave and during the second year she was on strike for 13 weeks. Emma has now been dismissed and wishes to know whether her length of employment entitles her to claim for redundancy or unfair dismissal. Advise her.

2. (a) In what circumstances may an employee be dismissed without notice?

(b) Kenneth took £5 from the petty cash in order to buy a birthday present for his girlfriend. He replaced the money the following day, but was discovered doing so and was summarily dismissed. Advise Kenneth.

To what extent, if at all, would your advice differ if Kenneth had been dismissed because of a deficit in the petty cash and the deficit had arisen because of an over-payment that he had carelessly made?

3. (a) Distinguish between an action for damages for wrongful dismissal and a claim for compensation for unfair dismissal.

(b) A firm of accountants holds an office party. Graves, a clerk, who is normally of impeccable behaviour, makes an insulting remark to Stade, the senior partner. When Stade objects, Hastie, another clerk, intervenes and knocks down Stade.

Discuss whether the behaviour of Graves and Hastie justifies their dismissal.

4. (a) A bus company is concerned about the number of accidents caused by careless driving, and a notice is therefore displayed in the garage stating that any driver who is involved in an accident will be instantly dismissed. The following day, two drivers, Alan and Brian, cause minor accidents and are dismissed without notice. Alan has been employed for 10 years and Brian for 10 months; both have clean driving records.

Advise Alan and Brian as to their possible rights arising from their dismissals.

(b) After the dismissals, the company discovers that both Alan and Brian have been keeping some of the fares paid by passengers.

To what extent may this new evidence be used to counter any actions brought by Alan and Brian?

5. It is easy today to engage workers but difficult either to dismiss them or to provide them with other than a full week's work.

Discuss this statement.

6. An employment tribunal yesterday upheld a claim for unfair dismissal by John Lamb. Lamb successfully contended that he had been unfairly dismissed for trade union activities. The tribunal made a basic award of £4000 and a compensatory award of £5000, in addition to ordering Lamb's reinstatement.

You are required to explain:

(a) the constitution and jurisdiction of an employment tribunal;

(b) any right of appeal that may be open to the employer;

(c) the difference between a basic award and a compensatory award;

(d) how reinstatement differs from re-engagement and the possible consequences if the employer ignores the order.

Unit 29. Redundancy Payments and Other Rights

When an employee loses his job the effects for him (or her) can be serious, and the rights to notice and to compensation for unfair or wrongful dismissal already discussed recognize this. The Redundancy Payments Act 1965 gave further recognition to a worker's 'property' rights in his job, which are deemed to become more valuable with increasing age and length of service with the same employer. These provisions now form Part XI of the Employment Rights Act 1996.

A. Redundancy payments

Qualifying period of continuous employment

An employee is not entitled to redundancy payment until he has been continuously employed with his employer for at least two years. Only years from the age of 18 count for this purpose. The rules to determine what amounts to continuous employment are as set out in Unit 28.

Dismissal, lay-off, short time

The right to a redundancy payment arises only if the employee has suffered one of these fates, usually dismissal.

For the purposes of the Employment Rights Act, Part XI, an employee can be treated as dismissed if, but only (section 136):

1. if the contract under which he is employed is terminated by the employer, whether with or without notice; or

333

2. where he is employed under a fixed-term contract which expires without being renewed; or
3. where the employee himself terminates the contract, with or without notice, in circumstances such that he is entitled to end it without notice because of his employer's misconduct or breach of the terms of the contract.

Under section 136(1)(c), therefore, an employee who leaves 'voluntarily' is still dismissed if the employer's misconduct has forced this on him: see *Marriott* v. *Oxford & District Co-operative Society Ltd* (Unit 26), *Donovan* v. *Invicta Airways Ltd* and *United Bank* v. *Akhtar* (Unit 27). Moreover, when a worker has been given notice of dismissal, there are detailed provisions entitling him to serve a counter-notice and thereby voluntarily leave early without loss of redundancy payment.

Subject to this, no redundancy payment is made when the employee leaves voluntarily.

> In *Morton Sundour Fabrics Ltd* v. *Shaw* (1966), Shaw was warned that his job in the velvet department was *likely* to end at an unspecified time some months in the future. He therefore sought and found another job, and left his present employer. He was held not entitled to a redundancy payment, because he had left voluntarily. He never actually received notice from his employer, and, therefore, did not come within the above provisions.

> In *Doble* v. *Firestone Tyre Co. Ltd* (1981), the company issued a statement towards the end of 1979 that a factory would close on 15 February 1980; employees were assured that the situation would be kept under review and any changes notified. Doble sought employment elsewhere and obtained another job on 17 December 1979. It was held that he had not been dismissed and therefore his claims for redundancy payment and unfair dismissal both failed.

Similarly, there is no dismissal, and, therefore, no redundancy payment, if the contract is frustrated as in cases such as *Morgan* v. *Manser* and *Hart* v. *A.R. Marshall Ltd* (Unit 28).

An employee is not taken to be dismissed if his contract is renewed, or he is re-engaged under a new contract on the same terms as hitherto, in pursuance of an offer, written or not, made by his employer before the end of his existing employment, so long as the renewal or re-engagement takes effect immediately or within four weeks of the end of his old job.

Alternatively, the employer may offer renewal or re-engagement on terms which differ, wholly or in part, from the old ones 'as to the capacity and place in which the employee is employed, and as to the other terms and conditions of his employment'. In this case, there must be a 'trial period' of at least four weeks under the new terms. If, during this trial period (a) the *employee* ends the employment for *whatever* reason, or (b) the employer ends it for a reason connected with or arising out of the change then, unless there is a further renewal or re-engagement, the worker is treated as dismissed as from the end of the original job.

The parties can, if they so wish, agree a trial period of longer than four weeks for the purpose of retraining the worker. Such an agreement must be in writing, before the employee starts work under the new employment; it must specify the end of the trial period, and the proposed terms of the worker's employment when the trial period ends. In either of the above cases, if the worker continues in his new employment after the trial period, he is regarded as not having been dismissed.

Since employers might attempt to avoid redundancy payments by using temporary lay-offs or short-time working, the Act provides for payment if either of these occurs. Lay-off occurs where a man, dependent upon being provided with work, is not so provided by his employer, and is consequently not entitled to remuneration. A claim may be based on short-time working where remuneration depends upon the hours worked, and work diminishes so that the remuneration for the week is less than half a week's pay. If the lay-off or short time lasts for at least 4 consecutive weeks in the last 8, or for any 6 of the last 13 weeks, the worker may give written 'notice of intention to claim' redundancy payment. The length of notice is either 4 or 6 weeks, depending upon which of the above periods of lay-off or short time the worker alleges. He must also give appropriate notice to terminate the employment. There are detailed provisions entitling the employer to serve a counter-notice if the work available is likely to increase in the immediate future.

Redundancy

The dismissal must have been due to redundancy and not, for example, to misconduct justifying instant dismissal. In a claim for redundancy payment before a tribunal, an employee who has been dismissed is presumed to have been dismissed for redundancy, so that the onus of proving misconduct or any other reason is on the employer.

By section 139 of the Act, redundancy occurs where the employee is dismissed because:

1. the employer has ceased or intends to cease to carry on the business for the purposes of which the employee was employed by him; or
2. the employer has ceased or intends to cease to carry on that business in the *place* where the employee was so employed; or
3. the requirements of that business for employees to carry out work of a particular kind, either generally or in the place where the employee was employed, have ceased or diminished or are expected to do so.

Where a *place* of business closes or moves (under 2 above), the main legal difficulty is to determine where, under his contract of employment, the worker has contracted to work. If, as in *UK Atomic Energy Authority* v. *Claydon* (1974), he has expressly agreed to work anywhere in the UK, he is not entitled either to redundancy payment or to compensation for unfair dismissal if he refuses to move. The 'place' where he is employed is the UK. The terms of the contract are not always so clear, however.

> In *O'Brien* v. *Associated Fire Alarms* (1969), an electrician who had lived and worked in Liverpool for many years was held impliedly to be bound to work only in the Liverpool area. He justifiably refused to move 120 miles to Barrow-in-Furness when the Liverpool branch closed, and was entitled to a redundancy payment (see also Unit 27).

335

In *Stevenson* v. *Tees-side Bridge and Engineering Ltd* (1971), on the other hand, a steel erector stated when applying for his job that he would be prepared to work away from home. There was no express term to this effect in the nationally agreed terms upon which he was employed, but there was provision for travelling expenses and subsistence allowances. Moreover, the very nature of the construction industry meant that when work on one site was completed, work would move to another building site. For some time, Stevenson worked at a site near his home, where he could earn a lot of overtime pay. When this was completed, he refused to move to a more distant site where he would have to live away from home. He was held not entitled to a redundancy payment.

The main problems arise where the business survives, but it is claimed that the job disappears. Has the requirement of the business for employees to carry out work of a particular kind ceased or diminished? This can still depend partly upon what *was* the requirement of the employer's business.

In *Vaux and Associated Breweries Ltd* v. *Ward* (1969), the landlord and the brewery decided to give a younger and more lively 'image' to a pub. The name was changed, a discotheque was opened, and younger barmaids were engaged. A barmaid aged 57 was dismissed and claimed redundancy payment. Her claim failed. Her particular kind of work was treated as 'serving customers', and this work had not ceased or diminished. (She might wish to claim compensation for unfair dismissal today, but this was only introduced after 1971.)

If the requirements of the employer's business have diminished or ceased, it must then be shown that the dismissal is 'attributable' to this.

In *Safeway Stores plc* v. *Burrell* (1997), B was employed by Safeway as a petrol station manager. Because of reorganization, the post of manager disappeared, but B was offered similar work (not exactly the same) as a 'petrol station controller', at lower pay. B refused and was dismissed. The need of the employer's business for work of this kind had not diminished or ceased, and the dismissal could not be attributed to this. Dismissal was due to reorganization, not redundancy. (B therefore successfully claimed unfair dismissal.)

In *Murray* v. *Foyle Meats Ltd* (1999), the work of a slaughterhouse had decreased, and its need for 'meat plant operatives' had diminished. After due consultations and proper procedures, M was one of those chosen for dismissal. The House of Lords held that M's claim for unfair dismissal compensation failed. The requirements of the business had genuinely diminished. The employer had acted properly in choosing for dismissal. Therefore dismissal was attributable wholly or mainly to the redundancy, and redundancy payment (a smaller amount) was M's proper entitlement. (Note again from Unit 28 that dismissal for redundancy is *not* normally *unfair*.)

Payment

Responsibility to make redundancy payments rests upon employers. However, if the former employer is insolvent, the state will meet the employer's statutory liability from the National Insurance Fund.

If the worker's statutory claim is contested by the employer, the claim must be pursued before an employment tribunal, normally within six months of dismissal.

The amount of payment is calculated by reckoning backwards from the end of the employment. For whole years of service after the 41st birthday (until retiring age) in which the worker has been continuously employed by this employer, he is entitled to one-and-a-half week's pay per year; for years from the 22nd birthday to the 41st, one week's pay per year; and for years between the 18th and 22nd birthdays, half a week's pay per year. The maximum number of years to be taken into account for this purpose is 20. 'Week's pay' will usually be calculated according to the gross pay to which the worker would normally have been entitled during the last week before dismissal, subject to a specified maximum. The employer must give the worker a written statement showing how the amount of redundancy payment has been calculated, non-compliance being a criminal offence.

Redundancy payment does not affect a right to unemployment benefit, and is independent of any claim for *wrongful* dismissal. The Secretary of State does have power under the Act, however, to make regulations modifying the amount of redundancy payment where there are also damages for wrongful dismissal.

Redundancy and *unfair* dismissal are normally mutually exclusive, because dismissal for redundancy is not 'unfair' (Unit 28). Where an employee is selected for redundancy because of union membership activity, or non-membership, however, or in contravention of a customary arrangement or agreed procedure without good reason, the dismissal will be unfair. This can benefit the claimant because compensatory or special awards may, under Part X of the Act, be added to his payment.

Exclusion from redundancy payment

Certain categories of people are not entitled to redundancy payment:
1. *Those over retiring age*: normally 65 for both men and women; the contract of employment can fix a lower age if it is the same for both.
2. *Persons rightfully dismissed for misconduct*, either without notice, or with notice where the employer had a right, which he did not exercise, to dismiss without notice.
3. *Those in excluded employments*: (a) share fishermen; (b) civil servants, members of the armed forces and various other public service employees; (c) those employed under the Government of an overseas territory; (d) an employee dismissed while abroad unless under his contract of employment he ordinarily worked in the UK; (e) those doing domestic work for a close relative. Regulations can also exclude those whose immediate occupational pension rights are sufficiently beneficial.
4. '*Contracting out*'. An employee engaged for a *fixed term of two years or more* entered into after the 1965 Act, shall not be entitled to a redundancy payment in respect of the expiry of that term without its being renewed (whether by the employer or by an associated employer of his), if before the term expires he has agreed in writing to exclude any right to a redundancy payment in that event. The exclusion may be either in the employment contract itself, or in a separate agreement.

Subject to this, any attempt to 'contract out' of redundancy entitlements is void. It should also be noted that if a 'fixed term' contract is terminable by notice by either party before the term expires, it is still a fixed term for this purpose, so that an exclusion in such a contract can be valid; see *Dixon* v. *BBC* (Unit 28).

5. *Unreasonable refusal of new employment.* If an employee *accepts* renewal or re-engagement, even (subject to the 'trial period') on new terms, he is treated as not having been dismissed at all (see page 334).

Conversely, he is disqualified from redundancy payment if he unreasonably *refuses* either an offer of renewal or re-engagement on the same terms as hitherto, or an offer of different terms which are *suitable* alternative employment for him. The offer must have been made before the end of the old employment, and have been to take effect either immediately or within four weeks. It need not have been in writing.

Similarly, an employee is disqualified if, having *accepted* different terms, apparently suitable, he then *unreasonably* leaves or gives notice during the trial period.

What is suitable, and whether refusal is unreasonable, depends on the facts of the particular case. A job in a nearby factory might be suitable, but perhaps not in a distant town. A married man with family commitments might reasonably refuse to move home, but perhaps not a single man.

> In *Cambridge and District Co-operative Society Ltd* v. *Ruse* (1993), the Co-op closed its butcher's shop in Cambridge, and asked the manager to move to a larger shop as manager of the butchery *department*. Here he was subordinate to the store manager, and previous responsibilities for the collection of cash and banking were no longer his. Within four weeks he resigned and claimed redundancy payment. His claim was upheld. Although the alternative employment was suitable, the loss of status made his refusal to accept it reasonable.

6. *An agreement between employers and trade unions* as to redundancy payments for certain workers may, on application by *all* parties, be approved by the Secretary of State in substitution for statutory provisions.

B. Procedure for handling redundancies

Because of the economic and social effects of redundancies, particularly on a large scale, specific duties are placed on employers by the Trade Union and Labour Relations (Consolidation) Act 1992, sections 188–194, and the Trade Union Reform and Employment Rights Act 1993 ('TURERA'), section 34.

Duty of employer to consult trade unions

In relation to *all* proposed redundancies, the employer must consult any independent trade union recognized by him in relation to the employees concerned. Consultation must be 'at the earliest opportunity', and must take place whether or not those to be dismissed are actually members of the union concerned.

Where 100 or more dismissals at one establishment are proposed within a period of 90 days, consultation must begin at least 90 days before the first dismissal takes effect. Where 10 or more dismissals at one establishment are proposed within a period of 30 days, consultation must begin at least 30 days before the first takes effect.

In consultation, the employer must disclose the following details in writing to the union representatives:

1. the reasons for his proposals;
2. the number and description of proposed redundant employees;
3. the total number of employees of that type at the establishment;
4. the proposed method of selection for redundancy;
5. proposed ways of carrying out the dismissals, with regard to any agreed procedure, including the period over which dismissals are to be spread.

By TURERA 1993, he must also consult over the proposed method of calculating any redundancy payments which exceed the statutory amounts; and about ways of avoiding dismissals or reducing their number, or mitigating the consequences of the redundancies.

The employer must consider any representations made by the union, reply to them and, if he rejects any representation, say why. Consultation must be undertaken with a view to reaching agreement with the union.

If circumstances render compliance with all of the above impracticable (e.g. because redundancy resulted from unexpected loss of a large order), then it is sufficient for the employer to do all that is reasonably practicable in the circumstances, so long as he does consult at the earliest opportunity.

If an employer fails to satisfy the above requirements, then a *trade union* (not an individual worker) may complain to an employment tribunal, normally within three months of the date set for dismissals. If the complaint is held to be well founded, the tribunal must make a declaration to this effect. It *may* also make a *protective award* to the employees concerned, under which the employer must continue to pay normal wages to the employees for such 'protected period' as the tribunal specifies.

The normal maximum protected period is 28 days, but up to 90 days' payment can be awarded if 100 or more dismissals are proposed within any 90 days, and up to 30 days' payment if 10 or more dismissals are proposed within any 30 days. Subject to these maxima, the length of any protected period is at the tribunal's discretion.

If an employer fails to comply with a protective award, the worker personally may complain to the tribunal, which will award payment if the complaint is well founded. The protective award is in addition to the redundancy payment. (Note that a worker is only entitled to a protective award if dismissal is for *redundancy* and not, for example, because of misconduct or because he unreasonably refuses re-engagement.)

Duty of employer to notify the Secretary of State

In addition to his duty to consult appropriate trade unions, an employer proposing 100 or more redundancies at one establishment within any 90 days must notify the

Secretary of State for Employment at least 90 days before the first dismissal takes effect. If 10 or more redundancies are proposed within any 30 days, 30 days' notification is required. The notification must identify any unions concerned, and contain such further particulars as the Secretary of State may direct.

If proper notice is not given, the employer may be prosecuted and subject to a maximum fine of £5000.

C. Death, winding up, etc. and insolvency

Of the employer

Death of an individual employer may still, because of the personal nature of the contract, sometimes end the employment. If so, an employee's *accrued* rights are not affected, and he is entitled to arrears of wages up to the date of the death. Employees who have the qualifying period of continuous employment will also be entitled to redundancy payments unless the personal representatives re-employ them, or offer to do so, within eight weeks of the death. An offer of re-employment can be implied if, simply, the business is continued as beforehand.

Dissolution of an ordinary partnership may similarly end the contracts of employees, but only if the identity of the partners is clearly material.

> In *Brace* v. *Calder* (1895), the claimant was employed for a fixed term by a partnership of solicitors, which was dissolved when two partners died. The business was carried on by the remaining partners, but the claimant, whose term had not expired, claimed that his employment had ended and demanded damages for breach of contract. He was held entitled to damages but, since the remaining partners had offered to re-engage him on the same terms, the damages were nominal because he had not taken the opportunity to mitigate his loss.

Note that a change of partners in a limited liability partnership (LLP) does not affect the employees, because an LLP is a separate legal entity.

Winding up of a company will end the employment if the business is ceasing, in which case rights to redundancy payments are likely to arise. Continuity of employment for statutory purposes is discussed in Unit 28 (page 320).

Bankruptcy or insolvency of the employer will often end the employments, although it might be possible to continue the business and/or transfer it to a new owner. If the employments end, employees have limited rights as preferred creditors, but this may be little comfort if the employer has no money at all. The 1996 Act section 182 therefore gives ex-employees of insolvent employers the right to claim certain sums from the Secretary of State for Employment.

Of the employee

Death of an employee obviously ends the employment. His estate is entitled to arrears of wages to the date of death. Insolvency of an employee will not automatically end the employment; it may or may not justify dismissal, depending upon the nature of his job.

Specimen questions

1. (a) When may an employee claim a redundancy payment?
   (b) John had been employed by Electrics Ltd for 20 years on security work at a factory making small electrical components. The factory was then bought by Panther Ltd, a motor manufacturer, for the purpose of producing electrical fittings for its cars. John's employment was continued by Panther Ltd for a period of 10 weeks. He was then told that his services were no longer required and he was given four weeks' notice. John found another job immediately, gave his employer one week's notice and left.

   Advise John of any rights he may have against Panther Ltd.

2. (a) Compare and contrast compensation for unfair dismissal and redundancy payment.
   (b) John is the chief accountant of an engineering company. His company is taken over by another company and John is offered the post of deputy accountant with the new organization at a lower salary. He writes a letter of protest to the managing director but takes up the new post and works for three weeks while looking for another appointment. Upon finding this, he leaves. Discuss the legal position.

3. Foreman is the manager of a warehouse that supplies a number of shops. The stock recording system is reorganized with the installation of a computer. Foreman is found to be unable to cope with the new method of working and is dismissed.

   The changes also mean that the services of two other employees, Smith and Jones, are no longer fully needed in the warehouse. Smith is offered a job by his employer as an assistant at a shop about 20 miles away. Jones is told that for the foreseeable future, he will be employed on a part-time basis in the warehouse for two days each week.

   All three employees seek compensation from their employer for redundancy. In addition, Foreman wishes to claim for unfair dismissal.

   You are required to advise:
   (a) Foreman;
   (b) Smith;
   (c) Jones.

4. On his 17th birthday, 1 January 1994, Eric was engaged by John as a trainee accountant. In April 1996, John died and Simon, his son, took over the business.

   In July 1997, Eric and other employees went on strike and they were told by Simon that they would be dismissed unless they returned to work immediately. They did not do so, and they were dismissed, but four days later the dispute was settled and they were re-engaged.

   Simon reorganized the business in September 1998, and told Eric that, in consequence of the reorganization, his services in his present capacity were no longer required. Simon offered Eric an alternative post as a storekeeper.

   Discuss Eric's right to claim a redundancy payment.

5. Albert is employed by a drug firm as the manager of a department in which new drugs are tested on animals. He refuses to administer a particular drug on the grounds that it would cause unnecessary suffering to the animals, whereupon the firm closes down the department and dismisses Albert without notice.

   Discuss Albert's right to claim:
   (a) compensation for unfair dismissal;
   (b) redundancy payment.

6. After five years' employment as chief cost accountant to a medium-sized engineering company, you have recently been appointed to the board of directors. Consultations are now taking place to appoint your successor. Draft a report for the other members of the board outlining the matters that should be included in the contract of employment of the person appointed.

Index

Note: Tables of Cases and Statutes with page references are on pages ix–xxi. Page references in italic indicate figures.

343